9210226

Corporate Profits and Cooptation

*Networks of Market Constraints
and Directorate Ties
in the American Economy*

QUANTITATIVE STUDIES IN SOCIAL RELATIONS

Consulting Editor: Peter H. Rossi

UNIVERSITY OF MASSACHUSETTS
AMHERST, MASSACHUSETTS

In Preparation

Michael D. Maltz, RECIDIVISM

Derek Hum and A. Basilevsky, THE ESTIMATION OF LABOR SUPPLY USING EXPERIMENTAL DATA: *The U. S. Guaranteed Income Experiments*

Peter Schmidt and Ann D. Witte, THE ECONOMICS OF CRIME: *Theory, Methods, and Applications*

Published

Walter R. Gove and Michael Hughes, with contributions by Omer R. Galle, OVERCROWDING IN THE HOUSEHOLD: *An Analysis of Determinants and Effects*

Ronald S. Burt, CORPORATE PROFITS AND COOPTATION: *Networks of Market Constraints and Directorate Ties in the American Economy*

Peter H. Rossi, James D. Wright, and Andy B. Anderson (Eds.), HANDBOOK OF SURVEY RESEARCH

Joan Huber and Glenna Spitze, SEX STRATIFICATION: *Children, Housework, and Jobs*

Toby L. Parcel and Charles W. Mueller, ASCRIPTION AND LABOR MARKETS: *Race and Sex Differences in Earnings*

Paul G. Schervish, THE STRUCTURAL DETERMINANTS OF UNEMPLOYMENT: *Vulnerability and Power in Market Relations*

Irving Tallman, Ramona Marotz-Baden, and Pablo Pindas, ADOLESCENT SOCIALIZATION IN CROSS-CULTURAL PERSPECTIVE: *Planning for Social Change*

Robert F. Boruch and Joe S. Cecil (Eds.), SOLUTIONS TO ETHICAL AND LEGAL PROBLEMS IN SOCIAL RESEARCH

J. Ronald Milavsky, Ronald C. Kessler, Horst H. Stipp, and William S. Rubens, TELEVISION AND AGGRESSION: *A Panel Study*

Ronald S. Burt, TOWARD A STRUCTURAL THEORY OF ACTION: *Network Models of Social Structure, Perception, and Action*

Peter H. Rossi, James D. Wright, and Eleanor Weber-Burdin, NATURAL HAZARDS AND PUBLIC CHOICE: *The Indifferent State and Local Politics of Hazard Mitigation*

The list of titles in this series continues on the last page of this volume

Corporate Profits and Cooptation

*Networks of Market Constraints
and Directorate Ties
in the American Economy*

RONALD S. BURT

*Department of Sociology and Center for the Social Sciences
Columbia University
New York, New York*

ACADEMIC PRESS

A Subsidiary of Harcourt Brace Jovanovich, Publishers

New York   London
Paris   San Diego   San Francisco   São Paulo   Sydney   Tokyo   Toronto

ACADEMIC PRESS, INC.
111 Fifth Avenue, New York, New York 10003

United Kingdom Edition published by
ACADEMIC PRESS, INC. (LONDON) LTD.
24/28 Oval Road, London NW1 7DX

Library of Congress Cataloging in Publication Data

Burt, Ronald S.
    Corporate profits and cooptation.

    (Quantitative studies in social relations)
    Includes bibliographical references and index.
    1. Interlocking directorates--United States.
2. Directors of corporations--United States.
I. Title. II. Series.
HD2785.B77 1983   338.8'7'0973   83-2578
ISBN 0-12-147180-2

PRINTED IN THE UNITED STATES OF AMERICA

83 84 85 86   9 8 7 6 5 4 3 2 1

Contents

3

Directorate Structure: Potentially Cooptive Interorganizational Relations   65

4

Directorate Structure: A Cooptive Response to Market Structure   117

5

Conclusions and Speculations   171

II

New Directions

6

A Note on Corporate Philanthropy   193

7
A Note on Corporation and Definitions of Constraint 223

8
Corporations in the Directorate Tie Market 237

9
Directors in the Directorate Tie Market 257

Foreword

The study of interorganizational behavior and the relationship between organizations and their environments enjoyed something of a fad beginning in the late 1960s. Ronald Burt's book should serve to give that line of research new and added impetus. His study of relationships among sectors of the economy and the implications of those relations for issues ranging from interlocking directorates to corporate philanthropy are important and provocative.

It is almost trite to note that we live in an organizational society and that the discipline of sociology is about the nature and structure of that society. Yet, organizational sociology has, at times, abandoned large areas of inquiry to economists and others. For the most part, the investigation of interorganizational relations has involved the study of relations among nonprofit and public organizations; few scholars have been bold or ambitious enough to tackle issues conventionally handled by industrial organization economists. But if economists like Easterlin can analyze fertility and marital stability, and Gary Becker can analyze marriage as an economic event, then it is only fitting to have Burt analyze the economic system in terms of the social relations among its actors, conceptualized in network terms. Whereas both economists and organization theorists have tended to analyze firms as focal units with respect to their environments, Burt's analysis recognizes the fundamentally relational nature of social life, and it incorporates network concepts to illuminate the structure of transactions and the consequences of that structure for various behaviors and outcomes.

The argument developed in this book is at once simple and powerful—firms occupy positions in economic sectors that, as a consequence of transaction pattern (purchases and sales) with other sectors, provide those firms with either more or less power to be used to earn profits. And, as a consequence of facing profit constraints because of network position, firms engage in strategies to attempt to coopt these market constraints. Such strategies range from ownership of subsidiaries to interlocking directorates to advertising and corporate philanthropy, which are also seen as cooptive acts in this analysis.

The analysis is powerful because it enables us to move well beyond previous research on a number of dimensions. For example, economists have been plagued with the problem of measuring market power, important because of its public policy implications and because it is an important predictor of profit margins. Slowly they have moved from simple four- and eight-firm concentration ratios to more refined indices. Using network methodology, Burt indicates how to assess precisely the relative power of sectors (or firms) and furthermore how to distinguish between power that derives from having few competitors within the sector, selling to a relatively unconcentrated market of end users, and buying from sellers who themselves face competition. Burt's analysis indicates that as a predictor of profit margins, the market power that comes from the position of the sector vis-à-vis its suppliers and customers is more important than the degree of competition within the sector.

As another example, cooptive intent has been assumed in most studies of interlocking directorates. The analysis in this book permits one to compare the pattern of interlocks with the pattern of structural constraints on profits. To the extent that interlocks follow patterns of market constraints, the inference of cooptive intent is strengthened. And, as yet another example, the network analysis can be transposed to consider the power of various individual directors, thereby permitting comparison of the perspective developed in this book with the intraclass perspective that has argued for a hegemony of the economic elite.

This book is not just formulas and statistics. One of its important contributions is to illustrate with examples how the concepts work and can be applied. Firestone Tire is examined to understand director interlocking, and the apparel industry is highlighted to show how the analytical techniques can explain something about its low level of profitability. Thus, the reader can use this book and the data generously provided in the Appendix to do his or her own analyses as well as to operationalize the concepts of structural autonomy and constraint with respect to other interorganizational issues.

I can recall serving on a dissertation committee with a colleague who warned ominously that the student we were advising would certainly get into trouble because he used profits as a dependent variable. This book examines the effects of director interlocking on profits and finds none, but the interpretation offered is that this lack of effect is because the structure of boards follows the pattern of constraints on profits so closely that there is no interlocking effect on profits net of market constraint effects. More fundamentally, this book is willing to tackle big issues head on—the intraclass perspective on the organization of economic elites, industrial organization economics, explaining variation in profits, and economic models of philanthropy. With that broad scope, and in his emphasis on the relational aspects of organizational social life, Burt has set a course that the discipline as a whole would be well served to follow.

—JEFFREY PFEFFER
Stanford University

Preface

This monograph is about the manner in which relations constrain the freedom to act and other relations are created to circumvent those constraints. More specifically, it is about the manner in which patterns of buying and selling among sectors of the American economy constrain the ability to make profits in manufacturing industries and the way firms in those industries use their boards of directors to create cooptive relations through which the constraints can be circumvented. I take a relatively unsophisticated network model of structural autonomy, adapt it to the substantive area of organizations and markets, and systematically trace empirical implications of the model for corporate profits and cooptive directorate ties in the American economy.

The analysis is presented for a stratified audience. For the general reader interested in organizations and markets, basic points are argued in prose, and evidence is presented in terms of means, correlations, and bar graphs. The bar graphs are especially helpful in illustrating the occasionally complex interaction effects evident in the data. These points are then captured in mathematical models for the specialized reader. Technical passages are introduced with a note to the lay reader indicating where the general argument can be picked up again. A quick overview and critique of the argument can be obtained by reading the introduction (Chapter 1) and conclusion (Chapter 5).

The work reported here began in the autumn of 1975 while I was a graduate student supported by the Corporate Actor Project at the National Opinion Research Center, University of Chicago (under National Science Foundation Grant SOC73-00504 to James S. Coleman). At the time, I had worked out a concept of jointly occupied network positions and had the idea that Simmel's notion of conflicting group-affiliations might be useful in capturing the extent to which occupations of a network position could be autonomous within their system. There was a similarity, in theory, between actors jointly occupying network positions and organizations operating within economic sectors. According to my initial network notions, the form of the relational pattern characterizing a sector's market transactions with suppliers and consumers had implications for the ability of organizations in the sector to control prices and so obtain high profits. The Corporate Actor Project provided an opportunity to assess my initial hunch and I took it. The network model applied to market constraint and cooptation turned out to be fruitful. I am grateful to Jim Coleman for providing that initial opportunity. In the spirit of that opportunity, data on market constraint and directorate ties are provided in an Appendix to this monograph.

This work has been supported by grants from the National Science Foundation (SOC77-22938, SOC79-25728) and carried out in facilities provided by the University of Chicago, the University of California at Berkeley, and the State University of New York at Albany. Of course, any opinions, findings, and conclusions or recommendations expressed in this publication are my own and do not necessarily reflect the views of the National Science Foundation. The excellent research facilities at the Berkeley Survey Research Center greatly assisted my work there. The administration of grant funds was efficient and unobtrusive. The computer and space accommodations were invaluable. I owe a special debt of gratitude to Percy H. Tannenbaum, the Center's Director, and to James S. Wiley, Assistant Director of the Center, for facilitating my access to center resources. The additional research time made available to me during a leave of absence spent in the Department of Sociology, State University of New York at Albany in 1978 and 1979 provided an unanticipated opportunity to analyze the data in greater detail than was originally planned. I greatly appreciate the efforts of Ronald A. Farrell, Richard H. Hall, and Nan Lin in making the facilities in Albany available to me. Janet Flack and Amy Ong helped in processing the four-digit market structure data. Able research assistance in coding the data on directors and establishments was provided by Nicholas Anderson, Kenneth Christman, Julie Geschwind, and Mark Lundgren under the supervision of Mr. Christman. In processing these data, I was aided by William Bittner, Harold Kilburn, Scott Pimley, and Ronald Simeone. Mr. Kilburn was a particularly consistent source of programming assistance and interesting substantive ideas. Finally, I am grateful to Miguel Guilarte and Linda Cranor of Columbia University for their thorough inspection of equations and text in the page proofs. A great many more people provided helpful comments on specific aspects of the work reported here and my acknowledgments to them are recorded in articles presenting the initial analyses refined and expanded here with much more detailed data. Drawn from the *Administrative Science Quarterly*, the *American Journal of Sociology*, the *American Sociological Review*, *Social Forces*, *Social Networks*, and *Social Science Research*, portions of these articles appear here in revised form with the kind permission of their publishers and are cited in the text where appropriate. In addition, I am grateful to the Graduate School of Business Administration, Division of Research at Harvard University for permission to excerpt illustrative quotes from Myles Mace's field work with directors in American corporations (Mace, 1948, 1971).

1
Introduction

In the United States there is a normative conception of the American economy as a perfect marketplace, a "free" market. Corporate bureaucracies as actors producing commodities for sale in this market are guided by two conflicting pressures in balance. They are motived by a desire to obtain profit so as to ensure their continued survival. They are constrained by competition from other corporate bureaucracies attempting to do the same thing for themselves. These profit-seeking actors are quick to develop profitable technological innovations, but are prevented from exploiting consumers because competing organizations are quick to imitate the profitable actions of innovators. The market motivation of profits ensures economic growth, and the market constraint of competition prevents exploitation.

As is characteristic of normative beliefs, this normative conception of the American economy is an ideal, a social prescription for empirical reality. The ideal is not realized in many ways. Corporate bureaucracies are not always independent and competitive. They are often instead coordinated as units in large corporate hierarchies; the hierarchies themselves are often connected by informal relations. These ties between ostensibly independent establishments are often interpreted as evidence of collusion enabling connected organizations to pursue profit interests without being subject to the constraint of competition. This freedom from the market constraint of competition could enable corporations to direct the American economy to suit their own interests. Far from the free market normative ideal, this alternative conception of the American economy suggests a managed market in which people as employees and consumers pay for the unbridled, self-interested actions of large corporations.

These concepts of managed and free markets are obviously both idealizations of empirical reality. Evidence can be found to support either characterization of the American economy: some features of the economy correspond to a free market, and some correspond to a managed market. There is intense competition among some corporate bureaucracies at the same time that there have been specific organizations acting in concert so as to manage competition to their own advantage. An accurate understanding of organizational behavior is unlikely to result from attempts to characterize the economy as a free or a managed market since either attempt alone must involve a misrepresentation of the social reality in which organizations are obliged to survive. The understanding must come from knowing the manner in which the economy is at once competitive and managed.

As a sociologist, I believe that this knowledge is to be found in the social structure of market and nonmarket relations among corporate bureaucracies in the economy. How does the structure of competitive buying and selling among organizations actually operate to constrain corporate profits? How could that competition be brought under control by the existence of nonmarket connections between organizations? To what extent has it been brought under control? These are my central concerns in this book.

Market constraints on corporate profits are discussed in Chapter 2. The structural conception of competition utilized there is distinct from, although related to, the microeconomic conception of competition in a free market. The microeconomic understanding focuses on competition between organizations producing the same commodity. Competition in the economy thus exists within sectors of the economy; organizations producing the same commodity constitute a sector of the economy (e.g., the tobacco sector, textile sector, or transportation equipment sector) and constrain one another's profits by undercutting one another's prices for the similar commodity they produce. The structural conception of competition advanced in Chapter 2 focuses on the sum of constraints inherent in the pattern of buying and selling an organization is obliged to perform in order to produce a commodity. Profits are not a direct result of producing a commodity. They come from being able to control the sales and purchase transactions involved in producing the commodity. The lower the price an organization must pay for its supplies and the higher the price it can charge for its product, the more profit it can make in producing the product. The structure of its buying and selling determines the extent to which it can control prices in those transactions. To the extent that a particular kind of transaction does not give an organization flexibility in determining the price of the commodity sold or purchased, the transaction is a market constraint on the organization's potential profits. My purpose in Chapter 2 is to describe how this is true in the American economy. Using data on sales and purchases involving manufacturing establishments in the 1967 American economy, I estimate elements in a network of market constraints on corporate profits, constraint occurring as a result of competition among organizations within a sector and as a result of the lack of competition in transactions with consumers and suppliers. I show that corporate profits were much more constrained by the lack of competition among suppliers and consumers than they were by the traditionally emphasized constraint of competition among organizations producing the same commodity.

In Chapter 3 I discuss some manners in which these market constraints could be brought under control through nonmarket connections between organizations. I focus on interorganizational relations through the corporate board of directors. Three types of these "directorate ties" are distinguished: ownership ties in which two organizations are jointly controlled by a single board of directors, direct interlock ties in which two corporations share one or more persons as members of their respective boards, and indirect interlock ties through financial institutions in which third-party financial corporations serve as brokers between two corporations. These directorate ties have the potential to direct the flow of information and influence among organizations selling and purchasing commodities. By so doing, directorate ties enable organizations to conduct their buying and selling with one another in a context free of the competition characterizing transactions between unconnected organizations. It is the creation of a less uncertain context in which business transactions can be conducted that enables connected organizations to circumvent market constraints on their profits. Directorate ties cannot eliminate the market constraint inherent in competitive buying and selling. They can provide a controlled, nonmarket context in which those transactions would be conducted.

There are political, empirical, and theoretical reasons for focusing on directorate ties. Stemming from seminal work by Adolf Berle, Gardner Means, and Philip Selznick, these reasons underlie an extensive literature in which the corporate board of directors is presented as a cooptive device.

In their now classic work, *The Modern Corporation and Private Property,* Berle and Means (1932) highlighted the political importance of directorates as the center of control in American corporations. The board is certainly the legal nerve center of the corporate bureaucracy. Typically composed of three or more persons, the directorate is legally deemed mind and soul of the corporate entity. What the directors do collectively as representatives of the firm, the corporation itself is deemed to do. For example, California law requires that "the corporation shall be managed and all corporate powers shall be exercised by or under the direction of the board. The board may delegate the management of the day-to-day operation of the business of the corporation to a management company or other person *provided that the business and affairs of the corporation shall be man-*

aged and all corporate power shall be exercised under the ultimate direction of the board'' (italics added, 1977, *Deerings California Code,* page 168). Boards traditionally have delegated the day-to-day operation of the firm to management, stepping in when operations were not going well. However, the legal responsibility of directors underlies the increasing involvement of the board in corporate control. With the social agitation of the 1960s and 1970s came litigation against directors as the persons responsible for corporate behavior. The Federal Trade Commission and the Securities and Exchange Commission led government agencies in taking a more active role in policing existing statutes and regulations at the same time that directors increasingly became the object of lawsuits initiated by shareholders seeking redress for consequences attributed to director mistakes or wrongdoings (e.g., see Bacon & Brown, 1975:1–3, 1977:9–10). This *realpolitik* recognition of the political importance of the board is reflected in at least two changes in board practice. The frequency with which legal indemnity is included in director compensation has increased, becoming a typical component by the end of the 1970s according to data on large and small firms in manufacturing and nonmanufacturing (Bacon, 1980:18–20). There has also been a clear increase in the prominence of the directorate audit committee as the mechanism ensuring that the company is keeping honest books and reporting accurate financial information on its operations. This increased prominence can be seen in the increased incidence of audit committees (increasing from a minority of publicly held firms in the 1960s up to nearly all firms by the late 1970s), the increased detail with which the rights and duties of the audit committee are written, the increased scope of those rights and duties, and the more frequent and longer audit committee meetings (Bacon, 1979). If not the source of day-to-day control, in short, the directorate is a politically important center in the distribution of corporate control.

The political importance of the board increases the importance of interdependent boards. Systematic empirical study of this issue began during the 1930s in the American economy. Having established the 1932 corporate control study with Berle, Means subsequently directed the National Resources Committee in describing controls among American corporations (Means, 1939). This study set the stage for later empirical work by introducing interlocking directorates as one method by which ostensibly competitive firms might coordinate their actions in a mutually profitable way. Two corporations are interlocked when one or more persons sit on the boards of both firms. To the extent that the directors of two corporations are the same, it is argued that the two firms could not act as independent competitors. Since the names of directors in large corporations are easily available to the public, interlocking directorates are easily tabulated for empirical research on nonmarket connections among large firms in the economy.

As centers of corporate control, finally, boards of directors constitute a theoretically interesting site for research on corporate cooptation. Struck with the manner in which the Tennessee Valley Authority (TVA) avoided conflicts with local voluntary organizations by appointing representatives of the organizations to positions in the TVA decision-making structure, Selznick (1949:13) proposed the now well-known concept of cooptation: "the process of absorbing new elements into the leadership or policy-determining structure of an organization as a means of averting threats to its stability or existence." Directorate ties between organizations can be understood as cooptive ties in the sense that the two organizations have brought outsiders into their respective policy-determining centers, their boards of directors.

Given its political importance as the center for corporate control, the ease with which data can be obtained on it, and its ready interpretation as a cooptive device, the directorate is a potentially useful focus for research. Social scientists have taken advantage of this opportunity. There is a directorate research tradition. This research can be brought together in an empirical generalization: There is extensive interlocking in the United States (especially in urban centers for corporate headquarters such as New York, Chicago, and Los Angeles), and those firms most involved in interlocking are large, capital intensive firms controlled by diffuse interest groups.

I continue this research tradition in Chapter 3. Evidence for this empirical generalization is discussed in some detail, and sample data representative of large corporations involved in American manufacturing in 1967 are used to extend the research tradition. Large corporations controlled by diffuse interest groups were not only especially likely to develop interlocking directorates with other firms, they tended to coordinate the three types of directorate ties mentioned before (ownership, interlocking, and indirect interlocking through financial institutions) so that they had multiplex directorate ties to sectors of the economy. I explain in Chapter 3 that these results provide even stronger support for the cooptive interpretation of directorates that has been advocated in traditional directorate research.

At the same time, I argue that this tradition falls far short of its intended goal. To show that directorate ties are extensive in the economy is not equivalent to demonstrating that they are being used to circumvent market constraints on corporate profits. Directorate ties have the potential to allow connected organizations to circumvent market constraints, and they are widespread in the American economy. But are they structured so as to enable establishments to circumvent market constraints on their profits? An answer to this question requires a comparison of the network of directorate ties among organizations to the network of market constraints. If directorate ties are being used to coopt sources of market constraint on corporate profits, then organizations connected by market constraint relations should be connected by directorate tie relations.

In Chapter 4 I show that this was precisely the situation in the American economy. The three types of directorate ties tended to be absent between organizations posing no market constraint for one another's profits. None of the three types tended to be absent between organizations posing a serious market constraint for one or the other's profits. Moreover, the frequency with which directorate ties occurred between sectors of the economy is predicted by the intensity of market constraint between sectors, frequency of ties increasing in proportion to intensity of constraint. In fact, the structure of directorate ties in the economy adds nothing to the prediction of corporate profits by market constraints since directorate ties were so closely patterned by—or so accurate a cooptive response to—market constraints. This point too is argued in Chapter 4.

In short, my purpose in this book is to present evidence of processes by which the American economy operates at once as a competitive market and as a managed market. Archival data are used to describe how corporate profts could have been significantly constrained by competitive forces created in the network of necessary buying and selling between specific supplier and consumer sectors. The data are then used to describe how a social network of directorate ties was superimposed on this initial economic network of buying and selling—where the network of directorate ties was structured in a manner that would have enabled connected organizations to lessen the uncertainty of market constraints on their profits. Nevertheless, the constraint of competitive market transactions on corporate profits endured despite the ostensibly strategic creation of directorate ties.

This poses a basic question for future research. Given the close association between directorate ties and market constraints on corporate profits, why are corporate profits still determined by the constraint of competitive market transactions? Why does this connection between profits and market constraint persist despite the availability of directorate ties through which those constraints could have been avoided?

Although I do not pretend to resolve this question within the scope of this book, I believe that the answer lies in the study of a directorate tie market, the social network of interorganizational directorate ties patterned on the economic network of market constraints on corporate profits. In Chapter 5 I discuss the directorate tie market as an implication of this study and discuss new lines of research aimed at revealing social processes responsible for the coordination of market constraints and directorate ties. Some of these lines are pursued in detail in the technical essays included as the second part of this book. The chapters in Part II build on specific results in the forthcoming analysis, so I shall postpone further discussion of them until I have summarized my conclusions from the study in Chapter 5.

PART I
THEORY AND EVIDENCE

2

Market Structure: Constraint on Profits from Competitive Market Transactions*

Profits are obtained by exploiting transactions. The lower the price paid to suppliers and the higher the price charged to consumers, the higher the profit. To the extent that an organization paying suppliers and charging consumers does not control the price in these transactions, the organization's freedom to obtain profits is constrained. My purpose in this chapter is to describe the manner in which a pattern of sales and purchase transactions contains such constraint on corporate profits. I first describe patterns of market transactions and profits in the 1967 American economy. These are my data. I then describe the constraint of competition among organizations producing a commodity, describe the constraint of imperfect competition among their suppliers and consumers, and close with a discussion of market constraints between specific sectors of the economy in 1967.

RELATIONAL PATTERNS AND PROFITS IN THE MARKET

An economy is a network of exchange transactions between persons and corporate bureaucracies as actors in the economy. The division of labor in the economy ensures considerable redundancy in this network. Those actors engaged

*Portions of this chapter are drawn from articles reprinted with the permission of the *American Journal of Sociology, Social Networks,* and *Social Science Research* (Burt 1980a, 1979b, 1979a).

9

in the production of similar commodities will have similar relations from other actors (i.e., will require similar proportions of types of commodities as inputs from suppliers) and to other actors (i.e., will offer similar types of commodities as outputs to consumers). Since business establishments producing similar types of goods can be expected to have similar patterns of relations (up to a limit of proportionality) with suppliers and consumers, they can be aggregated into "sectors" within an input–output table representation of the economy, establishments within a single sector having similar levels of purchases from other sectors of establishments as suppliers and having similar levels of sales to other sectors of establishments as consumers. Instead of analyzing transactions between individual establishments, aggregate transactions between sectors of establishments can be analyzed. Replacing individual interorganizational transactions with aggregate intersector transactions is analytically feasible here since the individual transactions are merely variations on the intersector transaction. The result of this aggregation is an input–output table representing unique patterns of market transactions between economic sectors (e.g., Leontief, 1951, 1968). The table appears as an (M, M) matrix Z representing transactions between establishments in M sectors, where the element in row j and column i is z_{ji}, the total dollars worth of commodities sold by establishments in sector j to establishments in sector i during some period of time.

The sales and purchase transactions characterizing establishments in some sector j of the economy are contained in the elements of row j in the input–output table (these would be sales transactions from establishments) and the elements of column j (these would be purchase transactions by the establishments). This is illustrated in Figure 2.1 for sector j. The total dollars of sales by establishments in sector j to those in sector 1 is given by element z_{j1}. The total dollars of purchases by establishments in sector j from those in sector 2 is given by element z_{2j}. Each element z_{ji} or z_{ij} in Figure 2.1 is a market transaction characteristic of establishments in sector j. This pattern of market transactions with suppliers and consumers is the relational pattern from which establishments in sector j must derive their profits.

A more concrete example of this network context is given in Table A.1 in the Appendix. These data are taken from the 1967 input–output study of the American economy (U.S. Department of Commerce, 1974). Because of limited census data on nonmanufacturing sectors, I have focused on the relational patterns characterizing those economic sectors engaged in manufacturing: 20 broadly defined two-digit Standard Industrial Classification (SIC) industries and 327 much more narrowly defined four-digit SIC industries. I refer throughout this book to sectors engaged in manufacturing as industries and reference economic sectors generally as sectors or industries. The four-digit industries correspond to unique sectors in the detailed input–output table and are subsumed by the two-digit industries. For example, the two-digit tobacco industry (SIC category 21)

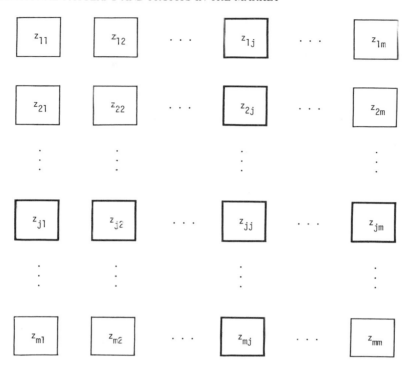

Figure 2.1. The pattern of market transactions defining economic sector j as a jointly occupied network position in the economy (z_{ji} is the dollars of sales by establishments in sector j to those in sector i).

contains four four-digit industries: the cigarette industry, the cigar industry, the chewing and smoking tobacco industry, and the tobacco stemming and drying industry (SIC categories 2111, 2121, 2131, 2141; note the common first two digits), each of which corresponds to a single sector in the detailed input–output study for 1967. The data in Table A.1 of the Appendix are relational patterns for the 20 two-digit industries. There are 51 sectors distinguished within the economy of which 20 are manufacturing industries. The market transactions in row and column j of this table define industry j as illustrated in Figure 2.1. The relational pattern characterizing the food industry, for example, is given by the elements in row and column 14 of the table. Establishments within the industry sold $3694 million worth of commodities to the livestock sector ($z_{14,1} = 3694$), nothing to the other agriculture sector ($z_{14,2} = 0$), and $24 million worth to the forestry/fishery sector ($z_{14,3} = 24$). They purchased $19,777 million worth of commodities from the livestock sector ($z_{1,14} = 19,777$), $6882 million worth from the other agriculture sector ($z_{2,14} = 6882$), and $423 million worth from the forestry/fishery sector ($z_{3,14}$). Each industry is defined in Table A.1 as a relational pattern of sales transactions to 51 sectors of the economy as consumers and purchase transactions from 51 sectors of the economy as suppliers. Each four-digit industry is similarly defined as a relational pattern of market transactions with economic sectors as suppliers and consumers, but there are a possible 483 sectors supplying or consuming output from four-digit industries rather than the mere 51 distinguished for two-digit industries. The size of the four-digit input–output table makes it awkward to consider in its entirety. I shall rely on the four-digit data to test hypotheses and on the two-digit data to illustrate them. At both the two-digit and four-digit industry level, however, the pattern of market transactions from which establishments in industry j derive their profits is given by elements in row and column j of the appropriately aggregated input–output table.

The input–output table representation of an economy is similar to topological network models of social structure (e.g., Burt, 1980b, 1982a:Chap. 2; Alba, 1982; Knoke & Kuklinski, 1982, for review). The fact that establishments producing similar commodities have similar patterns of market transactions with establishments in other sectors as suppliers and consumers means that they are structurally equivalent within the economy. They jointly occupy their sector as a network position within the economy, where Figure 2.1 presents the relational pattern defining position j. In place of an input–output table representation, sociologists construct density table representations of social structure. Element z_{ji} in the (M, M) density table corresponding to an input–output table is the typical (rather than the total) relation from actors jointly occupying position j, or status S_j as it is called, to actors jointly occupying status S_i. In other words, the economist's sector within an input–output table corresponds to the sociologist's jointly occupied position, or status, within a density table.[1]

In and of itself, this similarity of metaphor in economics and sociology is merely interesting. The similarity is useful here, however, because there is a network model of constraint available in sociology that can be used to represent market constraints in the economy. This model, a model of structural autonomy, uses the relational pattern defining a jointly occupied status to determine the extent to which its occupants are free to pursue their interests without constraint from other actors. As discussed in detail elsewhere (Burt, 1982a:Chap. 7), the model takes the patterns of relations among occupants of separate statuses as input and predicts the relative freedom each status offers its occupants as well as the extent to which that freedom is constrained by relations with each specific other status. In a sentence, the occupants of a status enjoy high structural autonomy to the extent that their relational pattern ensures low competition with one another while simultaneously ensuring high competition among the nonoccupant actors with

---

[1]See the Appendix to this chapter for a detailed discussion of the structural equivalence of competitors.

whom they have relations. Their structural autonomy is severely constrained by their relations with occupants of a particular other status to the extent that they only have relations with occupants of that status and those occupants are perfectly centralized so as to pursue their own interests collectively.

Treating an input–output table of market transactions as if it were a density table of social relations, the network model of structural autonomy defines the intensity of constraint that establishments in any one sector pose for profits in any other sector. Establishments in a manufacturing industry can obtain high profits to the extent that they can control price in their market transactions with suppliers and consumers. In other words, they can obtain high profits to the extent that they have high structural autonomy. Restating for establishments the preceding definition of structural autonomy, the establishments in an industry are free to obtain high profits (i.e., enjoy high structural autonomy) to the extent that their pattern of market transactions ensures low competition with one another while simultaneously ensuring high competition among their suppliers and consumers. Their ability to obtain high profits is severely constrained by their market transactions with establishments in a particular other sector to the extent that the bulk of their buying and selling is with establishments in that sector and the establishments in that sector are coordinated as a single corporate hierarchy so as to pursue their own interests collectively. In this case, establishments in the sector have control over price in the bulk of the market transactions involving establishments in the industry. Since the industry establishments do not control price in their market transactions, their ability to obtain profits is constrained. I shall make these general remarks more specific in a moment.[2]

These remarks suggest systematic differences in the ability of establishments in different sectors to obtain profits, some establishments having more control over price in transactions than do others. If there were perfect competition in the economy, then each establishment would have negligible control over price so that there would be little difference in the average profits obtained in one industry versus another. There would be little difference between the cost of producing a commodity and the price for which it could be sold.

In fact, price usually exceeds cost so that profits are well above zero. More to the point, profit margins are not equally greater than zero across different man-

---

[2]My emphasis is on autonomy rather than power, on the ability to pursue interests *without* constraint rather than on the ability to pursue interests *despite* constraint. A discussion of power in terms of an actor's network position is given elsewhere (Burt, 1977, 1979c) as an ability quite distinct from autonomy. Although a hermit can have high autonomy, few would consider him powerful. To be sure, powerful corporate actors will be able to obtain high profits from their investors. However, there can be corporate actors that are autonomous yet not powerful, and these autonomous corporate actors too will be able to obtain high profits. In order to obtain high profits, an establishment need not dominate the economy (as a powerful actor) so much as it must be free of severe market constraints within the economy (as an autonomous actor).

ufacturing industries. Establishments in some industries seem to be able to maintain prices further in excess of production costs than are establishments in other industries.

These statements are based on comparisons of price–cost margins across manufacturing industries. Collins and Preston (1968:13–17, 54–57, 1969) are to be credited with introducing the idea of measuring average profits within an industry (for the purpose of making comparisons across industries) as a price–cost margin. The total dollars of sales by establishments in an industry is the "value of shipments" (VS) for the industry. This corresponds to the sum of elements in one row of an input–output table. The sum of elements in a column of the table is the total costs of producing the commodities sold to obtain the value of shipments. The difference between the value of shipments for an industry and the sum of direct costs including materials, supplies, fuel, electric energy, cost of resales, and contract work done by others, is the "value added" (VA) by the industry. This is the dollars of income above and beyond direct costs that establishments in the industry were able to obtain from the sales they were able to make. Money given to employees as wages and salaries is considered part of the value added by an industry. The total net income for an industry could then be computed as the difference between dollars of value added (VA) and dollars given to labor costs (L). The price–cost margin (PCM) for the industry is the ratio of this net income over value of shipments as the gross industry income: $PCM = (VA - L)/VS$. The industry price–cost margin is then a measure of the proportion of an average dollar of sales that can be treated as profit. Since this proportion does not reflect industry capital costs (the production of steel, for example, requires more expensive equipment than the production of apparel), raw price–cost margins should be adjusted for capital requirements in order to measure industry profit margins more accurately for comparisons across industries. Capital-intensive industries would be expected to make high profits in order to cover their high capital costs. *The profit margin in industry j, p_j, is the raw industry price–cost margin adjusted for the extent to which the industry has high capital requirements.*[3] *A value of p_j equal to .5, for example, would show that 50¢ of the average dollar of sales by establishments in industry j went to cover production costs and 50¢ was left over as discretionary income, profit, for the establishments.*

---

[3]Capital requirements (CR) are computed as the gross book value of depreciable assets for industry j ($ASSETS_j$) divided by the value of shipments for the industry (VS_j), $CR_j = ASSETS_j/VS_j$, both taken from the 1970 *Annual Survey of Manufactures* (U.S. Department of Commerce, 1973). The raw price–cost margin in the industry is then specified as the sum of the industry profit margin p_j and a weighted capital requirements term $b(CR_j - \overline{CR})$, where $\overline{CR}$ is the average value of CR across the 327 four-digit industries: $PCM_j = p_j + b(CR_j - \overline{CR})$. To the extent that the capital requirements in industry j are above average, raw price–cost margins are expected to be high to cover the added costs of capital. For the four-digit industries, the least-squares estimate of b is .076; it is .064 for the two-

TABLE 2.1
Industry Profit Margins

	Two-digit industries $(N = 20)$	Four-digit industries $(N = 327)$
Mean	.258	.265
Standard deviation	.066	.081
Minimum	.169	.048
Maximum	.387	.601

Profit margins have been computed for the four-digit manufacturing industries and the two-digit industries using data on expenditures in 1967 as reported in the *Census of Manufactures* (U.S. Department of Commerce, 1971). Profit margins for the two-digit industries are given in Table A.3 of the Appendix. Four-digit data are given in Table A.2.

Instead of being low and equal for all industries in 1967, profit margins varied from industry to industry. This variation is summarized in Table 2.1. For the two-digit and four-digit industries, the mean profit margin across industries is .26 indicating that about a quarter of each dollar of sales by establishments on average could be interpreted as profit.[4] Individual industries varied from this

---

digit industries. Profit margins were then computed by adjusting raw price–cost margins for the capital requirements effect:

$$p_j = PCM_j - b(CR_j - \overline{CR}).$$

Although previous studies have controlled for interindustry differences in capital requirements by specifying such differences as an additional variable in regression equations predicting profit margins (e.g., Collins & Preston, 1969; Rhoades, 1973, 1974; Khalilzadeh-Shirazi, 1974; Lustgarten, 1975; Kwoka, 1979; Porter, 1979), I have taken the more conservative tack of completely removing the effect from raw price–cost margins. The difference is slight (raw and corrected price–cost margins have a .98 correlation for the two-digit industries and a .97 correlation for the four-digit), and I do not wish to carry CR as a variable throughout the analysis.

[4]The income reported as profit to the Internal Revenue Service is much lower than these numbers suggest. Using the tax return data compiled in the *Statistics of Income: Corporation Income Tax Returns* (Internal Revenue Service, 1971) for firms showing a profit during 1967, the mean ratio for two-digit industries of income taxes (profit) over total receipts (total income) is only .048 in contrast to the .258 reported in Table 2.1. Nevertheless, the census and tax return measures of profit margin are strongly correlated ($r = .80$), the industries showing a high profit margin in their tax returns also have a high price–cost margin. However, the tax return data are less adequate to the task of analyzing market constraints. Although the tax data can be useful in the absence of other data (see Chapter 6), there are two good reasons for not using them here. (a) The tax data are based on whole corporations being assigned to a single industry. The 1120 tax return form includes a list of economic sectors distinguished by the Standard Enterprise Classification system. The 20 broadly defined two-digit SIC industries correspond to aggregate SEC categories. The person filling out a corporation's income tax return is asked to indicate which industry group provided the ''largest percentage of total receipts'' for the firm's activities during the year. Since large firms are typically diversified into many eco-

mean. Among the four-digit industries, the lowest profit margin was endured by textile establishments engaged in scouring and combing (SIC category 2297, p_j = .048) and the highest profit margin was enjoyed by chemical establishments engaged in toilet preparations (SIC category 2844, p_j = .601). At the two-digit level, establishments in the apparel industry had the lowest average profit margin (SIC category 23, p_j = .169), and those in the chemical industry enjoyed the highest average profit margin (SIC category 28, p_j = .387). Attributing this observed variation in profit margins to imperfect competition, the industries with low average margins should have been more subject to market constraint on their profits than were the industries with high average profit margins.

THE CONSTRAINT OF COMPETITORS

The most widely understood market constraint on profits is the constraint created by competition among establishments in an industry. Ideally, this competition prevents any one establishment in the industry from being able to control price in its market transactions with suppliers and consumers. If, in order to obtain unusually high profits, one establishment lowered the prices it was willing to pay for supplies and raised the price to be charged to consumers, other establishments in the industry could offer prices more favorable to suppliers and consumers. In the interest of their own profits, suppliers and consumers could be expected to shift their market transactions to the other establishments. The establishment seeking unusually high profits by controlling price would be forced to offer more attractive prices before it perished for want of trade partners. But if

---

nomic sectors, this self-assignment to a single sector is increasingly likely to be unreliable as economic sectors are increasingly narrowly defined. Large firms cut across even the two-digit industries (as described in Chapter 3), let alone the much more narrowly defined four-digit industries. (b) In addition to the problem of corporate self-assignment to a single sector, the tax return data are not census compilations. The 1967 data are tabulated from returns for almost all firms owning assets over $10 million; however, smaller firms are sampled and sample tabulations are then used to project population totals (Internal Revenue Service, 1971:145–146). Firms with assets over $1 million but less than $10 million were sampled at a rate of 37.21% for the 1967 data, but smaller firms were sampled at a rate of no more than 6.1%, the smallest firms being sampled at a rate of 2.49%. This means that data on industries with typically small firms tend to be less reliable than those on industries with typically large firms. Firms in the lumber industry, for example, are typically smaller than those in the petroleum industry. A .67 confidence interval around the dollars distributed to stockholders in 1967 for the firms showing a profit is the reported figure ±10.38% for the lumber industry whereas the same interval for the petroleum industry is given by the reported figure ±0.09% (Internal Revenue Service, 1971:154). For reasons of reliability and accuracy, the census data used to compute price–cost margins seem preferable to tax return data. Still, it is worth noting that p_j probably overstates the actual profit margin in industry j even though it is strongly correlated with that margin.

establishments in the industry could coordinate their pricing decisions as a collective decision (i.e., if they were cooperative rather than competitive), then they would be free to obtain high profits. Any supplier wishing to sell to their industry would be obliged to sell at the industry price, and any consumer wishing to purchase their commodity would be obliged to pay the industry price. I am, for the moment, ignoring the possibility that suppliers and consumers too could be cooperative rather than competitive.

At this point it is convenient to distinguish the establishment and corporate levels of organization explicitly. Corporations are fictive persons created under corporate law. General Motors is a corporation. Corporations own and operate establishments. Establishments are the organizational units in which commodities are produced. Indirectly, of course, corporations as the owners of establishments are also organizational units in which commodities are produced. Although corporations typically own multiple establishments in multiple sectors of the economy, a single establishment specializes in producing a single type of commodity. I shall refer to a corporation's holdings in one sector of the economy as its establishment in the sector. Following the terminology of the Department of Commerce, an industry consists of all such establishments engaged in the manufacture of a single type of commodity. If a corporation owns two factories, one manufacturing bread and the other cigars, then it owns two establishments, one in the food industry and another in the tobacco industry. If it owns two factories at separate locations but both are engaged in the production of bread, then it owns a single establishment in the food industry.[5]

If the many organizations producing a commodity are owned and operated by the same corporation, then it is in the interest of the corporation to control competition among them so as to control the price of the commodity they sell. In respect to pricing decisions, the ostensibly competitive organizations in the industry can be treated as if they were a single establishment. In essence, there is a single establishment making pricing decisions within the industry. An empirical measure of the extent to which a corporation's establishment represents all of the output from an industry is the corporation's market share in the industry, the sum of all sales by the corporation's factories as an establishment divided by the industry value of shipments. Let s_1 be the largest market share of any corporation within an industry, s_2 be the second-largest market share, s_3 be the third-largest, and so on. If s_1 equals a fraction close to one, then a single corporation holds a

[5]This treatment differs slightly from that employed by the Commerce Department. The Commerce Department considers each factory within a sector as a separate establishment whether or not the factories are owned by a single corporation. Since establishment-level data are not available for a national sample of firms and since my principal concern is the coordination of establishments owned by separate corporations and operating in separate sectors, two or more Commerce Department establishments that are owned by a single firm in a single sector are treated as a single establishment.

monopoly over the industry. The firm's control over industry price is expected to result in prices favorable to the industry so that the average profit margin in the industry is high.

Even if the organizations producing a commodity are owned and operated by a small number of corporations (rather than just one corporation), it would be easier for them to act cooperatively in setting prices than it would be for a large number of corporations to act cooperatively. Each corporation would coordinate the prices charged by the organizations it owns. The fewer competitive corporations there were in the industry, the easier it would be for the corporations to agree informally on a pricing policy they could then enforce within their respective establishments. If the many organizations producing a commodity are owned by four corporations so that the four largest market shares in the industry sum to a fraction close to one, then there are only four competitors within the industry. The four corporations constitute an oligopoly within the industry. Their ability to control industry price collectively is expected to result in informal pricing agreements within the industry setting prices favorable to the industry so that the average profit margin in the industry is high.

The problem of monopolies and oligopolies having control over prices so that they can obtain high profits is a standard textbook problem in economics (e.g., Shepherd, 1970; Caves, 1982). Not surprisingly, there is empirical support for the received theory. The U.S. Department of Commerce publishes aggregate market shares for manufacturing industries. The four largest market shares in each industry are summed and published as the four-firm concentration ratio for the industry (i.e., $s_1 + s_2 + s_3 + s_4 = C14$, which is the four-firm concentration ratio for an industry). If there are four or fewer separate corporations owning all establishments in an industry, this concentration ratio equals one. There is replicated evidence that industry concentration is positively associated with industry profit margin (e.g., Collins & Preston, 1968, 1969).[6] The association is replicated here using four-firm concentration ratios reported for the four-digit industries in the 1967 *Census of Manufactures* (U.S. Department of Commerce,

---

[6]Although this association appears to be robust over studies of industries as a general population, it is not consistent across types of industries. For example, Collins and Preston (1969) report that the association between concentration and profits is higher for consumer goods industries than it is for producer goods industries. Even more striking, Porter (1974) reports that among consumer goods industries, the direct effect of concentration on profits is positive for nonconvenience goods but negative for convenience goods, convenience goods being items with low unit price and to which the consumer would be expected to want easy access (e.g., meat and dairy products, soft drinks, or tobacco products). I shall represent the potentially variable association between profits and concentration as an interaction between concentration and external constraints on an industry in the analysis of imperfect competition among suppliers and consumers. The association between concentration and profits is depressed for those industries subject to high constraint from their suppliers and consumers.

1971). Pooled ratios have been computed for each two-digit industry from the four-digit data.[7] These ratios allow high concentration within subsectors of each two-digit industry. As I mentioned earlier, however, I am relying on the four-digit data for testing hypotheses and the highly aggregate two-digit data for illustration.[8] On average, the four largest establishments in a four-digit industry accounted for 40% of industry sales in 1967 (i.e., $C14 = .40$). Among the two-digit industries, this average drops to a somewhat smaller 36% ($C14 = .36$). Even in the highly aggregate two-digit industries, concentration varied considerably, from a minimum in the lumber industry ($C14 = .16$) to a maximum in the tobacco industry ($C14 = .74$). If industry profit margins are regressed over these concentration ratios, the expected positive effect of oligopoly on profit margin is observed. On average, a .1 increase in the market share of the four largest establishments in an industry is associated with a .01 increase in the industry profit margin. Earlier studies have reported on the same level of effect for 1958 and 1963 data (e.g., Collins & Preston, 1969). Where $C14_j$ is the four-firm concentration ratio in industry j, e_j is an error term, and t-tests are given in parentheses, this effect is statistically negligible across the 20 two-digit industries,

[7]Two-digit ratios are computed as the weighted sum of four-digit ratios: $C14_j = \Sigma_k(VS_kC14_k)/VS_j$, where VS_k is the value of shipments from four-digit industry k subsumed by two-digit industry j (i.e., $VS_j = \Sigma_k VS_k$) and $C14_k$ is the four-firm concentration ratio for four-digit industry k. This aggregate measure of two-digit concentration preserves high levels of concentration within subsectors of a two-digit industry responsible for a high proportion of the value of shipments from the two-digit industry.

[8]Note in Table 2.1 that the aggregation of four-digit industries into two-digit industries has eliminated the extremely high profit margins found at the four-digit level. The range and variance in profit margins is lower across two-digit industries than it is across four-digit industries. The same regression toward the mean phenomenon is observed in aggregating four-digit measures of imperfect competition (Y_1 and $C14$) into two-digit measures. In other words, the two-digit data obscure processes of market constraint generating extremely high profit margins observed in the four-digit data. With these extremes eliminated, a fixed level of random variance in the data becomes a higher proportion of total variance in the two-digit data than it is in the four-digit data so that the two-digit data can be expected to offer less support for any hypotheses proposing processes of market constraint. At the same time, there is reason to expect a conservative bias even in the more accurate estimates computed from the four-digit data. As pointed out in the chapter Appendix, there is reason to expect some four-digit industries to be too finely drawn, multiple four-digit industries in fact being subsectors of a single industry. This oversegregation of industries can be expected to inflate the effective concentration within industries artificially because increasingly narrow production activities are increasingly likely to be performed by a single firm. These upwardly biased concentration ratios can then be expected to downwardly bias estimates of parameters involving concentration ratios since oversegregated sectors would have lower profit margins than those predicted by their inflated concentration ratios. In short, I expect a conservative bias in effects estimated from the two-digit data or the four-digit data because of their respective misrepresentations of structural equivalence in the economy, however, the bias in the two-digit data would be greater because of the gross aggregation of economic sectors involved in compiling the two-digit data.

$$p_j = .214 + .123 \ C14_j + e_j,$$
$$(1.29)$$

but quite significant across the 327 four-digit industries,

$$p_j = .228 + .093 \ C14_j + e_j.$$
$$(4.57)$$

These results are based on the assumption that the summed market shares of the four largest establishments in an industry measure the extent to which a small number of establishments in the industry have the power to determine, or influence strongly, industry prices in market transactions. This assumption ignores industry establishments smaller than the four largest. Many different market structures with different implications for the ability of industry establishments to control industry prices could generate a single four-firm industry concentration ratio. Consider the distribution of market shares across the eight largest establishments in three hypothetical industries with equivalent four-firm concentration (cf. Caves, 1982:8–10, for a related illustration). Industry A is dominated by one corporation's establishment holding a 57% market share, and the seven next-largest establishments each hold 1% market shares (i.e., $s_1 = .57$, $s_2 = s_3 = \cdots = s_8 = .01$). Industry B is dominated by the establishments of four corporations where no one corporation has a market share larger than the others ($s_1 = s_2 = s_3 = s_4 = .15$, and the remaining market shares are all .01). Industry C has the same distribution of market shares among the top four establishments that is found in industry B, but in this industry the remaining four establishments also hold strong market shares ($s_1 = s_2 = s_3 = s_4 = .15$, and $s_5 = s_6 = s_7 = s_8 = .10$). The four largest establishments in these hypothetical industries have equivalent aggregate market shares, the four-firm concentration ratio being .6 in all three industries, but they do not have equivalent control over industry prices. The dominant establishment in industry A is in the best position to control industry prices. It is least subject to the constraint of competition within the industry since it controls 57 times as much of the industry sales as any one of its competitors. It can offer much larger purchasing contracts to industry suppliers and can meet much larger purchasing orders from industry consumers than can its competitors within the industry. It is not entirely free from the constraint of intraindustry competition, but it is clearly the establishment least subject to such constraint in these three industries. There is no one dominant establishment in industry B, however; the four largest establishments are much larger than the many remaining establishments in the industry. If the four largest could coordinate their pricing decisions, they would be able to control industry prices as well as the dominant establishment in industry A can. They would be jointly responsible for 60% of industry sales and would be opposed by many competitors individually holding 1% market shares. This situation is significantly altered in industry C. The four largest establishments in industries B and C all have 15% market shares in their respective industries. The four largest in industry B are in competition with many, much smaller, establishments; however, the four largest in industry C are opposed by only four, almost as large, establishments. If the four largest establishments in industry B could coordinate their pricing decisions, it would be difficult for the industry's remaining establishments to threaten the agreed upon industry price. The four smallest establishments in industry C, however, pose a severe threat to any pricing agreement reached by the four largest establishments. The 60% market share represented by the four largest could be opposed by the 40% market share represented by the four smallest.

Across these three hypothetical industries with equal four-firm concentration, in short, there are different probabilities of industry prices being free from the constraint of competition. Prices in industry A would be least subject to constraint because there is a single dominant establishment in competition with many small establishments in the industry. Prices in industry B would be more subject to constraint because the four largest establishments must coordinate their pricing decisions in order to achieve the same level of control enjoyed by the dominant firm in industry A. Prices in industry C would be still more subject to constraint because the four largest establishments must coordinate their pricing decisions in order to hold a 60% market share jointly, but even if they were able to coordinate their pricing decisions their collusion could provoke a coalition of the remaining four establishments in the industry, and that competitive coalition would enjoy a large market share in the industry.

There are two analytically distinguishable dimensions operating here. The industries differ in the extent to which a small number of large establishments could jointly hold a large market share in the industry so as to be able to control industry prices. Industry A with its single dominant establishment is higher on this dimension than industries B and C with their respective four equally dominant competitors. The industries also differ in the extent to which a coalition of the largest establishments is free from the threat of a coalition among the remaining industry establishments. On this dimension, industry A is higher than industry B, which is much higher than industry C. If the ninth-largest through the smallest establishments in industries A and B each held a 1% market share, then a coalition of small establishments against the one dominant establishment in industry A would require the coordination of pricing decisions in 43 independent competitors. A coalition of small establishments against a coalition of the four largest establishments in industry B would require the coordination of pricing decisions in 40 independent competitors. Of course, a pricing agreement between three of the largest firms in industry B (which would provide a 45% market share) could be threatened by a coalition of the fourth-largest establishment with fewer than all 40 remaining establishments. Still, it would be difficult to coordinate the pricing decisions reached in so many different boards of directors. In industry C, however, a coalition of the four largest establishments would be no easier to coordinate than a competitive coalition of the remaining industry establishments. Both would require agreement on prices determined by four separate corporate directorates. Both would result in large aggregate market shares in the industry. This second dimension to imperfect competition, in short, is the extent to which nondominant establishments in an industry could not easily threaten a pricing agreement imposed on their industry by a coalition of the largest firms.[9]

Imperfect competition within an industry is defined simultaneously by these two dimensions. *Let y_{j1} vary between zero and one as the extent to which there is imperfect competition in industry j in the sense that a small number of establishments jointly hold a large market share in the industry so as to be able to control, or strongly influence, industry prices and they are free from the threat of competitive prices being offered by a coalition of other establishments in the industry.* Ideally, y_{j1} would be computed from the distribution of market shares across each corporate establishment in the industry. In order to preserve confidentiality, the Commerce Department cannot release such data.[10] However, aggregate data are available in public archives: the aggregate market share held by the four largest corporate establishments in an industry and the aggregate market share of the next four largest establishments. I have previously discussed the former as $C14$ and shall refer to the latter as $C58$. To the extent that a small number of establishments in an industry hold a large aggregate market share, $C14$ will be high. I shall use $C14$ as a measure of the first dimension of imperfect competition. To the extent that the fifth-largest through the smallest establishments in the industry hold a negligible market share (i.e., there are many small competitors), $C58$ will be low. I shall use $C58$ as a reversed measure of the second dimension of imperfect competition.[11] Imperfect competition within an industry, Y_1, would be high to the extent that $C14$ is high and $C58$ is low.

[9]Conceptually, this dimension of imperfect competition is closely related to the idea of group "completeness" described by Simmel (1908:95; cf. Merton, 1957:342ff) and the game theoretic concept of power discussed by Shapley and Shubik (1954; cf. Riker & Ordeshook, 1973:154ff).

[10]There is reason for wishing such data to be available in public archives. Using sample data modified by the Federal Trade Commission, Kwoka (1979) shows that the aggregate market shares held by the two largest firms in an industry are the most crucial for obtaining high profits. Using data on four-digit industries in 1972, he shows that price–cost margins were strongly, positively affected by two-firm concentration ratios, but were negatively affected by the market share of the third-largest firm in the industry. In other words, the countervailing power of the fifth- through the eighth-largest firms discussed in the text appears to begin with the third-largest firm. Unfortunately, these market share data are not available in public archives such as the *Census of Manufactures*.

[11]The 1967 *Census of Manufactures* reports concentration ratios for the 4 largest, 8 largest, 20 largest, and 50 largest firms in four-digit industries. The aggregate market shares for the four largest firms ($C14$), the fifth- through the eighth-largest ($C58$), the ninth- through the twentieth-largest ($C9–20$), and the twenty-first- through the fiftieth-largest ($C21–50$) firms in each industry can be

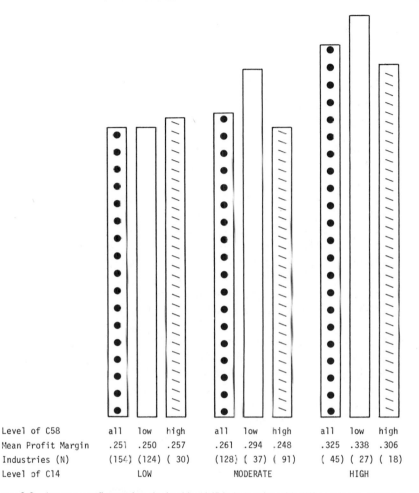

Level of C58	all	low	high	all	low	high	all	low	high
Mean Profit Margin	.251	.250	.257	.261	.294	.248	.325	.338	.306
Industries (N)	(154)	(124)	(30)	(128)	(37)	(91)	(45)	(27)	(18)
Level of C14		LOW			MODERATE			HIGH	

Figure 2.2. Average profit margins obtained in 1967 in industries with different levels of $C14$ (low, moderate, high) and $C58$ (low versus high).

---

computed from these cumulative concentration ratios. If profit margins in the 327 four-digit industries are regressed across these four market share measures, the following results are obtained (t-tests are given in parentheses):

$$P = .244 + .0014(C14) - .0033(C58) + .0003(C9\text{--}20) + .0005(C21\text{--}50) + E,$$
$$(4.27)(2.84)(0.23)(0.43)$$

indicating the negligibility of aggregate market share data available on any but the largest eight firms. I have accordingly ignored establishments smaller than the largest eight in the text. The squared multiple correlation for this equation is .099, which is about the same as the squared correlation between profit margins and the certainty measure in Eq. (2.2) combining $C14$ and $C58$ into Y_1 ($r^2 = .106$).

In other words, profit margins should be high in industries with high values of $C14$ and low values of $C58$. In fact, these two variables interact in association with profit margins. The bar graphs of 1967 data in Figure 2.2 illustrate the interaction.

The most obvious feature of the bar graphs in Figure 2.2 is the positive association between industry concentration and profit. Four-digit industries have been divided into three categories: those with low concentration ($.00 < C14 \leq .33$), those with moderate concentration ($.33 < C14 \leq .66$), and those with high concentration ($.66 < C14 < 1.0$).[12] The height of a bar in the figure reflects an average industry profit margin. An average profit margin of 25% was observed in all industries with low concentraion (i.e., $\bar{p} = .25$ when $C14$ is less than or equal to .33). This is the speckled bar over low concentration industries in the figure. The speckled bar over moderate concentration industries is slightly higher reflecting the average profit margin of 26% in these industries (i.e., $\bar{p} = .26$ when $C14$ is greater than .33 but less than or equal to .66). Finally, the speckled bar over high concentration industries is highest of all reflecting the average profit margin of 33% in these industries (i.e., $\bar{p} = .33$ when $C14$ is greater than .66). As would be expected from the earlier regression results, average industry profit margins increase across categories of increasing industry concentration.

A second feature of the bar graphs in Figure 2.2 is the inconsistency of this association across differences in the aggregate market share of the fifth- through the eighth-largest establishments. Across the 327 four-digit industries, the average aggregate market share of the fifth- through the eighth-largest establishments in an industry was 13% in 1967 ($\overline{C58} = .131$). For the purposes of illustration in Figure 2.2, I have divided industries into two categories: those with low aggregate market shares held by the fifth- through eighth-largest establishments ($C58 \leq .131$) versus those with high aggregate market shares ($C58 > .131$).[13] Indus-

---

[12]I shall use $C14$ and $C58$ as continuous variables in the following in order to measure imperfect competition as Y_1. The broad categories adopted for the illustrative purposes of Figure 2.2 are based on an analysis of much more narrowly defined categories; ten .1-width categories of $C14$ and six .05-width categories of $C58$. These categories were used to define a 10×6 table of $C14$ by $C58$ in which cell (i,j) was the average profit margin for industries in the ith category of $C14$ and the jth category of $C58$. I found that the interaction effect between $C14$ and $C58$ occurs within the categories distinguished in Figure 2.2; profit margins in industries with $C14$ less than .4 tended to be low regardless of the value of $C58$, margins tended to be high in industries with $C14$ greater than .69, although slightly depressed by high values of $C58$, and they tended to be high in industries with values of $C14$ between .39 and .69 if $C58$ was less than .15 but low in these industries if $C58$ was greater than .15. Since .15 is close to the mean value of $C58$, I have dichotomized $C58$ at its mean for Figure 2.2. I have trichotomized $C14$ at $\frac{1}{3}$ and $\frac{2}{3}$, roughly the breaking points for the $C14$ interaction with $C58$ in determining profits in the detailed table.

[13]This dichotomy is adopted for illustrative purposes in Figure 2.2 based on the analysis of more narrowly defined categories as described in footnote 12.

try profit margins were higher in moderately and highly concentrated industries when the second four largest establishments had a low market share. They were smaller when the second four largest establishments had a high market share. In terms of Figure 2.2, the white bars (industries in which $C58$ was low) are higher than the striped bars (industries in which $C58$ was high) in moderately and highly concentrated industries. Industry profits were lowered by the fifth- through the eighth-largest establishments in an industry posing a threat to the four largest establishments being able to control industry prices.

The third feature of the bar graphs in Figure 2.2 is the varying magnitude of this threat across different levels of industry concentration. It was least at low levels of concentration, greatest at moderate levels of concentration, and moderate at high levels of concentration. Consider the three categories of concentration individually. The average profit margin among low concentration industries was .251, which remained the same among those in which $C58$ was low and increased slightly among those in which $C58$ was high (these are the speckled, white, and striped bars, respectively, in Figure 2.2). In other words, the aggregate market share of the fifth- through the eighth-largest establishments did not have much effect on imperfect competition in an industry if the aggregate market share of the four largest establishments was low. Such an industry was highly competitive. In moderate concentration industries the average profit margin was .261, which increased to .294 among those in which $C58$ was low and decreased to .248 among those in which $C58$ was high. In other words, the aggregate market share of the fifth- through the eighth-largest establishments had a discernible effect on imperfect competition in an industry of moderate concentration. High profits were obtained if the four largest establishments could ignore the next four largest establishments (i.e., if $C58$ was low). But if the next four largest establishments held a high market share in the industry ($C58$ was high), then industry profits in these moderately concentrated industries decreased to a level observed in the low concentration industries: The striped bar in Figure 2.2 for moderate concentration industries is about the same height as the bars for low concentration industries. A similar, but less pronounced, difference in profits is observed in high concentration industries. These industries had the highest profits, all bars for high concentration industries being the highest in Figure 2.2. However, the average profit margin of .325 increased to an even higher .338 if $C58$ was low and decreased to a somewhat lower .306 if $C58$ was high.

An appropriate measure of Y_1 will be one in which $C14$ and $C58$ are combined so as to re-create the three features of the data distribution in Figure 2.2. Readers not interested in the details of how I shall do this may wish to skip to the next section, where imperfectly competitive suppliers and consumers are included in the prediction of industry profits.

Four measures of imperfect competition within the 327 four-digit industries are distinguished in Table 2.2. Industry profit margins (P) and four-firm con-

TABLE 2.2
Mean Measures of Imperfect Competition within Industries[a]

Levels of four-firm concentration	Levels of aggregate market shares held by the fifth- through eighth-largest establishments			
	All	Low	High	High/low
Mean profit margin (P)				
Low	.251	.250	.257	1.03
Moderate	.261	.294	.248	.84
High	.325	.338	.306	.91
Mean concentration (C14)				
Low	.215	.200	.276	1.38
Moderate	.479	.471	.482	1.02
High	.775	.800	.737	.92
Mean probability (C14 − C14 × C58)				
Low	.190	.181	.230	1.27
Moderate	.399	.422	.390	.92
High	.678	.724	.608	.84
Mean certainty ($Y_1 = C14 − C14 × C58 × U$)				
Low	.167	.166	.173	1.04
Moderate	.205	.304	.164	.54
High	.596	.687	.459	.67

[a]Categories of concentration and aggregate market shares for the fifth- through the eighth-largest establishments are given in the discussion of Figure 2.2. These means are computed from data on the 327 four-digit industries.

centration ratios ($C14$) have already been introduced. The rows of Table 2.2 distinguish the three categories of industry concentration introduced in Figure 2.2: low, moderate, and high. Columns present mean scores across and within the two categories of $C58$ introduced in Figure 2.2: low versus high. The first three rows of the table present the means given in Figure 2.2, the average profit margin in low concentration industries being .251 (left-most speckled bar in Figure 2.2), the average in moderate concentration industries being .261 (the middle speckled bar in Figure 2.2), the average in high concentration industries with high values of $C58$ being .306 (the right-most striped bar in Figure 2.2), and so on. An appropriate measure of Y_1 will combine $C14$ and $C58$ so as to re-create the relative magnitudes of these mean profit margins.

The second three rows of Table 2.2 present mean four-firm concentration ratios. Differences in the relative magnitudes of these means and the relative magnitudes of the corresponding mean profit margins indicate where $C14$ is a biased measure of imperfect competition. Overall, $C14$ is a poor measure of imperfect competition because it exaggerates the importance of moderate levels of concentration for control over industry prices. Three comparisons in Table 2.2 illustrate this. The mean concentration ratio in moderately concentrated industries was more than twice as large as the mean for low concentration industries (.479 versus .215), but the mean profit margin in moderately concentrated industries was about the same as that in the low concentration industries (.261 versus .251). Among low concentration industries, the mean concentration ratio when $C58$ was high was almost 1.5 times as large as the mean when $C58$ was low (.276 is 1.38 times as large as .200 as reported in row 4 of Table 2.2). But the mean profit margins are about the same in these two categories (.257 is 1.03 times as large as .250 as reported in row 1 of Table 2.2). Finally, the mean concentration ratio in moderately concentrated industries with a high value of $C58$ was about the same as that observed when $C58$ was low (.482 is 1.02 times as large as .471). But this is precisely the point at which the fifth- through the eighth-largest establishments posed the greatest threat to the four largest establishments being able to control industry prices. The mean profit margin in these industries was much lower when $C58$ was high than when it was low (.248 is .84 of .294 as reported in the second row of Table 2.2).

One strategy for obtaining a more accurate measure of imperfect competition within an industry is to think of market shares as probabilities of successful control over industry prices.[14] The market share s_i would be the probability of the ith largest establishment in an industry being able to control industry prices. Establishments owned by separate firms represent nonoverlapping market shares, so they could improve the probability of successfully controlling industry prices by coordinating their actions. The higher the aggregate market share of the four largest establishments, the more likely their success in controlling industry prices if they attempt to do so. The probability of their success would be $C14$. The higher the aggregate market share of the fifth- through the eighth-largest establishments, the more likely that they could successfully control industry prices if they chose to do so. The probability of their success would be $C58$.

A measure of imperfect competition could now be defined as the joint probability of successful control over industry prices by the four largest establishments

---

[14]I pursued several other strategies focusing on measures of marginal control; however, they did not yield results as accurate as those obtained with the strategy to be presented. Of course, the analogy between market shares and probabilities is merely an intuitive guide here.

and failure to control by the next four largest establishments. The probability of the fifth- through the eighth-largest establishments failing to control industry prices is one minus the probability of their success, $1 - C58$. The joint probability measure of imperfect competition would be the product of the preceding two probabilities assuming, for the moment, that the two attempts at control would be independent, $C14(1 - C58)$. The difference between this measure and raw four-firm concentration ratios is clearer when the measure is expressed without parentheses; $C14 - C14 \times C58$. The measure adjusts concentration downward to the extent that $C58$ is high when $C14$ is high. In other words, a high aggregate market share held by the fifth- through the eight-largest establishments will have little effect on industry competition unless the four largest establishments are in a position to successfully control industry prices. In this circumstance, the effect of the second four largest establishments would be one of decreasing the probability of successful control over prices by the four largest.

This measure offers a slightly stronger correlation with industry profit margins than the correlation obtained using raw four-firm concentration ratios; however, the improvement is slight (.272 rather than the earlier .246). The mean values of this joint probability measure are given in the third group of three rows of Table 2.2 and indicate the measure's weaknesses. The importance of moderate concentration is still exaggerated. The mean probability score for moderately concentrated industries is twice as large as the mean for low concentration industries (.399 versus .190). However, the joint probability measure does capture the depressive effect of high $C58$ on moderate $C14$. The mean probability score for low concentration industries is .230 when $C58$ is high and .181 when $C58$ is low, a ratio of 1.27 rather than the too high ratio of 1.38 implied by raw concentration ratios. The mean probability score for moderate concentration ratios is .390 when $C58$ is high and .422 when it is low, a ratio of .92 rather than the too high 1.02 implied by raw concentration ratios. In other words, $C58$ does have its desired depressive effect at moderate levels of concentration. At the same time, this joint probability measure is not accurately depicting the interaction of $C14$ and $C58$ in determining profit margins. The depressive effect of $C58$ at moderate levels of concentration is not sufficiently strong, and it is greatest when concentration is high whereas the observed profit margins show that it was greatest when concentration was moderate.

What is needed is a measure that emphasizes the depressive effect of $C58$ at moderate levels of concentration while decreasing its effect at extreme levels of concentration. One measure that does this introduces uncertainty into the preceding probability measure.

View imperfect competition from the perspective of the four largest establishments in an industry. The probability of them successfully controlling industry prices is given by $C14$, and the probability of the second four largest establishments being able to control price in competition with them is given by $C58$. But suppose that the four largest firms, in attempting to control industry prices, do not react objectively to $C58$. Suppose that they evaluate it subjectively from their own position in the industry. The more uncertain their own ability to control industry prices, the more threatening any probability of success by the second four largest firms would appear to be. If $C14$ is very low, then it is clear that the four largest firms could not control industry prices. If it is very high, then it is clear that they have a good chance of controlling industry prices. But if $C14$ is close to .5, then they are in a very uncertain position. They have a 50:50 chance of success. A high probability of the second four largest firms being able to control industry prices would be most threatening at this point. If this uncertainty has a normal distribution with maximum uncertainty occurring when $C14$ is .5, then the uncertainty of successful control by the four largest firms in an industry, U, can be expressed in the following form:

$$U = \left[\frac{k}{(2\pi\sigma^2)^{1/2}} \right] e^{-(C14 - .5)^2/2\sigma^2}, \tag{2.1}$$

where π and e are well-known mathematical constants σ^2 is the variance of four-firm concentration ratios across industries, and k is a constant to be estimated. This equation is the height of the normal distribution for a level of concentration $C14$. The height of the distribution is adjusted by the constant in brackets so that the area covered by the distribution has a particular value. When k is one, the area is one and is interpreted as a probability in unit normal test statistics. The constant in brackets is of secondary interest here. The shape of the distribution is defined by e raised to its exponent $-(C14 - .5)^2/2\sigma^2$. This exponent will be large to the extent that concentration in an industry is very different from .5 (either very much lower or very much higher) and concentration does not vary much across industries so that σ^2 is small.[15] Across the 327 four-digit industries, four-firm concentration had a variance ($\hat{\sigma}^2$) in 1967 of .0451. To the extent that concentration in an industry was less different from .5 than twice the variance in concentration across all industries, this exponent would be small. For example, an industry in which the

[15]The exponent is $-.5$ times a squared z-score concentration ratio centered on a mean of .5: $-.5[(C14 - .5)/\sigma]^2$. For substantive reasons, I have used .5 as the center for the distribution of uncertainty rather than the actual mean of .4 because uncertainty should be greatest when a set of firms hold combined market shares equal to half the market. There are other values of concentration that could be used to center the distribution of uncertainty and other measures of variation that could be used to scale the spread of the distribution of uncertainty as the denominator in the exponent. For example, I considered $C58$ as an alternative to the standard deviation σ. This would imply that the four largest firms have uncertain control to the extent that their aggregate market shares are less than $C58$ away from a 50% market share. The second four largest firms would matter to the first four to the extent that the market shares of the second four could reduce $C14$ to less than .5 or increase it to over .5. This and several other substantively plausible quantities were considered as alternatives for the .5 center and σ spread of the uncertainty distribution, but the values discussed in the text provided the measure of Y_1 best correlated with profit margins.

four largest establishments held a 49% market share would have an exponent of $-(.49 - .5)^2/2(.0451)$, which is $-.0001/.0902$ or $-.0011$. The exponent becomes more negative as industry concentration deviates more from $.5$: $-.2838$ for an industry with concentration equal to $.34$ or $.66$ and -1.7738 for an industry with concentration equal to $.10$ or $.90$. As the exponent becomes more negative, e raised to the exponent becomes smaller: the 49% market share generating $e^{-.0011}$, which is $.9989$; the 34% or 66% market share generating $e^{-.2838}$, which is $.7529$; and the 10% or 90% market share generating $e^{-1.7738}$, which is $.1697$. As e raised to the exponent becomes smaller, uncertainty decreases as the product of e raised to its exponent quantity multiplied by the bracketed constant in Eq. (2.1). The constant is 3.7927 for the 327 four-digit industries in 1967.[16] In other words, uncertainty has a maximum of 3.7927, which is obtained when industry concentration is $.5$ exactly. In the preceding example the 49% market share would generate a value of U equal to 3.7885, which is 3.7927 times $e^{-.0011}$. The more that concentration in an industry deviates from $.5$ relative to the standard deviation of concentration across the 327 industries, the less uncertain the success of the four largest firms in controlling industry prices and the closer to zero the level of uncertainty defined by Eq. (2.1). A market share of 34% or 66% would generate a value of U equal to 2.8555, which is 3.7927 times $e^{-.2838}$, and a market share of 10% or 90% would generate an uncertainty of $.6436$, which is 3.7927 times $e^{-1.7738}$.

The uncertainty of their own success in controlling industry prices is expected to increase the four largest firms's subjective evaluation of the probability of successful control by the second four largest firms. The subjective probability of successful control by the second four firms, as perceived by the four largest firms, could be written as $C58 \times U$, where the objective probability was given by $C58$ alone. With this change, the perceived probability of failure in an attempt by the second four firms to control industry prices changes to $(1 - C58) \times U$.

A measure of imperfect competition could now be defined as the joint probability of successful control over industry prices by the four largest firms and their evaluation of failure to control by the next four largest. In essence, the earlier probability measure is being modified to take into account an interaction between

---

[16]The constant has been estimated from the four-digit data in Eq. (2.2). Given the variance in four-firm concentration ratios, the bracketed constant in Eq. (2.1) equals $k/.5324$. Let X represent the remainder of Eq. (2.1);

$$X = e^{-(C14 - .5)^2/2\sigma^2},$$

so that $U = [k/.5324]X$. Profit margins were regressed over Y_1 as it is expressed in Eq. (2.2) yielding the following results:

$$P = .229 + .15038(C14) - .57034(C14 \times C58 \times X) + E,$$

which can be rewritten

$$P = .229 + .150(C14 - 3.7927[C14 \times C58 \times X]) + E.$$

The term in parentheses is Y_1 (cf. Eq. 2.2), and 3.7927 is the value of the bracketed constant in Eq. (2.1). This means that 3.7927 equals $[k/.5324]$, so the unknown k is slightly over two ($k = 2.0192$).

$C14$ and $C58$ as probabilities of successful control. The proposed measure defines imperfect competition within industry j, y_{j1}, as the following function of market shares held by the four largest establishments, $C14_j$, market shares held by the next four largest establishments, $C58_j$, and the uncertainty of control by the largest establishments, U_j, which determines the significance of $C58$ for control by the largest establishments[17]:

$$y_{j1} = C14_j(1 - C58_jU_j) = C14_j - C14_jC58_jU_j. \qquad (2.2)$$

I have computed two-digit values of Y_1 from the four-digit data, obtained from the 1967 *Census of Manufactures* and various census sources, in the same manner that two-digit concentration was computed from four-digit concentration. The Appendix provides computational details and scores for the four-digit (Table A.2) and two-digit (Table A.3) industries.

This measure offers a significantly stronger correlation with industry profit margins than the correlations obtained earlier. The correlation is .325 rather than the .246 obtained with raw concentration ratios. The positive effect of imperfect competition within industry j remains statistically negligible across the 20 two-digit industries (where e_j is an error term and t-tests are given in parentheses):

$$p_j = .215 + .186\, y_{j1} + e_j,$$
$$(1.28)$$

but is more significant than before across the 327 four-digit industries:

$$p_j = .229 + .152\, y_{j1} + e_j.$$
$$(6.21)$$

A comparison of these regression results with those obtained using raw concentration ratios (p. 20) shows that the intercepts are roughly the same here but the slopes are higher, rounding to .2 rather than the .1 obtained earlier. This higher slope is a result of moderate levels of concentration being adjusted downward when $C58$ is high. The mean and standard deviation of Y_1 are accordingly

---

[17]It is possible for Y_1 to take on negative values because U can be much greater than one. The maximum negative value would occur when $C14$ and $C58$ equal .5. Eq. (2.2) would equal .5 $-$ .25U, and U would equal $3.7927e^0$, so Y_1 would equal .5 $-$ .948 or $-$.448. Nothing this extreme occurred in the 327 four-digit industries. An industry containing only eight firms of roughly equal size is not an industry in the empirical world. However, there were three instances in which Eq. (2.2) yielded slightly negative values: $-$.007 in the chewing and smoking tobacco industry (SIC category 2131), $-$.004 in the primary zinc industry (SIC category 3333), and $-$.002 in the collapsible tubes industry (SIC category 3496). These values were a narrow range within the overall range of Y_1, the remaining values ranging from .00 to .96 with a mean of .24 and a standard deviation of .17. In order to avoid the need to give special attention to negative values of Y in the discussion of partial derivatives later in the analysis, I have rounded these three negative values of Y_1 up to zero so that all observed values of Y_1 lie between zero and one.

smaller than corresponding statistics for raw concentration. Across the 327 four-digit industries, .241 and .173 are the mean and standard deviation of Y_1 and .395 and .212 are the corresponding statistics for $C14$.

The bottom three rows of Table 2.2 illustrate the changes to raw concentration made by the certainty measure in Eq. (2.2). The relative magnitudes of the means in these rows should mirror corresponding magnitudes in the first three rows. The principal improvement over raw concentration is the downward adjustment of imperfect competition implied by moderate levels of concentration. The average value of Y_1 in low concentration industries is .167 and in the moderately concentrated industries is .205, both of which are lower and more similar to one another than the average of .596 observed in high concentration industries. This is an ordering observed in the mean profit margins, but not reproduced by raw concentration data. Among low concentration industries, the average value of Y_1 is about the same for those in which $C58$ is low and those in which $C58$ is high. This too is a feature of the observed profit margins not reproduced by raw concentration data. The respective means in Table 2.2 are .166 and .173 for a high-$C58$-to-low-$C58$ ratio of 1.04, which compares with the 1.03 ratio observed in the mean profit margins and greatly improves the 1.38 ratio implied by raw concentration. Finally, the depressive effect of $C58$ is strongest in moderately concentrated industries and weaker in high concentration industries. This is the pattern observed in the mean profit margins, a pattern reversed by raw concentration data. The bottom line is that Y_1 improves on raw concentration ratios as a measure of imperfect competition by combining values of $C14$ and $C58$ so as to reproduce the observed pattern of interaction with profit margins illustrated in Figure 2.2.

THE CONSTRAINT OF UNCOMPETITIVE
SUPPLIERS AND CONSUMERS

Market transactions with suppliers and consumers involve at least two parties, one organization buying and another selling. The constraint of competition among establishments in an industry only attends to one side of market transactions. To the extent that y_{j1} is greater than zero and approaches its maximum value of one, a small number of large establishments in industry j are free to obtain high profits by controlling industry prices in their transactions with suppliers and consumers in some other sector i of the economy.

To the extent that y_{i1} is greater than zero, however, the same lack of competition exists in supplier–consumer sector i so that transactions with the sector could pose an external constraint on profits in industry j. To the extent that establishments in an industry depend on suppliers and consumers operating in oligopolistic sectors, efforts by the establishments to control industry prices in their own favor are subject to being overturned by the similarly self-interested efforts of suppliers and consumers, suppliers increasing the price for which they can sell commodities needed in the industry as input and consumers decreasing the price they are willing to pay for commodities manufactured in the industry as output.

Market transactions with many different sectors can protect industry profits from the constraint of an oligopolistic supplier–consumer sector. High profits derived from transactions with sectors composed of many small competitors can be used to compensate for the constrained profits obtained in transactions with oligopolistic sectors. Consider a heuristic example. Industry j is an oligopolistic industry with two supplier–consumer sectors, one an oligopoly itself while the other is composed of many small competitors. It is in the interest of the industry oligopoly to control industry prices so as to increase industry profits. These prices would be opposed by the industry's suppliers and consumers. Although the competitive sector could not effectively oppose the artificial industry prices since its constituent establishments could not effectively control price in their market transactions, the large establishments in the oligopolistic sector could exercise some control over the prices they will accept in their market transactions. But the price paid for a commodity can be different in different market transactions. Facing competitive and oligopolistic sectors of consumers and suppliers, industry establishments could impose prices favorable to themselves on transactions with the competitive sector while negotiating less favorable prices for long-term or large-scale transactions with the oligopolistic sector. By so doing, the constrained profits they obtain in their market transactions with the oligopolistic sector can be supplemented with higher profits obtained by exploiting their transactions with establishments in the more competitive sector.

In short, establishments in sector i pose an external constraint on profits in industry j to the extent that two conditions occur: The sector is the principal supplier and consumer for the industry (i.e., z_{ij} and z_{ji}, respectively, represent the bulk of the purchases and sales made by establishments in industry j), and there is low competition among establishments in the sector (i.e., y_{i1} is high). An index of the extent to which these two conditions occur together for industry j and sector i has been proposed elsewhere as a component in the structural autonomy of the industry establishments. I shall discuss coefficients of market constraint in detail shortly, but for the moment let a_{ji} be the extent to which sector i is an oligopoly and its establishments are the principal suppliers and consumers for establishments in industry j. The higher the sum of the a_{ji} for industry j, the more constraint its suppliers and consumers pose for establishments in the industry controlling industry prices. Therefore, profit margins should be higher in industries faced with negligible external constraint (a_{ji} negligible for industry j) than they are in industries faced with strong external constraint (a_{ji} for industry j sum to a high value). The bar graphs in Figure 2.3

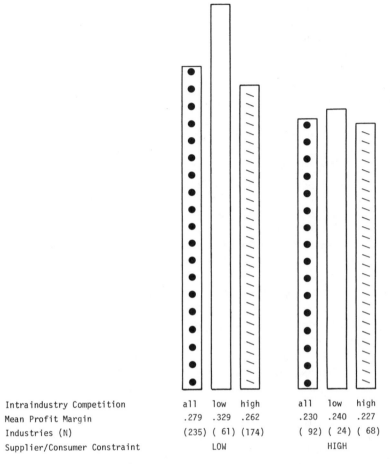

Intraindustry Competition	all	low	high	all	low	high
Mean Profit Margin	.279	.329	.262	.230	.240	.227
Industries (N)	(235)	(61)	(174)	(92)	(24)	(68)
Supplier/Consumer Constraint		LOW			HIGH	

Figure 2.3. Average profit margins obtained in 1967 in industries facing different levels of constraint from suppliers and consumers (low versus high) with different levels of intraindustry competition (low versus high).

illustrate how this was true for the 327 four-digit industries taken from the 1967 American economy. I wish to make three points before discussing market constraints in detail.

First, the bar graphs in Figure 2.3 show a negative association between profit and external constraint. Industries have been divided into two categories: those facing little or no constraint from suppliers and consumers (in the sense of the a_{ji} being negligible for industry j) versus those facing strong constraint from suppliers and consumers (in the sense that the a_{ji} for industry j sum to a value higher than the average sum across all 327 industries).[18] The height of a bar in the figure, as in Figure 2.2, reflects an average industry profit margin. An average profit margin of 28% was observed in all industries facing negligible constraint from suppliers and consumers. This is the speckled bar over low constraint industries in the figure. The speckled bar is lower over high constraint industries reflecting a 23% profit margin in industries faced with constraint from suppliers and consumers. In short, there is reason to believe that imperfectly competitive suppliers and consumers constrained the ability of establishments within an industry to control industry prices so as to raise industry profits.

At the same time, the absence of external constraint from suppliers and consumers exacerbated the ability of industry oligopolies to control industry prices. The second point illustrated by Figure 2.3 is the interaction between external constraint and competition among establishments in an industry. Industries within each category of external constraint have been further dichotomized: those in which there is low competition among establishments (y_{j1} is greater than the mean value of Y_1 across all 327 industries) versus those in which there is extensive competition (y_{j1} is less than the mean of Y_1). The mean profit margins in competitive industries are represented by the height of striped bars in Figure 2.3, and the mean profit margins in oligopolistic industries, those in which there is below-average competition, are represented by white bars. Comparatively low profit margins were obtained in industries facing strong constraint from suppliers and consumers—regardless of the level of competition within the industry. Note the roughly equivalent heights of the bars for the high constraint industries in Figure 2.3. On average, the profit margin in these industries was 23%, and this average increased only slightly to 24% if there was below-average competition among establishments in the industry. However, intraindustry competition had a strong effect on profits obtained in industries facing negligible constraint from suppliers and consumers. Note the quite unequal heights of the bars in Figure 2.3 for low contraint industries. The average profit margin obtained in industries facing low constraint from suppliers and consumers was 28%, but this average increased to 33% if the industry contained large, dominant establishments and decreased to 26% if there were many small establishments competing within the industry. In short, external and internal market constraints interact in determining industry prices. A lack of competition among suppliers and consumers constrained the ability of industry establishments, even an industry oligopoly, to obtain more than a below-average level of profit. In the absence of such constraint, however, industry oligopolies were free to exercise, and accordingly had

---

[18]As in Figure 2.2, Figure 2.3 is presented as no more than a heuristic device pending the analysis of continuous measures. The sum of the a_{ji} is presented in Eq. (2.3) in variable Y_2. Scores on Y_2 are dichotomized at their mean value of .9649, industry j being constrained if y_{j2} is less than this mean.

an incentive to develop, control over industry prices so as to obtain high industry profits.

Of course, and this is my third point, these results make no distinction between the manner in which suppliers versus consumers constrain the ability of industry establishments to obtain high profits. There is reason to expect this difference to be substantively important. Suppliers and consumers constrain profits at opposite ends of the production process. Suppliers constrain profits by keeping direct production costs in an industry high, and consumers constrain profits by keeping industry selling prices low. At these opposite ends of the production process, competition is among establishments in different mixtures of product markets, the pool of potential buyers for a specific commodity as a product. When constraining profits in an industry by keeping prices paid by consumers low, imperfect competition operates within a single product market—the market for the commodity manufactured in the industry. If there are only a few independent establishments buying in the market, each buyer can have a significant impact on market price. This impact, in turn, promotes collusion among the buyers to keep market price low. In contrast, imperfect competition operates across multiple product markets when it operates through suppliers to keep direct production costs high. The multiple markets are the separate economic sectors in which industry establishments purchase supplies. Here again, if there are few independent sellers in these sectors, each seller can have a significant impact on price and is accordingly encouraged to act in collusion with other sellers so as to keep the industry price for supplies high. As an industry's suppliers, however, establishments in separate product markets are unlikely to come into direct competition except where the markets are for substitutable commodities. Collusion among suppliers is particularly limited, therefore, by the extent to which suppliers are in different product markets. This reasoning can be condensed into a single sentence: Only one type of product flows *from* any given industry to its consumers, who have no trouble seeing the value of collusion despite the multiple sectors in which their own products are sold; however, products from different sectors can flow *to* the industry without creating the competition among suppliers that prompts collusion. In addition to requiring an index of market constraint that reproduces the pattern of direct and interaction effects on industry profits illustrated in Figure 2.3, there is reason to expect systematic differences between constraint from suppliers and constraint from consumers.

STRUCTURAL AUTONOMY AND MARKET CONSTRAINT RELATIONS

The points raised in the preceding two sections come together in defining processes by which a market transaction pattern would give establishments in an industry structural autonomy from market constraint. The market transaction pattern for industry j is illustrated in Figure 2.1. The structure of the pattern defines the extent to which industry establishments are free to control industry prices and so obtain high industry profits. Three features of the pattern have been stressed:

1. The many establishments in the industry should be owned and operated by a small number of large corporations dominating the industry. This condition concerns the relations among establishments in the industry, cell (j,j) in Figure 2.1.
2. The industry should be supplied by establishments in many different sectors of the economy. This condition concerns the relations to establishments in the industry, the z_{ij} in Figure 2.1.
3. The industry commodity should be sold to sectors in which there are many small competitive establishments. This condition concerns the relations from establishments in the industry, the z_{ji} in Figure 2.1.

In addition to the positive effect of these conditions on industry profits, the results in Figure 2.3 suggest that a lack of competition within the industry (condition 1) occurring with a lack of constraint from suppliers and consumers (conditions 2 and 3) is likely to have an interaction effect increasing profits above and beyond the level to be expected from either condition alone.

I now wish to present the technical details of a network model defining the structural autonomy of establishments in industry j, a_j, and the extent to which market transactions between the industry and some other sector i contribute to industry autonomy, a_{ji}. To the extent that the market constraint relation a_{ji} is negative, buying and selling between establishments in industry j and sector i is a potential constraint on profits obtained in industry j. Readers not interested in the technical details of the formulation may prefer to skip ahead to the numerical illustration provided in the next section.

Structural Autonomy: The Industry Profit Margin Predicted from Market Structure

Drawing on two classic discussions of freedom from social constraint, Émile Durkheim's *The Division of Labor in Society* and Georg Simmel's *Web of Group-Affiliations,* I have elsewhere discussed the following index of constraint on occupants of network position j from their relations with occupants of position i (Burt, 1980a:899, 1982a:Eq. 7.1);

$$a_{ji} = \left[\left(z_{ij} \Big/ \sum_q z_{qj} \right)^2 + \left(z_{ji} \Big/ \sum_q z_{iq} \right)^2 \right] y_i,$$

where y_i is a measure of the lack of competition among occupants of position i and z_{ji} is the strength of the relation from occupants of position j to those occupying position i.

This simple index is an aid to interpreting an industry's pattern of buying and selling transactions, where z_{ji} is the dollars of sales from establishments in industry j to establishments in sector i as reported in input–output table. To the extent that some sector i is the principal supplier and consumer for some industry j, the squared proportion of industry purchases obtained from the sector, $(z_{ij}/\Sigma_q z_{qj})^2$, will be close to one. The squared proportion of industry sales made to the sector, $(z_{ji}/\Sigma_q z_{jq})^2$, will also be close to one. Squaring proportionate market transactions highlights the sectors responsible for the bulk of an industry's buying and selling. To the extent that sector i is industry j's principal supplier and consumer, the bracketed term in the preceding expression will be close to two. Proportionate market transactions for two-digit and four-digit industries have been computed from the 1967 input–output data.[19] I have used four-firm concentration ratios to measure the lack of competition among establishments in supplier–consumer sector i, i.e., $C14_i = y_i$. The modified concentration measure, Y_1 in Eq. (2.2), more accurately reflects the extent to which a small number of large firms dominate a sector. However, accurate data on aggregate market shares held by the four largest versus the second four largest firms are not available on all sectors, so I have measured y_i in terms of the more easily approximated four-firm concentration ratio.[20] So measured, y_i varies from zero

[19]The two-digit indices of market constraint from other sectors do not involve intraindustry buying and selling. The two-digit industries are so highly aggregated that a considerable portion of interindustry buying and selling at the four-digit level is intraindustry activity at the two-digit level (note the high diagonal elements in Table A.1 of the Appendix). In order to capture constraints from other sectors more clearly, I have deleted two-digit intraindustry transactions from the constraint indices. In other words, z_{jj} is deleted from the sums $\Sigma_q z_{jq}$ and $\Sigma_q z_{qj}$. Given the much more narrow set of manufacturing activities encompassed by four-digit industries and the many more potential supplier–consumer sectors, intraindustry buying and selling is included in the constraint index sum of sales and purchases as discussed in the text.

[20]Sources of census data used to approximate four-firm concentration ratios for input–output sectors corresponding to multiple SIC categories in manufacturing and nonmanufacturing are given in the Appendix. I considered the possibility of measuring intrasector oligopoly using Y_1 where possible and relying on approximations to four-firm concentration ratios where accurate concentration data were not available. Since Y_1 is a downward adjustment to four-firm concentration, this use of Y_1 in some supplier–consumer sectors and $C14$ in others had the effect of lowering the level of oligopoly, on average, in those sectors in which I could estimate Y_1. The resulting correlations between profit margins and external constraint were similar in pattern to those obtained using $C14$ to measure Y, but they were consistently lower than the associations obtained with $C14$. For example, there is a strong correlation between P and Y_2 (relative to the correlations with other market constraint indicators) when Y_1 is used to define the a_{ji} ($r = .241$) and when $C14$ is used to define the a_{ji} ($r = .287$), but the correlation is slightly lower using the Y_1 measure, which is correcting $C14$ for some sectors and not for others.

to one as the extent to which sector i consists of four or fewer independent competitors. The index a_{ji} in the above expression varies from zero to its maximum of two as the extent to which sector i poses an external market constraint on establishments in industry j. These sector-specific constraints can be aggregated to measure the extent to which the industry establishments are free from such external constraint (where $q \neq j$):

$$y_{j2} = \left[2 - \sum_q a_{jq} \right] \Big/ 2. \qquad (2.3)$$

This index will very from zero to one as the extent to which establishments in industry j are free from supplier–consumer constraint. As would be expected from the illustration in Figure 2.3, industries free from such constraint tended to have high profit margins. The correlation between Y_2 and P is .382 across the 20 two-digit industries and .287 across the 327 four-digit industries.

The bar graphs in Figure 2.3 indicate an interaction effect between this lack of market constraint from industry suppliers and consumers, Y_2, and the lack of market constraint within an industry, Y_1. The highest profit margins were observed in oligopolistic industries free from supplier and consumer constraint. The product of Y_1 and Y_2 for an industry measures the extent to which this combination of conditions is true of the industry:

$$x_{j2} = y_{j1}y_{j2},$$

which will vary from zero to one. The magnitude of Y_1 is adjusted downward to the extent that the industry is subject to constraint from its suppliers and consumers. As would be expected from the illustration in Figure 2.3, oligopolies free from supplier–consumer constraint tended to enjoy high profit margins. The correlation between X_2 and P is .307 across the two-digit industries, .360 across the four-digit.

The network model of structural autonomy would define the autonomy of establishments in industry j, a_j, to be a weighted sum of the preceding three variables (cf. Burt, 1982a:Eq. 7.2):

$$a_j = b + b_1 y_{j1} + b_2 y_{j2} + b_x x_{j2}.$$

where b is an arbitrary constant (arbitrary because structural autonomy is an interval rather than a ratio scale) and the remaining coefficients weight the relative importance of Y_1, Y_2, and their interaction as X_2 in determining structural autonomy from market constraint. To the extent that all three variables are high, establishments in industry j enjoy high structural autonomy from market constraint. In a sentence, their pattern of market transactions ensures low competition with one another while ensuring high competition among their suppliers and consumers. The profit margin observed in the industry, p_j, can be expressed as the sum of two components, industry structural autonomy a_j and a residual component e_j:

$$p_j = [a_j] + e_j, \tag{2.4a}$$

so that industry structural autonomy can be measured as the profit margin in industry j predicted from its pattern of market transactions,

$$p_j = [b + b_1 y_{j1} + b_2 y_{j2} + b_x x_{j2}] + e_j, \tag{2.4b}$$

where b, b_1, b_2, and b_x are ordinary least-squares regression coefficients. However, unbiased estimates of market constraint effects are obtained in the following specification, where Y_1 and Y_2 are expressed as deviations from their mean values in the interaction term,

$$p_j = [\beta + \beta_1 y_{j1} + \beta_2 y_{j2} + \beta_x (y_{j1} - \bar{y}_1)(y_{j2} - \bar{y}_2)] + e_j. \tag{2.4c}$$

The bracketed terms in Eqs. (2.4b) and (2.4c) are identical, a_j being the same in both expressions. The interaction effects are identical, $b_x = \beta_x$. However, the positive effect of industry oligopoly, β_1, is understated by b_1, and the positive effect of freedom from supplier–consumer constraint, β_2, is understated by b_2.[21] The three effects on structural autonomy from market constraint, β_1, β_2, and β_x, should be positive.

In 1967 they were positive according to the results presented in Table 2.3. Industry profit margins increased with a lack of competition within the industry. Holding constant interindustry differences in constraint from suppliers and consumers does not eliminate the strong positive association between profit margins and industry oligopoly. The four-digit data allow the null hypothesis that β_1 equals zero to be rejected at well beyond the .001 level of confidence (*t*-test statistic of 7.3). Moreover, industry oligopoly increased industry profits in the

---

[21]The conservative bias in estimates specified in Eq. (2.4b) relative to Eq. (2.4c) is discussed elsewhere with specific reference to structural autonomy (Burt, 1982a:Chap. 7, footnote 11). In brief, the direct effects of Y_1 and Y_2 are estimated at the zero point on the interaction variable. In Eq. (2.4b), b_1 represents the effect of Y_1 on profits when Y_2 equals zero,

$$b_1 = \beta_1 - \beta_x \bar{y}_2,$$

and b_2 represents the effect of Y_2 on profits when Y_1 equals zero,

$$b_2 = \beta_2 - \beta_x \bar{y}_1.$$

Since the scores on these two variables are typically well above zero, the effects b_1 and b_2 refer to conditions outside the range of observed industries. Moreover, Y_1 and Y_2 are interval rather than ratio scales (in the sense that they, respectively, measure the *relative* lack of competition within industries and the *relative* lack of supplier–consumer constraint on industries), so b_1 and b_2 refer to conditions that would be difficult to interpret substantively even if they did exist. I have taken the center of the distributions as a reference point for evaluating market constraint effects. The effect of Y_1 on profits when Y_2 equals its mean value is given by β_1. The effect of Y_2 on profits when Y_1 equals its mean value is given by β_2.

TABLE 2.3
Structural Effects on Industry Profit Margins[a]

Structural indicators	Two-digit industries		Four-digit industries	
	Raw	Standardized	Raw	Standardized
Multiple correlation	.518		.463	
Y_1	.038	.057	.169	.364
	(0.22)		(7.30)	
Y_2	1.100	.487	.477	.279
	(2.00)		(5.16)	
$(Y_1 - \bar{Y}_1)(Y_2 - \bar{Y}_2)$	10.737	.335	.691	.099
	(1.23)		(1.83)	

[a]Parentheses contain t-tests for the null hypothesis and effects are specified in Eq. (2.4c).

absence of constraint from suppliers and consumers above and beyond its direct effect on profits. The interaction effect of Y_1 with Y_2, β_x, is positive. The four-digit data allow the null hypothesis that β_x equals zero to be rejected at beyond the .05 level of confidence (t-test statistic of 1.8). Finally, the lack of constraint from suppliers and consumers was associated with high industry profit margins. The null hypothesis of no direct effect, $\beta_2 = 0$, can be rejected at well beyond the .001 level of confidence with the four-digit data (t-test statistic of 5.16). This strong showing by supplier–consumer constraint, both as a direct determinant of profits and as an indirect determinant through industry oligopoly, makes the distinction raised in the preceding section between suppliers versus consumers all the more substantively interesting.

There has always been an explicit distinction between suppliers and consumers in empirical market structure research; however, the distinction more often than not has been a focus on consumers at the expense of suppliers. Given the emphasis in economic theory on buyers and sellers within a single product market, it is not surprising to find a focus in economic research on the pattern of market transactions between industry establishments and their consumers. In essence, these are the transactions within a single product market, the market for the industry's product. Key orienting concepts for this research are vertical integration (the coordination of establishments in separate sectors [e.g., Stigler, 1951]) and countervailing power (the coordination of buyers against oligopolistic sellers [Galbraith, 1952]). Empirical findings have been reported using 1963 and 1967 input–output table data.[22] Let c_{ji} be the proportion of all sales by establishments in industry j made to establishments in sector i,

[22]I am ignoring research measuring vertical integration in an industry as the ratio of value added to value of shipments (e.g., Tucker & Wilder, 1977). Such a measure is inappropriate here because it is too similar to the dependent variable, adjusted price–cost margins.

$$c_{ji} = z_{ji} \Big/ \sum_q z_{jq} = z_{ji}/VS_j,$$

so that c_{ji} is the ratio of z_{ji} over the sum of the jth row of an input–output table of dollar flow coefficients. Brooks (1973) computes a measure of imperfect competition among an industry's consumers by weighting the c_{ji} for industry j by the levels of concentration in each sector i ($j \neq i$),

$$\sum_i c_{ji} y_i,$$

where y_i is the four-firm concentration ratio for sector i. A value of one for this index of buyer concentration indicates that industry j sold all of its products to sectors containing four or fewer independent firms. As would be expected, buyer concentration is negatively associated with industry income at the level of two-digit SIC industries (Brooks, 1973; Clevenger & Campbell, 1977) and negatively associated with price–cost margins across four-digit industries (Lustgarten, 1975). Lustgarten further demonstrates that simply selling products to a small number of separate sectors is negatively associated with price–cost margins. He sums c_{ji}^2 across all sectors i (excluding industry j) to obtain an index that is high to the extent that industry j sells all of its product to a single consumer sector. He then reports a negative association between this index and price–cost margins. In sum, there is evidence suggesting a negative association between industry profits and the extent to which all industry output is sold to a small number of oligopolistic consumer sectors.

This condition is contained within the aggregate constraint measure in Eq. (2.3) along with an identical measure of supplier constraint. The extent to which establishments in industry j sell all of their product to a small number of oligopolistic consumer sectors is given as ($q \neq j$)

$$\sum_q c_{jq}^2 y_q.$$

The extent to which industry establishments purchase all of their supplies from a small number of oligopolistic supplier sectors is given by the corresponding measure ($q \neq j$)

$$\sum_q s_{jq}^2 y_q,$$

where s_{jq} is the proportion of all their purchases the establishments obtain from sector q ($s_{jq} = z_{qj}/\sum_q z_{qj}$). Total supplier–consumer constraint on the industry is then the sum of these two sums ($q \neq j$)

$$\sum_q (s_{jq}^2 + c_{jq}^2) y_q,$$

which has a maximum value of two. Y_2 is the lack of supplier–consumer constraint computed as the extent to which this sum is less than its maximum,

$$y_{j2} = \left[2 - \sum_q (s_{jq}^2 + c_{jq}^2)y_q \right] \bigg/ 2 = \left[2 - \sum_q a_{jq} \right] \bigg/ 2,$$

where industry j is excluded from the summation ($j \neq q$). In order to explore differences in the manner that market constraint operates through consumers versus suppliers, I have disaggregated this summary index of market constraint into six component indices.

The indices are defined in Table 2.4. The three indicators Y_3, Y_4, and Y_5 measure constraint from an industry's consumers, and Y_6, Y_7, and Y_8 measure corresponding aspects of constraint from industry suppliers.

Overall constraint is divided into a component originating with sectors as consumers (Y_3) and a component originating with sectors as suppliers (Y_6). These indices capture the same structural conditions measured by Y_2. In fact, y_{j2} is merely the average of consumer constraint y_{j3} and constraint from suppliers y_{j6} (where $q \neq j$),

$$y_{j2} = (y_{j6} + y_{j3})/2$$
$$= \left(1 - \sum_q s_{jq}^2 y_q + 1 - \sum_q c_{jq}^2 y_q \right) \bigg/ 2$$
$$= \left(2 - \sum_q a_{jq} \right) \bigg/ 2.$$

The constraint of having few separate sectors as suppliers or consumers is separated in Table 2.4 from the extent to which there are few competitive firms

TABLE 2.4
Measuring the Lack of Market Constraint on Establishments in Industry j from Their Suppliers and Consumers[a]

	Consumers	Suppliers
Freedom from reliance on a small number of oligopolistic product markets	$y_{j3} = 1 - \sum_q c_{jq}^2 y_q$	$y_{j6} = 1 - \sum_q s_{jq}^2 y_q$
Freedom from reliance on a small number of product markets	$y_{j4} = 1 - \sum_q c_{jq}^2$	$y_{j7} = 1 - \sum_q s_{jq}^2$
Freedom from oligopolistic product markets	$y_{j5} = 1 - \sum_q c_{jq} y_q$	$y_{j8} = 1 - \sum_q s_{jq} y_q$

[a]Summation is across all sectors q excluding industry j itself, c_{jq} is the proportion of industry j's sales consumed by sector q, s_{jq} is the proportion of industry j's purchases supplied by sector q, and y_i is the four-firm concentration ratio for sector i or some approximation to it (see the Appendix).

operating within those sectors. Y_4 measures the extent to which industry product is sold in many separate sectors of the economy, and Y_7 measures the extent to which the industry supplies are purchased in many separate sectors.[23] Y_5 measures the extent to which there is intense competition within the sectors consuming industry product, and Y_8 measures the extent to which intensely competitive sectors supply the industry.[24]

All of the measures in Table 2.4 vary from zero to one and should have positive correlations with industry profit margins. The correlations in Table 2.5 show that this is true of all but three negligibly negative correlations. The least-squares regression results in Table 2.5 report the relative unique associations between industry profits and the diverse constraint indicators. The aggregate constraint index Y_2 in regression equation (2.4c) has been replaced by its constituent component indices, Y_3 to Y_8, in the following regression equation:

$$p_j = \beta + \beta_1 y_{j1} + \sum_{k=3}^{8} \beta_k y_{jk} + \sum_{k=3}^{8} \beta_{xk}(y_{j1} - \bar{y}_1)(y_{jk} - \bar{y}_k) + e_j,$$

where β_k is the direct effect of constraint index Y_k in Table 2.4 and β_{xk} is its interaction effect with Y_1. A more detailed discussion of the correlations among the structural indictors in Table 2.4 and their separate effects on profit margins is given elsewhere (Burt, 1979a:120–135). Results for the two-digit industries are

---

[23]The sum of squared proportionate sales in Y_4, $\Sigma_q c_{jq}^2$ $(j \neq q)$, corresponds in content to Lustgarten's (1975) index of sector dispersion, *DSPH*. Instead of being stated in terms of two-digit SIC categories as is *DSPH*, however, all 483 sectors in the disaggregate input–output table for 1967 are potential consumer sectors q (excluding industry j itself).

[24]The weighted concentration in consumer sectors used to compute Y_5, $\Sigma_q c_{jq} y_q$ $(j \neq q)$, corresponds in content to the buyer concentration measures Brooks (1973) and Lustgarten (1975) utilize in their analyses. The weighted concentration in supplier sectors used to compute Y_8, $\Sigma_q s_{jq} y_q$ $(q \neq j)$, corresponds in content to the supplier concentration measure Clevenger and Campbell (1977) adopt as an empirical extension of Brook's analysis. As pointed out by Guth *et al.* (1976, 1977), this weighted concentration in consumer sectors (and correspondingly, weighted concentration in supplier sectors) overestimates the extent to which an industry's buyers are a small number of large, dominant establishments. However, their modifications of the index both ignore structural differentiation among sectors by only considering the m largest sectors (all consumers are grouped together versus all sellers in an industry) and require substantial truncation of the sample size from over 300 to about 50 manufacturing industries (cf. Guth *et al.*, 1976:489–490, 1977:242–243, and the response by Lustgarten, 1976:492–493, to the former). My purpose is not to measure accurately a condition among consumers and suppliers equivalent to the certainty measure for establishments within an industry (Y_1). The lack of accurate data on concentration even within supplier–consumer sectors makes that an impossibility (footnote 20 and the text referencing it). What is more, the indices in Table 2.4 only measure the *relative* extent to which different industries were exposed to oligopolies in their market transactions. This interval rather than ratio nature of the constraint indices has implications for the specification of market effects as I have already discussed (footnote 21 and the text referencing it); however, the indices are sufficient for my purpose in this chapter of measuring relative market constraint relations.

TABLE 2.5
Structural Effects on Industry Profit Margins[a]

Structural indicators	Correlation with profit margin	Regression coefficients		
		Raw	Standardized	t-test (df = 313)
Y_1	.326	.161	.346	5.89
Consumers indicators				
Y_3	.289	.276	.242	2.84
Y_4	−.042	−.055	−.157	2.35
Y_5	.220	−.015	−.029	0.33
X_3	.143	.825	.151	1.53
X_4	−.052	−.418	−.174	2.58
X_5	.106	−.237	−.079	0.81
Supplier indicators				
Y_6	.148	−.344	−.192	1.63
Y_7	.394	.279	.392	3.93
Y_8	−.060	.071	.079	0.86
X_6	.141	.543	.080	0.48
X_7	.028	−.124	−.027	0.22
X_8	.153	.330	.078	0.67

[a]Indicator Y_k is defined in Table 2.4 and its interaction term X_k is a product with Y_1 for the correlations [cf. Eq. (2.4b)] and a product of deviation scores in the estimation of regression coefficients [cf. Eq. (2.4c) and the 13 predictor equations in the text].

not considered here because there are so few two-digit industries and so many predictors in the preceding equation. The results in Table 2.5 show that suppliers and consumers do have different effects on industry profits. The effects they do have are in accord with the discussion of product markets in the preceding section.

Once again, a lack of competition within an industry has a strong positive effect on industry profits. The null hypothesis that β_1 equals zero can be rejected at well beyond the .001 level of confidence (t-test statistic of 5.89).

The crucial determinant of an industry's profit margin vis-à-vis market transactions with its suppliers is the extent to which supplies are purchased from establishments in many separate sectors of the economy. To the extent that establishments in an industry purchased supplies from a single sector, in other words, their industry had a low profit margin. Purchasing supplies from many sectors is measured by Y_7 and no other index of market constraint from suppliers or consumers had as strong an effect on industry profits. The null hypothesis that β_7 is zero can be rejected at well beyond the .001 level of confidence (t-test statistic of 3.93). Purchasing supplies from intensely competitive sectors (Y_6 and

Y_8) had a negligible effect on profits when other indicators are held constant.[25] None of the indicators of freedom from supplier constraint has a significant interaction with Y_1 in increasing industry profits (i.e., β_{x6}, β_{x7}, and β_{x8} are negligible, with t-test statistics almost equal to zero).

In contrast to market transactions with suppliers, transactions with consumers constrained industry profits to the extent that few separate sectors consumed industry product *and* those sectors contained few competitors. The strongest effect under the consumer constraint indicators in Table 2.5 is β_3, the tendency for industry profits to be high to the extent that industry product is purchased by establishments in many separate sectors within which competition is intense. Having to sell to oligopolistic sectors by itself did not have a direct effect on industry profits ($\hat{\beta}_5 \simeq 0$) despite the positive correlation between P and Y_5.[26] In contrast to expectations, selling to many separate sectors (Y_4) has a negative direct and interaction effect on industry profits. However, the association is negligible when the other indicators in Table 2.4 are not held constant.[27]

These results call for a respecification of the initial network model of structural autonomy in Eq. (2.4). The profit margin observed in industry j, p_j, is increased

---

[25]The contradictory negative effect of Y_6 is being ignored on the assumption that its effect is an artifact of its high correlation with Y_7 ($r_{67} = .526$) and the stronger association between profits and Y_7 ($r_{6p} = .148$ and $r_{7p} = .394$, both in Table 2.5). When Y_7 is held constant, in other words, its multicollinearity with Y_6 and its stronger association with profits suppress the positive zero-order association between Y_6 and profits. If profit margins are regressed over industry oligopoly, y_{j1}, and the extent to which supplies are purchased from a few, oligopolistic sectors, y_{j6}, as was done in Eq. (2.4c) for the aggregate constraint index, y_{j2}, then y_{j6} has the expected positive effect on profits:

$$p_j = .02 + .16\ y_{j1} + .21\ y_{j6} + 1.05\ (y_{j1} - \bar{y}_1)(y_{j6} - \bar{y}_6) + e_j,$$
$$\quad\quad (6.8)\quad\quad (2.2)\quad\quad (2.9)$$

where the t-tests (in parentheses) demonstrate the strong effect on profits from Y_6. This strong effect, however, seems to reflect the importance of having diverse supplier sectors since Y_7 (an index contained in Y_6) has a much stronger effect on profits in Table 2.5 than does Y_6.

[26]The lack of a direct effect from Y_5 has the same explanation as the contradictory effect of Y_6 described in footnote 25. The positive correlation between Y_5 and profit margins is still strong when intraindustry competition is held constant, as was done in Table 2.3 in testing the effect of the aggregate constraint index Y_2 (t-tests in parentheses);

$$p_j = .12 + .17\ y_{j1} + .13\ y_{j5} + .44\ (y_{j1} - \bar{y}_1)(y_{j5} - \bar{y}_5) + e_j.$$
$$\quad\quad (7.3)\quad\quad (4.8)\quad\quad (2.9)$$

However, Y_5 is strongly correlated with Y_3 ($r_{35} = .734$), and Y_3 has a slightly stronger correlation with profit margins ($r_{3p} = .289$ versus $r_{5p} = .220$ in Table 2.5), so the direct effect of Y_3 is the dominant consumer constraint effect when all indicators are in the same regression equation.

[27]The correlation between Y_4 and profit margins is negligible in Table 2.4 ($r_{4p} = -.042$), and a similarly negligible direct effect from Y_4 is obtained when it is specified as a predictor of profits in place of the aggregate constraint index Y_2 in Table 2.3 (t-tests in parentheses);

$$p_j = .24 + .15\ y_{j1} - .02\ y_{j4} - .18\ (y_{j1} - \bar{y}_1)(y_{j4} - \bar{y}_4) + e_j.$$
$$\quad\quad (6.2)\quad\quad (0.8)\quad\quad (1.4)$$

by the lack of competition within the industry, y_{j1}, increased by the extent to which many separate sectors supply the industry, y_{j7}, and increased by the extent to which industry product is sold in many separate sectors within which there is intense competition, y_{j3}, so that its reflection of industry structural autonomy, $\mathbf{a}_j$, can be written

$$p_j = [\mathbf{a}_j] + e_j \tag{2.5a}$$

$$= [b + b_1 y_{j1} + b_7 y_{j7} + b_3 y_{j3} + b_x y_{j1} y_{j3}] + e_j \tag{2.5b}$$

$$= [\beta + \beta_1 y_{j1} + \beta_7 y_{j7} + \beta_3 y_{j3} + \beta_x (y_{j1} - \bar{y}_1)(y_{j3} - \bar{y}_3)] + e_j, \tag{2.5c}$$

where Eqs. (2.5b) and (2.5c), respectively, correspond to Eqs. (2.4b) and (2.4c). The positive effect of industry oligopoly on industry profits is captured by β_1. The positive effect of having the industry's suppliers scattered across many separate sectors of the economy is captured by β_7. The positive effect of having the industry's product purchased in many separate sectors within which there is intense competition is captured by β_3, and β_x captures the positive effect of industry oligopoly being able to exploit the intense competition among industry consumers. There is no interaction effect between Y_1 and Y_7. An industry oligopoly cannot obtain special advantage from having suppliers scattered across many economic sectors in the same way that it can take advantage of intensely competitive consumers.[28] Table 2.6 presents ordinary least-squares estimates of the parameters in Eq. (2.5c). Two-digit and four-digit results are presented. The estimated market constraint effects are all positive and the four-digit data allow the null hypothesis to be rejected with considerable confidence for each of the effects specified in Eq. (2.5c). These estimates can be used to compute the coefficients in Eq. (2.5b). The interaction and supplier effects will be identical in the two equations, but the oligopoly and consumer constraint effects in Eq. (2.5b) understate the direct effects of Y_1 and Y_3, respectively.[29]

As in Eq. (2.4), structural autonomy in Eq. (2.5) is the profit margin predicted

---

[28]This is a statement of empirical conditions, not a derived conclusion. The interaction effect in Table 2.5 involving Y_7 is negligible ($\hat{\beta}_{x7} \simeq 0$). A similarly negligible interaction effect from Y_7 is obtained if Eq. (2.5) is respecified to include $b_{x7} y_{j1} y_{j7}$ as an interaction term ($\hat{\beta}_{x7} = -.04$, with a t-test statistic for the null hypothesis of 0.2).

[29]See footnote 21 for details on the bias. The connections between parameters in Eqs. (2.5b) and (2.5c) can be quickly demonstrated following Allison's (1977) succinct discussion of interaction terms in regression models. The bracketed term in Eq. (2.5c) can be rewritten

$$[(\beta + \beta_x \bar{y}_1 \bar{y}_3) + (\beta_1 - \beta_x \bar{y}_3) y_{j1} + \beta_7 y_{j7} + (\beta_3 - \beta_x \bar{y}_1) y_{j3} + \beta_x y_{j1} y_{j3}],$$

which is equivalent to the bracketed term in Eq. (2.5b), so corresponding coefficients in the two expressions are equivalent; i.e.,

$$b = \beta + \beta_x \bar{y}_1 \bar{y}_3, \qquad b_1 = \beta_1 - \beta_x \bar{y}_3, \qquad b_7 = \beta_7,$$
$$b_x = \beta_x, \qquad \text{and} \qquad b_3 = \beta_3 - \beta_x \bar{y}_1.$$

TABLE 2.6
Final Structural Effects on Industry Profit Margins[a]

	Two-digit industries		Four-digit industries	
Effects	Raw	Standardized	Raw	Standardized
Multiple correlation		.592		.546
β	-1.066	.000	$-.186$	.000
β_1	.047	.071	.151	.323
	(0.26)		(6.83)	
β_7	.179	.335	.217	.305
	(1.37)		(6.25)	
β_3	1.195	.466	.234	.205
	(2.20)		(3.97)	
β_x	10.831	.263	.503	.092
	(0.90)		(1.84)	

[a]Parentheses contain t-tests for the null hypothesis and effects are specified in Eq. (2.5c).

for industry j from its market transaction pattern with competitors, suppliers, and consumers. I refer to structural autonomy in Eq. (2.5) with the boldface character $\mathbf{a}_j$ as opposed to the a_j in Eq. (2.4) in order to identify it clearly as the network model of structural autonomy to be used in the forthcoming analysis. The higher multiple correlations in Table 2.6 relative to corresponding multiple correlations in Table 2.3 indicate the much improved accuracy of these final structural autonomy scores. The $\mathbf{a}_j$ for four-digit industries, as well as the market constraint data on Y_2, Y_3, and Y_7, are reported in Table A.2 of the Appendix. Corresponding data for the two-digit industries are reported in Table A.3.

Market Constraint Relations: Sector Contributions to
Industry Structural Autonomy

Since the constraint indices in Eqs. (2.5) are merely summed subindices describing an industry's market transactions with individual sectors as suppliers or consumers, the equation can be disaggregated to define the contribution each sector makes to industry structural autonomy. The bracketed term in Eq. (2.5b) expressing structural autonomy for industry j can be rewritten in terms of the components summed in the constraint indices given in Table 2.4 ($q \neq j$)

$$\mathbf{a}_j = b + b_1 y_{j1} + b_7\left(1 - \sum_q s_{jq}^2\right) + b_3\left(1 - \sum_q c_{jq}^2 y_q\right) + b_x y_{j1}\left(1 - \sum_q c_{jq}^2 y_q\right),$$

which can be rewritten, continuing the assumption of additive effects from components of market constraint, as a series of summed constraint effects (where industry j is again excluded from the summed sectors q),

$$\mathbf{a}_j = b + b_1 y_{j1} + b_7 - \sum_q b_7 s_{jq}^2 + b_3 - \sum_q b_3 c_{jq}^2 y_q + b_x y_{j1} - \sum_q b_x y_{j1} c_{jq}^2 y_q$$

$$= (b + b_7 + b_3) + (b_1 + b_x) y_{j1} + \sum_q (-b_7 s_{jq}^2 - b_3 c_{jq}^2 y_q - b_x y_{j1} c_{jq}^2 y_q)$$

$$= (b^*) + (b_1 + b_x) y_{j1} + \sum_q (-b_7 s_{jq}^2 - [b_3 + b_x y_{j1}] c_{jq}^2 y_q),$$

$$= b^* + \sum_i a_{ji}^*,$$

where a_{ji}^* is the contribution market transactions between industry j and sector i make to industry autonomy. The direct contribution of having the industry establishments owned and operated by a small number of large, dominant firms is positive:

$$a_{jj}^* = (b_1 + b_x) y_{j1},$$

and the contribution of buying and selling with establishments in some other sector i is typically negative as a result of the sector being the industry's sole supplier (s_{ji}^2) and/or containing few competitors while consuming a large proportion of the industry's output ($c_{ji}^2 y_i$):

$$a_{ji}^* = -(b_7 s_{ji}^2 + [b_3 + b_x y_{j1}] c_{ji}^2 y_i).$$

In order to facilitate comparisons across industries, these raw coefficients have been normalized by the profit margin predicted for the industry and intersector coefficients have been multiplied by two ($j \neq i$);

$$\mathbf{a}_{ji} = 2 a_{ji}^* / a_j, \tag{2.6a}$$

$$\mathbf{a}_{jj} = a_{jj}^* / a_j. \tag{2.6b}$$

This coefficient $\mathbf{a}_{ji}$ can be interpreted as a market constraint relation, a constraint on industry j from sector i. It is the extent to which market transactions between establishments in the industry and sector contribute to industry autonomy and so to industry profits. To the extent that the market constraint relation $\mathbf{a}_{ji}$ is negative, establishments in sector i are the principal source of supplies for industry j and/or are owned by a small number of independent firms that are the principal consumers of the industry's product. To the extent that $\mathbf{a}_{ji}$ is negative, in other words, sector i poses a market constraint for obtaining profits in industry j.

Here again, I am using the boldface character $\mathbf{a}_{ji}$ as opposed to a_{ji} or a_{ji}^* to indicate the final definition of the market constraint sector i posed for industry j. Using the results in Table 2.6 and the mean values of Y_1 and Y_3, the 483 $\mathbf{a}_{ji}$ for each four-digit industry j, and the 51 $\mathbf{a}_{ji}$ for each two-digit industry j have been computed. The two-digit market constraint relations are reported in Table A.4 of the Appendix.

A deeper understanding of the market constraint relations can be obtained by analyzing them as market incentives to develop cooptive interestablishment ties. Establishments have a market incentive to develop cooptive relations wherever such relations have the potential to increase their structural autonomy within the market to give them more control over their profit margins.

Within an industry, establishments could develop relations with one another so that they could act more easily in concert as an oligopoly. The extent to which the profit margin in industry j would increase with an increase in y_{j1}, the lack of competition among industry establishments, is given by the partial derivative of Eq. (2.5) with respect to y_{j1}:

$$\partial \mathbf{a}_j / \partial y_{j1} = \partial p_j / \partial y_{j1} = b_1 + b_x y_{j3}$$

$$= \beta_1 - \beta_x \bar{y}_3 + \beta_x y_{j3}$$

$$= \beta_1 + \beta_x (y_{j3} - \bar{y}_3), \qquad (2.7)$$

assuming that the infinitesimal increase in y_{j1} would not affect its mean value across all industries ($\bar{y}_1$). This partial derivative will be positive for all industries except those facing severe consumer constraint. Parameters β_1 and β_x should be positive in theory, and estimates of them for the 1967 data are positive. Since Y_3 only varies between zero and one, the partial derivative will be positive for industry j as long as y_{j3}, freedom from consumer constraint, does not fall below a certain level; specifically, as long as y_{j3} is greater than $\bar{y}_3 - \beta_1/\beta_x$. To the extent that y_{j3} is above average, $\bar{y}_3$, showing that industry j confronted below-average consumer constraint, the partial derivative is positive. A small increase in industry oligopoly would be expected to yield increased industry profits. Even if y_{j3} is no less than average by the ratio of the direct over the interaction effect of oligopoly on profits, β_1/β_x, the partial derivative will be positive. A small increase in industry oligopoly would be expected to yield increased industry profits even in the face of moderately severe consumer constraint. However, if establishments in the industry are so severely constrained by their consumers that y_{j3} is less than $\bar{y}_3 - \beta_1/\beta_x$, the partial derivative is negative showing that a small increase in industry oligopoly is not expected to yield increased industry profits. Establishments in these industries are repressed by their consumers in the sense that they depend on a small number of oligopolies to purchase their product at a reasonable price. In order to increase their industry profit margin, establishments in these "repressed industries" would have to coopt the sources of consumer constraint and/or drastically increase industry oligopoly. Establishments within "unrepressed industries" on the other hand, industries for which the partial derivative in Eq. (2.7) is positive, could expect to increase their industry profit margin with even a small increase in industry oligopoly facilitating their joint control over industry prices.

These remarks inform the interpretation of the intraindustry market constraint relation $\mathbf{a}_{jj}$. Under the assumption that the profit margin increase obtained with increased industry oligopoly is linear over the whole range of scores on y_{j1}, as is implicit in the regression parameters estimated, the partial derivative in Eq. (2.7) multiplied by a large or small change in y_{j1} is the expected change in industry profits. The increased profit margin to be expected from industry oligopoly increasing from zero to its existing level, y_{j1}, would then be the partial derivative multiplied by y_{j1}. This would also be the expected increase in the industry structural autonomy so that the marginal increase in structural autonomy it represented for the existing industry would be that product divided by existing industry autonomy. In other words, $[\partial \mathbf{a}_j / \partial y_{j1}] y_{j1}$ would be the expected increase in structural autonomy so that the ratio of this increase to the existing autonomy $\mathbf{a}_j$ would be the marginal increase

$$[\partial \mathbf{a}_j / \partial y_{j1}] y_{j1} / \mathbf{a}_j,$$

which equals the following expression upon substituting the expression in Eq. (2.7) for the partial derivative:

$$[\beta_1 + \beta_x(y_{j3} - \bar{y}_3)] y_{j1} / \mathbf{a}_j. \tag{2.8}$$

This expression is quite similar, but not identical, to the intraindustry market constraint relation $\mathbf{a}_{jj}$ defined in Eq. (2.6b) as

$$[b_1 + b_x] y_{j1} / \mathbf{a}_j,$$

which equals the following expression when the b coefficients are replaced by the corresponding betas:

$$[\beta_1 + \beta_x(1 - \bar{y}_3)] y_{j1} / \mathbf{a}_j. \tag{2.9}$$

The sole difference between Eqs. (2.8) and (2.9) is the replacement of actual freedom from consumer constraint [y_{j3} in Eq. (2.8)] with the maximum freedom from consumer constraint [1 in Eq. (2.9)]. The term $y_{j3} - \bar{y}_3$ in Eq. (2.8) measures the relative extent to which industry j is free from consumer constraint whereas the term $1 - \bar{y}_3$ in Eq. (2.9) measures the extent to which industries on the whole are free from consumer constraint. To the extent that industries on average face severe consumer constraint so that $\bar{y}_3$ is low, the term $1 - \bar{y}_3$ will be high, so that the potential interaction effect of industry oligopoly on profits in the rare instances of industry freedom from consumer constraint is high (i.e., $\beta_x(1 - \bar{y}_3)$ is high). *In other words, the intraindustry market constraint relation $\mathbf{a}_{jj}$ can be interpreted as the marginal contribution to industry structural autonomy represented by the lack of competition within the industry, a contribution made directly and indirectly in interaction with the level of consumer constraint facing establishments on average across all industries.*

Turning to market transactions with industry consumers and suppliers, suppose that cooptive interorganizational relations between industry and sector could enable industry establishments to conduct needed buying and selling in a nonmarket context more subject to their control than would be possible in an open market context. This process is the central idea discussed in Chapter 3. For the moment, however, imagine that industry establishments could decrease their dollars of sales to sector i, z_{ji}, or their dollars of purchases from the sector, z_{ij}, by conducting those transactions in nonmarket contexts created by cooptive interorganizational relations with establishments in the sector. The market constraint relation from the sector, a_{ji}, indicates the extent to which such action could be profitable to the industry establishments.

The increase in industry profit margin that could be expected from a decrease in open market purchases from sector i as a supplier is given by the partial derivative of Eq. (2.5) with respect to a decrease in the total dollars of purchases by the industry from the sector:

$$\partial a_j / - \partial z_{ij} = \partial p_j / - \partial z_{ij} = 2b_7 z_{ij} \bigg/ \bigg(\sum_q z_{qj}\bigg)^2 = 2\beta_7 z_{ij} \bigg/ \bigg(\sum_q z_{qj}\bigg)^2, \qquad (2.10)$$

assuming that the infinitesimal decrease in market purchases from sector i would not affect the total volume of industry purchasing nor the mean value of Y_7 across industries [$\bar{y}_7$, contained in the intercept terms for Eqs. (2.5), b and β]. Since the effect on profits of purchasing supplies from many separate sectors, β_7, is strongly positive, this partial derivative is nonnegative for all industries. In other words, establishments in every industry could improve their control over industry prices and so increase industry profits by developing cooptive relations to sectors from which they purchased a large proportion of their supplies.

The incentive to coopt consumers is slightly less obvious. The increase in industry profit margin that could be expected from a decrease in open market sales to sector i is given by the partial derivative of Eq. (2.5) with respect to a decrease in the total dollars of sales to the sector:

$$\partial a_j / - \partial z_{ij} = \partial p_j / - \partial z_{ji} = 2[b_3 + b_x y_{j1}] y_i z_{ji} \bigg/ \bigg(\sum_q z_{jq}\bigg) 2.$$

This equals the following expression when the b coefficients are replaced by the corresponding betas:

$$2[\beta_3 + \beta_x (y_{j1} - \bar{y}_1)] y_i z_{ji} \bigg/ \bigg(\sum_q z_{jq}\bigg)^2, \qquad (2.11)$$

assuming that the infinitesimal decrease in market sales to the sector would not affect the total volume of industry sales nor the mean value of Y_3 across all industries [$\bar{y}_3$, contained in the effect of industry oligopoly and the intercept terms in Eq. (2.5)]. Since freedom from consumer constraint has a positive effect on industry profits (directly, β_3, and indirectly in interaction with industry oligopoly, β_x) and Y_1 varies from zero to one, this partial derivative typically will be positive. In other words, establishments in most industries could improve their control over industry prices and so increase industry profits by developing cooptive relations to oligopolistic sectors in which they sold a large proportion of their output. Competition within the industry is the key unknown here. The partial derivative will be negative if the bracketed term is negative, and that will occur if the industry is intensely competitive such that y_{j1} is well below average. Specifically, it will be negative if y_{j1} is less than industry oligopoly on average minus the ratio of the direct effect of consumer constraint on profits over its interaction effect with industry oligopoly, i.e., if y_{j1} is less than $\bar{y}_1 - \beta_3/\beta_x$ (cf. the condition under which $\partial a_j/\partial y_{j1}$ is negative). A negative value for the partial derivative shows that industry establishments have too uncertain a control over industry prices to be able to exploit cooptive relations with oligopolistic consumers. Among the two-digit industries in 1967, $\bar{y}_1 - \beta_3/\beta_x = .123$, and the only industry with a value of Y_1 less than this criterion was the petroleum industry. Among the four-digit industries, $\bar{y}_1 - \beta_3/\beta_x$ is less than zero, so it would be impossible for y_{j1} to be less than the criterion. Viewed within the context of the more narrowly defined four-digit industries then, establishments in each industry could have expected increased industry profits to have resulted from increased control over their sales to oligopolistic consumers.

These remarks inform the interpretation of the interindustry market constraint relation $\mathbf{a}_{ji}$. Under the assumption that the profit margin increase obtained by decreasing open market buying and selling is linear over the whole dollar range of z_{ij} and z_{ji}, the partial derivatives in Eqs. (2.10) and (2.11) describe the change in profit margin to be expected from a large or small decrease in open market transactions with sector i. The increase in profit margin to be expected by only purchasing supplies from coopted establishments in sector i is given by the product of the partial derivative in Eq. (2.10) and the dollars of commodity purchased from the sector:

$$[\partial \mathbf{a}_j/-\partial z_{ij}]z_{ij} = \left[2b_7 z_{ij} \Big/ \left(\sum_q z_{qj}\right)^2 \right] z_{ij}$$

$$= 2b_7 z_{ij}^2 \Big/ \left(\sum_q z_{qj}\right)^2$$

$$= 2b_7 s_{ji}^2. \tag{2.12}$$

The increase to be expected by only selling to coopted establishments in sector i is given by the product of the partial derivative in Eq. (2.11) and the dollars of commodity sold to the sector:

$$[\partial \mathbf{a}_j/-\partial z_{ji}]z_{ji} = \left[2(b_3 + b_x y_{j1})y_i z_{ji} \Big/ \left(\sum_q z_{jq}\right)^2 \right] z_{ji}$$

$$= 2(b_3 + b_x y_{j1})y_i z_{ji}^2 \Big/ \left(\sum_q z_{jq}\right)^2$$

$$= 2(b_3 + b_x y_{j1})y_i c_{ji}^2. \tag{2.13}$$

The sum of Eqs. (2.12) and (2.13) represents the increase in profit margin to be expected from only buying and selling with coopted establishments in sector i:

$$[\partial \mathbf{a}_j / - \partial z_{ij}]z_{ij} + [\partial \mathbf{a}_j / - \partial z_{ji}]z_{ji} = 2(b_7 s_{ji}^2 + [b_3 + b_x y_{j1}]y_i c_{ji}^2).$$

The ratio of this quantity over the structural autonomy of the industry as it existed would be the marginal increase in structural autonomy that coopting the sector would represent to industry establishments as a whole:

$$2(b_7 s_{ji}^2 + [b_3 + b_x y_{j1}]y_i c_{ji}^2)/\mathbf{a}_j,$$

which is negative one times the market constraint relation from sector i to industry j as defined in Eq. (2.6a):

$$\mathbf{a}_{ji} = 2a_{ji}^*/\mathbf{a}_j,$$
$$= -2(b_7 s_{ji}^2 + [b_3 + b_x y_{j1}]y_i c_{ji}^2)/\mathbf{a}_j.$$

In other words, the market constraint relation $\mathbf{a}_{ji}$ can be interpreted as the marginal increase in structural autonomy for industry j that is forgone if industry establishments conduct their buying and selling with sector i establishments on the open market. Alternatively, $-\mathbf{a}_{ji}$ can be interpreted as the marginal increase in industry structural autonomy to be obtained by developing cooptive relations to sector i. This market incentive to develop cooptive relations to the sector will be high (i.e., the market constraint posed by the sector for industry profits will be severe) to the extent that the sector establishments are the industry's principal suppliers and/or they constitute an oligopoly purchasing a large proportion of industry output. I have multiplied the raw constraint a_{ji}^* by two in Eq. (2.6a) in order to make precise this analogy between the market constraint relation $\mathbf{a}_{ji}$ and a marginal increase in industry structural autonomy, i.e., profits.

NUMERICAL ILLUSTRATION:
THE APPAREL INDUSTRY

The two-digit apparel industry nicely illustrates the connection between market structure and profits. The industry is SIC category 23, which consists of several (33) four-digit categories including the men's and boy's suits industry (SIC category 2311), the corsets industry (SIC category 2342), the fur goods industry (SIC category 2371), the curtains and drapes industry (SIC category 2391), the pleating and stitching industry (SIC category 2395), and the fabricated textile products not elsewhere classified industry (SIC category 2399). The two-digit apparel industry contains many different four-digit industries as subsectors.

Apparel establishments did not enjoy high profit margins in 1967. The industry's corrected price–cost margin indicates that 17¢ out of the average dollar of product sold was profit above and beyond direct production costs ($p_j = .169$).

This is the lowest profit margin observed in any of the two-digit industries and is well below the 26¢ on the dollar average profit margin observed across all 20 of the two-digit industries that year. This low profit margin indicates that the industry's market transaction pattern defined severe market constraints for establishments in the industry.

Features of the market transaction pattern involving apparel establishments in 1967 are presented in Table 2.7: proportionate purchases from suppliers, proportionate sales to consumers, approximate aggregate market share held by the four largest firms in each sector, and market constraint relations (the a_{ji}).

TABLE 2.7
Market Structure for the Apparel Industry in 1967

Supplier–consumer sectors	Percentage of nonapparel buying and selling that is transacted with sector		Four-firm concentration approximation, y_i	Market constraint relation, a_{ji}
	Buying	Selling		
Livestock	.00	.00	.000	.0000
Other agriculture	.00	1.84	.000	.0000
Forestry/fishery	1.37	.00	.000	−.0004
Agribusiness services	.00	.21	.000	.0000
Iron mining	.00	00	.435	.0000
Nonferrous metal mining	.00	.00	.302	.0000
Coal mining	.03	.13	.025	.0000
Petroleum/gas	.00	.00	.028	.0000
Stone/clay mining	.00	.47	.116	.0000
Chemicals mining	.00	.00	.290	.0000
New construction	.00	2.14	.032	−.0001
Maintenance/repair	.24	.17	.033	.0000
Ordnance	.00	.56	.083	.0000
Food	.00	5.25	.323	−.0043
Tobacco	.00	.09	.736	.0000
Textiles	65.74	8.80	.380	−.8265
Apparel (intraindustry)	—	—	.201	.3010
Lumber	.07	1.03	.163	−.0001
Furniture	.07	2.43	.185	−.0005
Paper	2.09	1.45	.311	−.0011
Printing	.08	.98	.189	−.0001
Chemicals	4.45	1.54	.417	−.0042
Petroleum	.19	.13	.329	.0000
Rubber	.92	1.67	.313	−.0006
Leather	.77	3.93	.251	−.0020
Stone, clay, and glass	.02	.64	.373	−.0001

(*continued*)

TABLE 2.7 (*Continued*)

Supplier–consumer sectors	Percentage of nonapparel buying and selling that is transacted with sector		Four-firm concentration approximation, y_i	Market constraint relation, a_{ji}
	Buying	Selling		
Primary metals	.00	1.41	.451	−.0004
Fabricated metals	.58	1.75	.283	−.0005
Mechanical machines	.25	1.79	.365	−.0006
Electrical machines	.05	1.50	.462	−.0005
Transportation equipment	.02	27.24	.669	−.2385
Instruments	.30	.73	.494	−.0001
Miscellaneous	2.87	1.54	.276	−.0019
Transportation/warehousing	1.48	4.74	.254	−.0031
Communications (not radio/TV)	.87	.21	.060	−.0001
Radio and television	.00	.00	.060	.0000
Utilities	1.00	.34	.999	−.0002
Wholesale and retail	6.44	9.14	.001	−.0078
Finance/insurance	1.04	.00	.014	−.0002
Real estate	2.92	2.31	.000	−.0016
Personal services	.10	9.01	.002	−.0001
Business services	3.45	.00	.002	−.0022
Automobile services	.20	.73	.001	.0000
Amusements	.00	.00	.004	.0000
Medical and educational services	.13	2.35	.000	.0000
Federal government	.47	.60	.999	.0000
State and local government	.01	.30	.999	.0000
Gross imports	.50	.00	.000	.0000
Expense accounts	1.07	.34	.000	−.0002
Office supplies	.21	.00	.000	.0000
Scrap	.00	.51	.000	.0000

One explanation for the low profit margin in the apparel industry is the intense competition among apparel establishments. The aggregate four-firm concentration ratio for the industry is .201: The four largest firms in a subsector of the two-digit apparel industry held 20% of the subsector market on average. This is well below average for industries generally. The four largest firms in a subsector of a two-digit industry on average held 36% of their subsector market. The mean value of $C14$ across the 20 two-digit industries is .359. This low concentration within the industry generates a low certainty measure of industry oligopoly. The value of Y_1 for apparel establishments is .165, a score well below the .233 average across all 20 two-digit industries.

At the same time, apparel establishments faced the highest level of market constraint from their suppliers and consumers. The well-below-average value of .889 for Y_2 is reported in Table A.3 of the Appendix ($\bar{y}_2$ = .967). This high constraint is easily explained by considering the pattern of market transactions between apparel establishments and other sectors.

Apparel establishments obtained supplies principally from a single sector, the textile industry. Looking down column 2 of Table 2.7, note the dominant purchasing from textile establishments; 65.74% of apparel purchases from other sectors came from textile establishments. There is no other supplier sector that was nearly this important. The closest is the apparel industry itself. As reported in Table A.1 of the Appendix, $5199 million worth of goods were exchanged among the apparel establishments, and $7924 million worth of textiles were purchased by the apparel establishments. Aside from the apparel industry itself, the next most prominent supplier was the chemical industry, which provided a mere 4.45% of the industry's purchases [$536 million in cell (22,17) of Table A.1]. As would be expected from this distribution of purchases, the apparel establishments faced severe supplier constraint. The index Y_7 is well below average for the apparel industry. In fact, the industry's score is the lowest of all 20 two-digit industries (y_{j7} = .557).

Apparel establishments had more diversified selling transactions. Looking down column 3 of Table 2.7 reveals that no one sector was the principal consumer of apparel product. However, the transportation equipment industry was a major consumer, purchasing 27.24% of the apparel product sold outside the apparel industry itself. These purchases amounted to $638 million worth of products, a volume of sales decidedly lower than apparel sales to other apparel establishments ($5199 million) but a high volume of sales in comparison to apparel sales to other sectors. The next highest rate of consumption outside the apparel industry was about a third the volume of sales to transportation equipment establishments and equal in three sectors: the textile industry ($206 million or 8.8% of sales), the wholesale and retail trade sector ($214 million or 9.14% of sales), and the personal services sector ($211 million or 9.01% of sales). In other words, the transportation equipment industry consumed 27% of the apparel products sold outside the apparel industry with the next highest consumer being the wholesale–retail trade sector, which consumed 9%. Unlike the wholesale–retail trade sector, however, the transportation equipment industry was highly concentrated, 70% of the industry's sales coming from establishments owned by the industry's four largest firms. The transportation equipment industry constituted an important, unfortunately oligopolistic, consumer for the apparel industry. Accordingly, the index measuring freedom from such a consumer, Y_3, is low for the apparel industry. Although not the lowest score among two-digit industries, it is well below average (y_{j3} = .944, which is a standard deviation below the average $\bar{y}_3$ = .972).

These features of the industry's market transactions determine the structural autonomy of apparel establishments. Industry structural autonomy, a_j, is defined by Eqs. (2.5) and appears as follows when parameter estimates from Table 2.6 are inserted:

$$a_j = -1.066 + .047\, y_{j1} + .179\, y_{j7} + 1.195\, y_{j3} + 10.831(y_{j1} - \bar{y}_1)(y_{j3} - \bar{y}_3)$$

$$= -1.066 + .008 + .100 + 1.129 + .020$$

$$= .191.$$

A profit margin of 19¢ on the dollar would be expected in the industry based on its pattern of market transactions. This is the sum of a constant for all industries (-1.066), plus a minor adjustment for industry oligopoly (.008), plus an adjustment for freedom from supplier constraint (.100), plus an adjustment for freedom from oligopolistic consumers (1.129), plus an adjustment for industry oligopoly allowing the exploitation of competitive consumers (.020). This expected 19¢ profit is close to the observed margin of 17¢ on the dollar. Moreover, the expected profit margin is well below the average expected margin ($\bar{a}_j = .258$). The only industry with a lower expected profit margin is the textile industry in which a 17¢ on the dollar profit is predicted ($a_j = .168$ in Table A.3 of the Appendix).

The market constraint relations in Table 2.7 indicate where the apparel establishments most needed to improve their control over industry prices in market transactions in order to improve their ability to obtain profits. A quick look down the column of a_{ji} in Table 2.7 is sufficient to conclude that the low expected profit margin in the apparel industry can be traced to market transactions with the textile industry (for which $a_{ji} = -.827$) and the transportation equipment industry (for which $a_{ji} = -.239$). The textile industry is the principal supplier for apparel establishments, and the transportation equipment industry constitutes an oligopoly purchasing a large proportion of apparel output. As would be expected from the preceding discussion of apparel market transactions, the remaining market constraint relations for the industry are quite small. In short, apparel establishments had strong market incentives in 1967 to develop cooptive relations with establishments in the textile and transportation equipment industries in order to improve their control over apparel prices. They had little incentive to develop such ties with establishments in any other sectors of the economy beyond the boundary of the apparel industry itself.

SUMMARY

I have argued that profits are obtained by exploiting market transactions through control over price in those transactions where control is a parameter in the structural autonomy of an economic sector. The structural autonomy of establishments within a manufacturing industry is defined by the pattern of market transactions characterizing the industry as a production activity intermediary between industry suppliers and industry consumers. The industry provides high structural autonomy to the extent that there is low competition within the industry (in the sense that all industry production is coordinated within a small number of firms) while there is intense competition among the industry's suppliers and consumers (in the sense that industry buying and selling is transacted with many different sectors in which many different firms operate). The greater the autonomy of industry establishments in this sense, the more control they have over industry prices in market transactions. The more control they have over industry prices, the greater their ability to exploit transactions to obtain high profits.

This reasoning is borne out in the analysis of market structure and profit data on American manufacturing industries in the late 1950s. An industry's price–cost margin, the proportion of sales in excess of direct costs, was high to the extent that the industry provided its establishments high structural autonomy. With increasing ability to control industry prices according to the structural autonomy model, observed profits increased. Subsequent data analysis, not reported here, using multiple indicators of profits in 1967 and 1972, shows that the results reported here with price–cost margins are conservative. Stronger market effects are evident when profits are measured with the profit data reported for aggregate input–output sectors or returns to equity measures (e.g., see Collins & Preston, 1968:Chap. 3). The proportions of profit margin variance attributable to the three structural autonomy effects, however, seem to be robust over alternative measures. A little less than a third of the variance in price–cost margins across four-digit manufacturing industries is explained by the model in Table 2.6 (multiple correlation of .546). The strongest of the three effects is supplier–consumer constraint. Extraindustry market constraint accounts for 60% of the explained variance in price–cost margins. In other words, profits were depressed in industries relying on a small number of supplier–consumer sectors dominated by a small number of large firms. The oligopoly effect accounts for 35% of the explained variance in price–cost margins. In other words, profits were heightened in industries dominated by a small number of large firms. Finally, profits were high in those few industries dominated by a small number of large firms buying and selling with highly competitive suppliers and consumers. This interaction effect accounts for a small, but significant, 5% of the explained variance in price–cost margins.

Focusing on the strong extraindustry market constraint effect, suppliers affected profits in a way distinct from consumer constraint. Only one type of product flows from an industry to its consumers, who have no trouble seeing the value of collusion despite the multiple sectors in which their products are sold, but products from different sectors can flow to the industry without creating the

competition among suppliers that prompts collusion. In the 1967 American economy, industry profits were constrained by suppliers to the extent that the industry
establishments purchased the bulk of their supplies from a single sector. In
contrast, industry profits were constrained by consumers to the extent that industry establishments sold the bulk of their product to a single oligopolistic sector.
Further, there is a significant interaction between industry oligopoly and consumer constraint. Industry profits were especially likely to be high if the industry
was dominated by a small number of large firms *and* the industry's consumers
were strongly competitive and therefore easy prey for the industry oligopoly.
There is no interaction between industry oligopoly and supplier constraint. An
industry oligopoly could not obtain an unusual profit advantage from having
suppliers scattered across many economic sectors in the same way that it could
take advantage of intensely competitive consumers.

These results define market constraint relations between sectors of the economy. The structural autonomy of establishments in industry j, $\mathbf{a}_j$, is the profit
margin predicted for the industry from its pattern of market transactions with all
sectors of the economy [Eq. (2.5)]. The market constraint relation $\mathbf{a}_{ji}$ is the
extent to which this predicted profit margin can be traced to market transactions
between industry establishments and establishments in sector i [Eq. (2.6)]. More
specifically, $\mathbf{a}_{jj}$ is the marginal contribution industry oligopoly makes to its
expected profit margin. The intersector constraint, $\mathbf{a}_{ji}$ is the marginal increase in
expected industry profit margin that is forgone if establishments in industry j
conduct their buying and selling with sector i establishments on the open market.
Alternatively, $-\mathbf{a}_{ji}$ is the marginal increase in industry structural autonomy to be
obtained by developing cooptive relations to sector i. This market incentive to
develop cooptive relations to the sector will be high (i.e., the market constraint
posed by the sector for industry profits will be severe) to the extent that the sector
establishments are the industry's principal suppliers and/or they constitute an
oligopoly purchasing a large proportion of industry output.

These market constraint relations describe the intensity of constraint a sector
poses for industry control over industry profits. They do not describe the manner
in which cooptive relations could operate. Within the context of this book in
particular, the question of how directorate ties could enable establishments to
circumvent market constraints now comes to center stage. Addressing that question is my purpose in Chapter 3.

APPENDIX

A detailed aside on structural equivalence is of some value here because the
correspondence between statuses and sectors can be obscured by the colloquial
labels used to reference them. A strong criterion for structural equivalence re-

quires that two actors i and j have identical relations with other actors in order for them to be treated as equivalent. In other words, actors i and j are structurally equivalent if the Euclidean distance d_{ij} between their respective network positions is zero, where

$$d_{ij} = \left[\sum_q (z_{iq} - z_{jq})^2 + \sum_q (z_{qi} - z_{qj})^2 \right]^{1/2}.$$

This definition is too stringent for use in empirical research, and there are substantive reasons for not expecting two actors to perform a role in identical manners. The strong criterion for equivalence is typically replaced with a weak one in which actors i and j are treated as structurally equivalent if the distance between them is negligible, i.e., if d_{ij} is less than some criterion distance. Structurally equivalent actors jointly occupy a status, and their pattern of relations with occupants of other statuses defines the role-set associated with their status. Viewing corporate bureaucracies, or groups of these producing organizations, as actors in the economy and given z_{ij} as the market relation from actor i to actor j measured as the dollars of sales by i to j during some time interval, actors i and j are structurally equivalent under a strong criterion to the extent that their respective patterns of market relations with suppliers and consumers are identical, i.e., to the extent that the Euclidean distance d_{ij} is zero. They would be structurally equivalent under a weak criterion if d_{ij} is negligible. A status jointly occupied by organizations structurally equivalent in the economy would then be a set of organizations with negligibly different market relations with suppliers and consumers.

This "status" corresponds to a "sector" or "industry" in input–output analysis. However, a less general concept of structural equivalence, based on input coefficients, is used to define input–output sectors. The pattern of purchase relations for some set of organizations as actor j is given by N relations from all N actors in the economy, $z_{1j}, z_{2j}, \ldots, z_{Nj}$. Let z_j be the dollars of actor j's output. The pattern of purchase relations by j can be expressed as proportions of this output: $z_{1j}/z_j, z_{2j}/z_j, \ldots, z_{Nj}/z_j$. These proportion relations are discussed as input coefficients where a_{ij} is the proportion of one unit of actor j output that comes directly from actor i input; i.e., $a_{ij} = z_{ij}/z_j$. (This use of a_{ij} is not to be confused with the market constraint coefficient a_{ij} used earlier in this chapter.) The pattern of input coefficients for actor j describes a production process of combining inputs into a commodity output by actor j. Separate actors are treated as operating in the same economic sector to the extent that they are involved in the same production process, i.e., to the extent that they have similar patterns of input coefficients. The lack of similarity between two patterns has been represented as a Euclidean distance

$$d_{ij}^* = \left[\sum_q (a_{qi} - a_{qj})^2 \right]^{1/-},$$

where actors i and j are treated as operating in the same sector of the economy to the extent that d_{ij}^* is negligible. A review of this literature with empirical application to the 1967 input–output study is given in Blin and Cohen (1977).

In two qualities, this definition of structural equivalence is less general than the definition given previously. First, actors i and j could differ in the volume of their relations (z_i being different from z_j) and still be in the same sector even though they would be separated by nonzero d_{ij}^* (i.e., a_{qj} could equal a_{qi} even though z_{qi} would not equal z_{qj}). Second, actors i and j could have different patterns of sales relations to consumers and still be in the same sector even though they would have nonzero d_{ij} (i.e., there is no term in d_{ij}^* that represents the differences between z_{iq} and z_{jq} across all consumers q as there is in d_{ij}).

These two differences between d_{ij}^* and d_{ij} need not be critical, however, in defining sectors as structurally equivalent organizations. Production processes are defined by input coefficients so that the difference in the volume of purchases by two actors does not indicate a structural difference between them so much as it indicates a difference in their market shares of a sector, an important measure of imperfect competition within the sector as discussed in the chapter. Further, two actors with similar input coefficients are producing the same commodity and so are likely to sell that commodity to similar sectors of consumers. In other words, two actors structurally equivalent with respect to their input coefficients are likely to be structurally equivalent with respect to the proportions of their product sold to other sectors as consumers.

In fact, the four-digit SIC categories appear to be too finely distinguished rather than being crude approximations to structural equivalence. Kaysen and Turner (1959:295–331) discuss the possibility of collapsing four-digit SIC categories into broader categories that maintain intracategory homogeneity. Their basic point is that four-digit SIC categories are so finely distinguished that substitutable and complementary commodities are sometimes placed in separate categories. The input–output manufacturing sectors correspond, with few exceptions, to four-digit SIC categories or combinations of four-digit categories, categories being combined into a single input–output sector when they are judged to have similar patterns of input coefficients. For example, the beet sugar industry (SIC category 2063) and the cane sugar industry (SIC category 2061) are combined in 1967 into a single sugar industry (IO sector 141900). Even these input–output sectors can be too finely drawn. A network analysis of the z_{ij} in the aggregate 1963 input–output table showed that several aggregate sectors—let alone the many more disaggregate sectors corresponding to four-digit SIC categories—could be treated as structurally equivalent. Similarly, Blin and Cohen (1977) conclude that their cluster analysis of the a_{ij} shows that several aggregate sectors in the 1967 input–output table could be combined into more aggregate sectors while maintaining intrasector homogeneity with respect to patterns of input coefficients. A network analysis of the z_{ij} among aggregate sectors of the

1967 input–output table in Table A.1 of the Appendix does not suggest that any of the two-digit SIC industries could be treated as structurally equivalent to one another. The "true" level of aggregation defining sectors as positions jointly occupied by structurally equivalent actors therefore seems to lie somewhere between the extremes of the data available in public archives. The aggregate sectors in Table A.1 of the Appendix are likely to contain subsectors non-equivalent to one another—two-digit SIC categories define industries composed of actors structurally equivalent under a very weak criterion. On the other hand, the disaggregate sectors corresponding to four-digit SIC categories are likely to be distinguishing subsectors within more general sectors—some of the four-digit SIC categories are structurally equivalent but treated as if they were non-equivalent. This aggregation problem creates a conservative bias in estimating market constraints as discussed in footnote 8; however, it seems reasonable in general to make an analogy between the sociologist's concept of status and the economist's concept of sector in the sense that both are network positions jointly occupied by structurally equivalent actors. More importantly, the analogy facilitates investigations into the social structure of markets that use the wealth of network models available to describe the extensive, reliable, relation data available in input–output studies.

3

Directorate Structure: Potentially Cooptive Interorganizational Relations*

Across generations and cultures, people have protected their economic, market exchanges with nonmarket, social relations. In Chapter 2, I described processes by which the structure of buying and selling typical of manufacturing some commodity defined the ability of establishments doing the manufacturing to control price in their purchase and sales transactions. In this chapter, I describe ways in which those establishments could have reached out with nonmarket relations to protect their purchases and sales from market constraints.

The nonmarket relations to be described are directorate ties: interorganizational connections through corporate boards of directors. My purpose in this chapter is to describe directorate ties as a nonmarket structure to the economy, a network of cooptive relations to sources of market constraint on profits. In particular, I am concerned with describing the manner in which such ties could have functioned as cooptive relations and did connect American manufacturing firms in 1967 to diverse sectors of the economy. In Chapter 4, I shall extend the analysis to describe the coordination of directorate ties with market constraints between individual sectors of the economy.

*Portions of this chapter are drawn from articles reprinted with the permission of the *Administrative Science Quarterly,* the *American Sociological Review,* and *Social Networks* (Burt, 1980d; Burt *et al.,* 1980; Burt, 1979b).

TYPES OF DIRECTORATE TIES

Establishments can be connected in different manners through boards of directors. Three types of connections often discussed in empirical research are illustrated in Figure 3.1 with selected directorate ties involving Firestone Tire and Rubber as of 1967.

Establishments versus Firms

At the outset, I wish to clarify a distinction I have been maintaining, if implicitly, between establishments as the object and source of market constraints, and corporate directorates as one medium through which establishments can be coordinated.

Research on market structure relative to corporate profits has demonstrated market constraints to be a function of the typical sales and purchase transactions characterizing an industry. Market constraints operate at the organizational level of establishments, the actual units of production. In Figure 3.1, sectors of establishments are represented by squares, and arrows represent market constraint relations; for example, establishments in the primary metals industry were constrained by their market transactions with the transportation equipment sector and the transportation and warehousing sector (as well as other sectors not presented in the diagram). The absence of an arrow represents the lack of constraint; for example, establishments in the finance sector did not constitute a market constraint for any sector in the diagram.[1]

Establishments as production actors are owned and operated by corporations as legal entities. An establishment is a corporate bureaucracy within a single economic sector. It consists of everything that one corporation owns within a sector. As a sector is defined by the pattern of buying and selling characterizing the production of a commodity, an establishment is a corporate bureaucracy engaged in the production of a specific commodity. A corporation, a firm, is the legal entity for which a directorate is defined. If a firm operates within a single economic sector, then the firm owns one establishment. If a firm operates within two sectors of the economy, it owns two establishments, one in each sector. In Figure 3.1, firms are indicated in capital letters and their ownership of establishments is indicated with solid lines; for example, Firestone owned an establish-

---

[1]This dichotomous treatment of market constraints as present versus absent, severe versus negligible, is based on constraint tables such as the one presented in Table 2.7 for the apparel industry. The dichotomous coding is explained and used briefly in Chapter 4. It is adopted here as a heuristic device for discussing directorate ties as cooptive relations.

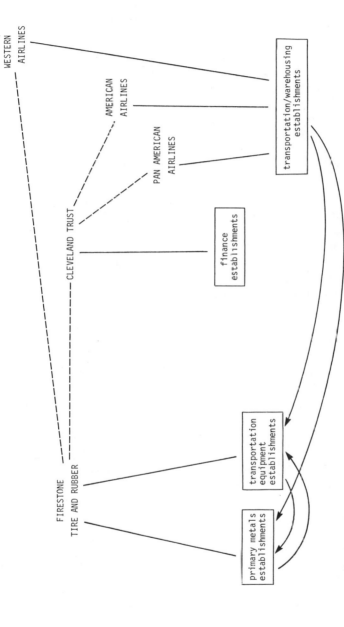

Figure 3.1. Illustration of three types of directorate ties involving two Firestone Tire and Rubber establishments in 1967 (arrows represent market constraint, solid lines represent ownership, and dashed lines represent interlocking).

ment in the primary metals industry and another in the transportation equipment industry (as well as several not presented in the diagram, cf. Figure 3.2).

Research on interorganizational ties through boards of directors has typically focused on the extent to which other corporations are represented on a firm's directorate. A dashed line between two firms in Figure 3.1 represents an interlocking directorate; for example, one of Firestone's directors also sat on the board of Cleveland Trust. The usual questions asked of such data in directorate research concern the number of Firestone's directors sitting on the boards of other firms, the number sitting on the boards of financial firms, and the number drawn from Firestone's own management. The assumption is that the composition of firms represented on Firestone's board reflects the market constraints confronting the firm. I shall return to this assumption in concluding this chapter.

The immediate problem is one of bringing market constraint data to bear on cooptive interpretations of directorate ties. The typical firm owns multiple establishments. Since each of a firm's establishments can be subject to different market constraints, the firm spanning several industries is subject to a complex mixture of market constraints. Further, there is no accurate method for using publicly available data to compare constraints and ties between firms by aggregating market constraints to the corporate level of analysis or disaggregating directorate ties to the establishment level of analysis.[2]

For the purposes of this study, I assume that individual establishments are efficiently managed and a corporate board of directors represents each establishment it owns no matter how small the establishment. My concern is the efficiency with which separate establishments could have been coordinated through

---

[2]Unfortunately, there are no reliable data in the public domain on the proportion of sales and profits a firm obtains from its operations in each of multiple sectors. Even if such data were available, there is no obvious criterion after which a firm should be assigned to a single sector. Is a firm in industry j when a third, a half, or three-fourths of its income results from its operations in the industry? The task of assigning firms to specific sectors seems impossible at this time without resorting to ad hoc procedures (e.g., see footnote 4 of Chapter 2 regarding tax return data, and footnote 5 of Chapter 8 regarding SEC Form 10-K data). The task of aggregating market constraints to the corporate level seems similarly intractable. The typical firm operates in multiple sectors. Each establishment it owns is subject to the market constraints characterizing its industry. The firm itself is subject to some mixture of these market constraints collectively confronting its multiple establishments. Further complicating this mixture is the lack of data on the extent to which the firm's sales and profits result from each of its establishments. For the purposes here, it seems preferable to oversimplify the situation by treating each of a firm's establishments as equally represented by the firm's board. This is probably not true empirically, but it has the advantage of a clear interpretation pending the development of some reliable method for quantitatively disaggregating firms into their component establishments. For the purposes of research building on the results reported here, a slightly less crude distinction is being made among establishments; a firm's primary establishments, its core production activities, are distinguished from secondary establishments. This distinction is discussed in Chapter 8.

directorate ties. The corporation is viewed less as the unit of cooptation than the means to cooptation. To be sure, when a representative from another firm sits on a corporate board, he represents the other firm. More important to an analysis of coopting sources of market constraint, however, he represents the establishments owned by the other firm. It is access to those represented establishments that might allow the corporation's own establishments to coopt sources of market constraint they confront. For example, consider the position of W. H. Vaughn, president of Firestone Steel Products in 1967. Firestone Steel Products was owned by Firestone Tire and Rubber and constituted the Firestone establishment indicated in Figure 3.1 for the transportation equipment industry.

The corporate bureaucracy Mr. Vaughn headed was organized to manufacture wheels, a production activity placing Firestone Steel Products within a subsector of the transportation equipment industry. Organization theory has much to say about the efficient management of Firestone Steel Products. The issues raised could range from the specialization of roles coordinated by authority relations as emphasized in Weber's (1925) conception of the efficient bureaucracy, to the coordination of people performing those roles with different, often conflicting, interests as highlighted by Barnard (1938) and Blau (1955) in their empirical research on bureaucracy. The most efficient scale of operations could be sought in the balance of cost curves, demand, and production volume discussed in microeconomic models of the firm (e.g., Shepherd, 1970:Chap. 3).

For the purposes here, however, I put these issues aside. I shall assume that a corporation's operations within a single industry are efficiently organized. Taking the efficient intraindustry organization of a corporate bureaucracy for granted, my concern is the interindustry organization of a corporation. In particular, my concern is the manner in which the Firestone Tire and Rubber board of directors could have enabled Mr. Vaughn's establishment to coopt sources of market constraint.

Looking beyond the structure of an establishment to the structure of its market environment, the industry in which Mr. Vaughn managed Firestone Steel Products was characterized by a structure of market constraints on his freedom to control pricing decisions. In the same way that market constraints on the apparel industry were described in Table 2.7, market constraints on Mr. Vaughn's industry can be described. The industry could be analyzed in much finer detail with respect to specific products, brand names, competitors, suppliers, consumers, and so on (e.g., see Hirsch, 1975, for illustration; Porter, 1980, for general methodology), but for the purposes of comparing many industries in this study I shall focus on the very basic market constraints defined by the structural autonomy model in Chapter 2. Among other sources of market constraint, Mr. Vaughn faced severe constraint from the primary metals industry and the transportation and warehousing sector. These are the arrows in Figure 3.1 pointing to the transportation equipment industry. How could Mr. Vaughn have used Firestone Tire and Rubber's directorate to circumvent those market constraints and so lower profit uncertainties for his establishment?[3]

Directorate Ties through Ownership

The most direct strategy for eliminating a source of market constraint would be to purchase an establishment in the constraint sector or create a new subsidiary establishment within the constraint sector. Since the previously owned establishments and the newly acquired/created establishment are controlled through the same board of directors, they are very closely interlocked through the directorate. The most obvious, and intimate, interestablishment directorate tie occurs when two establishments are owned by a single firm and so governed by a single directorate.

There are several advantages to conducting market transactions within the domain of a single corporate actor rather than conducting them between separate firms. These advantages have been discussed from a perspective that Williamson has aptly named the "transaction cost" approach (Williamson, 1975, 1981; cf. Arrow, 1974, esp. Chap. 2, and Ouchi, 1980). Within this approach, management is assumed to ask the question articulated by Coase (1937) in his classic paper on the firm: When is it advantageous to conduct market transactions under the authority of a corporate bureaucracy rather than conducting them on the open market under the authority of market price mechanisms? Williamson (1975) offers a comprehensive discussion of the general advantages that ownership ties

---

[3]The structural approach I am taking here shares with the population ecology approach (Hannan & Freeman, 1977; Aldrich, 1979, esp. Chap. 2) a general focus on the match between organizational form and environmental constraints. A population ecology treatment of adaptation to market constraint, however, would emphasize different features of this match. I am focusing on the structure of relations—the structure of market constraints to which a firm must adapt, and the structure of directorate ties with which it could adapt. Survival rates of different organizational forms over time are the focus of population ecology analyses. Were this a population ecology study, different firms would have been assumed to have stable directorate structures that were variably adapted to their environment, and those best adapted would be most likely to survive through any given time period (e.g., see Brittain & Freeman, 1980; Delacroix & Carroll, 1982). Unfortunately, the insights of population ecology are not pertinent to this study because the time path to adaptation is not at issue. This is a cross-sectional analysis of American manufacturing industries during the late 1960s. Whether the corporate directorate ties to be described were formed with the emergence of individual industries (Stinchcombe, 1965), with the spread of decentralization as the accepted structure for large firms (Chandler, 1962), or with short-term adaptation such as joint ventures (e.g., Pfeffer & Nowak, 1976) or replacing broken ties (e.g., Koenig et al., 1979; Ornstein, 1982; Palmer, 1983); my sole concern in this book is the extent to which directorate ties were coordinated with market constraint relations in 1967. The etiology of such a condition over time is a topic set aside for subsequent research (see Chapter 5).

can provide. In his corporate hierarchy terms (Williamson, 1975:151–154), the discussion here of establishments versus corporations would translate into a discussion of U-form (unitary) versus M-form (multidivisional) corporations. Williamson summarizes his discussion in terms of six advantages provided by ownership ties (cf., Williamson, 1975:257–258, original terms are given here in parentheses). A corporate hierarchy of establishments has the advantage of improving efficiency by improving the flow of trustworthy information. An establishment has (in the ideal) perfect audit information on other establishments in the hierarchy (information impactedness) thereby freeing it to specialize in making internal decisions without having to glean information on its environment (bounded rationality). Further, the corporate hierarchy provides security from the environment by allowing a less Machiavellian exchange process than typifies the market (atmosphere), preventing dishonesty (small numbers and opportunism), and permitting adaptation to environmental contingencies by means of coordination among its constituent establishments (uncertainty). These advantages are an elaboration of three general points articulated in Coase's (1937:336–339) analysis. The conduct of market transactions within a corporate bureaucracy offers advantages of information, influence, and privacy: (a) Ready access to information on other establishments within the firm means that the costs of searching for relevant supplier–consumer prices on the open market are avoided. (b) The influence each establishment has over others within the firm, through the joint interest in them from the firm's directorate, means that excessive costs of buying and selling on the open market can be avoided by buying and selling with comembers of the firm. (c) The privacy of exchanges within a firm protects those exchanges from interested outside parties. There are competitors interested in doing business with the same supplier–consumer sectors. There are government agencies interested in taxing purchases and sales or, worse, regulating those transactions according to quotas or price controls.

Where these advantages exist in general, they are more pronounced for transactions with a source of severe market constraint. For the reasons discussed in Chapter 2, an industry establishment has low control over price in such transactions, so the costs of buying and selling on the open market are especially high. The ownership tie advantages of information, influence and privacy have, at minimum, the potential to lower uncertainty in conducting severely constrained transactions. At maximum, they have the potential to increase an establishment's profit margin by decreasing excessive supplier prices and increasing depressed consumer prices.

This point is illustrated in Figure 3.1. Firestone Tire and Rubber owned establishments in both the primary metals industry and the transporation equipment industry. Establishments in the transportation equipment industry were owned by few competitive firms and consumed a large proportion of the output from the primary metals industry (see the concentration and transactions data in

Table A.1 of the Appendix). At the same time, the primary metals industry was the largest supplier for the transportation equipment industry. As would be expected from the discussion of market constraint in Chapter 2 and as is indicated in Figure 3.1, each industry was a source of market constraint on profits in the other. In this context, it was advantageous to both of Firestone's establishments to be governed by the same directorate. The head executive of its transportation equipment establishments, Mr. Vaughn, knew that his supply of primary metals product was secure. Moreover, he could be sure that the price he was charged for that supply would be the lowest price reasonable since establishment profits—the profit Firestone's primary metals establishment made from the sale and the profit Mr. Vaughn made from manufacturing transportation equipment from the primary metals product purchased—were both Firestone's profits. Ignoring bureaucratic infighting, there would have been no reason for Firestone's directorate to have given one of its establishments a high profit margin at the expense of profits in another of its establishments.

It is worth noting that the coordination of ownership ties with market constraint implies neither a change in the structure of market transactions nor a change in the pattern of market constraints on profits. Establishments within an industry were obliged to engage in market transactions with specific other sectors, and the pattern of those transactions defined constraints on industry profits. For example, under the technology used by Firestone Steel Products to manufacture wheels, a large proportion of supplies had to be purchased from the primary metals industry. There was no discretion; primary metals product had to be purchased somewhere. However, the establishment did have a choice in the specific primary metals establishment from which supplies were purchased. Ownership ties could have affected this choice by creating favored trade partners, partners with whom buying and selling carried information, influence, and privacy advantages decreasing the uncertainty of buying and selling on the open market. The general point here is that market transactions were conducted in accordance with technological requirements whether ownership ties were present or not, but the uncertainty of those transactions could have been reduced by the availability of ownership ties.

This line of reasoning can be extrapolated to pose an analytically fruitful question. Given the many advantages of transacting economic exchange within a corporate bureaucracy, why were any exchanges conducted on the open market? As Coase (1937:340) expressed the question in his initial inquiry, "Why is not all production carried on by one big firm?" It is fruitful to consider answers to this obviously rhetorical question because such consideration sets the stage for moving beyond ownership ties to analyze other types of ties that might enable establishments to circumvent market constraint while avoiding some ownership tie disadvantages.

Diseconomies of scale provide the most obvious reason for there being many (rather than one) large corporations responsible for production. With an increasing number and diversity of supplier–consumer transactions being conducted within a firm, there are increasing coordination costs—not the least of which is an increased probability of inefficient resource allocations to individual establishments. This point, referenced summarily by Coase (1937:340), is nicely elaborated in Lindblom's (1977:Chap. 5) discussion of systems coordination by authority relations alone as having strong thumbs, but no fingers; the corporate bureaucracy has the control required to coordinate establishments, but not the delicacy required to fine tune the coordination of many, diverse establishments.

There are also disadvantages to ownership ties that involve errors in entrepreneurial strategy. Diseconomies of scale involve an error in fine tuning a firm's production activities. Beyond these asceptically analytic errors in organization, there are social structural inefficiencies to consider. With the control provided by ownership ties comes commitment. An establishment not only has the advantages of access to other establishments within its parent firm, it has the responsibility of sharing their profit margins. This means that there are at least two structural conditions under which an establishment would be very ill served by an ownership tie.

First of all, an ownership tie would eliminate opportunities to exploit a consumer or supplier sector. Where a sector is poorly organized, highly competitive, there are advantages to buying and selling on the open market with the sector. Sector establishments would not be able to control sector prices. They could be forced to accept prices yielding them a low profit margin. If a low profit margin is to be endured by some sector of establishments, better they remain outside the corporation. An ownership tie to the sector would give a sector establishment access to much more favorable prices than would be possible on the open market—at the expense of profits available in buying and selling with the sector on the open market.

Second, an ownership tie could expose the establishment to severe market constraints beyond those it currently faces. A misleading feature of the transaction cost approach is the assumption that market transactions can be conducted on a one-by-one basis within a firm. This assumption is explicit in Coase's (1937:341) definition of the point at which it will no longer be efficient for a firm to expand, "a firm will tend to expand until the costs of organizing an extra transaction within the firm become equal to the costs of carrying out the same transaction by means of an exchange on the open market," and the assumption is explicit in Williamson's (1981:559–560) more recent formulation. In fact, market transactions exist in patterns as discussed in Chapter 2. The technology available for producing some commodity involves buying supplies from particular supplier sectors and selling the commodity to typical consumer sectors. This pattern of buying and selling defines an industry as a network position within the economy. When an establishment is brought into the firm with an ownership tie, the whole pattern of supplier–consumer transactions characterizing the establishment's industry is brought into the firm. In other words, the firm exposes itself to any market constraints confronting the establishment's industry. This will be a problem for the firm when those sources of market constraint are beyond the reach of the firm's current directorate ties. In such a situation, the firm has exposed its establishments to new sources of market constraint through the ownership tie to the recently acquired establishment. In both this situation and the situation of a highly competitive sector, the firm's establishments would be best served by a nonownership tie—some type of relationship providing the monitoring advantages of an ownership tie without the responsibilities of an ownership tie. Interlocking directorates provide one such tie.

Directorate Ties through Direct Interlocking

The preceding discussion implies that a firm's directorate governs the firm's establishments. In fact, the firm's management governs its establishments, and that management is represented to varying extents on the firm's directorate, some directorates being composed principally of corporate management, and so serving what Zald (1969) termed an internal control function. One of the shifts in directorate behavior observed during the late 1960s through the mid 1970s was a shift in the balance between so-called "inside" and "outside" directors. An increasing proportion of directors in large American firms consisted of outsiders: persons not employed by the firm, persons typically employed by some other firm. The presence of these outsiders on the board created interlocks with the firms from which they were drawn.

Relationships created by interlocked directorates provide a flexible surrogate for ownership ties. Instead of actually owning an establishment in a constraint sector, a firm can create a tie between itself and some other firm owning an establishment in the sector. In addition to ownership ties, interestablishment ties through a corporate board of directors occur when two establishments are owned by separate firms that share one or more directors. I shall refer to these relationships as interlock ties. The tie involves no more responsibility than a commitment to an individual director—a commitment easily formed by invitation, easily dissolved by resignation.

Strategic recruitment of directors from other firms can be advantageous. Mace (1971) provides a particularly useful discussion of such directors based on fieldwork he conducted during the 1960s, the fieldwork consisting of participation on directorates and interviews with other directors.[4] These directors are typically

---

[4]The functions of outside directors have been discussed in several informative books by persons involved in business administration (e.g., Vance, 1964; Koontz, 1967; Bacon & Brown, 1975; Mueller, 1978; Louden, 1982; cf., Pfeffer & Salancik, 1978:Chap. 7; Aldrich, 1979:Chaps. 12, 13); however, Mace's fieldwork provides a uniquely rich insider's description of outside directors. I rely on Mace's fieldwork extensively in quoting director and chief executive officer remarks communicating their sense of directorate life.

selected by a firm's chief executive, typically do not interfere with the firm's management, and do not attack proposals put forth by its management during board meetings. At the same time, outside directors do play three important roles within a firm: (a) Within their respective areas of expertise, outside directors offer advice and counsel to the management. (b) They constitute a corporate superego in the sense that, in order to avoid embarrassing questions during board meetings, the management takes particular care in preparing proposals before bringing them to the board for approval. As one president put it (Mace, 1971:24), ''The mere existence of outside directors makes us think a little bit harder, makes us organize our thoughts. It sharpens up the whole organization.'' (c) Finally, they offer the firm stability by being collectively empowered to replace the firm's chief executive in the event of death or incompetence. Since they have been appointed by the same office, however, the latter event is most likely to result in their resignations from the board or their collective request for an evaluation of the current management's performance by an outside consulting firm—a subtle hint to the reigning chief. There are exceptions to these typical roles, but the roles as general patterns of behavior are quite in keeping with the kinds of people one would expect to fulfill them: bright, successful individuals who are absorbed in other activities that leave little time to get involved in another firm's problems.

The advice and counsel role of the outside director most clearly animates the potential of a direct interlock tie as a means for circumventing market constraint. This potential could be tapped by treating the tie as a weakened version of an ownership tie. The potential could also be tapped by using the tie as no more than a channel for trustworthy information.

A direct interlock is in one sense a weakened ownership tie between establishments. In the same manner that the intensity of competition between establishments is decreased when both are owned by a single firm—the firm creating a community of interest between them—competition intensity can be decreased by a direct interlock tie. The general Federal Trade Commission report on interlocking directorates offers a common sense account of this (U.S. Federal Trade Commission, 1951):

> A director of two competing corporations cannot in good conscience recommend that either shall undertake a type of competition that is likely to injure the other. A director of two corporations that are respectively buyer and seller of the same commodities or services cannot in good conscience recommend that either concern prefer unrelated sources of supply or customers instead of the company in which he is interested, nor that either concern press to the limits its ability to strike a good bargain at the expense of the other. . . . Thus, the inherent tendency of interlocking directorates between companies that have dealings with each other as buyers or sellers, or that have relations to each other as competitors, is to blunt the edge of rivalry between corporations, to seek out ways of compromising opposing interests, and to develop alliances where the interest of one of the corporations is jeopardized by third parties [p. 21].

In other words, a direct interlock tie between two establishments could decrease competition between them because intense competition would create a conflict of interest for the director(s) constituting the interlock.

Although commonly mentioned in reports advocating stricter federal regulation of interlocking directorates, this potential of interlock ties to function as a type of ownership tie is rarely mentioned—for any of several possible reasons— in reports of personal interviews with directors describing the uses to which interlocks are actually put. More typical of those reports are references to interlocks as channels for trustworthy information.

Even if interlock ties were no more than channels for trustworthy information, they could lessen the uncertainty of market constraints. Given some sector posing severe market constraint on an establishment, a direct interlock tie to a firm operating in the sector would provide a source of insider information on developments being undertaken within the sector as well as probable sector response to developments being considered within the establishment. Mace (1948:28–37) discusses this point at length with illustrative examples (cf. W. F. Rockwell's remarks to the Corporate Directors Conference [1975, esp. pp. 53–54] on the use that his firm, Rockwell International, made of outside directors). As one corporate president summarized the matter in Mace's (1971) fieldwork,

> The board of directors serves as a sounding board—a wall to bounce the ball against. It is a kind of screen on major moves, whether it be acquisitions, or whether it be major shifts of policy or product line—the broad directions of the business. Board members serve as sources of information. . . . The decision is not made by the board, but the directors are a checkpoint for the management in adding their experience and knowledge to the program [p. 13].

Naturally, the flow of information is symmetric: The outside director advises the corporate president as well as carrying his observations during the board meeting back to his own firm. This ability to obtain information is a frequent motivation for serving as an outside director. One of Mace's (1971:105) respondents put the matter in the following way when asked to explain why he accepted positions as an outside director: "Because I want to learn, I want to broaden my contacts and to get inputs from outside the group I live with and work with on a daily basis. I went on the board of a company recently which is strong on consumer marketing—that's an area I want to know more about." Opinions such as this, opinions emphasizing the opportunity to learn about corporate practice in another firm's industry, are among the most often expressed as explanation for serving as an outside director (e.g., Mace, 1948:85, 1971:101–105, and see Bacon & Brown, 1975:56–59, for a similar conclusion drawn from personal interviews with directors).

In sum, the direct interlock tie can decrease the uncertainty created by market constraints. In the case of sectors constraining the establishment's profit margin, a direct interlock tie to the sector can lower competitive uncertainty for the establishment in any of several ways, such as (a) increasing the establishment's ability to identify the most advantageous of available trade partners in the sector, (b) increasing its ability to determine which potential trade partners pose the greatest risk as sources of supplies or consumption, (c) increasing its ability to predict future developments in the sector, and (d) increasing its ability to anticipate sector response to future price or product changes being considered in the establishment. In a sentence, direct interlock ties can improve an establishment's access to, and accuracy of information on, trade partners available in those economic sectors of interest to the establishment.

It is interesting to consider Figure 3.1 in this light. Firestone interlocked with Western Airlines, which in turn owned an establishment in the transportation and warehousing sector. A quick reference to the Appendix shows that this sector was highly concentrated for a nonmanufacturing sector and was the third-largest consumer of output from the transportation equipment industry. Table A.4 shows that transportation and warehousing posed a severe market constraint on profits in the transportation equipment industry. This constraint is indicated by an arrow in Figure 3.1. In this market context, Firestone's transportation equipment establishment had the good fortune of having Leonard K. Firestone as the man interlocking Firestone with Western. A member of the board of Firestone Tire and Rubber Company and president of Firestone Tire and Rubber of California (a division of the parent company), Mr. Firestone provided an eminently prestigious and partisan spokesman for Firestone products when Western planned its purchases of transportation equipment. At the same time, he provided a communication channel back to Firestone for his inferences regarding developments in the transportation/warehousing sector based on his participation in Western's directorate. This example of a potentially useful direct interlock tie between supplier and consumer is repeated throughout the economy, as will be clear in Chapter 4. A great variety of examples are described in the 1951 study conducted by the Federal Trade Commission.

Directorate Ties through Indirect Financial Interlocking

Firestone's other interlock in Figure 3.1 is an example of the ubiquitous financial interlock, Firestone's being with Cleveland Trust Company. This interlock was created by the president of Cleveland Trust, George F. Karch, serving as an outside director on Firestone's board. As the president of Cleveland Trust, Mr. Karch provided Firestone's establishments with the often-mentioned corporate need for financial advice and counsel. As one corporation president explained it to Mace (1971),

> I believe that today we in top management need sophisticated financial advice on the board. We cannot maintain these skills internally, and besides, the financial environment is constantly changing. . . . In my experience, the average top executive—including me—in relation to his role and financial responsibility is technically naive about the intricacies of finance today. I don't mean just the mechanics of a specific deal, but what is the impact of what we are doing on the whole company [p. 18].

Still, this need for financial counsel must be weighed against the obligations of having a financial firm represented on the board. In the case of commercial banks, there is room for secondary transactions with banks not represented on the board.[5] In the case of investment banks, the interlock can be limiting to the point that constraint was one of two reasons most often given for why management preferred not to have them on the board (Mace, 1971:144–148). In a response nicely illustrating the creation of favored trade partners through interlocking, one of Mace's (1971) respondents put it the following way:

> If you've got an investment banker on your board, you're sort of a little bit tied in with him, and I prefer not to have one on our board. An investment banker on the board restricts one's freedom of action—I mean you might or might not want to use his firm in some transaction, and *if he is on the board he thinks he is entitled to that business* [p. 146, italics added].

Here again, however, there is a symmetry to the interlock tie that can work to the nonfinancial firm's advantage. Restrictions firm A faces as a result of its interlock with a financial institution can also be imposed on other firms interlocked with it and imposed in a manner advantageous to firm A. A banker-director represents more than his financial establishment on the board. He represents all the sectors in which his firm controls establishments as well as those in which his firm has expert knowledge.

Looking beyond direct interlocks with financial institutions, a third type of interestablishment directorate tie occurs when two establishments owned by separate firms are connected indirectly through a financial institution interlocked with the two firms. Mintz and Schwartz (1981a, 1981b) offer a useful discussion of such ties through financial institutions as ''hubs'' in the network of interlocking directorates. As the banker on Firestone's board, for example, Mr. Karch provided an indirect channel of communication to all the firms over which Cleveland Trust held some influence. Looking past the direct interlock between Firestone and Cleveland Trust in Figure 3.1, note the indirect interlock that

---

[5]A firm–client relation is implied by even a commercial bank representative sitting on the board. One corporate president drew a distinction between commercial versus investment banks for Mace (1971:153); ''The commercial banker-director probably represents the company's lead bank but most large and medium-sized companies deal with many other banks so management is not limited to that one bank.''

Firestone has through Cleveland Trust to American Airlines and Pan American Airlines. It could be coincidence, but by interlocking with Cleveland Trust, Firestone tripled the number of establishments with which it had an interlock tie in the transportation and warehousing sector—a sector for which 53% of the total manufacturing purchases are provided by industries in which Firestone owned an establishment.

In one sense, indirect interlocks by means of financial institutions provide a market advantage similar to that provided by direct interlocks. They can channel the flow of information among establishments in the same manner possible through direct interlock ties. For example, Mace (1948) describes the situation of a small firm in the leather industry,

> price fluctuations in the raw hide market had a significant bearing on the company's profitability. Raw material costs represented 90% of the finished goods price, and with narrow profit margins in this competitive segment of the industry, small changes in these costs could determine the loss or profit for the period. . . . Not having the time to study and keep abreast of conditions in the leather market, the company's manager scheduled a weekly luncheon meeting with one of the directors, a vice president of one of the city's large banks, who had considerable experience with companies engaged in various segments of the leather industry. As part of his banking responsibilities, the banker-director studied the leather market on a day-to-day basis. Many of the bank loans which he handled were made to leather trade enterprises, and the banker felt impelled to understand as well as he could the purchasing and inventory problems of the bank's borrowers. The advice and counsel on leather price trends which were thus provided to the manager of the leather company constituted a real contribution to the efficiency of the management job accomplished in the company [pp. 30–31].

Relative to direct interlock ties, in fact, indirect financial ties could provide more efficient—if less accurate—channels for information on other sectors. The random and nonrandom errors to be expected during interpersonal communication imply that the accuracy of information transmitted across multiple interlock ties would decline with the number of different interlocks the information has passed over. Ceteris paribus, information communicated over indirect interlock ties should be less accurate than information communicated directly between directorates. However, the banker-director as an indirect connection to many sectors is efficient since information on all sectors is probably not needed at any one time and he takes only a single seat on the board as opposed to the many seats required to directly represent the sectors he indirectly represents. In the interest of maintaining some privacy in board meetings and maintaining a balance of voting power on the board, the efficiency of a financial interlock would seem to outweigh the possible distortion of information indirectly obtained by means of the interlock. Once aware of an idea, a firm's management could always pursue it outside the board meeting in order to obtain more accurate information on it. As an information source, financial interlocks seem to function in this manner.

Summarizing his observations, Mace (1971) felt that investment bankers in particular

> through exposure to many different companies in many different industries and regions, bring to company presidents and company boards of directors what one president described as "a treasury of information." Bankers, as they practice their profession, are collectors of information—they hear the problems faced and approaches followed by presidents of a substantial number of other companies. Thus investment bankers as directors were described as "great pollenizers"—they lift ideas from one company and deposit them in other companies [p. 200].

In a second sense, indirect financial interlocks are stronger than direct interlocks between nonfinancial firms and so offer a market advantage similar to ownership ties. With the growth of pension funds and insurance premium capital during the post–World War II period, stock ownership in American firms has become increasingly concentrated in banks and insurance companies (Kotz, 1978:60–71; Metcalf, 1978). In the same sense that a firm's establishments obtain advantages in conducting their market transactions with one another, it is in a financial firm's interest to maintain profit margins in its diverse holdings since those profits directly and indirectly translate into its own profits. This is the typical reason given for financial control being a threat to competition (although there seems to be little or no systematic evidence on the point).[6] For example, Representative Patman's (1968) report on commercial banks summarizes with a conclusion reached in an earlier study by the Federal Trade Commission,

> A director who is on the board of an industrial company and a financial institution cannot in good conscience encourage the latter to finance expansion by competitors of the former which may jeopardize the former's prosperity; nor can he in good conscience encourage the industrial company to obtain its credit through other channels. Thus the inherent tendency of interlocking directorates between companies that have dealings with each other as buyers and sellers, or that have relations to each other as competitors, is to blunt the edge of rivalry between corporations, to seek out ways of compromising opposing interests, and to develop alliances where the interest of one of the corporations is jeopardized by third parties [p. 25].

[6]Nevertheless, this is a basis for antitrust action against financial firms serving as intermediaries. Kotz (1978:133–134) describes an antitrust suit brought against Cleveland Trust Company in 1970. Cleveland Trust (the financial firm in Figure 3.1) held significant portions of common stock in four of the largest American firms engaged in manufacturing automatic screw machinery, had a representative on the board of each firm, and did "substantial banking business" with each firm. As of 1967, the four firms together accounted for 50.6% of the industry's sales, so Cleveland Trust constituted an intermediary between major competitors within the industry at the time. The complaint charged that Cleveland Trust used its voting rights to determine the directors selected and policy determined for the firms. In so doing, it was charged, Cleveland Trust was in the position of being able to inhibit competition among the firms. The case was settled in 1975 by prohibiting Cleveland Trust's officers from sitting on the boards of two of the four firms.

Patman's report then gives an example drawn from an earlier study of the General Motors Corporation:

> Several of the witnesses claimed that General Motors obtained business because directors of various transit companies were bankers who were anxious to obtain General Motors' banking business, and therefore urged their managers to purchase General Motors buses. These witnesses claimed that the managers of certain transit companies, although well satisfied with non General Motors products which they had used for many years, switched to General Motors at the urging of their directors [p. 25].

The director from a financial firm brings to the board more than information; he brings preferential trade partners according to the influence his firm has over potential trade partners.

Given a limited supply of elegible officers and the keen eye of federal agencies enforcing antitrust violations (see footnote 6), a financial institution might not maintain interlocks with every firm over which it exercises influence. Describing instances of financial control in 1967–1969, for example, Kotz (1978:121–123) reports a tendency for financial firms to have a representative on the boards of corporations in which they have extensive stock ownership but not on the boards of firms in which they have low, albeit significant, stock ownership.[7] Where they do occur, however, indirect interlock ties through financial institutions combine features of ownership ties and direct interlock ties in providing a market advantage to establishments connected by them.

THE COOPTIVE POTENTIAL OF DIRECTORATE TIES

Directorate ties have the potential to be cooptive in the sense of Selznick's (1949:13) initial presentation of cooptation as "the process of absorbing new elements into the leadership or policy-determining structure of an organization as a means of averting threats to its stability or existence." All three types of directorate ties provide a mechanism for absorbing new elements into management and averting the threat of market constraint. Summarizing the preceding discussion, four features of directorate ties define their cooptive potential: access to trustworthy information, the exercise of influence, privacy, and commitment.

Access to trustworthy information is the most often mentioned feature of directorate ties giving them a cooptive potential. All three types of directorate

---

[7]This does not mean that financial interlocks generally underestimate financial control. Kotz only considers interlocks created when a representative of a financial institution sits on the controlled firm, and he does not consider the instances in which interlocks occur between firms and financial institutions in the absence of financial control.

ties provide information, but are distinct in the kind of information provided and the manner in which it is provided. Across the three types of directorate ties, easy access to accurate information is balanced against information scope. The information obtained through ownership ties is easily obtained and highly accurate. Intrafirm audits ensure accuracy and intrafirm authority relations to a single directorate ensure access. In contrast, interlock ties operate by an informant providing advice and counsel. Rather than providing facts, as would be expected of company audits, outside directors provide advice and counsel on significant activities beyond the firm. They provide an early warning system monitoring trends and conditions in markets important to management. What is lost in accuracy and ease of access to information is balanced by the scope of information provided. In sum, ownership and interlock ties complement one another as information channels between managers in separate establishments.

Influence is a second feature animating the cooptive potential of directorate ties. The three types of directorate ties differ in the extent to which, and manner in which, each provides a channel for interestablishment influence. Weakest among them are direct interlock ties, ties in which influence operates by conflict of interest. The director of two firms cannot in good conscience encourage either to take action against the interests of the other. This is the reason typically cited for prohibiting interlocks between competitors as described in the preceding discussion of interlock ties, but it is also the reason cited by management for not appointing certain outsiders to the board. Interlocks with principal suppliers or consumers infringe on management's autonomy, making it difficult to develop relations with new trade partners. The frequent combination of credit with a financial interlock makes indirect financial interlock ties a more likely basis for interestablishment influence. The financial institution can function as a third party broker between establishments in supplier–consumer or competitor conflicts. As described in the preceding discussion of financial interlocks, this is the basis for the community of interest that banks are reputed to create among firms with which they are affiliated. The influence a financial firm has on the firms to which it extends credit is taken to its extreme in ownership ties. Ownership ties between establishments not only provide ready access to accurate information on other establishments, they provide access to the authority of the directorate responsible for each establishment. That authority makes ownership ties the relations through which an establishment could most reliably influence the production activities of other establishments.

A third issue is the privacy with which influence could be exerted or information could be obtained: privacy from the tax or price monitoring of government agencies, privacy from competitors interested in supply purchases indicating future production plans. The three types of directorate ties are ranked relatively easily in terms of the privacy they provide. Ownership ties offer maximum privacy; communication is intrafirm. In a sense, ownership ties offer the privacy of the black market. Buying, selling, and planning the future coordination of the firm's establishments are conducted in-house, masked from market forces unless it is in the firm's interests to make particular of its actions public. This privacy is greatly eroded in interlock ties. Communication through an interlock tie involves transmission across the boundaries of separate firms. Privacy in this interfirm connection is conditional on the joint interests of both firms. Instead of information being distributed according to one firm's interests, the potentially conflicting interests of two firms determine privacy. The difficulty of maintaining privacy in communication between two firms is only increased in communication through indirect financial interlocks inasmuch as the potentially conflicting interests of multiple firms associated with a central financial firm determine privacy.

   Commitment is the cost at which directorate ties provide ready access to accurate information, the ability to exert influence, and privacy. In particular, commitment is the complement to influence in directorate ties; the greater the influence possible in a directorate tie, the greater the commitment involved in the tie. Ownership ties represent a maximum commitment. If one of a firm's establishments fails to return a profit, the loss is covered with income obtained from the firm's other establishments. Interlock ties are much more flexible because they involve a commitment to a person rather than an establishment. The commitment in an interlock tie is to the person constituting the interlock; there is no commitment to ensure the profitability of the other directorates on which he sits. This commitment is formed with the ease of an invitation and dissolved with the same ease. The weaker provision of information, influence, and privacy in interlock ties, in other words, is to be balanced against the weaker commitment they entail. When the profit margin in a sector is lower than the profit margin typical of firm's establishments, it is in the firm's interest to monitor the sector's production activities with interlock ties while transacting business with the sector on the open market. It is not in the firm's interest to create an ownership tie to the sector because such a tie would commit the firm to an establishment likely to earn a lower profit margin than is typical of the firm's other establishments.

   All three types of directorate ties offer a means of averting threats to the stability and existence of establishments by enabling them to circumvent market constraints, this in turn decreasing profit uncertainties. Market constraints are circumvented through the creation of favored trade partners. The verb is important in this sentence. Market constraints are not eliminated by directorate ties— they are avoided. An establishment in the apparel industry must purchase supplies from the textile industry, an establishment in the transportation equipment industry must purchase supplies from the primary metals industry, and in both cases the supplier sector poses a market constraint for industry profits. However, there is a choice of supplier establishments within a supplier sector. Directorate ties make some establishments more attractive trade partners than other establishments. Ownership ties create the information, influence, and privacy advantages of conducting market transactions in the nonmarket context of a corporate hierarchy. Buying and selling can be conducted more efficiently in this context than they can on the open market—efficiency translating into stable, increased profits for buyers and sellers, especially in the context of severe constraint on the open market. Direct interlock ties channel the flow of adverse and favorable information on trade partners available in other sectors, again making some establishments more attractive than others as suppliers or consumers. This same function is fulfilled by indirect financial interlocks, at a greater efficiency if a potentially lower accuracy. Moreover, the outside director brings to the board the influence that his firm can exercise over potential trade partners.

In sum, market transactions between industry and sector occur as described in an input–output table whether or not there are directorate ties between the industry and sector. The more that all three types of directorate ties connect industry and sector, however, the lower the proportion of buying and selling that must be transacted on the imperfectly competitive open market. Together, the three types of directorate ties create favored trade partners as establishments with which buying and selling can be conducted to better advantage and with lower uncertainty than would be possible in the absence of directorate ties. In this sense of defining trade partners with which necessary buying and selling can be conducted in a nonmarket context, directorate ties have the potential to coopt sources of market constraint.[8]

DESCRIBING DIRECTORATE TIES

Given the cooptive potential of the three types of directorate ties, I wish to describe the frequency with which each type connected manufacturing establishments in 1967 to competitors, suppliers, and consumers. It would be impossible to describe all ties among all establishments. There were too many firms owning

---

[8]This function is hardly unique to directorate ties. Corporations, let alone directorate ties, are a relatively recent addition to economic systems. Kinship and ceremonial relations serve, in many economic systems, the cooptive functions that directorate ties serve in the corporate economy. In some cases, the analogy to directorate ties in a primitive economy can be striking; for example, the Kula exchange relations among the Trobriand Islanders described by Malinowski (1922, see Burt, 1982a:325n, for more specific references) or the kinship, and kin-like, relations among the Nuer described by Evans-Pritchard (1940, cf. Light's, 1972, description of credit associations among Chinese and Japanese immigrants to the United States). General themes on this topic are nicely reviewed in Sahlins's (1972:Chap. 5) discussion of the "sociology of primitive exchange." There has yet to be a comparative historical analysis of directorate ties as a corporate enactment of the age-old practice of creating nonmarket, social relations to integrate trade partners in potentially conflictual economic exchange relations.

too many establishments. This raises the problem of how to draw sample data. There is also the problem of organizing sample data so as to represent cooptive relations in terms of directorate ties. I shall first address the sampling problem. Readers not interested in computational details might prefer to skip ahead to the section in which the sample data are used to replicate basic findings in directorate research.

Sample Values of Directorate Tie Frequencies

Firms are typically sampled for directorate research by size, large firms having extensive assets and/or extensive annual sales. For example, the pace-setting study by the National Resources Committee (Means, 1939) describes interlocks among the 200 largest nonfinancial corporations and the 50 largest financial institutions. Dooley (1969) and Allen (1974) describe identical samples for later points in time (1964 and 1970, respectively). In a similar vein, the 1951 U.S. Federal Trade Commission study describes post–World War II interlocks among the 1000 largest manufacturing firms based on Department of Commerce data (and considering indirect interlocks among 330 of the largest nonmanufacturing firms), and Representative Patman's Subcommittee on Domestic Finance report (Patman, 1968) describes the 500 largest industrial, and 200 largest nonindustrial, firms in the 1966 *Fortune* listing (together with 49 large banks in urban centers). More recent work continues this tradition. Mariolis (1975) and Pennings (1980) describe the 500 largest manufacturing firms and the 247 largest nonmanufacturing firms drawing principally from the 1970 *Fortune* listing. Bearden *et al.* (1975) describe the 1131 largest firms drawn principally from *Fortune* listings between 1963 and 1974. Senator Metcalf's Subcommittee on Reports, Accounting and Management report (Turner, 1978) describes interlocking directorates involving 130 of the largest firms in 1976.

This sampling on a size criterion is justified by Berle and Means's (1932) finding that the top 200 nonbanking firms in 1929 controlled between 45% and 53% of all assets in nonbanking firms. Given the increasing concentration of assets in large corporations since 1929, there is little need to analyze more than the largest firms if analysis is intended to allow one to make inferences about corporate assets in the economy as a whole.

Nevertheless, an innovative twist on this size criterion is proposed by Warner and Unwalla (1967). Defining a population of 20,989 firms listed in the 1961 *Fortune* compilation of the 750 largest American firms and the 1961 *Million Dollar Directory* from Dun and Bradstreet (a listing of firms with a million dollars or more of annual sales), a stratified random sample of 500 firms was drawn with the aid of *Moody's Industrial Manual*. The sample was stratified into 11 SIC categories, and the number of sampled firms within each category approximated the proportion of total net worth of firms in the population that was accounted for by the net worth of firms in the category (Warner and Unwalla, 1967:24,124).

My purpose here requires a slight variation on the usual size criterion in directorate research, a variation anticipated by Warner and Unwalla. I am concerned neither with describing the control of assets in the overall economy nor with interlocking among firms generally. Instead, I wish to describe the manner in which establishments jointly occupying manufacturing industries as network positions are connected by directorate ties to establishments in sectors generally. A two-stage sampling procedure seems appropriate. The first stage yields a positional sample representative of manufacturing industries, and the second stage snowballs that sample into nonmanufacturing sectors.

The purpose of the positional sample is to ensure that directorates operating in each manufacturing industry, and likely to be responsible for directorate ties, are represented in the analysis. Since interlocking is more typical of large firms than small firms, the largest firm-owning establishments in an industry are most likely to be responsible for any directorate ties linking establishments in the industry to sectors generally. Beginning with the 1968 *Fortune* listing of the 500 largest American manufacturing firms in 1967, the four largest firms owning an establishment in any one of the two-digit SIC manufacturing industries have been located using the SIC listing for each firm in the 1968 *Poor's Directory of Corporations, Directors and Executives*. The resulting 42 firms represent large American firms engaged in manufacturing. Since a single firm could have been the largest firm owning an establishment in more than one industry, the sample does not contain four unique firms from each industry. Among the 42 sampled firms are the four largest owning an establishment in any one of the two-digit manufacturing industries. Although not the 42 largest manufacturing firms, the sampled firms are quite large. Liggett and Myers Tobacco is the smallest of the firms with its 1967 sales rank of 220 in the nation, yet it sold an impressive $384,801,000 worth of product that year.

At the four-digit level, 559 firms represent large firms operating in manufacturing industries. Only 339 of these firms are on the 1968 *Fortune* listing. The remaining firms on the *Fortune* listing operated in industries in which four larger firms operated. There were many industries, however, in which fewer or none of the firms on the *Fortune* listing operated. The five industries in which only one large firm owned an establishment have been deleted as objects of constraint since directorate ties from the industries would have been based principally on the activities of a single firm. If two or more large firms operated in an industry, however, *Poor's* has been used to complete the industry's representation in the positional sample. Where possible, approximate sales data were used to locate the next largest firms in incomplete industries. After exhausting the sales data listed in *Poor's*, firms were drawn at random from *Poor's* listing of firms operating within the industry. Of the 559 manufacturing firms in the four-digit sample, 165 were drawn based on approximate sales data and 55 were drawn at random within incomplete industries. These 55 randomly drawn firms were smaller than the other 504 firms inasmuch as they had few employees and only sold product within a single industry.

The purpose of the snowball sample is to locate large nonmanufacturing firms that the sampled manufacturing firms represented on their boards. Directors of the largest 250 nonindustrials in the 1968 *Fortune* listing were coded from *Poor's* and compared to the boards of the sampled manufacturing firms. Any nonmanufacturing firm that was interlocked with one or more of the sampled manufacturing firms was added to the sample. In effect, directors of the sampled manufacturing firms are being used as sociometric citations to nonmanufacturing firms in which they are also directors so as to snowball the initial sample into nonmanufacturing sectors. Of the 250 largest nonindustrials, 110 interlocked with one or more of the 42 manufacturing firms in the two-digit sample, and 227 interlocked with one or more of the 559 manufacturing firms in the four-digit sample.[9]

The final samples of firms are representative of large firms involved in 1967 American manufacturing, involved either directly by owning manufacturing establishment(s) or involved indirectly by interlocking with at least one firm that did own manufacturing establishment(s). The two-digit sample consists of 152 firms, and the four-digit sample consists of 786 firms.

Sample frequencies of directorate ties can now be computed from two types of information coded for each sampled firm (where divisions and subsidiaries are considered part of a sampled firm). Using the directors of firms a and k given in the 1968 *Poor's*, b_{ak} and b_{ka} are set equal to zero unless one or more of the directors in firm a is also a director in firm k, whereupon they both equal one. A nonzero value of b_{ak} indicates an interlock between the directorates of firms a and k. *Poor's* also lists the SIC categories in which firms sell product. Using the input–output study's listing of SIC categories corresponding to input–output sectors, d_{kj} is set equal to zero unless firm k is listed as selling product in an SIC category corresponding to input–output sector j, whereupon it is set equal to one. A nonzero value of d_{kj} indicates that firm k owned an establishment in sector j.

Ownership ties are defined by the d_{kj}. If a manufacturing firm in industry j also owned an establishment in sector i, then the product $d_{kj}d_{ki}$ will equal one; otherwise it will equal zero. The number of establishments in sector i that were owned by manufacturing firms operating in industry j is therefore given as

$$w_{ji(o)} = \sum_{k} d_{kj} d_{ki} \tag{3.1}$$

---

[9]Of the 110 nonmanufacturing firms in the two-digit sample, 32 are banks, 22 are insurance companies, 21 are transportation firms, 20 are utilities, and 15 are merchandising firms. Of the 227 such firms in the four-digit sample, 49 are banks, 50 are insurance firms, 41 are transportation firms, 48 are utilities, and 39 are merchandising firms.

where summation is across all manufacturing firms k. Only manufacturing firms are considered since the sample has been drawn to represent only large firms involved in the 1967 manufacturing industries. Ownership ties between non-manufacturing sectors could be computed from Eq. (3.1) using the sample data; however, the frequencies would refer not to large nonmanufacturing firms per se so much as large nonmanufacturing firms involved in manufacturing.

Direct interlock ties are defined by the b_{ka} and d_{kj}. If a manufacturing firm k interlocked with some other firm a, which in turn owned an establishment in sector i, then the product $b_{ka}d_{ai}$ will equal one; otherwise it will equal zero. The number of establishments in sector i that were represented on the board of manufacturing firm k is therefore given as

$$\sum_a b_{ka}d_{ai}, \tag{3.2}$$

where summation is across all manufacturing and nonmanufacturing firms a, excluding k itself. The number of interestablishment direct interlock ties from industry j to the sector is given by the following sum across all manufacturing firms k:

$$w_{ji(d)} = \sum_k d_{kj}\left(\sum_a b_{ka}d_{ai}\right), \qquad k \neq a. \tag{3.3}$$

Indirect financial interlock ties are defined by the d_{kj} and a modification of the b_{ka}. Firm k had an indirect interlock tie through a financial firm c to firm a if the product $b_{kc}b_{ca}$ equals one. The product is zero otherwise. In the parlance of graph theory, a value of $b_{kc}b_{ca}$ equal to one indicates a two-step chain of interlocks between firms k and a with financial firm c as an intermediary. The number of indirect connections between firms k and a by means of financial institutions is given by the sum

$$\sum_c b_{kc}b_{ca}, \tag{3.4}$$

where c is any sampled bank or insurance firm. Let b_{ka}^* and b_{ak}^* equal zero unless the sum in Eq. (3.4) is positive (indicating indirect financial interlocking between firms a and k), whereupon they both equal one. The number of establishments in sector i that were represented on the board of manufacturing firm k indirectly by means of financial institutions is now given as [cf. Eq. (3.2)]

$$\sum_a b_{ka}^* d_{ai}, \tag{3.5}$$

where summation is across all manufacturing and nonmanufacturing firms a, excluding k itself. The number of establishment interlock ties from industry j to sector i by means of financial institutions is given by the following sum across all manufacturing firms k [cf. Eq. (3.3)]

$$w_{ji(i)} = \sum_k d_{kj}\left(\sum_a b^*_{ka}d_{ci} \right) \qquad k \neq a. \tag{3.6}$$

Directorate ties linking establishments in each industry to each possible economic sector have been computed. For each of the 20 two-digit industries j, there are three w_{ji} to 45 economic sectors i: $w_{ji(o)}$ being the frequency of ownership ties, $w_{ji(d)}$ the frequency of direct interlock ties, and $w_{ji(i)}$ the frequency of indirect financial interlock ties. Six of the 51 intput–output sectors used to compute market constraints are not included because they have no corresponding SIC categories. In other words, it is impossible for these sectors to be connected to manufacturing industries by directorate ties as ties are operationalized here. Two-digit directorate tie frequencies are reported in Tables A.5, A.6, and A.7 of the Appendix. Again at the four-digit level, government and special industry sectors (a total of 15 sectors) are deleted because they have no corresponding SIC codes. Further, the 75 agricultural, mining, and construction sectors in the detailed input–output table have been collapsed into 13 sectors because many of the original sectors used to compute market constraints correspond to the same SIC categories. In other words, a directorate tie to one of these sectors was simultaneously a tie to multiple sectors. The redundant sectors have been combined. For each of 322 four-digit industries j, there are three estimates of w_{ji} to 405 sectors i, 359 of which are manufacturing industries and 46 of which represent nonmanufacturing.[10]

At both the two-digit and four-digit levels, w_{ji} is the frequency with which establishments in industry j had directorate ties to sector i in 1967 based on the sampled firms. This sample is designed to allow inferences to be made regarding the manner in which manufacturing establishments were connected in 1967 through directorates to establishments more generally as their competitiors, suppliers, and consumers. The sample, in short, provides a basis for describing directorate ties involving manufacturing establishments and the types of firms most responsible for those ties.

Replicating Past Research Findings

The computed directorate tie frequencies are based on sample data and are further restricted by the fact that the sample is specifically designed to describe directorate ties through large firms involved in manufacturing. These are both divergences from traditional directorate research in which the population of all large firms is described. It is important therefore to know if these sample data replicate past research findings, findings used to interpret directorate ties as cooptive relations. This is particularly true of the two-digit data since they are

---

[10]There are 322 industries rather than the 327 analyzed in Chapter 2 because 5 industries were inadequately represented in the positional sample as discussed earlier in the text.

based on a comparatively small number of firms. If the sample data do replicate past research findings, then my subsequent analysis of them clearly adds to the cumulative understanding of such ties. If the sample data do not replicate past research findings, then it is not clear whether new findings are new knowledge or merely a result of the manner in which firms have been sampled.

Past research findings can be brought together in an empirical generalization: There is extensive interlocking in the United States (especially in urban centers for corporate headquarters such as New York, Chicago, and Los Angeles), and those firms most likely to be involved in interlocking are large firms operating in capital-intensive industries where the firm is controlled by diffuse interest groups. Putting to one side the overall tendency for interlocks to occur, there are three principal findings to this empirical generalization. Each can be interpreted in terms of cooptation.[11]

Large firms tend to interlock extensively with other firms. Measuring firm size in terms of dollars of assets or annual sales, a ubiquitous finding in directorate research is the positive correlation between firm size and the number of different corporations represented on the firm's board (e.g., Warner & Unwalla, 1967; Dooley, 1969; Pfeffer, 1972a; Allen, 1974; Pennings, 1980). This finding has an interpretation in terms of cooptation. The larger a firm is, the more impact its actions have on other organizations and accordingly the more the firm needs representatives who can integrate and legitimate the firm in its external environment (cf. Dooley, 1969:316; Pfeffer, 1972a:223; Allen, 1974:395).

Firms operating in capital-intensive industries extensively interlock with other firms. This finding occurs in two manners. The most extensively interlocked of all firms are those operating in finance, particularly banks. Among the many firms represented on the typical directorate, there is commonly a representative from a major bank, usually a bank in the same geographical region as the firm itself (see, Warner & Unwalla, 1967; Dooley, 1969; Levine, 1972; Pfeffer, 1972a; Allen, 1974, 1978b; Bearden et al., 1975; Mariolis, 1975; Sonquist & Koenig, 1975; Turner, 1978; Pennings, 1980; Mintz & Schwartz, 1981a, 1981b). Arguing for a cooptive interpretation of interlocking, Allen (1974) suggests that extensive financial interlocking is to be expected since capital is a "very generalized resource with a very dispersed demand from such economic organizations as corporations [p. 395]." This view is clearly reflected in the preceding discussion of indirect interlocks through financial firms as intermediaries. An implication of this line of reasoning is that firms with high capital requirements should have disproportionate representation on their boards from

---

[11] I am only concerned here with very basic features of directorate research. For discussion of this research in the more general context of how organizations cope with their environment, see Aldrich and Pfeffer (1976), Pfeffer and Salancik (1978), Aldrich (1979), Aldrich and Whetten (1981); the last work provides a review with an emphasis on network concepts.

other firms. Measuring capital requirements as a firm's ratio of debt to equity, Pfeffer (1972a:224) and Pennings (1980:115) report the expected positive correlation. However, Pennings (1980:115) also reports a slight negative correlation between his measure of capital requirements and the number of interlocks in which firms are involved. Using the ratio of assets to employees as a measure of a firm's capital intensiveness, Allen (1974:400) reports a low negative correlation with financial interlocking.[12] Similarly, Pennings reports a negative correlation between a firm's debt-to-equity ratio and its interlocks with financial institutions.

Finally, firms controlled by diffuse interest groups tend to interlock extensively with other firms. This finding is supported by research addressing the question of corporate control. The "management control" thesis advanced by Berle and Means (1932) and supported in subsequent research (Larner, 1970; Allen, 1976) says that the corporate officers as "management" have come to power as a result of the diffusion of shares among so many owners that individual owners no longer exercise control over the corporate use of capital. Berle and Means (1932:196) refer to management as "a board of directors and the senior officers of the corporation," but the term is more often reserved for officers only—few or many of whom can also be directors. In contrast to this management control thesis, there is a "family control" thesis: extensive stock ownership by members of a family enables a kinship group to be the ultimate source of corporate control (e.g., Burch, 1972; Zeitlin, 1974, 1976).[13] Research on these two theses has produced a basic result: Concentration of corporate control in either a kinship group or a firm's management is associated with infrequent interlocking. Measuring management control as the percentage of directors who are also officers in a corporation, Dooley (1969) and Pfeffer (1972a) report a negative correlation between management control and number of interlocks. Pennings (1980:90) reports a negative correlation between interlocking and the proportion of the board drawn from within the firm. Identifying family-controlled firms as those in which a kinship group holds more than 10% of available

---

[12]Both Allen and Pennings present correlations with size of firm held constant. Pennings (1980:115) also measures capital intensiveness as the ratio of assets to employees. Unlike Allen, however, Pennings holds the number of employees constant before presenting correlations, so the low correlations he reports between this measure of capital intensiveness and interlocking are difficult to interpret or compare to Allen's.

[13]A third basis of corporate control has been discussed at length by Kotz (1978) as financial control. In the same research style of Larner and Burch, Kotz shows that many large American firms can be viewed as operating under the full or partial control of financial institutions. Kotz's study raises the question of how differences in financial control over a firm are associated with corporate interlocking. Pennings (1980:107–134) provides a detailed report on financial interlocking; however, financial interlocking is only vaguely related to financial control since it need not imply that the financial firm(s) represented on a directorate have any influence over it. The association between financial control and patterns of directorate ties has yet to be described systematically.

stock, Allen (1976) finds fewer interlocks in family-owned firms than in other firms. This negative correlation between concentration of corporate control and interlocking can be interpreted in terms of cooptation. The more control is concentrated in a single group, the greater the loss of control incurred with the addition of a single outside group on the directorate. Selznick's analysis of the TVA demonstrates that cooptive efforts can backfire. When the TVA brought representatives of local organizations into its own decision-making structure, it was forced into some actions more beneficial to the local organizations than to the TVA (see Selznick, 1949:113–114, 145–153, 205–213, 217, 259–261). But where control of a corporation is already dispersed such that each individual interest group sharing control has little control over eventual decisions, the addition of yet another voice on the directorate entails little loss of control for each person already on it. Indeed, the balance of power in such a directorate could well require outside directors in order to avoid one group becoming more powerful than others already represented on the board. In order to maintain a decision-making capacity unimpaired by their corporate environment, in short, a dominant kinship or management group on a directorate would be expected to oppose extensive interlocking with other firms (cf. Dooley, 1969:332; Pfeffer, 1972a:224). In Zald's (1969) terms, concentration of corporate control in a single interest group (kinship or management) results in the directorate serving an "internal control" function rather than an "external representation" function.

In order to replicate these findings with the sample data to be used in this analysis, measures of firm size, capital intensiveness, and sources of control are required. Unfortunately, the lack of data on even a majority of the 559 manufacturing firms in the four-digit sample prohibits such an analysis at the four-digit level. I shall describe the manner in which the directorates of the 42 manufacturing firms in the two-digit sample represented establishments across 45 economic sectors.[14] Fortunately, this is the sample for which replication most needs to be demonstrated given the small number of firms it contains.

The sample data do replicate past research findings according to the correlations in Table 3.1. Firms with extensive assets tended to have frequent interlocks with other firms and a high number of interlocks per director. Of the

---

[14]It would seem curious to code extensive data on the boards of all firms in the 152 firm sample and then only compute correlations using the 42 manufacturing firms as units of analysis. This is done for reasons of inference. The 42 manufacturing firms represent manufacturing industries. An analysis of these firms allows inferences to be drawn about American manufacturing. The 110 nonmanufacturing firms have not been sampled to represent similarly nonmanufacturing sectors of the economy. They have been sampled to represent directorate ties from manufacturing into nonmanufacturing sectors. An analysis of the 110 nonmanufacturing firms would, therefore, only allow inferences to be drawn about nonmanufacturing firms as they are interlocked with large manufacturing firms.

TABLE 3.1

Moments for Corporation Variables and Interlocking[a]

| Variables[b] | Mean | S.D. | Corporate variables | | | |
			Assets	Capital–output ratio	Management control	Family control
Assets, X_1	3191.45	3269.21	1.00			
Capital–output ratio, X_2	.95	.42	.32	1.00		
Management control, X_3	39.39	15.83	.09	.05	1.00	
Family control, X_4	1.79	.78	−.05	−.06	.29	1.00
Number of interlocks with financial firms	5.40	3.54	.21	−.23	−.38	−.17
Number of interlocks with nonfinancial firms	6.07	5.13	.30	−.18	−.35	−.29
Total number of interlocks	11.48	8.15	.28	−.21	−.39	−.26
Per capita number of interlocks with financial firms	.35	.24	.14	−.13	−.36	−.20
Per capita number of interlocks with nonfinancial firms	.38	.30	.23	−.10	−.38	−.30
Per capita number of total interlocks	.73	.51	.20	−.12	−.40	−.28

[a]Moments are computed using the 42 firm sample representative of manufacturing industries. A correlation greater in absolute magnitude than .25 is significant beyond a .05 level of confidence.

[b]X_1, millions of dollars of assets as given in 1968 *Fortune* 500 listings; X_2, dollars of assets over dollars of sales as given in 1968 *Fortune* 500 listings; X_3, percentage of firm's directors who are also its officers as given in 1968 *Poor's*; X_4, three levels measuring kinship group control of a firm (see footnote 15). Interlocks are coded from *Poor's*, and per capita interlocks are the ratio of number of interlocks over number of directors in firm.

mean 11.5 interlocks per manufacturing firm, 5.4 were with financial firms and 6.1 were with nonfinancial firms. Standardizing by the relative number of financial (54) versus nonfinancial (98) firms in the sample, the typical manufacturing firm had a .06 tendency to interlock with each nonfinancial firm and a .10 tendency to interlock with each financial firm. A higher tendency to interlock with financial firms is typical of past research findings; however, capital intensiveness is negatively correlated with interlocking. Table 3.1 supports the negative correlations Allen (1974) reports between interlocking and capital intensiveness. Family control of a firm is negatively correlated with interlocking where control has been measured on a three-point scale: three points if a single kinship group owned more than 10% of the firm's stock, two points if such a group owned less than 10% but more than 2%, and one point if the firm was probably not controlled by any one kinship group (cf. Larner, 1970:70–117; Burch,

1972:36–67).[15] Measuring the probable percentage of stock held by a single kinship group yields correlations nearly identical to those reported.[16] As found in past research, management control is negatively correlated with interlocking where control has been measured as the percentage of the firm's directors who are also officers.

The correlations among the corporation variables also replicate earlier research findings. Management control is uncorrelated with firm size (cf. Dooley,

[15]Larner's study provided sufficient data to allow the 42 manufacturing firms to be classified as controlled by management or an external minority (any kinship group holding 10% or more of a firm's stock). Burch's more detailed data on stock holdings grouped the firms into three categories: probably family controlled, possibly family controlled, and probably not family controlled. All of the firms Burch classified as possibly family controlled or probably not family controlled, Larner classified as nonminority controlled. Of the 15 firms classified as probably family controlled by Burch, however, Larner only classified 5 as controlled by an external minority. Of the 10 disputed firms, Burch reported single kinship groups controlling more than 10% of the stock in 4 firms (R. J. Reynolds Tobacco, Ling-Temco-Vought, U.S. Plywood-Champion Papers, and Uniroyal, previously known as U.S. Rubber). Given the greater detail of, and support for, Burch's figures, these 4 firms were assumed to be minority-controlled firms. The remaining 6 of the disputed firms involved indirect control by a family or a family holding of less than 10% of a firm's stock. These 6 firms were, therefore, classified as possibly family controlled. Of the 42 manufacturing firms, the family-control variable classifies 9 as probably family controlled, 15 as possibly family controlled, and 18 as probably not family controlled.

[16]A continuous measure of family control was considered for two reasons. First, it seemed inelegant to have a continuous measure of management control and an ordinal measure of family control. Second, the three levels of family control represent quite unequal percentages of stock ownership. Using the data in Burch's study, an average of 26.3% of a firm's stock was owned by a family in the nine firms classified here as probably family controlled. For the firms classified as under possible family control, the average ownership by a family dropped to 5.9% of the firm's stock. Further, the minimum percentage control in the probable family control category was 14%, whereas the maximum in the possible family control category was 8%. No data are presented for firms Burch classifies as probably not under family control. Some inferences can be made about the concentration of stock ownership in firms in all three categories, however, using data from a subcommittee report on stock ownership in large American corporations (Metcalf, 1978). Of the 42 manufacturing firms in the three categories of family control (3, 2, 1), the sample of firms in Metcalf's report include 4, 8, and 10, respectively. The mean percentages of stock in these firms that was controlled by the five largest investors were 27.3%, 6.7%, and 8.4%, respectively. Using Burch's or Metcalf's data, in other words, the category of probably family control represents a quantum leap in concentrated stock ownership over the lower two categories. The question is whether or not the unequal differences in stock ownership between family-control categories are matched by similarly unequal differences in interlocking, differences not accurately matched by the ordinal measure of family control. A continuous variable of family control was constructed. Each firm's score on the variable was the percentage of stock held by a family group according to Burch's study. Where specific figures were not given for a firm, the firm was assigned the mean level of stock ownership for its category. Firms in the category of probably not family controlled were assigned scores of zero. The ordinal and continuous measures of family control are highly correlated ($r = .89$). Since the continuous variable yields correlations almost identical to those obtained using the simple three-point ordinal scale and since the exact estimates of stock ownership in Burch's study involve guesswork, the less complex ordinal scale has been retained in the analysis.

1969:317). As argued by Zeitlin (1976), contradicting Allen (1976), family control is also uncorrelated with firm size. Since firms controlled by diverse interest groups are low on both the management-control variable and family-control variable, there is a positive correlation between the two variables (cf. Allen, 1976:887).

In short, the types of firms most, and least, likely to represent outsiders on their boards in the sample data are the same types found in traditional directorate research. I now want to consider this replication in more detail and from a different perspective. I turn to the question of how the three types of directorate ties differed, and were coordinated, in representing diverse economic sectors on the boards of manufacturing firms in 1967.

COOPTIVE CORPORATE ACTOR NETWORKS

I take an approach quite compatible conceptually with the tradition of work established by Berle, Means, and Selznick. Methodologically, however, I depart from that tradition. A firm's involvement in directorate ties is described in terms of its network of directorate ties. The possessive reference to network is significant here. The corporate structure of the economy in terms of directorate ties is not analyzed. Neither the centrality of specific types of firms (such as banks) nor the formation of interest groups as cliques of firms is my concern here. Rather, the network of relations involving a single firm is analyzed. The concept of a corporate actor network is taken from a mode of network analysis popular in anthropology and sociology[17] and bears a close resemblance to Evan's concept of an "organization-set," although the two concepts are by no means iso-morphic.[18] As a representation of a firm's involvement in directorate ties as

[17]Largely pursued by European anthropologists, the ego-network mode of network analysis has been fruitfully employed by a handful of American sociologists analyzing the social psychology of urban life (e.g., Laumann, 1973; Wellman, 1978; Fischer, 1982). Extracting a person from his position in social structure and describing the relations involving the person as an anchoring point, this research provides a method of understanding how persons coordinate different types of relations within their social environment (see Burt, 1982a:Chap. 2; Burt & Minor, 1983, for references and review). What I am doing here is similarly representing cooptive corporate relations. Extracting a corporation from the social structure of firms and describing the relations involving the corporation as an anchoring point, I wish to describe the manner in which firms coordinate different types of potentially cooptive relations.

[18]The concept of actor network is similar to Evan's (1966, 1972) concept of an organization-set in the sense that a "focal organization" is taken as an anchoring point and the set of organizations connected to the focal organization constitute nodes in the firm's network. In contrast to an organiza-tion-set, however, there is no distinction here between input versus output organizations. The concern is with symmetric cooptive relations rather than asymmetric flows of goods. Further, the organizations constituting nodes here are establishments rather than corporations. Instead of tamper-ing with Evan's concept of organization-set as he has described it, I have chosen to import the concept of actor network from anthropology.

potentially cooptive relations, its cooptive network is the total set of establishments represented on the firm's board by ownership, direct interlocking, and indirect interlocking by means of financial institutions.

Figure 3.2 is a diagrammatic representation of Firestone's cooptive network based on the two-digit data. Interlocking and ownership are indicated in the same manner used in Figure 3.1 earlier. Figure 3.1 presented a portion of Firestone's network. Taking Firestone as what Evan terms a "focal" organization, Figure 3.2 diagrams the basic threads connecting Firestone's directorate to establishments throughout the economy. The diagram shows that Firestone owned establishments in eight manufacturing industries, had direct interlock ties to establishments in two sectors, and had indirect interlock ties through Cleveland Trust as a financial institution to establishments in five sectors.

Figure 3.2 offers an immediately comprehensible picture of the full set of establishments represented on Firestone's board through ownership, direct interlocking, and indirect financial interlocking. Just like the sociograms typical of early sociometry in which relations between persons were presented as arrows between points in a diagram, Figure 3.2 has an analytical value in presenting Firestone's cooptive network all at once so that basic features of the network can be grasped immediately. However, Firestone had an exceedingly simple cooptive network. A diagram such as Figure 3.2 for General Motors's cooptive network, one of the most complex in the two-digit sample, would be very difficult to analyze visually. Just like sociograms, diagrams of cooptive networks have limited utility in the comparative analysis of networks across corporations because the complexity of the diagrams would constrain analysis more than facilitate it.

Table 3.2 presents a representation of cooptive networks that is more useful analytically. Rows in the table correspond to the 45 sectors distinguished in the two-digit data. Columns in the table indicate the number of establishmens in each sector represented on a firm's board by a specific type of directorate tie. The number of establishments in sector i represented through ownership is binary: either the firm owned an establishment in the sector or it did not [d_{ki} in Eq. (3.1)]. The number of establishments in sector i represented on the board through direct interlocking is given by Eq. (3.2), and the number represented through indirect financial interlocking is given by Eq. (3.5).

A comparison of Figure 3.2 and Table 3.2 clarifies the meaning of these data on cooptive networks. Figure 3.2 shows that Firestone owned eight establishments. These are given in Table 3.2 as ones in the ownership column under Firestone (the column labeled "O"). The two establishments represented on Firestone's board through direct interlocking are given in Table 3.2 as ones in the direct interlocking column (note the ones in rows 34 and 39 of the column labeled "D"). Finally, the five establishments represented on its board by indirect financial interlocking are given in the appropriate rows of the indirect in-

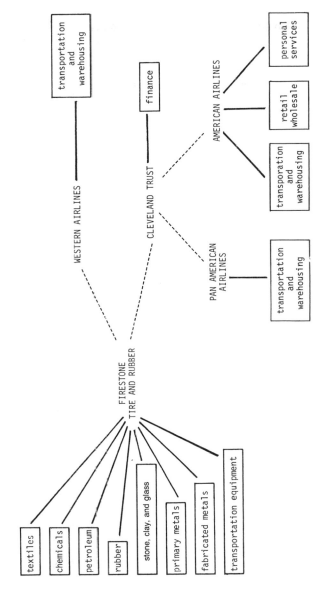

Figure 3.2. Firestone's cooptive network as of 1967 (ownership relations given by solid lines and interlocking is represented by dashed lines).

TABLE 3.2

Cooptive Networks of Firestone and General Motors

Establishments[a]	Firestone Tire and Rubber			General Motors		
	O	D	I	O	D	I
1. Livestock	0	0	0	0	0	0
2. Other agriculture	0	0	0	0	0	0
3. Forestry/fishery	0	0	0	0	1	1
4. Agribusiness services	0	0	0	0	0	0
5. Iron mining	0	0	0	0	0	1
6. Nonferrous metal mining	0	0	0	0	0	1
7. Coal mining	0	0	0	0	3	4
8. Petroleum/gas	0	0	0	0	5	8
9. Stone/clay mining	0	0	0	0	0	0
10. Chemicals mining	0	0	0	0	0	0
11. New construction	0	0	0	0	1	3
12. Maintenance/repair	0	0	0	0	1	3
13. Ordnance	0	0	0	0	1	4
14. Food	0	0	0	0	2	7
15. Tobacco	0	0	0	0	0	0
16. Textiles	1	0	0	0	1	3
17. Apparel	0	0	0	0	1	2
18. Lumber	0	0	0	0	1	2
19. Furniture	0	0	0	0	0	2
20. Paper	0	0	0	0	3	7
21. Printing	0	0	0	1	1	2
22. Chemicals	1	0	0	1	4	13
23. Petroleum	1	0	0	0	4	5
24. Rubber	1	0	0	1	1	6
25. Leather	0	0	0	0	0	2
26. Stone, clay, glass	1	0	0	1	1	6
27. Primary metals	1	0	0	1	2	6
28. Fabricated metals	1	0	0	1	2	8
29. Mechanical machines	0	0	0	1	3	12
30. Electrical machines	0	0	0	1	1	10
31. Transportation equipment	1	0	0	1	1	6
32. Instruments	0	0	0	0	0	6
33. Miscellaneous	0	0	0	1	1	3
34. Transportation/warehousing	0	1	2	0	3	11
35. Communications	0	0	0	0	1	3
36. Radio/television	0	0	0	0	0	0
37. Utilities	0	0	0	0	6	11
38. Wholesale/retail	0	0	1	1	4	12
39. Finance/insurance	0	1	1	0	10	25
40. Real estate	0	0	0	0	1	2
41. Personal services	0	0	1	0	0	2
42. Business services	0	0	0	0	1	6
43. Automobile services	0	0	0	0	0	1
44. Amusements	0	0	0	0	0	0
45. Medical/educational services	0	0	0	0	0	0
Total establishments	8	2	5	11	67	206

[a]The establishments in rows 13–33 are manufacturing industries.

terlocking column (labeled "I"): two establishments in transportation/warehousing (one owned by Pan American Airlines and the other owned by American Airlines, as illustrated in Figure 3.2), and one establishment each in wholesale/retail (owned by American Airlines), finance (owned by Cleveland Trust), and personal services (owned by American Airlines).

Corresponding to Firestone's network, Table 3.2 presents the cooptive network for General Motors. Imagine a diagram such as Figure 3.2 constructed for this network. In contrast to Firestone's 15 directorate ties to establishments (8 ownership, 2 direct interlock, and 5 indirect interlock), General Motors had 284 directorate ties (11 ownership, 67 direct interlock, and 206 indirect interlock). Within manufacturing, General Motors owned establishments in 10 industries, had direct interlock ties to establishments in all but 4 industries, and the only industry it is unable to reach by indirect interlocking ties through financial institutions is the tobacco industry. Even when stated compactly as in Table 3.2, in other words, relational data must be condensed in order to compare cooptive networks across firms.

NETWORK RANGE

Perhaps the least pretentious structural concept in network analysis is ego-network range (e.g., Mitchell, 1969:19–20; Burt, 1980b:90, 1983a). A firm's cooptive network has range to the extent that it encompasses a diversity of establishments, many establishments in many sectors.

Table 3.3 presents moments on network range variables across the 42 manufacturing firms. Network range is measured in two ways—as the total number of establishments represented on a corporate board (column totals in Table 3.2) and as the number of different sectors from which these establishments were drawn (number of nonzero entries in columns of Table 3.2). In the case of ownership, these two measures of network range are identical by definition since all a firm's holdings in a single sector are grouped together here as a single establishment. In the cases of representation through direct or indirect interlocking, the two measures can differ. For example, Firestone represented five establishments on its board by indirect interlocking through financial firms, but these establishments were drawn from four different sectors.

I draw two conclusions from Table 3.3. Overall, network range was least in the case of representation through ownership, intermediate in the case of direct interlocking, and most extensive in the case of indirect interlocking through financial firms. Second, this relative range of networks differed across firms. If similar relative ranges existed for each firm, then the network range variables would be highly correlated, each firm's network through ownership consistently being the least extensive and its network through indirect interlocking con-

TABLE 3.3
Network Range[a]

	O	D	I	Mean	S.D.
Number of establishments represented on corporate board by					
Ownership (O)	1.00	.12	.02	6.19	3.84
Direct interlocks (D)	.16	1.00	.79	24.00	17.42
Indirect interlocks (I)	.03	.80	1.00	111.60	67.65
Number of sectors represented on corporate board by					
Ownership (O)	1.00	.09	−.03	6.19	3.84
Direct interlocks (D)	.17	1.00	.65	13.36	8.09
Indirect interlocks (I)	−.02	.70	1.00	28.55	9.03

[a]Correlations are computed across the 42 manufacturing firms. A correlation greater in absolute magnitude than .25 is significant beyond the .05 level of confidence. Coefficients above the diagonal are product model correlations and those below are rank-order correlations (Kendall's tau). Each firm's score on the "number of establishments" variables corresponds to column totals in a table such as Table 3.2, and its score on the "number of sectors" variables corresponds to the number of nonzero entries in a column of a table such as Table 3.2.

sistently being the most extensive. In fact, the variables are not perfectly correlated. Direct and indirect interlock range are correlated such that it seems reasonable to say that a firm's network of direct interlock ties usually had less range than its network of indirect interlock ties. Network range in terms of ownership ties, however, is uncorrelated with network range in terms of the interlock ties. As is illustrated by Firestone in Figure 3.2 and Table 3.2, there were some firms whose network range was greater by ownership than by the interlock methods of representation.

As a concept, network range is closely linked to the traditional analysis of corporate involvement in interlocking. Firms whose networks have the greatest range should be the firms that have the greatest need to coopt their environment. Based on past directorate research, therefore, the most extensive cooptive corporate actor networks are to be expected for large, capital-intensive firms not controlled by a kinship or management group.

Table 3.4 presents correlations between network range and corporation variables corresponding in part to the correlations in Table 3.1. Two sets of network range variables are given, one using establishments as nodes and the other using sectors as nodes. Summary canonical indices for each of the two sets of measures are also given. The summary index is the weighted combination of the three network range variables that is maximally correlated with the corporate variables.

As might be expected from Table 3.3, overall network range is least indicated

TABLE 3.4
Correlations between Corporate and Network Range Variables[a]

Network range variables	Corporate variables					
	Assets	Capital–output ratio	Management control	Family control	R_1	R_2
Number of establishments represented on corporate board by						
Ownership (O)	−.02	−.01	−.27	−.02	.16	.21
Direct interlocks (D)	.39	−.07	−.29	−.37	.91	.89
Indirect interlocks (I)	.38	−.19	−.28	−.35	.97	.82
Summary canonical index (R_1)	.40	−.15	−.32	−.37	1.00	.90
Number of sectors represented on corporate board by						
Ownership (O)	−.02	−.01	−.27	−.02	.16	.21
Direct interlocks (D)	.42	.01	−.30	−.29	.84	.95
Indirect interlocks (I)	.31	−.16	−.24	−.23	.79	.82
Summary canonical index (R_2)	.41	−.06	−.34	−.29	.90	1.00

[a]Correlations are computed across the 42 manufacturing firms. A correlation greater in absolute magnitude than .25 is significant beyond a .05 level of confidence. Network range variables are defined in Table 3.3. The summary canonical indices are taken from canonical correlation models relating network range variables to the four corporate variables. Second canonical correlations are negligible at even the .10 level of confidence. R_1 is completely determined by the number-of-establishments variables. R_2 is completely determined by the number-of-sectors variables.

by network range in terms of ownership. The best indicator of network range is the range of direct interlock ties. This means that network range by means of direct interlocking (of the three methods of representing establishments) has the highest correlations with the corporate variables and is the best correlated of the three network range variables.

Using either set of measures of network range, number of establishments in network or number of sectors in network, the greatest network range tended to occur in large firms not controlled by a kinship or management group. Firms with extensive assets tended to have a large number of establishments represented on their boards ($r = .40$) and a large number of sectors represented on their boards ($r = .41$). Once again, there is a low negative association between a firm's capital intensiveness and the range of its cooptive network. Finally, firms under the control of a kinship or management group, respectively, tended to have few establishments represented on their board ($r = −.37$ and $−.32$, respectively) and tended to have few sectors represented on their board ($r = −.29$ and $−.34$, respectively). Representation through ownership is an exception. Although management-controlled firms tended to own few establishments, the number of establishments a firm owned is not correlated with its size, capital intensiveness, or level of family control.

These results take sectors of the economy as given and describe the manner in which directorates represented establishments in the sectors. Alternatively, the firm's network can be taken as given so as to describe the manner in which establishments in sectors were represented. Table 3.5 presents data on the absolute and relative numbers of establishments represented through direct interlocking on corporate boards in manufacturing. Direct interlocking has been selected here since it is the best indicator of network range according to Table 3.4. Three classes of establishments are distinguished: finance, manufacturing, and other. The same pattern of correlations given in Table 3.5 is obtained if manufacturing establishments are separated into durable versus nondurable manufacturing or if the "other" establishments are separated into six one-digit SIC categories (agribusiness, mining, construction, transportation/utilities, wholesale/retail, and services).

Looking at the absolute number of establishments represented on a firm's board, Table 3.5 shows that the mean 24 establishments in Table 3.3 were typically 5 financial establishments, 13 manufacturing establishments, and 6 other types of establishments. The representation of all three classes of establish-

TABLE 3.5
Absolute and Proportionate Representation through Direct Interlocking[a]

Network range variables	Corporate variables				Mean	S.D.
	Assets	Capital–output ratio	Management control	Family control		
Number of establishments represented on corporate board from						
Finance	.18	−.21	−.34	−.39	5.00	2.99
Manufacturing	.43	.05	−.20	−.32	12.60	10.96
Other	.27	−.20	−.32	−.31	6.29	5.35
Proportion of establishments on corporate board that is drawn from						
Finance	−.31	−.16	.11	.33	29.59	20.53
Manufacturing	.49	.24	−.11	−.18	42.35	23.82
Other	−.24	−.23	−.12	−.01	26.68	15.10

[a]Correlations are computed across the 42 manufacturing firms. A correlation greater in absolute magnitude than .25 is significant beyond a .05 level of confidence. Number of establishments in each class is computed by summing across sectors within each class. The proportion of establishments in each class is then determined by dividing the number of establishments in the class by the total number of establishments represented on the firm's board by direct interlocking.

ments is similarly determined by the attributes of the firm. Firms with extensive assets tended to have high numbers of finance, manufacturing, and other types of establishments represented on their boards. Firms controlled by management or a kinship group tended to have little representation from any of the three classes of establishments.

This consistency across the three classes dissolves when proportionate representation is considered. The percentage of a network drawn from the three classes of establishments suggests that representation of financial firms on a corporate board was ubiquitous, but not without its limits. On the average, about 30% of the establishments represented on a firm's board were financial, 42% were manufacturing establishments, and 27% were other types of establishments. For large, capital-intensive firms, however, the proportionate representation of manufacturing establishments increased. After an initial representation of financial establishments on its board, a firm did not continue to augment such representation on a par with the firm's growth. This could be explained by the fact that it was predominantly with other manufacturing firms that any one manufacturing firm had transactions. It is market constraints on these transactions that were supposedly coopted by representation on the board. Ceteris paribus, growth of a manufacturing firm in terms of assets should therefore have been accompanied by a growing representation on the firm's board from other manufacturing firms. As given in Table 3.5, assets are positively correlated with percentage representation from manufacturing and negatively correlated with percentage representation from financial and other establishments. The same process of differential growth into the three types of economic sectors ensured a different pattern of correlations for firms dominated by a single interest group. Since few establishments in general were represented on the board of directors in such corporations, the ubiquitous representation of financial establishments in their case constituted a high proportion of the total establishments represented on their boards. Thus there should be a positive correlation between percentage representation of financial establishments on a firm's board and the extent to which the firm was dominated by a single interest group. This correlation is documented in Table 3.5 to exist if the dominant group was management ($r = .11$) and to be significant if the dominant group was a family ($r = .33$).[19]

---

[19]This sparks the intriguing notion, fostered by some sociologists (e.g., Zeitlin, 1974, 1976), that powerful families use financial institutions to reach establishments in the sectors constraining their corporate interests, thus avoiding the direct representation that would impair the family's decision-making perogatives. This interpretation of Table 3.5 is rejected in part by the positive association between assets and percentage representation from manufacturing for the 18 firms classified as probably not under family control ($r = .29$) as well as the 9 classified as probably under family control ($r = .63$). These correlations are comparable to those in the fifth row of Table 3.5. There is additional evidence. If family-controlled firms used financial institutions to coopt market constraints, assets should be positively correlated with network range in terms of indirect interlocking but

NETWORK MULTIPLEXITY

The preceding description of network range concerns structural form, the extent to which many establishments in many sectors were represented on a corporate board. Looking more closely now at the content of the cooptive relations a firm used to reach establishments, how were ownership versus direct interlocking versus indirect interlocking coordinated so as to represent establishments on a corporate board?

The coordination of relations with different contents is captured by the concept of multiplexity (e.g., Mitchell, 1969:20–24; Burt, 1980b:90–91). A firm's network has high multiplexity to the extent that establishments in each sector of the firm's network were represented through ownership, direct interlocking and indirect interlocking through financial institutions. Figure 3.3 presents Venn diagrams of three ideal-type cooptive networks in terms of which multiplexity could be analyzed. The area of the circles indicates network range defined by the number of sectors from which establishments were represented on a corporate board by means of ownership, direct interlocking, and indirect interlocking through financial institutions. Circles overlap to the extent that each type of directorate tie reached establishments in the same sectors. The relative areas of the circles correspond to the mean numbers of sectors in which establishments were reached using the three types of directorate ties (cf. Table 3.3).

If the three types of directorate ties were used as alternative methods of reaching establishments, then cooptive networks would have been patterned as given in Figure 3.3a. In this diagram, establishments in some sectors (say, manufacturing) are represented on a corporate board through ownership, establishments in other sectors (say, finance and manufacturing sectors not represented through ownership) are represented by means of direct interlocking, and establishments in still other sectors (say, all nonmanufacturing sectors) are represented by means of indirect interlocking through financial institutions. Since

uncorrelated with network range in terms of direct interlocking. This is to be expected since family-controlled firms would have represented establishments on their board indirectly through their financial agents and restricted direct representation on the board to the financial agents themselves. In fact, the 9 family-controlled firms behaved just like the 18 non-family-controlled firms. The number of sectors and establishments represented on a family-controlled firm's board increased with the firm's assets ($r = .71$ and .66, respectively, for representation by direct interlocking; $r = .48$ and .42, respectively, for indirect interlocking) and the number of sectors and establishments represented on a board probably not controlled by a family increased with the firm's assets ($r = .51$ and .47, respectively, for direct interlocking; $r = .28$ and .37, respectively, for indirect interlocking). Further, the number of establishments by which network range in terms of indirect interlocking exceeded network range in terms of direct interlocking is positively correlated with assets for both family- and non-family-controlled firms ($r = .21$ and .30, respectively). Family-controlled firms, in short, were not systematically using financial institutions as intermediaries to coopt establishments in preference to interlocking directly with the establishments.

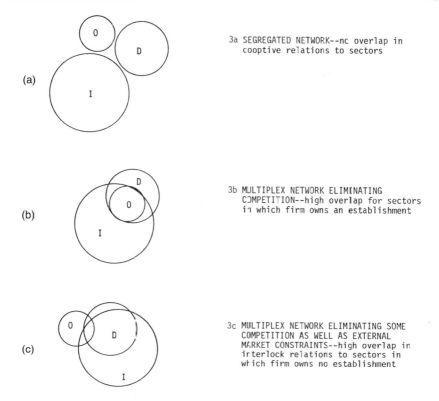

(a)

3a SEGREGATED NETWORK--nc overlap in cooptive relations to sectors

(b)

3b MULTIPLEX NETWORK ELIMINATING COMPETITION--high overlap for sectors in which firm owns an establishment

(c)

3c MULTIPLEX NETWORK ELIMINATING SOME COMPETITION AS WELL AS EXTERNAL MARKET CONSTRAINTS--high overlap in interlock relations to sectors in which firm owns no establishment

Figure 3.3. Ideal-type cooptive corporate actor networks. Circles refer to the number of sectors represented on a corporate board by ownership (O), direct interlocking (D), or indirect interlocking through financial institutions (I).

each type of cooptive relation is directed at a unique class of sectors, there is no network multiplexity.

But there is reason to expect cooptive networks to have exhibited some multiplexity. For one thing, multiple types of directorate ties to a sector are more likely to endure in the sense that a firm can maintain at least some tie to the sector when others are dissolved by market changes, corporate failures, or federal antitrust actions. Moreover, the different types of directorate ties are potentially cooptive in different ways, direct interlock ties providing information on operations beyond the firm's own establishments and indirect interlock ties through financial institutions providing the additional possibility of influencing the actions of establishments beyond those the firm actually owns. These features of the different types of directorate ties were discussed previously in the chapter. Figures 3.3b and 3.3c illustrate two types of cooptive networks that might result from firms deliberately coordinating their directorate ties to create multiplex directorate ties as cooptive relations.

If the three types of directorate ties were coordinated solely to eliminate competition with the establishments a firm owned, then networks should have been structured as illustrated in Figure 3.3b. In this network, establishments from all sectors in which a firm owns an establishment are linked to the firm by the other two types of directorate ties. Since interlocks with other firms, particularly indirect interlocks through financial firms, can result in representation of sectors that are of no actual concern to the firm, its network can extend beyond the range required by the firm. The distinct feature of this network is that all sectors in which a firm owns establishments are sectors represented on the firm's board by direct and indirect interlocking.

If the three types of directorate ties were coordinated to reduce competition within the sectors in which a firm owned establishments and also to eliminate market constraints from sectors with which the firm had transactions but in which the firm owned no establishments (e.g., the transportation/warehousing sector for Firestone in Figures 3.1 and 3.2), then networks should have been structured as illustrated in Figure 3.3c. In this network, some sectors in which a firm owns an establishment are linked to the firm by all three types of directorate ties. In addition, however, there is significant multiplexity in the interlock relations directed toward sectors in which the firm owns no establishments. It is this significant multiplexity toward sectors in which a firm owns no establishments that is the distinct feature of the network in Figure 3.3c.

Table 3.6 presents means and standard deviations for measures of multiplexity in the observed cooptive networks.[20] A directorate tie linking a firm with

[20]To my knowledge, Galaskiewicz and Marsden (1978) provide the first systematic study of interorganizational multiplexity. Within the community they describe, if an organization's agent cites some other organization as a source of financial income, then he also tends to cite it as a source of social support as well as information on community affairs. Conversely, the absence of a citation for any one reason is associated with the absence of citations for the other two reasons. In a similar vein, the three types of directorate ties considered here were contingent on one another. Where establishments in a sector were represented on a board by one type of directorate tie, the sector also tended to be represented on the board by the other two types of ties. Where one type of tie was absent, the other types tended to be absent. This contingency existed after controlling for the marginal tendencies for each type of tie to occur. Demonstrating contingency between directorate ties, however, need not demonstrate multiplexity in the relations (see footnote 7 of Chapter 4 for a more detailed statement). To a considerable extent in sparse networks, contingency between relations is a result of the simultaneous absence of relations. Multiplexity, in contrast, is concerned with the simultaneous presence of relations. Consider an isolated person. This person has no friendship relations to others, no kinship relations to others, no advice relations to others, and so on. Such a person is not usually discussed as having coordinated his relations to others so as to have achieved complete multiplexity. Rather, he is considered to have no relations. Instead of describing multiplexity in terms of the contingency between directorate ties in cooptive networks, in short, I have focused on the coordination of existing ties.

TABLE 3.6
Network Multiplexity[a]

Multiplexity	45-sector results			405-sector results		
	Mean	S.D.	t-test	Mean	S.D.	t-test
Number of sectors represented on corporate board by multiplex relations						
ODI	2.60	2.55	6.67	9.21	8.50	7.02
OD	2.60	2.55	6.67	9.21	8.50	7.02
OI	4.05	3.37	9.52	13.52	10.92	8.02
DI	13.10	8.10	10.48	191.67	55.85	22.24
Percentage of sectors in which firm owns an establishment that are also represented on corporate board by interlocking						
ODI	41.42	37.16	7.24	63.47	22.18	18.55
OD	41.42	37.16	7.24	63.47	22.18	18.55
OI	78.44	28.93	12.10	97.56	6.55	96.53
Percentage of all sectors represented on corporate board that are represented by multiplex relations						
ODI	8.26	8.21	6.52	2.82	2.96	6.17
OD	12.44	11.01	7.32	4.62	3.71	8.07
OI	16.52	11.63	9.21	3.57	2.85	8.12
DI	71.29	61.27	7.54	50.55	13.80	23.74

[a]Moments are computed across the 42 manufacturing firms. A t-test of 3.55 indicates a mean significantly greater than zero at beyond the .001 level of confidence. ODI refers to a sector represented on a board by ownership (O), direct interlocking (D), and indirect financial interlocking (I). The first set of percentages is computed by dividing the number of multiplex relations of some type in a network by the network range by ownership. The second set of percentages is computed by dividing the number of multiplex relations of some type in a network by the number of sectors in the network reached by the relevant relations (e.g., for Firestone in Table 3.2, ODI is 0/12, OD is 0/10, OI is 0/12, and DI is 2/4).

establishments in a sector is coded as multiplex if one or more establishments in the sector were represented on the firm's board by ownership and direct interlocking (this is OD multiplexity in Table 3.6), or by ownership and indirect interlocking (OI multiplexity), or by direct and indirect interlocking (DI multiplexity). For example, consider the networks in Table 3.2. The two multiplex relations in Firestone's network were DI multiplex relations to the transportation/warehousing and finance/insurance sectors. These sectors were represented on Firestone's board by direct interlocking and indirect financial interlocking. Establishments in no sector were represented on the Firestone board by ownership and interlocking simultaneously. On the General Motors board, in contrast, all three types of directorate ties reached each of 11 sectors. The General Motors example raises a question. Since there are only 45 economic sectors distinguished at the two-digit level, the firms with the most extensive networks might have highly multiplex networks simply because so few sectors are distinguished. Therefore, Table 3.6 presents multiplexity results for the 42 manufacturing firms as they had multiplex directorate ties to the 45 two-digit sectors and as they had multiplex directorate ties (through all 786 firms) to the 405 four-digit sectors. If the same multiplexity results are obtained for cooptive networks representing the 45 sectors and the 405 sectors, they cannot be attributed to the limited number of two-digit sectors.

Table 3.6 presents t-tests of the significance of mean levels of multiplexity. Multiplexity is zero if firms directed each type of relation to separate sectors. If this tended to be the case, then t-tests in Table 3.6 would be insignificant. They would also be insignificant if the multiplexity of cooptive networks varied so much across firms that the mean level of multiplexity was, in comparison, little different from the total absence of multiplexity. The t-tests in Table 3.6 show that neither of these conditions occurs. The same conclusion holds for two-digit and four-digit sectors. High multiplexity occurred in terms of the absolute number of multiplex ties, the percentage of ownership relations coordinated with interlock ties, and the percentage of sectors represented on a board that are represented by multiplex ties.

The mean levels of multiplexity shown in Table 3.6 indicate that the network structure in Figure 3.3c was typical of the manufacturing firms. Multiplex relations were coordinated as if to coopt both sources of competition with a firm's own establishments and to coopt establishments in sectors external to the firm but constraining the firm's establishments. Clearly, the segregated network in Figure 3.3a is rejected. Cooptive relations were not used as alternatives to one another since there was significant overall multiplexity. Neither were they coordinated so as to generate the network in Figure 3.3b. In support of Figure 3.3b, many sectors in which a firm owned an establishment were also represented on the firm's board by interlock ties. As expected under Figure 3.3c, however, there was high multiplexity among the interlock relations. Both types of interlock relations seem to have been directed at the same sectors beyond those in which a firm owned an establishment. Of all two-digit sectors represented on a firm's board by interlocking, 71% were represented by both direct and indirect interlocking simultaneously. Of the sectors represented on a firm's board by direct interlocking, 95% are also represented on the board by indirect financial interlocking (which is quite different from zero, having a t-test of 37.3).

Although the network structure illustrated in Figure 3.3c seems to typify manufacturing firms in general, deviations from this form can be expected for individual firms as a consequence of their capital and control characteristics.

Recall from Table 3.5 that corporate growth in terms of assets was accompanied by increasing representation of manufacturing industries on the corporate board once an initial representation from financial institutions existed. Assuming that this spread into industries was an attempt to coopt sources of market constraint, then the relations linking the firm to new industries should have been multiplex. Since these firms already owned establishments in manufacturing industries, it was the networks that had begun to interlock extensively in manufacturing that would have been the most multiplex. Since it is firms with extensive assets controlled by diffuse interest groups that interlocked most extensively in manufacturing (Table 3.5), these are the firms that should have had the most multiplex networks.

This conclusion is supported by Table 3.7 for both the two-digit and four-digit sectors, although the results are weaker at the four-digit level.[21] Four multiplexity variables in Table 3.7 demonstrate that the network structure illustrated in Figure 3.3c was most closely approximated by large firms not dominated by management or a family group. Firms with extensive assets tended to have large numbers of sectors represented on their board by all three types of directorate ties ($r = .44$), tended to have a high proportion of the industries in which they own establishments be represented on the board by interlocking ($r = .36$), and tended to have a high proportion of all sectors represented on their boards be represented by all three types of directorate ties simultaneously ($r = .36$). Conversely, firms dominated by management or a family group tended to have a low proportion of all sectors represented on their boards be represented by all three types of directorate ties simultaneously ($r = -.34$ and $-.16$, respectively). Further, the distinctive coordination of direct and indirect interlocking illustrated in Figure 3.3c was associated with large, diffusely controlled firms. The proportion of sectors represented on a corporate board by direct interlocking also represented by indirect interlocking through financial firms is positively correlated with assets ($r = .30$). The proportion is negatively correlated with the percentage of directors who were officers in the firm ($r = -.29$) and negatively correlated, weakly, with the level of family control over the firm ($r = -.24$). As in previous tables, Table 3.7 reveals no association between capital intensiveness and multiplexity.

Table 3.8 sheds some light on the counterintuitive absence of a strong, positive correlation between capital intensiveness and directorate ties. Table 3.8 presents correlations between the four corporate variables and three dummy

[21]Controlling for the number of different two-digit sectors represented on a firm's board, however, does not eliminate the positive correlation between the number of sectors represented on the board by all three types of directorate ties simultaneously (ODI multiplexity) and assets (partial $r = .38$, $p = .01$). Neither does a control for network range eliminate the negative correlation with the percentage of directors who are officers in the firm (partial $r = -.32$, $p = .02$), although it does reduce the already weak negative correlation with the level of control by a single kinship group (partial $r = -.15$).

TABLE 3.7

Correlations between Corporate and Network Multiplexity Variables[a]

	Corporate variables			
Multiplexity	Assets	Capital–output ratio	Management control	Family control
Number of sectors represented on corporate board by all three types of directorate ties				
45 sectors	.44	.11	−.38	−.22
405 sectors	.14	−.05	−.30	−.21
Percentage of sectors in which firm owns an establishment that are also represented on corporate board by interlocking				
45 sectors	.36	.00	−.34	−.22
405 sectors	.39	.28	−.27	−.08
Percentage of all sectors represented on corporate board that are represented by all three types of directorate ties				
45 sectors	.36	.21	−.34	−.16
405 sectors	.17	−.05	−.29	−.23
Percentage of sectors represented by direct interlocking that are also represented by indirect interlocking				
45 sectors	.30	.15	−.29	−.24
405 sectors	.21	.04	−.17	−.02

[a]Correlations are computed across the 42 manufacturing firms. A correlation greater in absolute magnitude than .25 is significant beyond a .05 level of confidence.

variables—the presence of a complete multiplex (ODI) relation to a finance sector, the presence of such a relation to a manufacturing sector, and the presence of such a relation to a sector other than finance or manufacturing. For example, Figure 3.2 shows that Firestone did not have a complete multiplex tie to finance. It did directly and indirectly interlock into the banking sector, but it did not own a banking or insurance establishment. Table 3.8 shows that it was large, capital-intensive firms that tended to have a complete multiplex relation to finance. Even after controlling for the number of different sectors represented in a firm's network, the firms tending to have a complete multiplex relation to finance were large (partial $r = .33$) and capital-intensive (partial $r = .39$). Since all firms tended to interlock with financial institutions, the variation across firms that is responsible for these correlations was a result of differences in their tendencies to own establishments in the finance sector. This conclusion is sup-

TABLE 3.8
Network Multiplexity to Different Sectors[a]

Presence of at least one complete multiplex (ODI) relation to one or more sectors of each type	Corporate variables					
	Assets	Capital-output ratio	Management control	Family control	Mean	S.D.
Financial						
45 sectors	.38	.35	−.17	−.02	.19	.40
	(.33)	(.39)	(−.08)	(.04)		
405 sectors	.27	.46	−.15	−.10	.24	.58
	(.27)	(.46)	(−.14)	(−.09)		
Manufacturing						
45 sectors	.25	−.04	−.28	−.34	.62	.49
	(.01)	(.10)	(.08)	(−.29)		
405 sectors	.11	−.18	−.29	−.20	8.00	7.70
	(.09)	(−.46)	(−.29)	(.06)		
Other						
45 sectors	.07	.29	−.37	.05	.31	.47
	(−.02)	(.35)	(−.28)	(.14)		
405 sectors	.12	.40	−.17	−.10	.98	1.70
	(.10)	(.39)	(−.12)	(.04)		

[a]Correlations are computed across the 42 manufacturing firms. A zero-order correlation greater in absolute magnitude than .25 is significant beyond a .05 level of confidence. Partial correlations controlling for the number of sectors in a firm's network by any of the three types of directorate ties (given in parentheses) are significant beyond the .05 level of confidence if greater than .26 in absolute magnitude. The multiplex relation variables are binary.

ported by looking at correlations between the four corporate variables and a dummy variable equal to one if the firm owned a finance establishment (these correlations are not presented). The firms owning a finance establishment were large ($r = .38$) and capital-intensive ($r = .35$). There is no significant association with management or family control. Similarly, the firms interlocking with financial institutions had no significant tendencies to be large ($r = .11$) or capital-intensive ($r = −.07$).

As explanation of the observed tendency for capital-intensive firms not to interlock extensively with financial institutions, these data suggest that such firms had no special need for financial interlocks. They had already extended their cooptive networks to the finance sector by directly owning establishments there.[22]

[22]This is not to say that the firms owning finance establishments owned major banking or insurance institutions. All eight firms owning a finance establishment owned a credit agency of some type (SIC categories 61 and/or 67).

SUMMARY

Three types of directorate ties between establishments have been distinguished as potentially cooptive interorganizational relations: ties through ownership (where one firm owns and operates both establishments), ties through direct interlocking (where each establishment is owned by a separate firm but the two firms share one or more directors), and ties through indirect financial interlocking (where each establishment is owned by a separate firm but the two firms share one or more directors with the same bank or insurance company).

These directorate ties are not cooptive in the sense of actually changing market transactions between economic sectors. Rather, they create favored trade partners within sectors. An establishment within the transportation equipment industry, for example, must purchase supplies from the primary metals industry in order to manufacture transportation equipment. However, it has a choice of supplier establishments within the primary metals industry. Directorate ties make some establishments more attractive than others. Ownership ties create the many advantages of conducting market transactions in the nonmarket context of a corporate hierarchy. Instead of buying and selling on the open market, transactions can be coordinated so as to be more efficient for both buyers and sellers owned by the same firm. Direct interlock ties channel the flow of adverse and favorable information regarding trade partners available in other sectors to make specific establishments more attractive as suppliers or consumers again. This same function is fulfilled by indirect interlocks through financial institutions, at a greater efficiency if a potentially lower accuracy, banker-directors in particular being a source of information on operations in many sectors. Moreover, the representative from a financial institution brings to the board the influence his firm can exercise over potential trade partners. In this sense of combining the function of patterning the flow of information with that of brokering market transactions between establishments, indirect financial interlocks combine features of direct interlock ties and ownership ties, respectively. Together, the three types of directorate ties create favored trade partners. These favored trade partners are establishments with which buying and selling can be conducted with lower uncertainty because of more accurate information and a third-party authority over the transactions, the higher authority of a shared board of directors and/or the brokered authority of an intermediary financial institution.

In other words, market transactions between industry and sector occur as described in an input–output table whether or not there are directorate ties from the industry to the sector. The more that all three types of directorate ties connect industry and sector, however, the lower the proportion of buying and selling that must be transacted on the imperfectly competitive open market, a social context fraught with uncertainties for the profits of buyer and seller. In this sense of defining trade partners with which necessary market transactions can be conducted in a nonmarket context, directorate ties have the potential to coopt sources of market constraint.

The relative frequencies with which directorate ties connected sectors in 1967 have been computed using a sample of firms representative of large American firms involved in manufacturing in 1967. Ties connecting the two-digit industries with economic sectors are based on 152 firms of which 42 are in manufacturing industries. Ties connecting the four-digit industries with economic sectors are based on 786 firms of which 559 are in manufacturing industries. From each industry to each economic sector there are three estimates of w_{ji} as a potentially cooptive relation: $w_{ji(o)}$ is the number of manufacturing firms owning an establishment in industry j and sector i, $w_{ji(d)}$ is the number of establishments in sector i represented on the boards of firms owning an establishment in industry j, and $w_{ji(i)}$ is the number of establishments in sector i represented through financial institutions on the boards of firms owning an establishment in industry j.

These sample directorate data were used to describe the manner in which establishments in diverse economic sectors were represented in 1967 on the typical board of directors. The concept of a cooptive corporate actor network was helpful in organizing the data. The description replicated basic findings in directorate research using more traditional methodology and extended those findings in a substantively meaningful way.

Substituting the concept of network range for the traditional measure of involvement in interlocking (the number of interlocks), the types of firms previously found to be highly involved in interlocking had the greatest cooptive network range. Firms with extensive assets controlled by diffuse interest groups had boards on which the greatest diversity of establishments were represented, the most establishments from the most sectors. Further, network range varied for different types of directorate ties. The smallest number of establishments and sectors was represented on directorates by ownership ties, a higher number was represented by direct interlocks with other firms, and the highest number was represented by indirect financial interlocking. Although this ranking was not observed in every firm (e.g., Firestone in Figure 3.2), it was typical of the manufacturing firms generally. Finally, networks did not appear to grow so as to maintain a constant proportion of establishments from specific sectors on the board. All but one of the firms considered here had financial institutions(s) represented on their boards. Of the total number of establishments represented on the boards of smaller firms, a high proportion were financial. As a firm grew in terms of assets (bearing in mind that only cross-sectional data were analyzed here), the firm increasingly represented manufacturing industries on its board rather than nonmanufacturing sectors. Of the total number of establishments represented on the boards of larger firms in the two-digit sample, a high proportion was from manufacturing industries.

The three types of directorate ties did not appear to be used as alternatives in the sense that one type was used to represent specific sectors on the board and another type was used to represent other sectors (as in Figure 3.3a). Rather, there was significant multiplexity in the relation between a firm and an economic sector. Sectors represented on the board by ownership tended also to be represented on the board by direct interlock ties and indirect financial interlock ties. Given the observed growth of networks by direct interlocking into other industries rather than into nonmanufacturing sectors, it appears that multiplexity was directed at those sectors in which a firm owned establishments (as in Figure 3.3b). This strategy would have reached competitors of a firm's own establishments. However, since there was significant multiplexity in direct and indirect interlock ties, a further strategy is involved. The significant multiplexity of directorate ties directed at sectors in which firms owned no establishments (as in Figure 3.3c) suggests that firms were striving to coopt sources of constraint external to the firm. Recall from Figure 3.1 that Firestone directly interlocked with Western Airlines and indirectly interlocked, through Cleveland Trust, with two additional transportation firms, American Airlines and Pan American Airlines. In this example, Firestone appears to have coordinated direct and indirect interlock ties to the transportation sector, a sector which is a major consumer of Firestone products. This multiplexity in direct and indirect financial interlock ties to sectors in which a firm owned no establishment makes sense in terms of the discussion of directorate ties as cooptive relations, interlock ties providing information on operations beyond the firm's own establishments and indirect interlock ties through financial institutions providing the additional possibility of influencing the actions of establishments beyond those the firm actually owned. As would be expected from past directorate research, the most multiplex cooptive networks were associated with firms having the greatest need to coopt their environment—firms with extensive assets controlled by diffuse interest groups.

Of course, a firm's cooptive network could be extended to include other types of interorganizational relations. Other measures of directorate ties could be considered such as the directed ties created when officers in one firm sit on the boards of other firms (e.g., Galaskiewicz & Wasserman, 1981; Mizruchi, 1982) or the broken ties replaced (Koenig et al., 1979; Ornstein, 1980, 1982; Palmer, 1983). There are also other types of potentially cooptive relations such as mergers (Pfeffer, 1972b), personnel flows (Baty et al., 1971; Pfeffer & Leblebici, 1973), joint ventures (Pfeffer & Nowak, 1976), or information and social support more generally (e.g., Turk, 1977; Bick & Müller, 1978; Galaskiewicz & Marsden, 1978; Laumann et al., 1978; Pfeffer and Salancik, 1978; Galaskiewicz, 1979). Moreover, relations within the network could be analyzed in terms of their formality as institutionalized ties (Litwak & Rothman, 1970). For example, Berkowitz et al. (1979) report that the structure of direct interlock ties is much clearer when analyzed in conjunction with stock ownership ties as ties between establishments within an enterprise. They interpret the combination of stock ownership and interlocking to be a more formal interorganizational relation than either kind of tie is by itself. Different types of relations will probably have distinct global structures within a system of firms (e.g., Berkowitz *et al.*, 1979; Galaskiewicz, 1979:71–73). However, I would expect a firm to direct formalized, multiplex relations at firms owning establishments in sectors constraining the firm's profitability. In other words, a firm is likely to have a great variety of potentially cooptive relations—ties formalized to the extent possible for each type of relation—with firms owning establishments in sectors most seriously constraining their profitability.

The question of market constraint raises a final point. In one very important regard, the analysis of cooptive corporate actor networks is quite in keeping with the traditional methods of analyzing interlocking directorates. It provides descriptive rather than theoretical analysis. The diversity of establishments or sectors represented on a corporate board is captured by network range, and the coordination of alternative ties with those establishments is captured by network multiplexity. The resulting description can be interpreted in terms of cooptive motivations on the part of the firm. I have reviewed these interpretations in this chapter, but these interpretations have yet to be justified with research demonstrating an association between directorate ties and the market constraints that they supposedly bring under control. Interpreting directorate ties as cooptive relations does not advance our understanding of such ties so much as it provides a sociological label for them.

Like instinct theories of action in which a person's behaviors are explained by attributing to the person an instinct for those behaviors, cooptation is a rationalization for action without a specification of parameters for action. In other words, there is no statement in traditional directorate research of the conditions under which a directorate tie would not be cooptive. Accordingly, there is no method of rejecting an argument interpreting directorate ties as cooptive. What is known, what I have argued in this chapter, is that directorate ties have the potential to be cooptive relations and some types of firms use their directorate in what can be interpreted to be a cooptive manner. Are these ostensibly cooptive uses of directorates merely a reflection of variations in corporate tastes, or are they patterned so as to lessen the profit uncertainties created by market constraints? This is the question to which I turn in Chapter 4.

A

4

Directorate Structure:
A Cooptive Response
to Market Structure*

To the extent that directorate ties were cooptive relations to sources of market constraint in 1967, directorate ties should have occurred where market constraint was intense. In other words, directorate tie frequencies as cooptive relations (the w_{ji} in Chapter 3) should be predictable from market constraint relations (the a_{ji} in Chapter 2). A specific example can illustrate the kind of association to be described. As described in Chapter 2, establishments in the apparel industry faced their most severe market constraint from the textile industry (cf. Table 2.7). Directorate ties should have connected the apparel industry to the textile industry. Four of the sampled manufacturing firms owned establishments in the apparel industry: Allied Chemical Corporation, Burlington Industries, Raytheon Company, and Uniroyal. The directorate tie relations for apparel establishments are based on the sectors represented on the directorates of these four firms. Allied Chemical, Burlington, and Uniroyal each owned a textiles establishment ($w_{ji(o)}$ = 3). There was only one direct interlock tie between the industries: Raytheon interlocked with International Paper, which owned a textiles establishment ($w_{ji(d)}$ = 1). There were four indirect interlock ties between the industries through financial institutions ($w_{ji(i)}$ = 4). Burlington interlocked with Wells Fargo Bank,

*Portions of this chapter are drawn from articles reprinted with the permission of the *American Journal of Sociology*, the *American Sociological Review*, and *Social Science Research* (Burt, 1980a; Burt et al., 1980; Burt, 1980c).

117

which in turn interlocked with International Paper. This gave Burlington an indirect interlock tie to International Paper's textiles establishment. Similarly, Allied Chemical interlocked with New York Life, which in turn interlocked with International Harvester. This gave Allied an indirect interlock tie to the textiles establishment owned by International Harvester. Finally, Raytheon had two indirect financial interlock ties to the textiles industry. Raytheon interlocked with John Hancock Mutual and State Mutual of America. The former gave Raytheon an indirect interlock tie to Textron's textiles establishment, and the latter provided a connection to International Paper's textiles establishment. In all, the market constraint posed for profits in the apparel industry by buying and selling between that industry and the textiles industry had several directorate ties superimposed on it: three ownership ties, one direct interlock tie, and four indirect financial interlock ties. These directorate ties had the potential, as described in Chapter 3, to enable connected establishments to circumvent market constraint.

My purpose in this chapter is to describe the extent to which there was a systematic tendency in 1967 for directorate ties to occur with market constraints so as to give constrained establishments a nonmarket context for conducting buying and selling with sources of constraint. As can be readily seen in the preceding illustration, there are a great many considerations that could be taken into account here. The four indirect financial interlock ties between the apparel and textiles industries, for example, are based on a complex web of ties among several corporations. I only propose to describe basic features of the association between market constraint and directorate ties in 1967, first in qualitative terms and then in quantitative terms. Subsequent analyses can attempt to capture the association in finer detail once these basic features have been documented.

THE ABSENCE OF DIRECTORATE TIES

The market constraint coefficient a_{ji} indicates the market incentive establishments in industry j had to develop cooptive relations to sector i in 1967. It says nothing, however, about the frequency of directorate ties (w_{ji}) to be expected as the manifestation of an industry-to-sector cooptive relation. How many ties would be required for the industry to have coopted the sector? Should each establishment in the industry have had a connection to each establishment in the sector, or would it have been sufficient for each to have had a connection to any one establishment?

Lacking guidance from available theory or directorate research, I have chosen to avoid this measurement issue for the moment by turning it around so as to make it more tractable. I shall focus on the absence of directorate ties. I can very clearly measure the lack of directorate ties between establishments in industry j and sector i: it is a zero value of w_{ji}. In the absence of any directorate ties, I know that establishments in the industry were ignoring the sector. If directorate ties were being used to coopt sources of market constraint, then this absence of directorate ties should not have occurred where there was a market incentive to develop cooptive relations. If there was any connection between industry and sector (i.e., if w_{ji} is nonzero), then I shall assume the presence of some industry to sector connection without attempting to interpret the level of cooptation it represented.[1]

Locating Sources of Severe Market Constraint

Establishments in industry j had a market incentive to develop cooptive relations to specific other sectors according to the results in Chapter 2. As cooptive relations, directorate ties should not have been absent within an industry (as long as the industry was not repressed by its market transactions with consumers), and they should not have been absent between the industry and some sector i to the extent that the sector posed a severe market constraint for profits in the industry. Market constraint is not an on–off condition. A sector posed some level of constraint for industry profits, a level given by the relevant $\mathbf{a}_{ji}$ coefficient. In keeping with the qualitative treatment of directorate ties as absent versus present, however, I shall, for the moment, treat market constraint as a qualitative dichotomy between severe and negligible constraint. The quantitative values of constraint given by the $\mathbf{a}_{ji}$ will be considered later in the chapter.

The severe market constraints confronting an industry in 1967 have been located in terms of the average constraint an industry faced and the variation in constraint facing it from each other sector. If the constraint posed by sector i for industry j, $\mathbf{a}_{ji}$, lies outside a 95% confidence interval around the average constraint facing the industry, then sector i is coded as being a source of severe market constraint for industry j.[2] Sector i posed a severe constraint for profits in

---

[1]This binary treatment of directorate ties between sectors of the economy is quite similar to the treatment of sociometric citations between statuses as a blockmodel of social structure (see White *et al.*, 1976, for the initial statement; Burt, 1980b:120–125, 1982a:Chap. 2, for review and literature in the context of network models generally). In proposing blockmodels, White and his colleagues call attention to the significance of holes in social structure (zero-blocks). The presence of a single contact between two statuses is sufficient for communication to occur between the statuses even though many contacts between the statuses would facilitate that communication. However the absence of any contact between two statuses indicates a hole in social structure, a communication gap in the structure. There is a qualitative difference between no contacts linking two statuses versus one contact. There is merely a quantitative difference between one, two, three, and so on, contacts between the statuses.

[2]Each two-digit industry j faced some mean level of constraint, $\bar{\mathbf{a}}_j$, from the 51 sectors distinguished, and this constraint varied from sector to sector with a standard deviation s_j; $s_j = (\Sigma_i[\mathbf{a}_{ji} - \bar{\mathbf{a}}_j]^2/50)^{1/2}$. A 95% confidence interval around the mean constraint for industry j can then be given as

industry j, in other words, if market transactions between the industry and sector posed a more severe constraint on the industry than the typical constraint posed by any one sector of the economy.

The typical constraint posed by a sector on industry profits was negligible. Given 20 two-digit industries and 44 other sectors that industry establishments could have reached with directorate ties, there are 880 possible instances in which a source of constraint could have been coopted ($20 \times 44 = 880$). Only 88 of these sector to industry constraints emerge as "severe" according to the coding. Given 322 four-digit industries being considered as the object of market constraint and 404 other sectors that industry establishments could have reached with directorate ties, there are 130,088 possible instances in which a source of constraint could have been coopted ($322 \times 404 = 130,088$). Of these potential constraints, only 3038 met the criterion of being especially severe constraints. Only a small fraction, in short, of potential market constraints in 1967 were severe constraints. Of the two-digit market relations 10% involved severe constraint, and slightly more than 2% of the four-digit relations involved severe constraint.

The Absence of Ties Is Contingent on Constraint

The absence of directorate ties should have been contingent on market constraint in a systematic way—to the extent that ties were being used as cooptive relations. Three contingency hypotheses can be derived from the arguments advanced in Chapters 2 and 3.

First, directorate ties should not have been absent among establishments within an industry. All intraindustry market constraints are significantly positive. This is not a surprising result since $\mathbf{a}_{jj}$ represents the contribution to the industry j profit margin made by a lack of competition within the industry and that contribution is positive (β_1 in Tables 2.3 and 2.6). However, not all establishments had a market incentive to develop intraindustry directorate ties. Establishments in six of the two-digit industries were so severely constrained by their buying and selling with other sectors that they had no immediate incentive to develop direc-

---

CI = $\bar{\mathbf{a}}_j \pm .28s_j$. Similarly, each four-digit industry faced some mean level of constraint $\bar{\mathbf{a}}_j$ with standard deviation s_j so that a 95% confidence interval around the mean could be given as CI = $\bar{\mathbf{a}}_j \pm .09s_j$. The distribution of $\mathbf{a}_{ji}$ for industry j is skewed with a small number of severe constraints and a large number of negligible constraints. The mean is typically near zero. If $\mathbf{a}_{ji}$ falls within the 95% confidence interval around the mean for industry j, then I have coded sector i as having a negligible effect on industry profits. If it falls below that interval, then I have coded sector i as a source of severe constraint on profits in industry j. This coding is arbitrary, but it is adequate for the purposes here since I shall be analyzing the $\mathbf{a}_{ji}$ directly in the next section. Also the data are highly skewed so that severe constraints could be identified by many different codings. Two-digit constraints are given in Table A.4 of the Appendix.

torate ties with one another. Their immediate concern was constraint from consumers. As discussed in Chapter 2, they were repressed by a dependence on
consumption by a small number of oligopolistic sectors. There was, however, a
market incentive for directorate ties to be developed among establishments in
each of the 322 four-digit industries and in each of the 14 unrepressed two-digit
industries.[3]

Second, directorate ties should not have been absent between an industry and
each sector posing a severe constraint for industry profits. Establishments in
every industry could have improved their control over industry prices, increasing
industry profits, by developing cooptive relations to sectors constraining industry
profits.[4] As cooptive relations, directorate ties should not have been absent either
in the 88 instances of severe market constraint on two-digit industries or the 3038
instances of severe constraint on four-digit industries.

At the same time that there was a market incentive to maintain cooptive
relations with some sectors, there was no incentive to maintain such relations
with other sectors. Sectors that posed a negligible constraint for industry profits
were either highly competitive internally or engaged in little buying and selling
with industry restablishments. Given the directorate tie costs described in Chapter 3—commitment and exposure to being coopted—there is no reason to expect
directorate ties to be maintained in the absence of a market incentive for them.
As cooptive relations, in other words, directorate ties should have been absent
between an industry and any sector posing negligible constraint for industry
profits.

[3]An industry j is treated as repressed if a decrease in intraindustry competition would not increase
the industry profit margin, i.e., if the value of the partial derivative in Eq. (2.7) is not positive. The
derivative is negative to the extent that the direct effect on profits from industry oligopoly (β_1) is
much smaller than its interaction effect with low consumer constraint (β_x). Among the four-digit
industries, the direct effect of industry oligopoly was sufficiently high and the interaction effect
sufficiently low for it to be impossible for the partial derivative in Eq. (2.7) to be negative ($\partial p_j / \partial y_{j1}$
$= .151 - .503(y_{j3} - .966) = .637 - .503y_{j3}$, where y_{j3} varies from zero to one). This is not true of
the two-digit industries among which the direct oligopoly effect on profits is much smaller than the
interaction effect ($\hat{\beta}_1 = .096$ and $\hat{\beta}_x = 10.831$, so that $\partial p_j / \partial y_{j1} = 10.577 - 10.831y_{j3}$). The six
repressed industries are textiles, apparel, furniture, primary metals, mechanical machines, and elec-
trical machines. Of course, this dichotomy between repressed and unrepressed industries is arbitrary.
There is considerable variation in the extent to which industries could be considered repressed. The
variation is the variation in the extent to which industries confronted oligopolistic consumers [y_{j3} in
Table 2.4, which is the variable in the partial derivative in Eq. (2.7)]. In the quantitative analysis that
follows, this variation, rather than the repressed–unrepressed dichotomy, is considered directly (see
Figures 4.7, 4.8, and 4.9).

[4]This statement is based on the fact that industry profit margins could be expected to increase if
buying and selling with sources of constraint could be conducted in a nonmarket context free from
constraint. In other words, the statement is based on the fact that the partial derivatives in Eqs. (2.10)
and (2.11) are nonnegative for all industries. The only exception is the two-digit petroleum industry,
for which coopted consumers need not increase industry profits [Eq. (2.11) is negative] but coopted
suppliers should [Eq. (2.10) is positive].

Directorate tie measurement affects the rigor with which these hypotheses can be tested. Directorate ties are not created on a tie-by-tie basis. They are created in blocks. When two firms interlock, all of their respective establishments become connected by directorate ties. If a board of directors wishes to coopt a specific sector constraining one of establishments owned by the board, the board can interlock with a second firm that owns a particularly attractive establishment in the constraint sector. By so doing, however, the board extends its relations to many sectors in addition to the one it wished to represent on the board. It would now represent all the sectors in which the second firm owned establishments. In short, interlock ties can be expected to be much more extensive than cooptive purposes require. It would be naive to treat each sector represented on a board as if it were of special, unique interest to the board. This overstatement of cooptive relations by directorate ties could create evidence in support of the second hypothesis and create evidence contradicting the third.

The problem lies less in the use of directorate ties per se than in their analysis. Analysis must explicitly consider the coordination of the three types of types. The overstatement of cooptive relations is probably least in the case of ownership ties since these ties are most nearly created on an establishment-by-establishment basis. It is higher for direct interlock ties, but especially high for indirect financial interlock ties since whole sets of firms tied to a bank are being represented on the board and financial institutions tend to have extensive interlocks with firms operating in each manufacturing industry. But when all three types of directorate ties occur together, it seems unlikely that they have been created by accident in the creation of other ties. It is when a type of directorate tie occurs as the only type of tie between industry and sector that the specter of incidental connections arises. This is not to say that every instance of all three types of ties occurring together is planned and every instance of uniplex ties is an accident. This is a statement of relative likelihood. The probability that indirect financial interlock ties were created by accident when those are the only type of tie between industry and sector is a high probability—high relative to the probability that accident is responsible for the simultaneous appearance of ownership, direct interlock, and indirect financial interlock ties between industry and sector.

As a specific third hypothesis, there should be a tendency for all three types of directorate ties to have been absent simultaneously between an industry and any nonfinancial sector posing negligible constraint for industry profits. There were 772 instances of negligible nonfinancial constraint on two-digit industries and 126,084 instances among four-digit industries. The finance sector is a special case here since it posed negligible constraint for profits in every industry (as constraint is based on patterns of buying and selling) yet was the medium for extensive interlock ties among industry establishments. Under the assumption that financial institutions are being used as a medium for coordinating the operations of nonfinance establishments, extensive directorate ties can be expected

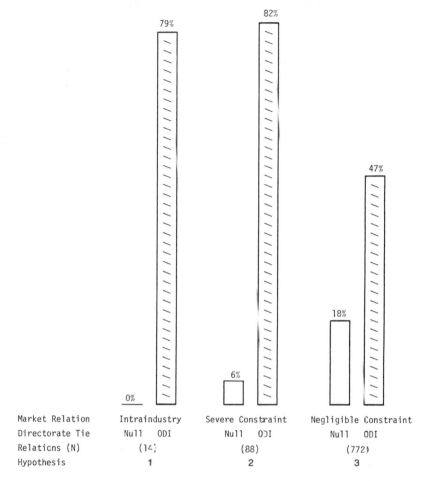

Figure 4.1. The absence of directorate ties was contingent on the absence of market constraint: two-digit results (excluding finance sector).

between industries and the finance sector despite the lack of market constraint from the sector. There are 20 two-digit industry-to-finance-sector relations and 966 such relations in the four-digit data.[5]

The manner in which these hypotheses were true in 1967 is illustrated by the bar graphs in Figure 4.1 (for two-digit industries) and Figure 4.2 (for four-digit

[5]There are three finance sectors per four-digit industry and one per two-digit industry. There is only one finance sector in the aggregate input–output table for 1967. The detailed table distinguishes banking, credit, and insurance establishments as separate sectors. Any one of these, or all three, could have had directorate ties to any four-digit industry.

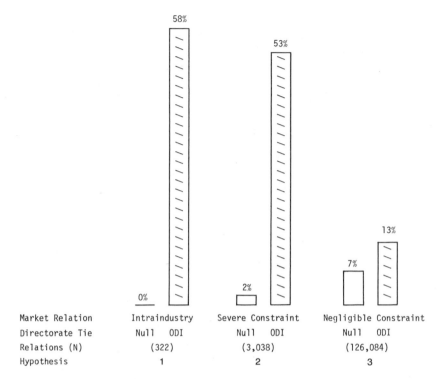

Figure 4.2. The absence of directorate ties was contingent on the absence of market constraint: four-digit results (excluding banking, credit, and insurance sectors).

industries). Within each class of market relations distinguished in the preceding hypotheses (intraindustry, severe constraint, and negligible constraint from non-financial sectors), two kinds of directorate tie relations are distinguished. The complete absence of directorate ties is referenced as a null relation (i.e., $w_{ji(o)} = w_{ji(d)} = w_{ji(i)} = 0$). The simultaneous presence of all three types of directorate ties is referenced as an ODI multiplex relation (i.e., $w_{ji(o)} > 0$, $w_{ji(d)} > 0$, $w_{ji(i)} > 0$).

The prevalence of null relations is indicated in Figures 4.1 and 4.2 by white bars. The highest white bars occur over hypothesis 3, the negligible market constraint relations. Among the four-digit industries, all three types of director-ate ties were absent in 7% of the instances where a sector posed negligible constraint for an industry's profit margin. This percentage dropped to 2% when a sector posed a severe constraint. All three types of ties were absent in 18% of those instances where a sector posed negligible constraint for profits in a two-digit industry. The percentage dropped to 6% when a sector posed severe constraint. There was no instance of a null relation within an industry.[6] Overall, directorate ties tended not to be absent where there was a market incentive for establishments to develop cooptive relations.

The prevalence of ODI multiplex relations is indicated in the figures by striped bars. The highest striped bars occur over hypotheses 1 and 2, the market relations where there was a profit incentive to develop cooptive relations. All three types of directorate ties occurred among establishments in 58% of the four-digit industries and 79% of the two-digit industries. Where a sector posed a severe constraint for profits in an industry, establishments in the industry and sector were connected by all three types of directorate ties in 53% of the instances involving four-digit industries and 82% of the instances involving two-digit industries. The simultaneous presence of all three types of directorate ties was much less prevalent in the absence of severe constraint. The striped bar over hypothesis 3 in both figures is clearly lower than those over hypotheses 1 and 2. Again, directorate ties tended not to be absent where there was a market incentive for cooptive relations to be developed.

These bar graphs illustrate the expected contingency between market constraint and directorate ties; however, there are two issues I wish to address in order to connect the evidence with the hypotheses more directly. First, there is the issue of marginal frequencies. How strong are the contingency effects when marginals are held constant? The ODI multiplex relations were more prevalent than null relations regardless of the type of market relation being considered. This is illustrated in Figures 4.1 and 4.2 by the striped bars being consistently higher than corresponding white bars. This should occur under hypotheses 1 and 2, but it contradicts hypothesis 3. It is possible that the evidence supporting the first two hypotheses is more a result of the overall tendency for ODI multiplex relations to occur than it is a result of the tendency for such relations to be maintained within industries and to sources of severe market constraint. Similarly supporting the hypotheses is the tendency for null relations to occur with negligible market relations three times as often as they occur with severe market constraint (18% versus 6% in Figure 4.1; 7% versus 2% in Figure 4.2). But there were many more negligible market relations than there were severe market constraints, so any type of directorate tie could be expected to occur more often with negligible market relations. Second, there is the issue of other combinations

---

[6]It would be impossible for a null relation to occur within an industry since $w_{jj(o)}$ is the number of establishments owned in the industry. The positional sample ensures that this frequency is four or more for each industry, so all three types of directorate ties cannot be simultaneously absent within any industry. There is no such assurance for interlock ties, however, and they did tend to occur within industries as illustrated by the high striped bars in Figures 4.1 and 4.2 over intraindustry. Nevertheless, intraindustry directorate ties are best understood by considering the quantitative data on intraindustry tie frequencies as described in the next section (see Figures 4.3 and 4.4).

of directorate ties than those represented by null relations and ODI multiplex relations. There were instances of uniplex relations (industry and sector being connected by a single type of directorate tie) and relations in which only two types of directorate ties were present. If all directorate tie relations were null or ODI multiplex, the percentages over adjacent white and striped bars in Figures 4.1 and 4.2 would sum to 100. As an extreme example, only 20% of negligible nonfinancial market relations involving four-digit industries are represented in Figure 4.2 (7% + 13% = 20%). The remaining 80% of the relations are other combinations of types of directorate ties. It is possible that specific combinations of ties other than the ODI and null combinations were contingent on market constraint relations.

Addressing these two issues does not change the basic result illustrated by the bar graphs in Figures 4.1 and 4.2; all three types of directorate ties tended to be present in the presence of market constraint and tended to be simultaneously absent in the absence of constraint. Readers not interested in a more detailed examination of the qualitative data may wish to skip ahead to the next section, where the distribution of directorate tie frequencies is compared to the intensity of market constraint.

Table 4.1 contains a tabulation of market relations with directorate tie relations. The table columns distinguish four kinds of market relations: intraindustry, severe constraint, negligible constraint from nonfinancial sectors, and negligible constraint from financial sectors. All relations to banking, credit, and insurance establishments are contained in the fourth column. The table rows distinguish eight combinations of directorate ties: null relations, three kinds of uniplex relations (O, D, and I), three kinds of relations in which only two types of directorate ties occurred (OD, OI, and DI), and ODI multiplex relations. Frequencies based on the two-digit industries are given in parentheses below the corresponding frequencies for four-digit industries.

In order to examine the contingency of directorate tie relations on market relations net of the marginal tendencies for different kinds of relations to occur, the frequencies in Table 4.1 can be described by the following model:

$$f_{mk}^{WA} = \gamma \ \gamma_m^W \ \gamma_k^A \ \gamma_{mk}^{WA}, \tag{4.1}$$

where γ is a constant similar to the overall mean in an analysis of variance, γ_k^A is the marginal tendency for the kth class (columns of Table 4.1) of market relations to have occurred, γ_m^W is the marginal tendency for the mth combination (rows of Table 4.1) of directorate ties not to have occurred, and γ_{mk}^{WA} is an interaction term expressing the tendency for the mth combination of directorate ties to have occurred with the kth class of market relations net of the marginal tendencies for each to have occurred. When a condition occurred more often than average, then

TABLE 4.1
Frequency of Market and Directorate Tie Relations[a]

Directorate tie relations	Market relations			
	Intraindustry	Severe constraint	Negligible constraint	Finance
Null	0	50	8859	15
	(0)	(5)	(138)	(0)
O	46	6	89	0
	(2)	(0)	(2)	(0)
D	0	0	38	0
	(0)	(0)	(3)	(0)
I	0	255	28,616	0
	(0)	(0)	(70)	(0)
OD	1	0	1	0
	(0)	(0)	(0)	(0)
OI	89	97	1525	0
	(1)	(5)	(70)	(0)
DI	0	1005	70,021	654
	(0)	(6)	(121)	(4)
ODI	186	1625	16,935	297
	(11)	(72)	(368)	(16)
Total	322	3038	126,084	966
	(14)	(88)	(772)	(20)

[a]Two-digit frequencies are given in parentheses below appropriate four-digit frequency. Only nonfinancial sectors are included in the negligible constraint frequencies. Null refers to the complete absence of any ties between establishments, O refers to one or more ownership ties, D refers to one or more direct interlock ties, and I refers to one or more indirect financial interlock ties. OD, OI, DI, and ODI refer to the simultaneous presence of combinations of the three types of directorate ties.

its parameter is greater than one. If the mth combination of directorate ties tended to occur with the kth class of market relations more often than would have been expected from the marginal tendencies for that combination to have occurred and that class to have occurred, then γ_{mk}^{WA} will be greater than one. The dependent variable in Eq. (4.1) is f_{mk}^{WA}, the frequency with which the mth combination of directorate ties occurred with the kth class of market relations. For example, there were several instances of null relations occurring in the absence of constraint from nonfinancial sectors ($f_{13}^{WA} = 8859$ for the four-digit data, 138 for the two-digit data) and fewer instances of them occurring with severe constraint from some other sector ($f_{12}^{WA} = 50$ for the four-digit data, 5 for the two-digit data). To the extent that null relations tended to occur with negligible market relations from nonfinancial sectors, above and beyond the marginal tendencies for null relations and negligible market relations to occur, $\gamma_{1\,3}^{WA}$ will be greater than one.[7]

Table 4.2 presents parameter estimates of Eq. (4.1) for the two-digit and four-digit data when directorate ties are coded as a trichotomy; null relations (row 1 of Table 4.1) mixed relations (rows 2–7 of Table 4.1) and ODI multiplex relations (row 8 of Table 4.1). To the extent that the bar graphs in Figures 4.1 and 4.2 support the hypotheses only because of marginal tendencies, rather than a con-

---

[7]It might appear to be more straightforward to estimate an unrestricted model for a four-way table (market relations by O by D by I) directly here; however, such a model would not capture directorate tie multiplexity. The specific problem is that interactions in the model would not capture multiplexity. Since this is not obvious, a quick explanation is in order. Consider a three-way tabulation of ownership ties (no = 1, yes = 2), direct interlock ties (no, yes), and market constraint (negligible, severe). In the presence of market constraint, OD multiplex ties should not have been absent. The frequency with which the ith level of ownership ties and jth level of direct interlock ties occurred with the kth class of market relations, f_{kij}^{AOD}, would be given in terms of eight parameters,

$$f_{kij}^{AOD} = \gamma \; \gamma_k^A \; \gamma_i^O \; \gamma_j^D \; \gamma_{ij}^{OD} \; (\gamma_{ki}^{AO} \; \gamma_{kj}^{AD} \; \gamma_{kij}^{AOD}),$$

where the parameters in parentheses capture the interaction of the two types of directorate ties with constraint. Note three points in this specification. (*a*) There is no parameter capturing the association between null ties (the simultaneous absence of ownership and direct interlock ties) and market constraint. This condition is absorbed into the other parameters. In other words, there is no independent test for the hypothesis that directorate ties tended to be simultaneously absent in the absence of market constraint. (*b*) The parameter capturing an interaction between ownership ties and direct interlock ties, γ^{OD}, is not the tendency for OD multiplexity to have occurred. It is the tendency for ownership ties and direct interlock ties to have occurred together and/or to have been simultaneously absent:

$$\gamma_{11}^{OD} = \gamma_{22}^{OD} = (\Pi^2{}_k[f_{k11}f_{k22}/f_{k21}f_{k12}])^{1/8},$$

which is the fourth power of the mean odds-ratio between O and D (e.g., Goodman, 1972:1042). In other words, if ownership ties and direct interlock ties tended to be simultaneously absent, but had only a random tendency to occur together, this interaction parameter would be high. This is not what is meant by relational multiplexity (e.g., Burt, 1980b:89–90, 1982a:Chap. 2, for review and references). A hermit has no relations with others and so at once has no social relation or economic relation to any particular other, but this does not mean that the hermit has coordinated his relations as multiplex ties to others. Rather, it means that he is an isolate. Multiplexity refers to the simultaneous presence of different types of relations from one actor to another. The simultaneous absence of relations is a wholly different concept. (*c*) The impropriety of γ^{OD} as a measure of multiplexity carries over to γ^{AOD} as the parameter capturing the interaction between constraint, ownership ties, and direct interlock ties. This third-order interaction is the tendency for O and D to have been simultaneously absent or present in the presence versus the absence of market constraint:

$$\gamma_{122}^{AOD} = \gamma_{111}^{AOD} = ([f_{111}f_{122}/f_{121}f_{112}]/[f_{211}f_{222}/f_{221}f_{212}])^{1/8},$$

which is proportional to the odds-ratio between O and D in the absence of market constraint over the odds-ratio in the presence of constraint. Again, it can be high either because O and D tended to occur together in the absence of constraint or because they tended to have been simultaneously absent in the absence of constraint.

TABLE 4.2
Null versus ODI Multiplex Relations in Association with Market Relations[a]

Directorate tie relations	Market relations				Marginal effect γ_m^W
	Intraindustry $\gamma_{m\,1}^{WA}$	Severe constraint $\gamma_{m\,2}^{WA}$	Negligible constraint $\gamma_{m\,3}^{WA}$	Finance $\gamma_{m\,4}^{WA}$	
Two-digit industries					
Null	.68	1.23	2.15	.56	.27
	(.5)	(.5)	(2.2)	(.8)	(3.8)
Mixed	1.20	.64	1.04	1.25	1.08
	(.4)	(1.6)	(.2)	(.5)	(.4)
ODI	1.23	1.27	.45	1.44	3.45
	(.5)	(1.0)	(4.1)	(.9)	(6.4)
Marginal	.20	1.21	17.33	.24	
Four-digit industries					
Null	.22	1.09	3.72	1.11	.10
	(2.1)	(.3)	(5.5)	(.4)	(9.7)
Mixed	1.40	.68	.97	1.08	4.18
	(.9)	(3.1)	(.2)	(.6)	(11.7)
ODI	3.22	1.36	.28	.83	2.48
	(3.3)	(2.4)	(10.6)	(1.4)	(7.5)
Marginal	.05	1.08	55.15	.32	

[a]Parameters are given in Eq. (4.1) and estimated from the frequencies in Table 4.1 as described in footnote 8. At the two-digit and four-digit levels, respectively, values of 13.77 and 447.62 were obtained for γ. Unit normal test statistics are given in parentheses. Parameter estimates with hypothesized values are significant at the .05 level of confidence if the unit normal statistic is 1.6 or more (but see footnote 9 on testing).

tingency between market relations and directorate tie relations, the interaction terms in Table 4.2 for null and ODI multiplex relations will equal one. This is obviously not the case.[8]

First, there is a strong overall interaction between the absence of directorate ties and market relations. Interactions between market relations and the three combinations of directorate ties can be tested for their collective significance by

[8]Because of some zero frequencies in the tables to be fit, all frequencies have been increased by .5 before estimating parameters (e.g., Goodman, 1970:299). The overall mean effect is the geometric-mean frequency in all $K \times M$ cells of a table (M is the number of directorate tie combinations distinguished, K is the number of classes of market relations distinguished):

$$\gamma = (\Pi_m \Pi_k f_{mk}^{WA})^{1/KM}.$$

The tendency for the kth class of market relations to have occurred is then the geometric mean of frequencies within the class given the overall mean:

imposing the restriction that all γ_{mk}^{WA} in Eq. (4.1) equal one and attempting to describe the observed frequencies with the marginal effects remaining. The hypothesis that the observed frequencies result from marginal effects alone can be rejected at well beyond the .001 level of confidence. With six degrees of freedom, the likelihood ratio χ^2 is 56.83 for the two-digit data and 3239.50 for the four-digit data. Unit normal test statistics indicate the significance of specific interaction effects contributing to the aggregate contingency between directorate relations and market constraint relations.[9]

Note that the parameters in Eq. (4.1) break observed frequencies into component effects. Each frequency is completely predicted by the parameters in the equation. For example, the 138 instances of all three directorate ties being simultaneously absent in the absence of market constraint ($f_{1\,3}^{WA} = 138$ for the two-digit data) consist of a mean effect ($\hat{\gamma} = 13.77$), multiplied by a tendency for all three types of ties not to have been absent simultaneously ($\hat{\gamma}_1^W = .27$, which is less than one), multiplied by a tendency for negligible market relations to have occurred frequently ($\hat{\gamma}_3 = 17.33$, which is greater than one), multiplied by an interaction term expressing the tendency for null relations to have occurred with negligible market relations above and beyond the marginal effects ($\hat{\gamma}_{1\,3}^{WA} = 2.15$, which is greater than one). In other words, $f_{1\,3}^{WA} = 13.77 \times .27 \times 17.33 \times 2.15$

$$\gamma_k^A = ([\Pi_m f_{mk}^{WA}]^{1/M})/\gamma.$$

The tendency for the mth combination of directorate ties not to have been absent is similarly given as

$$\gamma_m^W = ([\Pi_k f_{mk}^{WA}]^{1/K})/\gamma,$$

and its tendency to have occurred when the kth class of market relations occurred is given as

$$\gamma_{mk}^{WA} = f_{mk}^{WA}/(\gamma\ \gamma_m^W\ \gamma_k^A).$$

[9]Statistical interpretations of the parameters in Eq. (4.1) assume each of the 894 two-digit w_{ji} and the 130,410 four-digit w_{ji} is independently observed. As with much of network analysis, it is difficult here to determine the correct number of independent observations underlying second-order coefficients. At the two-digit level, directorate ties have been computed from 152 separate firms for which 2903 different persons served as directors, and the firms together owned 414 of what I am treating here as establishments (a conservative estimate of what the Department of Commerce treats as establishments in constructing the input–output table; see footnote 5 to Chapter 2). At the four-digit level, these alternative numbers of observations increase dramatically with the increase in market relations. Any one, or some mixture, of these numbers could be the correct number of independent observations. Further complicating the situation, the independence of observations is not equal across the classes of market relations. There is more likely interdependence between w_{ij} and w_{ik} than between w_{jj} and w_{kk}, separate firms being more likely across two separate industries j and k than within an industry i. In the absence of a more appropriate treatment, I have merely assumed the w_{ji} to be independent and reported routine statistical interpretations of the gammas and their significance (cf. Fienberg and Wasserman, 1981:158; Holland and Leinhardt, 1981:36, for very similar working assumptions in their applications of log-linear models to network data).

$= 138.5$, where the additional .5 is a constant added to the observed frequencies in order to eliminate zero frequencies (see footnote 8).

Figures 4.1 and 4.2 illustrate the tendency for null relations to have occurred in the absence of market constraint. Table 4.2 shows that this tendency was net of marginal effects. Negligible market constraint from nonfinancial sectors tended to be the rule rather than the exception for both two-digit and four-digit industries ($\hat{\gamma}_3^A \gg 1$). But the number of null relations to be expected in the absence of market constraint as a function of infrequent null relations and frequent negligible constraint is significantly less than the number observed. There are over twice as many instances in the two-digit data ($\hat{\gamma}_{1\ 3}^{WA} = 2.15$ with a unit normal test of 2.2). There are almost four times as many instances in the four-digit data ($\hat{\gamma}_{1\ 3}^{WA} = 3.72$ with a unit normal test statistic of 5.5).

Figures 4.1 and 4.2 illustrate the tendency for ODI multiplex relations to have occurred where there was a market incentive for cooptive relations and to have been absent in the absence of market constraint. Table 4.2 shows that portions of this tendency were net of marginal effects. ODI ties did occur more often than would be expected from marginal effects within industries and with sectors posing a severe constraint ($\hat{\gamma}_{3\ 1}^{WA}$ is greater than one, and $\hat{\gamma}_{3\ 2}^{WA}$ is greater than one). However, these tendencies are statistically negligible among the two-digit industries. Among the four-digit industries, there is a strong tendency for ODI ties within industries and a slight tendency for such ties to connect an industry with sectors posing a severe constraint for the industry's profits. The strongest interaction effect involving two-digit or four-digit ODI ties, however, is with the absence of constraint. The number of ODI multiplex relations to be expected in the absence of market constraint—as a function of frequent ODI ties and frequent negligible constraint—is significantly more than the number observed. These complete multiplex relations occurred less than half as often among two-digit industries as would be expected from marginal effects ($\hat{\gamma}_{3\ 3}^{WA} = .45$ with a unit normal test statistic of 4.1) and occurred about a quarter as often as would be expected from marginal effects in the four-digit data ($\hat{\gamma}_{3\ 3}^{WA} = .28$ with a test statistic of 10.6). In short, the strong marginal tendency for ODI multiplex relations to have occurred among two-digit and four-digit industries ($\hat{\gamma}_3^W \gg 1$) is a major component in the tendency for such relations to have been observed where there was a market incentive for cooptive relations to have been developed. At the same time, this marginal tendency was not solely responsible for the observed tendency ($\hat{\gamma}_{3\ 1}^{WA}$ and $\hat{\gamma}_{3\ 2}^{WA}$ are greater than one). Moreover, the marginal tendency for ODI multiplex relations to have occurred serves to obscure the fact that they occurred relatively infrequently in the absence of market constraint ($\hat{\gamma}_{3\ 3}^{WA}$ is much less than one).

The second issue to be addressed is the question of how specific combinations of directorate ties (other than null and ODI relations) were associated with

market constraint. Table 4.1 distinguishes eight possible combinations of directorate ties. Table 4.3 presents parameter estimates for Eq. (4.1) expressing the
extent to which each combination was contingent on market constraint.[10]

There are no effects in Table 4.3 for OD multiplex relations. Direct interlock
ties almost never occurred with ownership ties in the absence of indirect financial
interlock ties. As reported in Table 4.1, there were no such relations involving
the two-digit industries and only two instances of such relations involving the
many four-digit industries. Given the rarity of OD multiplex relations, I have not
attempted to estimate interaction effects between them and classes of market
relations.

There are no effects in Table 4.3 for relations to banking, credit, and insurance
establishments as a finance sector. The typical directorate tie relation to finance
was a DI or ODI multiplex relation. Every two-digit industry had interlock ties to
finance establishments. Four out of five industries had an ODI multiplex tie to
finance. All but five of the four-digit industries had interlock ties to finance
establishments. The five that did not contained very small establishments in
which narrowly defined manufacturing activities took place.[11] These five industries did not have interlock ties to any other sector of the economy; however, they
did have ownership ties. Slightly less than a third of the four-digit industries had
ownership ties as well as interlock ties to finance establishments. Given the rarity
of directorate tie relations (other than DI and ODI relations) to finance establishments, Table 4.3 does not present interaction terms expressing the tendency for
each combination of directorate ties to have reached finance from manufacturing.
The simple summary statement here is that profits in no industry were severely
constrained by market transactions with finance establishments, but all three
types of directorate ties tended to connect those establishments with manufacturing industries.[12] Finance is clearly a special case in the association between
market constraint and cooptive directorate ties.

Turning to the detailed association between market constraint and combina-

---

[10]Parameters were estimated as described in footnote 8 except that the frequencies in Table 4.1
were fit directly rather than aggregating rows 2–7 as mixed ties. The absence of OD frequencies
means that M in footnote 8 is a 7 for Table 4.3 rather than its value of 3 for Table 4.2. The deletion of
relations to the finance sector (column 4 of Table 4.1) means that K in footnote 8 is a 3 for Table 4.3
rather than its value of 4 for Table 4.2

[11]The industries are industrial patterns (a subsector of mechanical machines), collapsible tubes,
house slippers (a subsector of the leather industry), wallpaper, and household furniture (not elsewhere classified—n.e.c.). The industries are marked with an asterisk (*) in Table A.2.

[12]This is clear for the two-digit industries (80% of which had ODI relations to the finance sector),
but even the four-digit industries tended to have such relations in the sense that there is a significant
interaction between ODI multiplex relations and finance relations ($\hat{\gamma}_{84}^W$ is 2.3 with a unit normal test
statistic of 2.5 for the four-digit data). A much stronger interaction effect is obtained for DI multiplex
relations, as would be expected from the frequencies in Table 4.1. These effects are not presented in
the text since they add little to the discussion. The two clearly dominant frequencies in column 4 of
Table 4.1 are those for DI and ODI multiplex relations.

TABLE 4.3

Directorate Tie Combinations and Market Constraint[a]

Directorate tie relations	Two-digit market relations				Four-digit market relations			
	Intraindustry γ^{WA}_{m1}	Severe constraint γ^{WA}_{m1}	Negligible constraint γ^{WA}_{m1}	Marginal effect γ^{W}_{m}	Intraindustry γ^{WA}_{m1}	Severe constraint γ^{WA}_{m1}	Negligible constraint γ^{WA}_{m1}	Marginal effect γ^{W}_{m}
Null	.31	1.37	2.33	1.38	.17	1.19	4.94	.63
	(1.3)	(.6)	(1.8)	(.7)	(2.1)	(.4)	(3.7)	(1.1)
O	7.78	.62	.21	.28	32.12	.31	.10	.31
	(3.2)	(.5)	(2.6)	(2.5)	(11.1)	(3.9)	(11.3)	(6.0)
D	2.37	.94	.45	.18	4.88	.34	.61	.02
	(.9)	(.1)	(1.2)	(2.8)	(1.7)	(1.2)	(.8)	(6.5)
I	.87	.35	3.31	.50	.07	2.37	6.28	1.59
	(.1)	(1.1)	(2.0)	(1.2)	(3.2)	(1.9)	(4.3)	(1.1)
OD	—	—	—	—	—	—	—	—
OI	.82	1.19	1.03	1.59	7.83	.59	.22	2.45
	(.4)	(.4)	(.1)	(1.4)	(7.2)	(2.6)	(9.6)	(5.7)
DI	.31	1.60	2.02	1.40	.03	4.37	7.22	3.38
	(1.4)	(.9)	(1.5)	(.7)	(4.1)	(3.3)	(4.6)	(2.9)
ODI	.78	1.93	.67	12.87	2.24	1.34	.33	17.81
	(.7)	(2.2)	(1.8)	(12.0)	(2.9)	(1.5)	(7.1)	(18.7)
Marginal	.22	.56	8.19	—	.05	.70	29.57	—

[a]Parameters are given in Eq. (4.1) and estimated from the frequencies in Table 4.1 as described in footnote 10. At the two-digit and four-digit levels, respectively, values of 5.24 and 96.87 were obtained for γ. Unit normal test statistics are given in parentheses. Parameter estimates are significantly nonnegligible at the .05 level of confidence if the unit normal statistic is 1.6 or more in a one-tail test, 2.0 or more in a two-tail test (but see footnote 9 on testing).

tions of directorate ties, the conclusions reached from Table 4.2 are corroborated at this more detailed level. There is a strong overall contingency between market constraint and combinations of directorate ties. The null hypothesis that the data are adequately described by marginal effects alone can be rejected at well beyond the .001 level of confidence (χ^2 is 71.18 for the two-digit data and 4425.24 for the four-digit data with 12 degrees of freedom). Again, ODI multiplex relations have a strong tendency to have occurred ($\hat{\gamma}_8^W >> 1$), but tended to be absent in the absence of market constraint ($\hat{\gamma}_{8\,3}^{WA} < 1$). At the other extreme, null relations tended to occur in the absence of severe market constraint ($\hat{\gamma}_{1\,3}^{WA} > 1$).

Beyond the earlier conclusions, Table 4.3 shows a tendency for DI multiplex ties to have occurred between industries and sectors posing a severe constraint for industry profits. Although $\hat{\gamma}_{7\,2}^{WA}$ is greater than one for both the two-digit and four-digit industries, it is only significantly so for the four-digit industries. On the other hand, other combinations of directorate ties do not tend to be high with constraint at the two-digit and four-digit levels. There is no tendency for direct interlock ties alone to have been coordinated with ownership ties in reaching sectors constraining industry profits; OD ties were almost nonexistent. More-over, there is no tendency for indirect financial interlock ties alone to be coordi-nated with ownership ties in reaching constraint sectors. In fact, OI ties are significantly infrequent between four-digit industries and constraint sectors ($\hat{\gamma}_{6\,2}^{WA}$ = .59). In other words, direct and indirect financial interlock ties do not appear to have been coordinated *only* so as to reach competitors within the constraint sectors in which a firm owned an establishment. As was suggested by the analysis of the cooptive networks of individual firms in Chapter 3, the two types of interlock ties were coordinated in reaching constraint sectors beyond those in which a firm owned establishments.

At the same time, this cooptive interpretation of DI multiplex relations should not be taken too far. Both two-digit and four-digit industries tended to be con-nected by DI multiplex relations to sectors posing a negligible constraint for industry profits ($\hat{\gamma}_{7\,3}^{WA} > 1$). If DI multiplex relations were intended to coopt sources of constraint, they should have occurred infrequently in the absence of market constraint—in the same manner that ODI multiplex relations occurred infrequently ($\hat{\gamma}_{8\,3}^{WA} < 1$).

One reason why DI relations occurred frequently in the absence of market constraint is the tendency for interlock ties to overstate the cooptive intent of firms. This point was discussed on page 122 where the nonseparability of estab-lishments was emphasized. When two firms interlock, all of their respective establishments become connected by directorate ties even if the interlock was created for the purpose of connecting only two establishments. As I have opera-tionalized it, an interlock tie cannot be created individually unless two firms own only one establishment each.

Judging from Table 4.3, this overstatement of cooptive relations does not seem to be too troublesome with respect to direct interlock ties. Direct interlock ties tended not to occur by themselves as uniplex relations ($\hat{\gamma}_3^W < 1$) and were almost never found with ownership ties alone (OD multiplex relations). The only instances in which direct interlock ties tended to occur in the absence of market constraint, in fact, was when they occurred with indirect financial interlock ties as DI multiplex relations.

Indirect financial interlock ties do appear to overstate cooptive relations. They were widespread throughout the economy, and the only cases in which director-ate ties actually tended to occur in the absence of constraint were cases involving indirect financial interlock ties. Such ties had a significant tendency to be the only type of directorate tie between an industry and a sector posing no constraint on its profits. These relations are referenced in Tables 4.1 and 4.3 as I-uniplex relations ($\hat{\gamma}_{4\,3}^{WA} \gg 1$ for both two-digit and four-digit industries). I have already pointed out the tendency for DI multiplex relations to have occurred in the absence of market constraint. This tendency seems more attributable to indirect financial interlocking than to direct interlocking since the latter, in all other circumstances, tended not to occur in the absence of market constraint.

THE FREQUENCY OF DIRECTORATE TIES

The preceding analysis is motivated by the lack of a function by which the frequency of directorate ties between an industry and sector can be transformed into a measure of the intensity of industry to sector cooptation. I have circum-vented this problem by only considering the absence of ties as a qualitative measure of industry establishments having no cooptive designs on a sector. However, there is much more information in the computed directorate tie fre-quencies than can be represented by collapsing frequencies into binary code, present versus absent.

Given the demonstrated contingency association between directorate ties and market constraint, I now propose to explore the possibility of a continuous association between directorate tie frequency, w_{ji}, and market constraint inten-sity, a_{ji}. I still have no theoretical interpretation of the w_{ji} as quantitative mea-sures of cooptation. My analysis in this section is purely empirical, but based on the knowledge that a_{ji} measures the market constraint sector i posed for industry j as well as the market incentive industry establishments had to develop cooptive relations with the sector. My situation here is the pleasant one of using a predic-tor variable firmly grounded in theory to understand better a dependent variable about which I have a hunch.

Intraindustry Results

At the outset, intraindustry ownership ties must be distinguished from interlock ties. Ownership ties within an industry are different in meaning from intraindustry interlock ties. Between an industry j and some sector i, $w_{ji(o)}$ is the number of ownership ties between industry and sector as discussed in Chapter 3. A comparable intraindustry figure would be the number of separate establishments within the industry that are owned by the same firm or perhaps the frequency of intraindustry mergers. However, $w_{jj(o)}$ is neither of these. It is the number of large corporations operating in the industry, not the number of competitors per se, but rather the number of sampled firms attracted to the industry (and representing large manufacturing firms as the positional sample). Intraindustry interlock ties, in contrast, conform to the discussion in Chapter 3; $w_{jj(d)}$ is the number of intraindustry direct interlock ties between establishments, and $w_{jj(i)}$ is the number of intraindustry indirect interlock ties through financial institutions.

Two features of an industry are predicted to make it attractive to large firms and encourage intraindustry interlock ties. First, the market constraint coefficient $\mathbf{a}_{jj}$ indicates the extent to which industry oligopoly contributed to industry profits. Specifically, $\mathbf{a}_{jj}$ is the marginal contribution control over industry prices by a small number of industry establishments makes to the industry's structural autonomy—which in turn is the industry profit margin predicted by market structure generally. To the extent that $\mathbf{a}_{jj}$ is positive, industry j should have been an attractive market to large firms since the low competition within it would ensure comparatively stable profits—assuming that the large, dominant firms within the industry would allow competitors to enter the market. Second, industry establishments had a market incentive to develop cooptive relations with one another to the extent that they were free from dependence on a single, oligopolistic consumer sector. The increased profit margin to be expected from increasing industry oligopoly is given by the partial derivative $\partial \mathbf{a}_j / \partial y_{j1}$ in Eq. (2.7). To the extent that this partial derivative is positive, industry establishments could have improved their control over industry price, and accordingly profits, by developing cooptive relations with one another. In other words, a high value of the partial derivative indicates that the industry was an attractive product market in which to own an establishment and provided a market incentive to develop directorate ties among competitors. A negative value of the partial derivative indicates that the industry was repressed by its dependence on oligopolistic consumers and so was not an attractive market in which to own an establishment.

On first inspection, neither of these arguments appears to be valid. Neither ownerships ($w_{jj(o)}$), nor direct interlock ties ($w_{jj(d)}$), nor indirect financial interlock ties ($w_{jj(i)}$) are correlated with the market coefficient $\mathbf{a}_{jj}$ or the market incentive $\partial a_j/\partial y_{j1}$. Statistically negligible correlations are implied by the two-digit data as well as the four-digit data.

A closer inspection of the data reveals a subtle association between intraindustry directorate ties and market conditions. The effect of the market coefficient a_{jj} is an inverted curvilinear effect. The effect of the market incentive $\partial a_j/\partial y_{j1}$ occurs in interaction with the effect of a_{jj}. The marginal contribution to industry profits from industry oligopoly (i.e., a_{jj}) is the dominant effect on intraindustry directorate ties.

Figures 4.3 and 4.4 illustrate the association between w_{jj} and a_{jj}. Figure 4.3

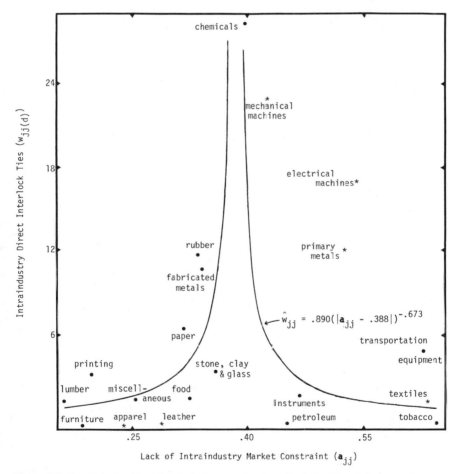

Figure 4.3. Intraindustry direct interlock ties as a function of a lack of intraindustry market constraint: two-digit results (repressed industries are marked with an asterisk).

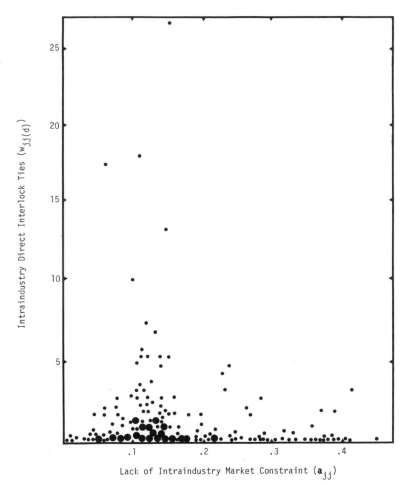

Figure 4.4. Intraindustry direct interlock ties as a function of a lack of intraindustry market constraint: four-digit industries (a large dot represents four or more industries).

presents a graph of direct interlock tie frequencies within two-digit industries, $w_{jj(d)}$, against the market coefficient $\mathbf{a}_{jj}$. Repressed industries, that is, industries confronted with oligopolistic consumers (so that the market incentive $\partial \mathbf{a}_j / \partial y_{j1}$ is less than zero), are marked by asterisks. Note that the asterisks do not stand apart from other industries in any systematic way. Figure 4.4 presents a corresponding graph for the 322 four-digit industries. The much larger number of four-digit industries makes it impossible to distinguish them all individually as is possible in Figure 4.3; however, the association observed in the two-digit data is also observed in the four-digit data. Similar graphs are obtained for ownership and indirect financial interlocking, so I have only presented a single graph for each data set, direct interlock ties being between separate establishments (unlike the ownerships) and less prone to overstating cooptive relations (unlike the indirect interlock ties as discussed in the preceding section). The graphs illustrate the association to be proposed.

The most striking feature of these data distributions is the tendency for directorate ties to have been most frequent among establishments in moderately competitive industries. Frequencies tend to be much lower in highly competitive industries (far left of the graphs) and in industries dominated by a small number of large firms (far right of the graphs). All three of the two-digit graphs and all three four-digit graphs show a sharp peak in tie frequencies before and after which tie frequency decreases rapidly. The principal difference between the two-digit and four-digit data is the greater frequency of oligopolistic industries implied by the four-digit data. The more narrowly defined production activities distinguished by the four-digit industry categories mean that it was easier for a small number of large firms to be responsible for all manufacturing in a four-digit industry relative to a broadly defined two-digit industry. This in turn means that it would be easier for a small number of competitors to appear to be able to control industry price according to the certainty measure y_{j1} in Eq. (2.2). There are accordingly many four-digit industries in which oligopoly was a large contributor to industry profits according to the market coefficient $\mathbf{a}_{jj}$ in Eq. (2.6). These industries are to the far right of the graph in Figure 4.4 and have been averaged with more competitive four-digit industries when data were aggregated to the two-digit industry level. The large number of four-digit industries with high values of $\mathbf{a}_{jj}$ and low values of w_{jj} makes it clear that the three two-digit industries in the lower right-hand corner of Figure 4.3 are not merely outliers in a positive, monotonic association between the frequency of ties within an industry and industry oligopoly. Rather, they represent a systematic tendency for directorate ties to be infrequent within an industry dominated by a small number of large firms.

The curvilinear association illustrated in Figures 4.3 and 4.4 can be represented by a kinked regression line. The frequency of directorate ties increased rapidly with increasing values of $\mathbf{a}_{jj}$ from zero through some criterion level of $\mathbf{a}_{jj}$. Let $\mathbf{a}$ be the mean value of $\mathbf{a}_{jj}$ across all industries. Visual inspection of the data distributions is sufficient to recommend the mean as one of several alternative criteria around which the distributions could be centered. The median is too low, and the mean has the dual advantage of having a statistical meaning as a center to the data as well as being in the midst of the highest directorate tie frequencies. With increasing values of $\mathbf{a}_{jj}$ beyond the average $\mathbf{a}$, the frequency of directorate ties decreases rapidly. This association can be represented by the following equation predicting w_{jj} from $\mathbf{a}_{jj}$:

$$w_{jj} = \alpha(|\mathbf{a}_{jj} - \mathbf{a}|)^{\beta} e_j = \hat{w}_{jj} e_j, \tag{4.2}$$

where $|\mathbf{a}_{jj} - \mathbf{a}|$ is the absolute value of the difference between $\mathbf{a}_{jj}$ and the mean $\mathbf{a}$, e_j is a residual term, and the unknown parameters α and β can be estimated by ordinary least-squares after taking the natural logarithms of both sides of the equation. The following regression equation results:

$$\ln w_{jj} = \ln \alpha + \beta[\ln(|\mathbf{a}_{jj} - \mathbf{a}|)] + \ln e_j.$$

The term in parentheses is high when $\mathbf{a}_{jj}$ is far above or below the criterion level $\mathbf{a}$. Low directorate ties frequencies occur at these extremes. Therefore, the regression coefficient β will be significantly negative to the extent that directorate ties increased rapidly in frequency with increasingly moderate competition.

Table 4.4 presents estimates of the parameters in Eq. (4.2) for the two-digit and four-digit industries.[13] Illustrating the form of the function, the number of direct interlock ties predicted within two-digit industries is graphed in Figure 4.3 as a broken, bold line. This is $\hat{w}_{jj(\mathrm{d})}$ in Eq. (4.2). A comparison of the correlations between raw scores and log scores of the variables shows that the association is more exponential than linear. The log score correlations (given in Table 4.4 as standardized β) are consistently stronger than corresponding raw score correlations. The kinked association between industry oligopoly and directorate

---

[13]A distinction is to be drawn here between the results for two-digit industries and those for the four-digit industries. For the four-digit industries, the certainty measure Y_1 is a better measure of industry oligopoly than the industry four-firm concentration ratio $C14$, better in the sense that Y_1 is better than $C14$ in predicting industry profit margins and $\mathbf{a}_{jj}$ based on Y_1 is a better predictor of intraindustry directorate ties than is $\mathbf{a}_{jj}$ based on $C14$. This is not true of the two-digit industries. The correlations between two-digit industry profit margins and the aggregate certainty measure and aggregate four-firm concentration ratios are virtually identical (.2829 for Y_1 and .2826 for $C14$). Since both measures are merely weighted averages of actual market conditions at the four-digit industry level, the stronger performance of the certainty measure in the four-digit data is the focus of attention in Chapter 2. However, two-digit market coefficients based on aggregate concentration are much more strongly correlated with intraindustry directorate ties than are market coefficients based on the certainty measure. For the purposes of illustrating the strength of the association between intraindustry ties and industry oligopoly, therefore, the two-digit market coefficients analyzed in this section are based on aggregate concentration ratios rather than aggregate certainty measures with the market effects adjusted for the larger standard deviation of concentration ratios. Specifically, $\mathbf{a}_{jj}$ in Figure 4.3 and Table 4.4 is $\mathbf{a}_{jj}(.8C14_j/y_{j1})$, where $\mathbf{a}_{jj}$ is defined in Eq. (2.6) and given in the Appendix. Basing the two-digit market coefficients on the certainty measure instead of concentration yields identical results, but they are consistently weaker; for example, the correlations reported in Table 4.4 round to $-.3$ rather than the $-.5$ results reported. Even stronger results are obtained from the two-digit data if the initial structural autonomy model is used to define market coefficients, the initial model being the one in which there is no distinction between supplier constraint and consumer constraint. A $-.7$ average correlation is obtained between intraindustry directorate ties and industry oligopoly. These results are reported elsewhere (Burt, 1982a:Table 8.5). The bottom line here is that the aggregate two-digit industries are best described by comparatively crude measures, the original concentration data and the initial structural autonomy model, whereas the four-digit industries are best described by the models emphasized here, the certainty measure of industry oligopoly and the structural autonomy model in which supplier constraint is distinguished from consumer constraint.

TABLE 4.4
Predicting Directorate Tie Frequency from a Lack of Intraindustry Market Constraint[a]

w_{jj}	α	β Raw	β Standardized	t-test	Raw score r	Mean	S.D.
Two-digit industries							
Owned establishments	3.290	−.413	−.632	3.5	−.593	2.173	.538
Direct interlock ties	.890	−.673	−.492	2.4	−.457	1.483	1.126
Indirect financial interlock ties	1.068	−1.111	−.548	2.8	−.456	2.705	1.665
Four-digit industries							
Owned establishments	5.878	−.088	−.157	2.9	−.098	2.005	.631
Direct interlock ties	2.531	−.118	−.098	1.8	−.056	1.242	1.367
Indirect financial interlock ties	10.642	−.189	−.118	2.1	−.051	2.868	1.815

[a]Parameters are specified in Eq. (4.2), the criterion **a** is .388 for the two-digit sample, .147 for the four-digit, and the regression line of predicted direct interlock ties is graphed in Figure 4.3 as a broken, bold line. Parameters have been estimated with ordinary least-squares after taking the natural logarithms of the two variables in Eq. (4.2). The mean log score for **|a**$_{jj}$ − **a|** is −2.376 for the two-digit industries and −2.769 for the four-digit with respective standard deviations of .822 and .889. In order to compute logs of the interlock ties, $w_{jj(d)}$ and $w_{jj(i)}$ have been increased by one before taking logs.

ties is statistically significant but low in magnitude; $\hat{\beta}$ is significantly less than zero for ownerships, direct interlock ties, and indirect financial interlock ties.[14]

The specific industries labeled in Figure 4.3 can be used to interpret the association. Industry competition is clearly the principal determinant of where an industry appears in the graph. At the left, where $\mathbf{a}_{jj}$ is low, one finds the highly competitive industries in which there are many small competitors rather than a small number of large, dominant firms. These are the lumber industry, the furniture industry, the apparel industry, printing, leather, and so on. At the right-hand extreme, where $\mathbf{a}_{jj}$ is relatively high, one finds the two industries most dominated by a small number of firms: the tobacco industry and the transportation equipment industry. At this level of extreme concentration, firms have no need for interlock ties with one another in order to coordinate their actions. They are so few in number that they can easily anticipate one another's behavior. This phenomenon is widely recognized in work by academics (e.g., Phillips, 1960; Galbraith, 1973; Pfeffer and Salancik, 1978) and in more journalistic accounts.[15] It is succinctly stated by Galbraith (1973) in his description of oligopolistic firms

[14]This negative association contradicts the monotonic, positive association Pennings (1980:94ff) reports in his analysis of interlocks among large American firms in 1969. He reports intraindustry interlocking to increase with industry concentration. A close look at his measures reveals the reason for this contradiction. Pennings assigns each of 386 large firms to a two-digit industry and then correlates the concentration in a firm's industry with the firm's involvement in interlocking (Pennings, 1980:101). The positive correlation he reports between concentration and intraindustry (horizontal) interlocking can be traced to two features of his operationalization: two-digit concentration ratios and firms as units of analysis. The two-digit industries aggregate four-digit industries so that many highly concentrated industries disappear. In fact, there are only two two-digit industries that stand out as highly concentrated: tobacco and transportation equipment. In an analysis of two-digit directorate ties, I found that there were few intraindustry directorate ties in these two industries as of 1967. I decided to put them aside as outliers, as I have explained with data distributions elsewhere (Burt, 1980c:156–161). With these two industries put to one side, I found a monotonic association between concentration [in terms of $\mathbf{a}_{jj}$ based on the initial constraint model in Eq. (2.4)] and intraindustry directorate ties, high levels of concentration being associated with more frequent directorate ties. The four-digit data quickly revealed, however, that the tobacco and transportation industries were not outliers so much as they were examples of high concentration industries. By taking firms as his units of analysis, Pennings de-emphasizes the tobacco and transportation equipment industries in his correlations. Few large firms operated in these industries (in keeping with the high concentration in them) so the bulk of his units of analysis are drawn from other industries. In these other industries, I too found a positive monotonic association between directorate ties and concentration. The four-digit data make it clear, however, that this monotonic association is quite wrong as a general understanding despite the fact that it is plausible for the two-digit industries (once tobacco and transportation equipment are ignored or given little weight). There is a systematic tendency for intraindustry interlocking to decrease as industry concentration increases past a criterion level.

[15]In the course of describing Robert McNamara's background in the transportation equipment industry, for example, journalist David Halberstam briefly describes in *The Best and the Brightest* why the Chevrolet was a more durable and expensive car than the Ford just after World War II:

as components in a managed market where industry prices are more a "gentlemen's agreement" than an end result of competition:

> the prices that serve the growth of one firm will, generally speaking, serve the growth of others. One firm, accordingly, can set prices knowing that others will find them broadly acceptable. And, the number of firms in the industry being small, the pacesetting firm can know or judge what will be acceptable to the other firms and be so guided. The others will then conform [p. 126].

This implicit coordination of actions by dominant firms within an industry presents a formidable barrier to entry by other firms so that the small number of firms operating within the industry ensures a low frequency of interlock ties. But industry oligopoly is not solely responsible for low directorate ties. Note that the textile industry appears to the far right of Figure 4.3 with a market coefficient a_{jj} just slightly lower than the values obtained for the tobacco and transportation equipment industries. The textile industry was moderately competitive more than it was dominated by a small number of large firms. Aggregate four-firm concentration in the industry was slightly above average and aggregate certainty of control over industry prices (Y_1) was slightly below average. But the textiles industry confronted severe market constraint from other sectors, so the average contribution of industry oligopoly to textile profits is a large proportion of the industry profit margin. It is this marginal contribution to profits from industry oligopoly that is captured by the market coefficient a_{jj} making the textiles industry appear to the far right of Figure 4.3. The negative values of β in Table 4.4 show that infrequent directorate ties among industry establishments were characteristic of industries that were oligopolistic in the absolute sense of containing a small number of dominant firms or oligopolistic in the marginal sense that a moderate level of oligopoly was the dominant market factor having a positive effect on industry profits.

At the same time, the kinked association evident from the results in Table 4.4 and the two graphs accounts for a very small amount of the variation in directorate tie frequencies. There are clearly more processes at work in producing such ties than the effect of industry oligopoly on industry profits.[16]

> GM had converted to war production, but it had been very careful to establish in its factory and production lines the kind of systems that could be easily converted to peace time production. Chevy thus had a massive lead; it could bring out a car for much less than it actually did, but if it lowered its prices it would kill Chrysler and bring the wrath of the Congress down for antitrust. ("Don't ever hire anyone from the auto industry," Gene McCarthy, one of McNamara's severest critics later said of him. "The way they have it rigged it's impossible to fail out there.") So Chevy kept its prices higher and produced a much better car than Ford [pp. 283–284].

[16]At this point, it is convenient to note the similarity between Eq. (4.2) and an equation estimated by Pfeffer and Salancik (1978:156). In terms of the symbols used here, Pfeffer and Salancik specify

One additional process is the market incentive an industry provided for intraindustry cooptation. This incentive was determined by industry market relations with consumers. To the extent that an industry was not repressed by dependence on purchases by an oligopolistic consumer sector, increasing industry oligopoly could increase industry profits. This effect of industry oligopoly on industry profits in the absence of constraint from consumers is illustrated by the bar graphs in Figure 2.3 in Chapter 2 and is measured by the extent to which the partial derivative $\partial \mathbf{a}_j / \partial y_{j1}$ is greater than zero. As cooptive relations, directorate ties should have been most frequent in the industries for which this partial derivative is high.

There is no immediate evidence of such an effect. Graphs of the w_{jj} by the market incentive $\partial \mathbf{a}_j / \partial y_{j1}$ appear random. Correlations between these variables for ownerships, direct interlock ties, and indirect financial interlock ties are almost perfectly zero (respectively, .05, .01, and .06 for the two-digit data, .03, .01, and .04 for the four-digit).

The large number of four-digit industries makes it possible to investigate this effect in greater detail. Figure 4.5 presents bar graphs illustrating a shifting interaction effect between industry oligopoly, industry market incentive for cooptive relations, and industry directorate ties. What the market incentive for cooptive relations appears to have done is amplify the curvilinear effect of industry oligopoly.

---

the following equation in which the number of interorganizational ties within industry j, w_{jj}, is predicted by the level of concentration within the industry, y_{j1}:

$$\ln w_{jj} = \ln a + b_1 \ln(y_{j1}) + b_2(\ln|y_{j1} - y|) + \ln e_j,$$

where y is the median value of y_{j1} for all industries. Describing frequencies of intraindustry joint ventures and aggregate direct interlock ties, Pfeffer and Salancik (1978:156, 166) report significantly negative estimates of b_2 and positive estimates of b_1. The principal implication of this equation for Eq. (4.2) is the monotonic effect of industry oligopoly, b_1. Pfeffer and Salancik (1978) specify the monotonic effect because "as the number of firms in the organizational field to be coordinated increases, the probability of developing an interorganization structure through informal or semiformal linkages decreases [p. 155]." In other words, b_1 should be positive as they report. To some extent this effect is captured by the kinked association in Eq. (4.2), infrequent directorate ties being expected in industries in which there are many competitors ($\mathbf{a}_{jj} \ll \mathbf{a}$) as well as those in which there are only a few ($\mathbf{a}_{jj} \gg \mathbf{a}$). Nevertheless, I reestimated (4.2) with a linear term included, $b_1[\ln \mathbf{a}_{jj}]$. In this equation, β is still significantly negative for all three types of directorate ties in both two-digit and four-digit industries. In keeping with the two-digit results Pfeffer and Salancik report, b_1 is consistently postive at the two-digit level with values of .56, .70, and 1.50, respectively, for ownerships, direct interlock ties, and indirect financial interlock ties (t-tests of 2.5, 1.2, and 1.9, respectively). Note that only ownerships show a strong monotonic effect and all three effects are much weaker than the corresponding kinked effects in Table 4.4. At the four-digit level, moreover, b_1 is consistently negligible with values of .02, .17, and .22, respectively, for the three types of directorate ties (t-tests of .4, 1.5, and 1.5, respectively). Faced with this weak evidence for a monotonic effect, I have only specified a kinked association in the text. That kinked association is closely related to the b_2 effect reported by Pfeffer and Salancik for joint ventures and aggregate direct interlock ties.

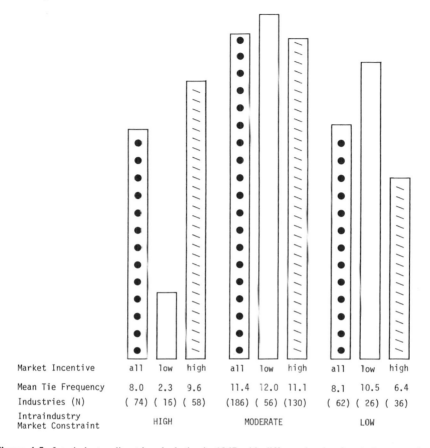

Market Incentive	all	low	high	all	low	high	all	low	high
Mean Tie Frequency	8.0	2.3	9.6	11.4	12.0	11.1	8.1	10.5	6.4
Industries (N)	(74)	(16)	(58)	(186)	(56)	(130)	(62)	(26)	(36)
Intraindustry Market Constraint		HIGH			MODERATE			LOW	

Figure 4.5. Intraindustry direct interlock ties in 1967 with different levels of an industry market incentive for cooptive relations ($\partial \mathbf{a}_j / \partial y_{j1}$ low versus high) and intraindustry market constraint (high, moderate, low, referring to values of $\mathbf{a}_{jj}$ that are low, moderate, high, respectively).

Industries have been divided into three groups on the basis of the market coefficient $\mathbf{a}_{jj}$: low, moderate, and high. The moderate group consists of industries with values of $\mathbf{a}_{jj}$ within half a standard deviation of the criterion mean $\mathbf{a}$. Industries with values of $\mathbf{a}_{jj}$ outside this range are classified as low or high depending on whether $\mathbf{a}_{jj}$ is below or above the range of moderate $\mathbf{a}_{jj}$. The dotted bars in Figure 4.5 show the average frequency of direct interlock ties within each group of industries. The documented curvilinear association between w_{jj} and $\mathbf{a}_{jj}$ is illustrated. An average of 11.4 ties occurred in moderately competitive industries. This average drops to 8 ties in highly competitive industries (low $\mathbf{a}_{jj}$) and relatively oligopolistic industries (high $\mathbf{a}_{jj}$).

Each group of industries has been further divided into two groups on the basis of the market incentive for cooptive relations: low incentive industries having a below-average value of $\partial \mathbf{a}_j / \partial y_{j1}$ and high incentive industries having an above-average value. The high incentive industries should have been attractive positions in which to own an establishment since they were not constrained by oligopolistic consumers. Further, directorate ties among industry establishments would offer the dual advantage of increased industry profits as a direct and interaction effect of increased coordination of industry pricing decisions. In other words, the white bars in Figure 4.5 (representing low market incentive industries) should be consistently lower than the striped bars (representing high market incentive industries). Instead, the bars illustrate an amplification of the curvilinear effect of industry oligopoly.

Among highly competitive industries, a market incentive for cooptive relations did increase the frequency of directorate ties. An average of 2.3 direct interlock ties occurred within highly competitive industries with a low market incentive for cooptive relations. This average increased to 9.6 ties within industries providing a high incentive. Freedom from oligopolistic consumers greatly increased the frequency of directorate ties among establishments in highly competitive industries.

This effect is greatly diminished, and eventually reversed, with decreasing industry competition. There is almost no difference in the average number of direct interlock ties observed in low versus high market incentive industries that were moderately competitive. The white and striped bars in the center of Figure 4.5 are about the same height. Among comparatively oligpolistic industries, however, there were actually fewer ties in high market incentive industries. An average of 10.5 direct interlock ties were observed in oligopolistic industries confronting an oligopolistic consumer sector. This average drops to 6.4 ties in the absence of an oligopolistic consumer sector.

These results can be interpreted in terms of the earlier noted association between directorate ties and industry oligopoly. Within the highly competitive industries (low $\mathbf{a}_{jj}$), a market incentive for cooptive relations greatly increased directorate ties among industry establishments. In the absence of an oligopolistic consumer sector determining demand for their product, establishments in highly competitive industries could—and were free to—greatly improve their control over industry prices and profits by developing directorate ties with one another. Within moderately competitive industries ($\mathbf{a}_{jj}$ about average), directorate ties reached their highest frequencies. As discussed in Chapter 2, control over industry prices by industry establishments would be maximally uncertain in such industries. Directorate ties among industry establishments would provide one strategy for coordinating pricing decisions to lessen that uncertainty. Whether an industry was faced by an oligopolistic consumer sector or was free from such constraint, a moderate level of competition within the industry was associated with the highest frequency of directorate ties. With increasing industry oligopoly (high a_{jj}), there was decreasing need for directorate ties in order for the largest firms to coordinate their pricing decisions so as to control industry prices. Coordination could be improved by such ties, however, and the threat to industry price control posed by oligopolistic consumers was sufficient to increase the frequency with which industry establishments were connected by interlock ties. The average frequency of direct interlocks in oligopolistic industries constrained by oligopolistic consumers is almost as high as the average observed in moderately competitive industries (10.5 in the former, 11.4 in the latter). In the absence of an oligopolistic consumer sector, on the other hand, oligopolistic firms had little need for directorate ties and few were observed in their industries.

This understanding makes sense theoretically in terms of the network model used to guide the market analysis in Chapter 2, i.e., in terms of a_{jj} as a measure of the importance of industry oligopoly to industry profits and $\partial a_j/\partial y_{j1}$ as a measure of industry market incentive for cooptive relations. However, the effects illustrated by the bar graphs in Figure 4.5 are very weak statistically. A two-way analysis of variance in which the three categories of a_{jj} and two categories of market incentive in Figure 4.5 are used to account for log directorate tie frequencies implies significant interaction effects as illustrated by the bar graphs in the figure. However, the significant effects are only significant at a .04 level of confidence for ownerships and indirect interlock ties through financial institutions. The interaction effects for direct interlock ties are negligible.[17] The illustrated interactions can be expressed more specifically by extending Eq. (4.2) to include the effects of market incentive:

$$w_{jj} = [\alpha(|a_{jj} - a|)^\beta e_j]M_j^{(\gamma + \delta_m\gamma_m + \delta_h\gamma_h)}, \tag{4.3}$$

where the bracketed expression is the kinked association in Eq. (4.2) between industry ties and industry oligopoly, M_j refers to the industry market incentive for cooptive relations ($M_j = \partial a_j/\partial y_{j1}$), and the exponent in parentheses is the effect of the market incentive. Dummy variables within this effect distinguish the three categories of industry oligopoly distinguished in Figure 4.5: δ_m equals zero unless industry j was moderately competitive (a_{jj} about average), whereupon it equals one; and δ_h equals zero unless industry j was relatively oligopolistic (a_{jj} high), whereupon it equals one. In other words, the effect on directorate ties of the market incentive within highly competitive industries is γ. For these industries δ_m and δ_h both equal zero, so the parenthetical exponent reduces to γ. The effect of the market incentive within moderately competitive industries is then γ

---

[17]Effects were estimated simultaneously with the main effects of each variable. With two degrees of freedom, the test statistics (F-tests) for interactions between industry oligopoly and industry market incentive on ownerships, direct interlocks, and indirect financial interlocks are 3.19, .63, and 3.28, respectively. Total variation in log frequencies accounted for by the six categories is higher, of course, since it includes the main effects of industry oligopoly (Table 4.4) and industry market incentive.

plus an adjustment γ_m (since δ_h equals zero). The effect of the market incentive within relatively oligopolistic industries is γ plus an adjustment γ_h (since δ_m equals zero). Based on the illustration in Figure 4.5, the market incentive effect within highly competitive industries should be positive ($\gamma > 0$), the adjustment for moderately competitive industries should reduce the strength of the association ($\gamma_m < 0$), and the adjustment for relatively competitive industries should strongly reduce the strength of the association ($\gamma_h \ll 0$). The result expected is a positive market incentive effect in highly competitive industries, a more negative effect in moderately competitive industries, and a still more negative effect in relatively oligopolistic industries; that is, $\gamma > (\gamma + \gamma_m) > (\gamma + \gamma_h)$. Like the analysis of variance results, estimates of the unknown parameters in Eq. (4.3) reveal weak effects. The parameters have been estimated by ordinary least squares after taking the natural logarithm of both sides of Eq. (4.3) and are presented in Table 4.5.[18] The negative estimates of β show the kinked association between directorate tie frequencies and industry oligopoly and the positive estimates of γ show the tendency for ties to increase in highly competitive industries with increasing market incentive for cooptive relations. However, all three γ estimates are statistically negligible. Similarly, adjustments to this effect for ownerships in moderately competitive industries (γ_m) and relatively oligopolistic industries (γ_h) are negligible. Adjustments to the effect for interlock ties are negative, but negligible, for moderately competitive industries. Statistically, the strongest adjustments to the market incentive effect within highly competitive industries are the negative adjustments for interlock ties within relatively oligopolistic industries—and these adjustments are only marginally signif-

---

[18]The effects estimated fall within the class discussed as the analysis of covariance. I have specified slope effects within an analysis of covariance using dummy variables. The specification is clearer when Eq. (4.3) is written in its log form. Taking the natural logarithms of both sides of Eq. (4.3) yields the following regression equation:

$$\ln w_{jj} = [\ln \alpha + \beta(|\mathbf{a}_{jj} - \mathbf{a}|) + \ln e_j]$$
$$+ \gamma(\ln M_j) + \gamma_m \delta_m(\ln M_j) + \gamma_h \delta_h(\ln M_j),$$

where the bracketed expression is the log form of Eq. (4.2) (ignoring the changed intercept term resulting from introducing M_j) and the gammas express slope effects in different contexts, contexts being defined by the three levels of $\mathbf{a}_{jj}$ in Figure 4.5. The slope of the association between $\ln w_{jj}$ and $\ln M_j$ within highly competitive industries is γ, the slope within moderately competitive industries is $\gamma + \gamma_m$, and the slope within relatively oligopolistic industries is $\gamma + \gamma_h$. The use of dummy variables in regression equations capturing analysis of covariance effects is relatively routine, so further details can be obtained elsewhere (e.g., Hanushek & Jackson, 1977:106–108). Although this model extends the analysis of variance effects to allow a continuous association between tie frequencies and market incentive for cooptive relations, it retains the inelegance of reducing $\mathbf{a}_{jj}$ to a trichotomy: low, moderate, high. Attempts to express with quantitative values of $\mathbf{a}_{jj}$ the interaction effects illustrated in Figure 4.5 were not informative. In all alternative specifications considered, however, the overall effect of market incentive was statistically negligible.

TABLE 4.5

Market Incentive Effects on Directorate Tie Frequencies[a]

	β	γ	γ_m	γ_h
Owned establishments	$-.101$	.084	.089	.033
	(2.6)	(0.2)	(0.7)	(0.7)
Direct interlock ties	$-.097$	.851	$-.414$	$-.545$
	(1.1)	(0.9)	(1.5)	(1.7)
Indirect financial interlock ties	$-.249$	1.774	$-.074$	$-.683$
	(2.2)	(1.4)	(0.2)	(1.6)

[a]Parameters are specified in Eq. (4.3), and estimates are based on the four-digit data. Parameters have been estimated by ordinary least-squares after taking the natural logarithms of both sides of Eq. (4.3); cf. the note to Table 4.4. The t-tests for slopes and adjustments are given in parentheses.

icant. The adjustment γ_h is significantly less than zero at the .05 level of confidence for direct interlock ties and indirect financial interlock ties if a one-tail test is made. It is only for these interlock ties that the expected rank order of market incentive effects is observed; the effect within highly competitive industries ($\hat{\gamma}$ of .85 and 1.77, respectively) being higher than the effect within moderately competitive industries ($\hat{\gamma} + \hat{\gamma}_m$ of .44 and 1.70, respectively), which is higher than the effect within relatively oligopolistic industries ($\hat{\gamma} + \hat{\gamma}_h$ of .31 and 1.09, respectively). As an aggregate, the three effects of market incentive contained in the parenthetical exponent in Eq. (4.3) do not significantly improve the prediction of tie frequencies from the prediction in Eq. (4.2), which captures only the kinked effect of the market coefficient a_{ij}.[19] That kinked association is the principal component in a quantitative function relating directorate tie frequency to the intensity of intraindustry market constraint.

In summary, intraindustry directorate ties were patterned by market constraint, but the patterning is a small, if statistically nonnegligible, portion of variation in frequencies across industries. The association with intraindustry competition is curvilinear. Within highly competitive industries there was no hope for a small number of establishments to control industry prices. With decreasing competition, large firms were attracted to the industry, and interlock ties occurred among industry establishments with an exponentially increasing frequency. Directorate ties were most frequent in industries where control over industry prices would have been most uncertain, i.e., in moderately competitive industries. This is not to say that directorate ties were especially frequent in every moderately competi-

[19]This statement is based on test statistics assessing the aggregate effect of all three gamma coefficients in Eq. (4.3). With 3 and 317 degrees of freedom, the F-statistics are .3, 1.2, and 1.1 for ownerships, direct interlock ties, and indirect financial interlock ties, respectively. All three statistics imply quite negligible effects.

tive industry. The modal frequency at every level of a_{jj} is low as illustrated by the dense band of observations across the bottom of the graphs in Figures 4.3 and 4.4. When the highest frequencies did occur, however, they tended to occur in moderately competitive industries. Past the maximum reached in moderately competitive industries, the association is reversed. As a small number of firms became increasingly dominant within the industry so as to increase industry concentration, decrease industry competition, and accordingly lower the uncertainty of their control over industry prices, they had less need for interlock ties with one another in order to coordinate their pricing decisions. Past an average level of a_{jj}, large firms were attracted to the industry and interlock ties occurred among industry establishments with an exponentially decreasing frequency. There were systematic deviations from this curvilinear association. Among highly competitive industries, interlock ties were frequent within industries free from oligopolistic consumers. This freedom provided both a market incentive for cooptive relations among industry establishments and the market tranquility to maintain them. Profitable increases in control over industry prices were to be expected from being involved in such ties. At the other extreme of a_{jj}, where industry oligopoly made a high marginal contribution to industry profits, interlock ties were infrequent in general—but frequent within those industries confronting oligopolistic consumers. This constraint from consumers posed a threat to industry control over industry prices, so there was advantage to maintaining intraindustry interlock ties despite industry oligopoly.

Extraindustry Results

    In comparison to the intraindustry association between market constraint and directorate tie frequency, extraindustry results are simple. The market constraint a_{ji} measures the extent to which the profit margin in industry j can be attributed to buying and selling between establishments in industry j and sector i. This buying and selling makes a negative contribution to industry profits (i.e., poses a market constraint for industry profits), to the extent that the sector had either or both of two role relations with the industry. The sector posed a constraint to the extent that the industry depended on the sector for a large proportion of input supplies purchased by industry establishments. The sector posed a constraint to the extent that it was dominated by a small number of large firms and those firms affected demand for industry output by consuming a large proportion of the output sold by industry establishments. These features of buying and selling with sector i are brought together in a_{ji} as the marginal increase in industry profit margin that would be forgone if industry establishments conducted their buying and selling with sector i on the open market. Alternatively, $-a_{ji}$ can be interpreted as the marginal increase to be obtained by developing cooptive relations to the sector. As cooptive relations, in short, directorate ties should have occurred between industry j and sector i as a function of the intensity of the market incentive industry establishments had to maintain such ties: w_{ji} should increase with increasingly negative $\mathbf{a}_{ji}$.[20]

In fact, directorate tie frequency is linearly proportional to market constraint intensity with some minor qualification. Table 4.6 presents ordinary-least-squares estimates for the following regression equation in which the frequency of directorate ties between industry j and sector i w_{ji}, is linearly proportional to the intensity of market constraint posed by the sector for industry profits, $\mathbf{a}_{ji}$:

$$w_{ji} = \alpha + \beta\mathbf{a}_{ji} + e_{ji} = \hat{w}_{ji} + e_{ji}. \tag{4.4}$$

Estimates are based on market and directorate tie relations with nonfinancial sectors, 855 relations with nonfinancial sectors generally and 83 relations with sources of severe constraint as identified earlier in the chapter.[21] Strong negative values of β are implied for all three types of directorate ties for variations in severe constraint as well as variations in market constraint more generally. Consistently weaker correlations are obtained between log scores indicating the linear, rather than exponential, nature of the association (cf. log score r and standardized β in Table 4.6). The log score correlations are positive because the negative $\mathbf{a}_{ji}$ had to be expressed as positive values before computing log scores. The significantly negative estimates of β in Table 4.6 show that with increasingly intense market constraint on industry j from sector i the industry and sector tended to be connected by increasingly frequent ownership ties, direct interlock ties, and indirect interlock ties through financial institutions.[22]

Illustrating the form of the association, Figure 4.6 presents a graph of direct interlock tie frequencies, $w_{ji(d)}$, against variations in market constraint, $\mathbf{a}_{ji}$, for

[20]This statement is based on the discussion of Eqs. (2.10) through (2.13) in Chapter 2. The positive values of the partial derivatives in Eqs. (2.10) and (2.11) imply that establishments in every industry could have improved their control over industry prices and thus improved industry profits by conducting their market transactions with constraint sectors in a nonmarket context.

[21]The financial sector is deleted from all computations here. Interlock ties occur more frequently with this sector than with any other sector, and yet the sector posed no market constraint for profits in any industry. This point is illustrated in Table 4.1 in qualitative terms. In the graph of interlock tie frequencies in Figure 4.6, the finance sector would occur well off the graph vertically at the right-hand extreme of the graph (cf. the graph in Burt, 1980c:155). Including the 20 industry-to-finance-sector relations (or the four-digit industry-to-finance relations) only lowers the strength of the correlations between $\mathbf{a}_{ji}$ and w_{ji} without adding to the scope of the argument. I am treating the finance sector less as the object of cooptive interlock ties than as a medium for cooptation through indirect financial interlock ties as discussed in Chapter 3.

[22]Again, I caution against a strict interpretation of statistical significance here given the ambiguity of the number of independent observations used to compute the w_{ji} (see footnote 9). I am reporting routine statistical tests of significance as if each industry-to-sector relation were independently observed. Routine tests will overstate significance to the extent that these observations are interdependent.

TABLE 4.6

Predicting Directorate Tie Frequency from Market Constraint Intensity: Two-Digit Results[a]

w_{ji}	α	β Raw	β Standardized	t-test	Log score r	Mean	Standard deviation
Nonfinancial sectors (N = 855)							
Owned establishments	1.454	−23.989	−.438	14.2	.31	1.643	2.123
Direct interlock ties	3.994	−32.551	−.222	6.6	.18	4.250	5.688
Indirect financial interlock ties	19.647	−190.481	−.277	8.4	.20	21.147	26.685
Sources of severe market constraint (N = 83)							
Owned establishments	3.526	−13.960	−.440	4.4	.34	4.554	3.295
Direct interlock ties	6.100	−20.553	−.372	3.6	.33	7.615	5.742
Indirect financial interlock ties	33.145	−116.446	−.381	3.7	.33	41.723	31.724

[a]Parameters are specified in Eq. (4.4), and the regression line of predicted direct interlock ties to sources of severe constraint is given as a bold line in Figure 4.6. Parameters have been estimated by ordinary least-squares where the mean market constraint is − .0079 for the 855 nonfinancial relations and − .0737 for the 83 severe constraint relations (respective standard deviations of .0388 and .1038). In order to compute log scores, w_{ji} have been increased by one, and the typically negative a_{ji} have been subtracted from one before taking logarithms. The sources of severe market constraint are identified on pages 119–120.

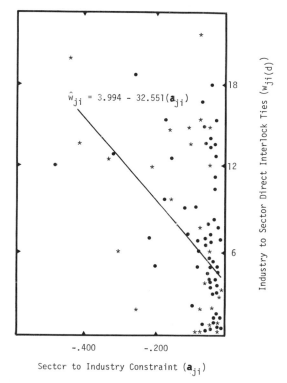

Figure 4.6. Extraindustry direct interlock ties as a function of market constraint: two-digit results (dots and asterisks are all severe market constraints).

the 83 severe market constraints used to compute the results in the lower half of Table 4.6. Sources of severe constraint are presented instead of all 855 nonfinancial relations in order to keep the graph simple. Very similar graphs are obtained for ownership and indirect interlock ties. As in Figure 4.3, relations involving one of the six repressed industries are marked with asterisks. The graph illustrates two points about the association between w_{ji} and a_{ji}.

First, there is no striking difference between relations involving repressed industries and those involving unrepressed industries. The asterisks in Figure 4.6 are scattered throughout the distribution of the data. Recomputing the standardized values of β in Table 4.6 using 256 relations a_{ji} for repressed industries j (as opposed to the 855 relations used in Table 4.6) yields estimates of $-.52$, $-.24$, and $-.30$, respectively, for ownership ties, direct interlock ties, and indirect financial interlock ties. Using 599 relations for unrepressed industries yields corresponding estimates of $-.39$, $-.19$, and $-.24$ for the three types of directorate ties. These effects show the pattern found in Table 4.6 of a strong association for ownership ties and equal, but weaker, associations for the two types of interlock ties. There is clearly no tendency for the industries repressed by oligopolistic consumers to have been less able than unrepressed industries to respond to market constraint with directorate ties. I shall return to this point with the four-digit data.

Second, it would not be correct to say that directorate ties only occurred as a function of market constraint. The least intense market constraints are found to the extreme right-hand side of the graph in Figure 4.6. There are several instances of direct interlock ties occurring with high frequency among these negligible constraints. This feature is true in similar graphs of ownership ties and indirect financial interlock ties, but it is particularly true of interlock ties as is reflected in the weaker correlations reported in Table 4.6 for interlock ties. This tendency is even more apparent in a graph including negligible constraints since all of the negligible constraints fall into a narrow band to the far right of the graph but directorate ties were often frequent. I interpret these high frequencies, in part, to be a result of directorate ties overstating cooptive relations. This point has already been discussed earlier in the chapter. It seems appropriate here because there were not equally numerous instances of low frequency directorate tie relations occurring with severe constraint. The data distribution in Figure 4.6—and this is a feature of all graphs of w_{ji} versus $\mathbf{a}_{ji}$—is triangular rather than square. Observations are conspicuously absent in the lower left-hand corner of the graph.

As with the intraindustry results, the patterning of extraindustry directorate ties by extraindustry market constraint is much more a tendency than an absolute. There is a significant tendency for all three types of directorate ties to have been infrequent in the absence of severe constraint and to have increased in frequency in proportion to constraint intensity. The principal component in a quantitative function relating directorate tie frequency to the market constraint intensity posed by a sector is the linear association expressed by β in Eq. (4.4).

There is a minor qualification to this conclusion. The linear association need not be robust over especially severe market constraint. Five of the 860 nonfinancial market relations to two-digit industries have been excluded from the above analysis. This is why there are 855 and 83 relations in Table 4.6 rather than the full 860 and 88 available. All 5 are among the 88 severe market constraints identified earlier in the chapter and are given in parentheses in Table A.4 of the Appendix. Two of them involve repressed industries: the constraint posed by the textiles industry for apparel and that posed by the apparel industry for textiles. The remaining three involve unrepressed industries: constraint on the food industry from the livestock sector, constraint on the tobacco industry from the other agriculture sector, and constraint on the petroleum industry from the crude petroleum and natural gas sector. These five relations had three qualities worth noting. First, they are clearly outliers from the association expressed by Eq.

(4.4). They represent a small proportion of all nonfinancial relations considered (0.5%), and they represent extreme levels of constraint. They represent an average a_{ji} of $-.683$ versus the $-.008$ average for the 855 other nonfinancial constraints or the $-.073$ average for the other 83 severe market constraints. The most severe among the five outliers is almost three times as severe as the most severe constraint represented in Figure 4.6 (-1.353 versus $-.481$). Despite the severity of constraint they represent, directorate ties were comparatively infrequent in response to them. The five w_{ji} corresponding to these five severe a_{ji} average 2.4 ownership ties, .4 direct interlock ties, and 6.8 indirect financial interlock ties. This is point two. Although outliers, directorate ties are not completely absent. Industries were responding to these constraints, but not in proportion to their severity. The apparel and textiles industries were connected by all three types of directorate ties. Two-thirds of the petroleum industry establishments was owned by firms that also owned crude petroleum and natural gas establishments.[23] In short, the five particularly severe constraints do not reject the linear association between extraindustry ties and constraint and are insufficiently numerous to warrant a curvilinear alternative to it. A third point about them, however, provides a clue to a systematic feature of the association between extraindustry ties and constraint.

This clue concerns the importance of supplier constraint. This third point is that four of the five outlier relations in the two-digit data reflected supplier, rather than consumer, constraint. The food industry depended on the livestock sector for meat supplies. The tobacco industry depended on the other agriculture sector for tobacco leaf. The apparel industry depended on the textiles industry for cloth. The petroleum industry depended on the crude petroleum and natural gas sector for the raw product it refined and distributed. There is no tendency for industries repressed by constraint from oligopolistic consumers to have been less able than unrepressed industries to respond with directorate ties to extraindustry market constraint. However, the constraint of dependence on a single supplier sector is not a component in the partial derivative $\partial a_j / \partial y_{j1}$ identifying repressed industries. The five outlier relations in the two-digit data call attention to the possible significance of supplier constraint for the maintenance of directorate ties to sources of constraint in proportion to constraint intensity. This possibility is reinforced by an analysis of the two-digit data if supplier and consumer con-

---

[23]No ties in the two-digit sample were recorded between the food and livestock sectors or between the tobacco and other agriculture sectors. It is possible that competition is so intense within the agricultural sectors that food and tobacco establishments have no need to coopt them. It is also possible that existing connections were missed in the sampling or coding of subsidiaries owned by firms operating in the food or tobacco industries. It is also possible that the food and tobacco industries—as the two industries most involved with agriculture—have developed some form of cooptive relation with agriculture other than directorate ties, e.g., long-term purchasing agreements, partial stock ownership, regional market monopolies.

straints are combined, but is clearly indicated by the four-digit data for which more detailed analysis is possible.[24]

The unknown parameters in Eq. (4.4) have been estimated for each of the 322 four-digit industries. In other words, there are 322 estimates of β for each type of directorate tie. The estimated β for any one industry is negative to the extent that the industry was connected by directorate ties to 399 other sectors with a frequency proportional to the market constraint each sector posed for industry profits.[25] The standardized estimates of β, that is, the correlation between $\mathbf{a}_{ji}$ and w_{ji} for industry j, are presented in Figures 4.7, 4.8, and 4.9. The upper graph in each figure presents the distribution of these correlations by the extent to which each industry was constrained by its suppliers ($1 - y_{j7}$; cf. Table 2.4). The lower graph presents the distribution by the extent to which an industry was constrained by its consumers ($1 - y_{j3}$). Graphs for all three types of directorate ties are presented because they show different strengths of association between market constraint and tie frequency. Figure 4.7 reports correlations for the frequency of ownership ties. Figure 4.8 reports correlations for direct interlock ties, and Figure 4.9 reports correlations for indirect financial interlock ties.

As suggested by the five outlier relations in the two-digit data, the strength of the association between tie frequency and constraint intensity varied across the four-digit industries by the extent to which an industry was constrained. Constraint from consumers had little or no effect on the association. The graphs at the bottom of Figures 4.7–4.9 show no systematic tendency for correlations to be less negative at high levels of constraint than at low levels. In other words, as was true of the two-digit data, there is no tendency for industries repressed by oligopolistic consumers to have been less able than unrepressed industries to counter market constraint with directorate ties. On the other hand, constraint from suppliers did lower the association—but only for interlock ties. In the

[24]My earlier analysis of the two-digit data found a strong difference between repressed and unrepressed industries in terms of their ability to develop directorate ties in proportion to market constraint, repressed industries being far less able (Burt, 1980c:161–167). However, that analysis used the initial structural autonomy model [Eq. (2.4)] in which repressed industries were those facing severe market constraint from suppliers and/or consumers. In the model refined here for the four-digit data [Eq. (2.5)], only consumer constraint defines repressed industries [Eq. (2.7)]. Since the association between w_{ji} and $\mathbf{a}_{ji}$ is not lower for repressed industries than it is for unrepressed industries in this analysis and the association was lower in the earlier analysis, it seems likely that supplier constraint is the reason. This inference is clearly supported by the four-digit data to be presented.

[25]Each estimate is based on 399 nonfinancial relations between a four-digit industry and other sectors. Five financial sectors are deleted from the initial 405 sectors: three corporate sectors (banking, credit agencies, insurance carriers) and two brokerage sectors (security and commodity brokers, insurance agents and brokers). Where two or more input–output sectors have been collapsed in computing directorate tie frequencies to an aggregate sector i, $\mathbf{a}_{ji}$ is the mean constraint they posed for industry j (see Chapter 3 on computing directorate tie frequencies to nonmanufacturing sectors).

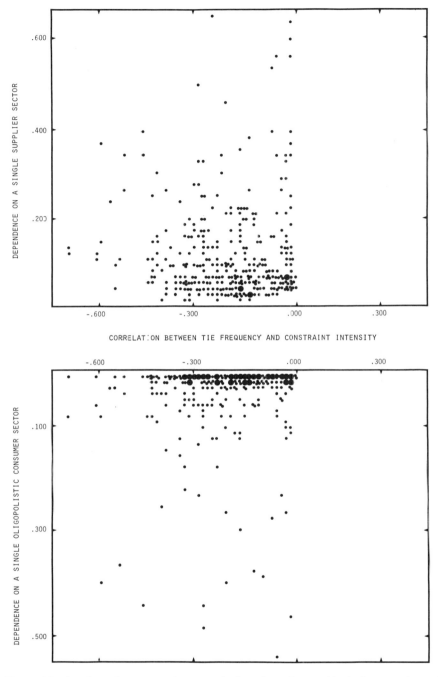

Figure 4.7. Correlation between market constraint intensity and ownership tie frequency by total level of constraint on industry.

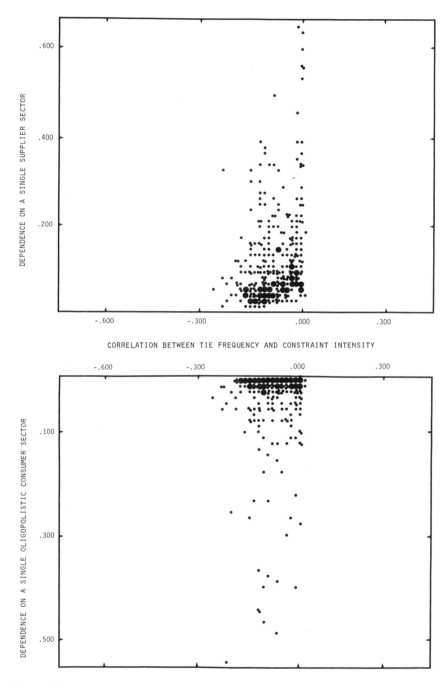

Figure 4.8. Correlation between market constraint intensity and direct interlock tie frequency by total level of constraint on industry.

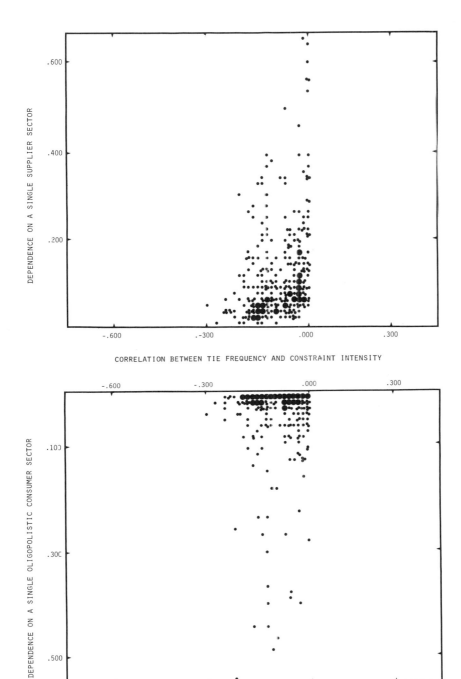

Figure 4.9. Correlation between market constraint intensity and indirect financial interlock tie frequency by total level of constraint on industry.

graphs at the top of Figures 4.7–4.9, note that more and stronger negative values of the association between $\mathbf{a}_{ji}$ and w_{ji} occur when industry j is free from supplier constraint (lower portion of graph) than occur when the industry is severely constrained (upper portion of graph). As one moves from the bottom of the graph to the top, moving across industries increasingly dependent on a single supplier sector, there is a systematic tendency for the correlation between market constraint intensity and directorate tie frequency to become less negative. For ownership ties this tendency is negligible, but for interlock ties it is significant at well beyond the .001 level of confidence. On average, a .1 increase in the extent to which an industry relied on a single supplier sector (i.e., a .1 increase in $1 - y_{j7}$) is associated with a .05 decrease in the magnitude of the correlation between extraindustry market constraints and interlock tie frequencies.[26]

A much more obvious feature of the distributions in Figures 4.7–4.9 is the tendency for w_{ji} to be negatively correlated with $\mathbf{a}_{ji}$. In each graph, the distribution of correlations is clearly to the negative side of zero. In fact, it rarely exceeds zero. In other words, there is a clear tendency for directorate tie frequencies to have increased with increasingly severe market constraint on the four-digit industries.

Table 4.7 summarizes the average prediction of tie frequencies from market constraints on an industry by industry basis. Given an estimate of β in Eq. (4.4) for each of the 322 four-digit industries, Table 4.7 presents the mean value of $\hat{\beta}$ across all industries. Reflecting the larger number of firms in the four-digit sample and the resulting geometric increase in interlock ties among establishments, the mean estimates of β in Table 4.7 are higher than corresponding estimates in the two-digit data. As was true of the two-digit data, these estimates are clearly negative.

Reflecting the strength of this negative association, Table 4.7 presents statistical tests implying that the negative estimates of β are significantly different from zero at well beyond the .001 level of confidence. The analysis of variance F-ratios are quite large, implying a significant amount of variation in directorate tie frequencies is accounted for by market constraint intensity. With the enormous

---

[26]These statements are based on a regression of the correlation between constraint intensity, $\mathbf{a}_{ji}$, and tie frequency, w_{ji}, for industry j over the extent to which the industry relied on a single supplier, $1 - y_{j7}$:

$$r_j = a + b(1 - y_{j7}) + e_j,$$

where r_j is the correlation between $\mathbf{a}_{ji}$ and w_{ji} for industry j. The estimates of b for ownership ties, direct interlock ties, and indirect financial interlock ties, respectively, are .015, .466, and .510 (with t-tests of 0.4, 5.0, and 6.3). Standardized values of b, the correlations between r_j and supplier constraint, are .02, .27, and .33, respectively, for the three types of directorate ties. With increasing supplier constraint, the typically negative association between market constraint intensity and interlock tie frequency becomes increasingly positive.

TABLE 4.7
Predicting Directorate Tie Frequency from Market Constraint Intensity: Four-Digit Results[a]

	β		Predicted sum of squares	Combined sum of squares	F-ratio
	Mean	99% confidence interval			
Ownership ties	−48.505	−64.5 to −32.6	7037	98,225	9181.2
Direct interlock ties	−237.505	−326.0 to −149.0	227,331	21,604,484	1348.5
Indirect financial interlock ties	2369.374	−3292.4 to −1446.4	18,938,788	1,053,347,600	2346.3

[a] Ordinary least-squares estimates on the β in Eq. (4.4) have been obtained for each industry and averaged across the 322 industries to obtain the mean β reported. Industry-specific estimates of β when standardized are given in Figures 4.7–4.9; confidence intervals are based on the variation in estimated betas across industries (see footnote 27), and the F-ratio is distributed with (1; 128,154) degrees of freedom (see footnote 28).

number of relations being considered, it would be difficult for any association not to be significant. This point makes the graphs in Figures 4.7–4.9 helpful once again. Regardless of ambiguities in the actual number of independent observations involved in computing statistical tests here, the distributions in Figures 4.7–4.9 show that a negative association between tie frequency and constraint intensity was characteristic of all four-digit industries. The observed variation in estimates of β across industries has been used to place a confidence interval around the mean estimate of β.[27] These results are presented in Table 4.7 as 99% confidence interval estimates of β and are all well below zero. There is clearly a negative association between $\mathbf{a}_{ji}$ and w_{ji}.[28]

As was true of the two-digit data, the strength of the association between tie

[27]Degrees of freedom problems are raised in footnotes 9 and 22 of this chapter. Using the standard deviations of the data distributions in Figures 4.7–4.9 to compute standard errors for the mean estimates in Table 4.7 yields standard errors of 6.161, 34.157, and 356.095 for ownership ties, direct interlock ties, and indirect financial interlock ties, respectively. An estimated mean β in Table 4.7 plus or minus 2.592 times the appropriate standard error defines the 99% confidence interval estimate in the table.

[28]In fact, the estimates of β in Table 4.7 are conservative in expressing the association between $\mathbf{a}_{ji}$ and w_{ji}. The covariation between $\mathbf{a}_{ji}$ and w_{ji} across industries has two components. One component results from covariation within each industry's relations with other sectors:

$$SS_w = \sum_i (\mathbf{a}_{ji} - \bar{\mathbf{a}}_j)(w_{ji} - \bar{w}_j),$$

where $i \neq j$, and $\bar{w}_j$ and $\bar{\mathbf{a}}_j$ are means for industry j computed across its relations with the other 399 nonfinancial sectors i. The second component results from covariation between the mean constraint facing an industry from other sectors ($\bar{\mathbf{a}}_j$) and its mean frequency of directorate ties to those sectors ($\bar{w}_j$):

$$SS_m = \sum_j (\bar{\mathbf{a}}_j - \bar{\mathbf{a}})(\bar{w}_j - \bar{w}),$$

across js where $\bar{w}$ and $\bar{\mathbf{a}}$ are means computed across all industries and all sectors. By computing regression coefficients for Eq. (4.4) on an industry by industry basis, the second covariance component is ignored. The estimated betas in Table 4.7 are determined by SS_w without regard to SS_m. Since the analysis in Chapter 8 shows that there is a tendency for industries confronted by market constraint to have been extensively involved in directorate ties, SS_m is nonnegligible and the estimates in Table 4.7 understate the association between $\mathbf{a}_{ji}$ and w_{ji} as it is described for the two-digit industries. This nonnegligible covariance is deleted from the F-ratios in Table 4.7. In other words, it is considered neither explained (as it should be) nor residual. The F-ratios are obtained by comparing the mean predicted sum of squares, $SS_w/1$, to the mean sum of squares not predicted by market constraint, SS_r/df_r, where SS_r is the residual variation in directorate ties ($\sum_j \sum_i (w_{ji} - \bar{w}_j) - SS_w$, $i \neq j$), and df_r equals the number of relations not used in the prediction ($322 \times 399 - 2 - 322$). The final subtraction of 322 degrees of freedom is required since means have been computed for each industry and removed from the sum of squares. In other words, SS_m is deleted from consideration. The F-ratios reported in Table 4.7 are then computed as $SS_w df_r/SS_r$ and distributed with (1; 128,154) degrees of freedom under the hypothesis that $\mathbf{a}_{ji}$ is independent of w_{ji} within each industry j. Although the results in Table 4.7 are conservative, they provide the flexibility of analyzing changes in $\hat{\beta}$ across industries and show a strong association between tie frequency and constraint intensity.

frequency and constraint intensity varied in the four-digit data across the types of directorate ties. Ownership ties were most closely patterned by market constraint and direct interlock ties were least patterned. Indirect interlock ties through financial institutions were more strongly patterned by constraint than direct interlock ties; however, both types of interlock ties were far less strongly associated with constraint than were ownership ties. In Tables 4.6 and 4.7, the strongest statistical tests for significant difference from zero are reported for ownership ties, weaker tests are reported for indirect financial interlock ties, and much weaker tests are reported for direct interlock ties. This point is made more vividly by the graphs in Figures 4.7–4.9. The industry-specific correlations for ownership ties (Figure 4.7) spread much further into negative values than do correlations for either of the interlock ties—although the correlations for indirect financial interlock ties spread further to the left of the graphs than do the correlations for direct interlock ties (Figure 4.9 versus Figure 4.8).

In summary, extraindustry directorate ties were patterned by market constraint, but the patterning—as was true of directorate ties within industries—represents a small, statistically nonnegligible portion of variation in tie frequencies. The association between tie frequency and constraint intensity is a simple linear one. Directorate ties occurred frequently between industry and sector to the extent that the sector posed a severe market constraint for industry profits. Ownership ties were most closely patterned by market constraint. The association between constraint intensity and the frequency of interlock ties is not only weaker on average, it is further weakened by supplier constraint. With increasing industry dependence on a single sector for supplies, the association between market constraint intensity and the two types of interlock ties weakens. Increasing industry dependence on a single oligopolistic consumer sector, in contrast, has no effect on the association.

COOPTIVE SUCCESS

It seems clear that the three types of directorate ties were patterned in 1967 as if they were intended to coopt sources of market constraint. This does not mean, however, that establishments in every industry were equally successful in coopting sources of market constraint. To the extent that those in some industries were more successful than establishments in other industries, ''successful'' cooptation should have translated into unexpectedly high profits.

This idea can be stated explicitly in terms of the analysis of market constraint in Chapter 2. Differences in industry profit margins were explained in terms of differences in market constraint. Establishments within an industry providing high structural autonomy were able to obtain correspondingly high profit margins. The proposed network model did not consider directorate ties as cooptive relations among establishments. But where establishments in an industry managed to circumvent market constraint on their industry—circumvent it in the sense of having directorate ties with the sources of constraint as described in Chapter 3—the network model overstates constraint *actually* imposed on the industry. The model assumes that all transactions represented in an input–output table are conducted on the open market. It is then used to determine the *potential* constraint posed for industry profits by its suppliers and consumers. By moving some or all of their market transactions with sector i off the open market and into the nonmarket context created by directorate ties, industry establishments need not be subject to all of the potential market constraint sector i posed for the industry. In other words, where establishments in industry j were able to develop cooptive directorate ties as of 1967 with sectors constraining industry profits, $\mathbf{a}_j$ is a conservatively biased prediction of the industry profit margin. The profit margin should have been higher than $\mathbf{a}_j$ since ostensible market constraints considered in predicting $\mathbf{a}_j$ had been circumvented. In this situation, the residual term in the prediction of profit margins should be positive ($p_j - \mathbf{a}_j = e_j > 0$) showing that the industry had a higher profit margin than would have been expected from the pattern of market transactions defining its network position in the economy.

This error in prediction is itself predictable from the estimated market constraints. The increased profit margin to be expected in industry j if buying and selling with sector i is never connected on the open market is negative two times the raw market constraint sector i posed for the industry ($-2a_{ji}^*$).[29] Under the assumption that the presence of ownership ties, direct interlock ties, and indirect financial interlock ties between industry j and sector i provided sufficient cooptive relations for establishments in the industry to circumvent market constraint from the sector, let w_{ji} be a crude measure of cooptation: w_{ji} equals zero unless all three types of directorate ties connected industry j and sector i, whereupon w_{ji} equals one. The product $-2a_{ji}^*w_{ji}$ is the increased profit margin in industry j to be expected by having coopted sector i. A measure of the overall increase to be expected by circumventing market constraints through directorate ties is then the sum of these products across all sectors i for which $\mathbf{a}_{ji}$ is negative[30]:

$$d(\mathbf{a}_j) = \Sigma_i - 2a_{ji}^*w_{ji} \qquad \text{for all} \quad \mathbf{a}_{ji} < 0. \qquad (4.5)$$

---

[29]Recall that the market constraint coefficient $\mathbf{a}_{ji}$ equals $2a_{ji}^*/\mathbf{a}_j$ as the marginal increase in industry profit margin to be expected by conducting all buying and selling with sector i in a controlled, nonmarket context. The numerator in this ratio is the absolute increase expected and is the focus in Eq. (4.5). Interpreting $2a_{ji}^*$ in this manner assumes that the partial derivatives in Eqs. (2.12) and (2.13) are true for large and small changes in sales to sector i, z_{ji} and purchases from sector i, z_{ij}.

[30]This summation automatically excludes the industry j itself since a_{jj}^* is always positive. Other measures have been considered and are discussed in the following as implying the same conclusion reached with this simple measure.

This index of successful cooptation will be high when establishments in industry j were subject to severe potential market constraints but had successfully developed ownership ties, direct interlock ties, and indirect financial interlock ties with those sectors that were the sources of that constraint. The error in predicting industry profits is expected to be high when industry establishments had cooptive relations with their suppliers and consumers. Accordingly, a high value of $d(\mathbf{a}_j)$ should have resulted in a high value of the error e_j.

There is modest empirical support for this idea. Values of $d(\mathbf{a}_j)$ have been computed for the two-digit and four-digit industries. At both levels of aggregation, the index of successful cooptation is positively correlated with the extent to which industry profit margin exceeds the value predicted from market structure; however, the correlation is very weak. At the two-digit industry level, e_j and $d(\mathbf{a}_j)$ are correlated .032; they are correlated .095 at the four-digit industry level. The correlation obtained from the two-digit data is negligible. That obtained from the four-digit data is obviously low in magnitude, but it is significantly greater than zero at the .04 level of confidence. Table 4.8 presents correlates of the index $d(\mathbf{a}_j)$ that suggest a reason for the low correlations observed.

The first three rows of Table 4.8 show that successful cooptation has a very weak association with excess profits and a negative association with observed profits. The weak correlations between e_j and $d(\mathbf{a}_j)$ are presented. These represent the correlation between p_j and $d(\mathbf{a}_j)$ after the market structure indicators in

TABLE 4.8
Successful Cooptation, Industry Performance, and Market Constraint[a]

	Successful cooptation	
Correlates	Two-digit $d(\mathbf{a}_j)$ ($N = 20$)	Four-digit $d(\mathbf{a}_j)$ ($N = 322$)
Industry performance		
Observed profit margin (p_j)	−.359	−.098
Excess profit margin (e_j)	.032	.095
Direct effect on profit margin	.444	.117
	(0.6)	(1.8)
Extraindustry market constraint		
Consumer constraint ($1 - y_{j3}$)	.741	.106
Supplier constraint ($1 - y_{j7}$)	.148	.314
Aggregate constraint	.772	.316

[a]Correlations are presented. Indices are explained in the text. Correlations with aggregate constraint are multiple correlations between successful cooptation, $d(\mathbf{a}_j)$ and three constraint variables: y_{j3}, y_{j7}, and the interaction term with consumer constraint $(y_{j1} - \bar{y}_1)(y_{j3} - \bar{y}_3)$. The direct effect of successful cooptation on the industry profit margin is the regression coefficient for $d(\mathbf{a}_j)$ when it is added to the prediction of industry profits in Eq. (2.5). The t-test for the direct effect is given in parentheses.

Eq. (2.5) have been held constant. Against the possibility that $d(\mathbf{a}_j)$ had a significant direct effect on profit margins, $d(\mathbf{a}_j)$ was added to the market structure variables used to predict profit margins (i.e., the certainty measure of industry oligopoly y_{j1}, the supplier constraint measure y_{j7}, the consumer constraint measure y_{j3}, and the interaction between y_{j1} and y_{j3}) in Eq. (2.5). The t-tests for this direct effect merely corroborate the inference to be made from the correlations between e_j and $d(\mathbf{a}_j)$. There is a negligible positive effect among two-digit industries and a weak, but nonnegligible, positive effect among four-digit industries. The first row of Table 4.8 shows that successful cooptation has a negative association with observed profits. The last three rows of the table offer an explanation.

The last three rows of Table 4.8 show that successful cooptation has a strong positive association with the level of extraindustry market constraint an industry confronted. These correlations are much stronger than the correlations with profit measures. To the extent that an industry depended on a single oligopolistic consumer sector, it tended to be cooptively successful. To the extent that it relied on a single sector for its supplies, it was cooptively successful. Further, the correlations between extraindustry market constraint and successful cooptation are proportional to the strength of the association between industry profits and the constraint measures. Consumer constraint $(1 - y_{j3})$ is a stronger predictor of two-digit industry profit margins than is supplier constraint $(1 - y_{j7})$ and has the stronger correlation with $d(\mathbf{a}_j)$ in Table 4.8 (cf. Table 2.6). Supplier constraint is a stronger predictor of four-digit industry profit margins than is consumer constraint and has the stronger correlation with $d(\mathbf{a}_j)$ in Table 4.8 (again, cf. Table 2.6).

My conclusion from these results is that the index of successful cooptation is in fact an ersatz measure of the aggregate market constraint an industry confronted from other sectors. This explains the strong positive correlations between $d(\mathbf{a}_j)$ and the indices of supplier and consumer constraint, correlations proportional to the weight given these indices in predicting industry profits. It also explains the negative correlations between $d(\mathbf{a}_j)$ and observed profit margins, margins being low in industries confronted with massive market constraint. And it also explains the weak correlations between $d(\mathbf{a}_j)$ and excess profits e_j. The market constraint indices are contained in the equation predicting profit margins for which e_j is a residual. Accordingly, they have no correlation with e_j as the residual term and $d(\mathbf{a}_j)$ as an ersatz measure of market constraint has little correlation with e_j.

In other words, establishments were successful in coopting constraint sectors with ODI multiplex ties to the extent that constraint existed to be coopted. In order for the index of successful cooptation, $d(\mathbf{a}_j)$, to have a strong positive correlation with profits, there must be variability in the cooptive success of establishments in different industries—cooptive success not only in the magnitude of constraint coopted [this is the condition captured by $d(\mathbf{a}_j)$, which does vary across industries] but also in the extent to which sources of constraint are coopted. There was little variability of the second type in 1967. There tended to be ODI multiplex directorate tie relations between each industry and sectors constraining profits in the industry. Since directorate ties were pervasive and patterned by market structure, their patterning among establishments adds little to the prediction of industry profit margins by market structure alone. This same conclusion extends to other measures of the extent to which industries were connected by potentially cooptive relations with sources of constraint. The results in Table 4.8 are replicated with merger data (Burt, 1980a) as well as alternative measures of $a(\mathbf{a}_j)$ focusing only on the severe constraints identified in the beginning of the chapter or focusing only on the absence of ODI multiplex ties. To the extent that any type of potentially cooptive interestablishment relation is strongly patterned by market structure, in short, successful cooptation as the level of market constraint coopted becomes an ersatz measure of market structure itself.

SUMMARY

The structure of directorate ties in 1967 was patterned by the structure of market constraints. There was, however, a great deal more variation in directorate ties than could be accounted for by market constraints. An apt summary here is that a small, statistically nonnegligible amount of variation in directorate tie structure is accounted for by market constraint. More to the point, directorate ties were systematically patterned by market constraint as if they were being used as cooptive relations to sources of constraint. This point has been demonstrated in three ways.

Qualitatively, the absence of directorate ties was contingent on market constraint. All three types of directorate ties tended to be absent between an industry and sectors having a negligible effect on industry profits. Where a sector had no effect on profits in a four-digit industry, the simultaneous absence of ownership ties, direct interlock ties, and indirect financial interlock ties occurred five times as often as would be expected from the tendencies for these null ties and negligible constraint to occur in the economy generally. There is a strong tendency for the three types of directorate ties to have occurred together, industry and sector being connected by ownership tie(s), direct interlock tie(s), and indirect financial interlock tie(s) simultaneously. No other combination of the types of directorate ties was as likely to occur as these ODI multiplex ties. Nevertheless, these ODI ties tended to be absent in the absence of constraint. Where a sector had no effect on profits in a four-digit industry, ODI multiplex ties occurred only a third as often between industry and sector as would be expected by the strong tendencies for both conditions to occur in the economy generally.

Not only was the absence of directorate ties contingent on market constraint, the quantitative frequency with which establishments in industry and sector were connected by directorate ties is a function of the severity of the market constraint posed by the sector for industry profits. The association is a simple linear one. Directorate ties occurred frequently between industry and sector to the extent that the sector posed a severe market constraint for industry profits. Ownership ties were most closely patterned by market constraint. The association between constraint intensity and frequency of interlock ties is not only weaker on average, it is further weakened by supplier constraint. With increasing industry dependence on a single sector for supplies, the association between market constraint intensity and the two types of interlock ties weakens. Increasing industry dependence on a single oligopolistic consumer sector, in contrast, has no effect on the association. Among establishments within an industry, directorate tie frequency has a kinked association with industry competition. Within highly competitive industries there was no hope for a small number of establishments to control industry prices. There were few large firms within these industries and few interlock ties. With decreasing competition, large firms were attracted to the industry and interlock ties occurred among industry establishments with an exponentially increasing frequency. Directorate ties were most frequent in industries where control over industry prices would have been most uncertain (i.e., in moderately competitive industries). This is not to say that directorate ties were especially frequent in every moderately competitive industry. When the highest frequencies did occur, they tended to occur in moderately competitive industries. Past the maximum reached in these industries, the association is reversed. As a small number of firms became increasingly dominant within an industry so as to increase industry concentration, decrease industry competition, and accordingly lower the uncertainty of their control over industry prices, they had less need for interlock ties with one another in order to coordinate their pricing decisions. Past an average level of industry competition, large firms were attracted to the industry and interlock ties occurred among industry establishments with an exponentially decreasing frequency. There were systematic deviations from this curvilinear association. The deviations too suggest a market constraint foundation for directorate ties. Among highly competitive industries, interlock ties were frequent within industries free from oligopolistic consumers. This freedom provided both a market incentive for cooptive relations among industry establishments and the market tranquility to maintain them. Profitable increases in control over industry prices were to be expected from being involved in such ties. At the other extreme of industry competition, interlock ties were infrequent within relatively oligopolistic industries—but frequent within those industries confronting oligopolistic consumers. This constraint from consumers posed a threat to industry control over industry prices, so there was advantage to maintaining intraindustry interlock ties despite industry oligopoly.

Finally, there was intriguingly modest support for the idea that having directorate ties with sources of market constraint increased industry profits. The two-digit results are negligible. However, the four-digit results imply that a non-negligible increase in industry profit margins could have resulted from successful cooptation. The extent to which the profit margin observed in an industry exceeded the margin expected from market structure alone is positively correlated with the extent to which ODI multiplex relations connected the industry to sectors posing the most severe constraint on industry profits. Moreover, successful cooptation had a unique positive effect on industry profit margins when the market constraint indicators are held constant. On the other hand, much stronger correlations are obtained between successful cooptation and the market constraint indicators themselves. With every industry maintaining ODI multiplex relations with sources of market constraint, successful cooptation is more a measure of the constraint available to be coopted than it is a measure of success relative to other industries. In other words, the weak association between successful cooptation and profit margins is yet further evidence of the fact that directorate ties were patterned by market constraints.

5

Conclusions and Speculations

Evidence of both managed and open competition has been found in the American economy. I have focused on ties through boards of directors as a general class of potentially cooptive relations through which competition within the economy could have been managed. I have focused on the buying and selling activities of manufacturing industries as the variably competitive market relations to be managed. These foci have been brought together in a simple question: Were corporate boards of directors used in the 1967 American economy as a device for managing competition to control uncertainty in corporate profits? Given the evidence, my answer is a qualified yes.

Affirmative answers to this question are not difficult to find in directorate research; however, the traditional analysis presents no systematic evidence to justify such an answer. The traditional analysis describes the existence of directorate ties—the structure and cooptive potential of directorate ties—without explicitly linking those ties to market constraints on corporate profits. Directorate ties do have the potential to coopt sources of market constraint, and they are extensive in the American economy. Thus the traditional analysis concludes on a pessimistic note. Witness the following, drawn from a U.S. Senate study in which the directorates of large American firms were once again found to be interlocked extensively (Turner, 1978):

Such interlocking directorates among the Nation's very largest corporations may provide mechanisms for stabilizing prices, controlling supply and restraining competition. They can have a profound effect on business attempts to influence Government policies. They can impact on corporate decisions as to the type and quality of products and services to be marketed in the United States and overseas. They can influence company policies with respect to employee rights, compensation and job conditions. They can bear on corporate policies with respect to environmental and social issues and possibly, control the shape and direction of the Nation's economy [pp. 280–281].

There is evidence to support these statements as descriptions of possibilities, but there is no systematic evidence in the traditional analysis to support them as facts. Note the verbs of action in the quoted material: may provide, can effect, can possibly control. These are verbs expressing the cooptive potential of directorate ties. There is no systematic evidence to support the use of verbs expressing the actual use of directorate ties as cooptive relations: do provide, do effect, do control. It would be impossible to gather and process data on all ties so as to be able to describe the extent to which ties are actually used in a cooptive manner. Short of that ideal, however, it would be possible to gather data on the market relations actually constraining corporate profits so as to describe the extent to which ties occur in places where it would be especially profitable for firms to abuse the cooptive potential of directorate ties. Like instinct theories of action, in other words, cooptive interpretations of directorate ties have high face validity and provide a sociological label for such ties—but they do not provide a criterion in terms of which directorate ties could be evaluated as cooptive relations to sources of market constraint.

The network perspective adopted in this study underlies two fundamental departures from traditional directorate research. First, the coordination of different types of directorate ties has been analyzed in terms of multiplexity in cooptive corporate networks. Second, a relatively unsophisticated network model of structural autonomy has been used to guide the analysis in terms of its definition of constraint. The model provides one definition of a crucial element missing in the traditional analysis of directorate ties. That missing element is the criterion market constraint that cooptive directorate ties purportedly hold in rein.

FIVE SUMMARY CONCLUSIONS

Without repeating details given in the summary sections of the preceding chapters, I draw five general conclusions from the evidence that has been presented.

Market Constraint Relations   The aggregate profit margin in an industry was significantly determined by the intensity of market constraints on the structural autonomy of industry establishments (Chapter 2).

An industry's pattern of buying and selling indicated the intensity and sources of market constraint on the industry. The analysis in Chapter 2 describes how an industry profit margin increased with the extent to which a small number of firms could control industry prices with certainty. This ability increased with (a) increasing domination of the industry by a small number of large firms, (b) decreasing reliance on a single supplier sector, and (c) decreasing reliance on sales to a single oligopolistic consumer sector.

> **Multiplex Directorate Tie Relations** Different types of potentially cooptive interorganizational ties through corporate boards of directors tended to be coordinated as multiplex ties between economic sectors (Chapter 3).

A sector reached by one type of tie tended to be reached by others whether a firm or an industry was the source of ties. Three types of directorate ties have been distinguished in Chapter 3 as potentially cooptive in the sense of providing a nonmarket context for transacting necessary buying and selling: ties through ownership, ties through interlocking directorates, and indirect interlock ties through financial institutions as intermediaries. As demonstrated in Chapter 3, the firms most extensively involved in these ties, and most extensively coordinating them as multiplex ties to diverse sectors, were large firms controlled by diffuse interest groups.

> **Intraindustry Cooptation** Directorate ties among establishments within an industry were patterned by market constraint (Chapter 4).

The frequency of ties had a kinked, exponential association with the intensity of competition in the industry. Ties were especially infrequent within highly competitive and comparatively oligopolistic industries. In the former, directorate ties could not provide a great marginal increase in control over industry prices by a small number of firms. In the latter industries, oligopolistic firms had no need for directorate ties in order to coordinate their pricing decisions and so determine industry prices. The highest frequency in directorate ties occurred in industries where control over industry prices would have been most uncertain—in moderately competitive industries.

Extraindustry market constraint created systematic deviations from this kinked association. Freedom from the constraint of oligopolistic consumers provided market incentives for cooptive relations among establishments in highly competitive industries. Although infrequent within highly competitive industries on average, directorate ties occurred with high frequency within such industries in the absence of oligopolistic consumers. Although infrequent within comparatively oligopolistic industries, directorate ties occurred with high frequency within such industries threatened by the constraint of oligopolistic consumers.

Extraindustry Cooptation   Directorate ties between establishments in separate sectors were patterned by market constraint (Chapter 4).

The three types of directorate ties tended to be simultaneously absent between establishments in an industry and establishments in a sector posing negligible market constraint for industry profits. Further, the frequency with which each type of directorate tie was observed between an industry and sector is a function of the severity of the constraint posed by the sector for industry profits. With increasingly severe constraint, the industry and sector were connected by increasingly frequent directorate ties. More specifically, increasing sector oligopoly and increasing industry dependency on the sector for purchases and supplies was associated with increasingly frequent ownership ties, direct interlock ties, and indirect financial interlock ties between industry and sector.

Cooptive Success   The presence of multiplex directorate ties to sectors constraining industry profits does not explain why profit margins in some industries were higher than would have been expected from market structure alone (Chapter 4).

There is some evidence of profits increasing from successful cooptation. There is much stronger evidence of successful cooptation being an ersatz measure of the magnitude of constraint to be coopted; the more constraint that suppliers and consumers posed for industry profits, the more constraint industry establishments could have circumvented through their strategically located directorate ties to those suppliers or consumers.

In short, directorate ties were patterned in the 1967 American economy as if they were intended to control uncertainty in industry profits. They appeared between an industry and sector to the extent that the sector posed a market constraint for industry profits. Since these ties occurred between every industry and those sectors constraining industry profits, however, no industry gained singular advantage from them in the sense of obtaining unusual profits. Interindustry differences in successful cooptation account for some differences in industry profit margins above and beyond predictions by market structure alone, but the added prediction is very weak. This does not rule out the possibility that directorate ties changed the nature of competition in the economy, but it does show that the mere strategic placement of such ties did not distinguish unusually profitable manufacturing industries from industries in which low profits were typically obtained.

THE DIRECTORATE TIE MARKET

The lack of a direct effect on industry profit margins from industry differences in successful cooptation need not mean that directorate ties had no effect on the nature of competition in the economy. By creating a nonmarket context in which necessary buying and selling could be transacted and by occurring wherever especially competitive market transactions had to be carried out, directorate ties could have ensured that little of the most competitive buying and selling actually occurred on the open market. Rather, such transactions would have been conducted between favored trade partners detected through directorate ties as described in Chapter 3. Establishments without directorate ties to constraint sectors would have been forced to conduct their buying and selling on the open market—a business context fraught with the profit constraints described in Chapter 2. In other words, directorate ties to sources of market constraint could have been a necessary precursor to corporate survival rather than an opportunity for exploiting market transactions to obtain unusual profits.

It is interesting to consider the implications of this being true. A whole new class of unanticipated corporate constraints would have to be recognized as a second market, a social mirror of the economic market. The economic market would consist of buying and selling commodities. The second market, a social market, would consist of interorganizational directorate ties. It is clear from the analysis in Chapter 4 that directorate ties were patterned by market constraint, but there were many ties occurring in the absence of constraint. I shall refer to the former class of directorate ties as relations in a directorate tie market, a social network of cooptive relations providing nonmarket contexts for what would otherwise be the most constrained buying and selling. When a directorate tie occurs with a severe market constraint, it is a component in this directorate tie market. It is a tie occurring in a structural context in which there is an economic incentive for a cooptive relation. When a tie occurs in the absence of constraint, it is not a component in the directorate tie market.

There is analytical value in recognizing the directorate tie market. At the very least, recognition of such a market focuses analytical attention on those directorate ties through which it would be most profitable for business establishments to manage competitive forces in the economic market. It is the relations in this social network of a market that are most likely to be fruitful sites for research on strategies of corporate cooptation.

Turning to the substantive implications of a directorate tie market, the necessary involvement of establishments in a directorate tie market could raise or lower their efficiency in manufacturing products. This, in turn, would raise or lower the efficiency of the economy as a whole. My inference is that a directorate tie market increases the efficiency of the economic market but not by as much as it could. This inference is more than a simple compromise between an optimistic and pessimistic interpretation of the market. It is based on the sources and nature of evidence for those extremes.

Beginning with the optimistic view, one could argue that a directorate tie market would increase the efficiency of production by facilitating the flow of trusted information among central actors in the economic market. From this perspective, the close association between market constraints and directorate ties would indicate merely that large corporations had overcome the inefficiency of barriers to the flow of information needed to coordinate the activities of diverse suppliers and consumers so as to bring a product to market at a minimal price. Thus the directorate tie market serves to lower the price of commodities eventually consumed as final demand—that final demand consisting of dollars we spend as individual consumers and those that the government spends as our proxy in making particularly large purchases. Evidence for this optimistic interpretation of a directorate tie market comes from personal interviews with corporate officers describing their actual behavior (as opposed to the behavior of which they are capable). One might say that it is in the interest of such respondents to present a benign view of themselves. This is certainly true, but it does not follow from that truth that field data on corporate officers are false or that corporate officers take social science so seriously as to misrepresent their behavior deliberately and systematically in order to curry favor with social science audiences. Ceteris paribus, it seems likely that the economic market would be significantly less efficient without directorate ties than it is with them. It would be too difficult for the management of an establisment constantly to obtain and process trustworthy information on the activities of significant actors in all sectors affecting their profits. This problem is alleviated by the advice, counsel, and influence functions of directorate ties. It is not surprising that these functions of directorate ties are typically highlighted in personal interviews with corporate officers. The people most likely to report the information value of directorate ties are the people who, in the course of making some decision, are most likely to have received some item of information that saved them from making a costly wrong move or revealed to them a profitable opportunity. This is not likely to happen in many of the myriad decisions that must be made in the course of manufacturing a product, so directorate ties are unlikely to be numbered among the factors most determining corporate policy—when corporate officers do the numbering. Corporate officers can be expected to report that directorate ties are a minor feature of day-to-day management, but a very significant feature of the decisions they do inform. The information they provide is knowledge that management would not be likely to integrate into planning in the absence of directorate ties, less because of a lack of access than because of an inability to obtain and process the scope of information relevant to their planning. Hunch and hope seem to be prominent features of pricing decisions at the directorate level of growing firms. The advice, counsel, and influence available through directorate ties reduce the uncertainty in those decisions so that production can be managed more efficiently.

At the same time, directorate ties do selectively facilitate the flow of information in creating favored trade partners. This is less likely to bring together establishments in maximizing the efficiency of their transactions than it is likely to stabilize those transactions and make them profitable. The community of interest created by directorate ties might seem a negligible issue to the people actually making price and product decisions; however, an effective performance of the director role almost requires the creation of such a community. At heart, the director's interest is to protect stockholder interests in the firms for which he is director. This interest is not furthered by intense competition between the establishments for which he is responsible. It is not furthered by passing profitable opportunities on to establishments competing with those for which he is responsible. It is not furthered by warning his competitors of incipient supplier or customer problems. Thus the directorate tie market could be viewed as a network of barriers to new competitors, a network maintaining markets for overpriced commodities. From this perspective, the close association between market constraints and directorate ties would indicate that large corporations had arrived at a point where they controlled the economy in a manner enabling them to raise, rather than lower, the prices of commodities eventually consumed as final demand. The key word here is enable. To be able to do something is not the same as actual behavior. The same self-interest responsible for communities of interest in a directorate tie market limits exploitation of that community. It is not in the director's interest to exploit directorate ties to destroy his competitors thereby courting antitrust litigation against a firm for which he is responsible.

The bottom line then is that a directorate tie market can be expected to increase the efficiency of the economic market but not by as much as it could. Such a view is distant from the gloomy picture painted in descriptions of the abuses of power possible through directorate ties (e.g., the material quoted on page 172), yet it does not contradict them. Directorate ties could be abused so as to eliminate competition. However, there is no evidence of systematic abuse, and available evidence on typical director behavior does not support a view of the directorate tie market as inherently antagonistic to the greater interests of society. Ties of diversification and interlocking directorates were patterned so as to facilitate necessary buying and selling within the economy—but had no direct effect on differences in industry profit margins above and beyond the effect of market structure alone.

I believe that the immediate challenge posed by the study's findings is twofold. The first task is to define the directorate tie market more generally. The second is to define the market in more detail. In other words, what has been provided here is little more than a start, a toehold on what seems to be a fruitful orientation for directorate research guided by structural theory. The symbiotic structure of organizations and markets has long received the attention of social scientists. Given the initial results reported here, I see great substantive promise in studies of the directorate tie market—studies describing how networks of cooptive directorate ties within an economy are sustained by a network of market constraints on corporate profits. More specifically, there are several lines of research within these two general tasks that seem especially ripe. I shall discuss these lines in a summary way here. More detailed discussion is given in Chapters 6–9.

GENERALIZING THE STUDY'S FINDINGS

This study was motivated by a curiosity about the extent to which directorate ties might be patterned on the market constraints implied by the network model of structural autonomy. Given the evidence of directorate ties being a cooptive response to market constraints in the 1967 American economy, there is reason to expand this limited study to more general substantive issues. Is the same tendency to coopt sources of market constraint observed with respect to diverse corporate behaviors, observed in diverse time periods, and observed in diverse economic systems?

Other Corporate Behaviors

In theory, the network model found useful here should be useful in any research concerned with corporate behavior as a response to market constraint. In order to illustrate the point, I pursue a line of research in Chapter 6 that fills in a gap left by Chapters 1–4, the gap of how corporate actors as producers behave toward people as final consumers. I use the structural autonomy model to measure the extent to which people as a consumer sector posed a market constraint for profits in each two-digit industry in 1967. Cooptive corporate relations to people as a sector should have been patterned by these constraints. An argument for viewing corporate philanthropy as a cooptive relation to people, a relation akin to advertising, is supported by the analysis. Industry differences in corporate expenditures for philanthropy and advertising are highly correlated and significantly associated with industry market incentives to establish cooptive relations with people. This same research strategy could be used to describe corporate behaviors toward other kinds of actors such as organized labor, elected officials, the military, government agencies more generally, as well as foreign markets.

Other Time Periods

An important consideration never raised in the preceding analysis is time. I have tested hypotheses with archival data on the American economy during the late 1960s, specifically 1967. I have been careful to use the past tense in discussing features of the 1967 American economy. Although I would have preferred more recent data for the sake of timeliness, such data are not essential to the purpose of this study, and, more importantly, timely data will never be available. Still, inferences about the directorate tie market over time can be drawn from available research to provide leads for future research.

First, consider the purpose of this study. As stated in the Preface, I set out to describe the manner in which patterns of buying and selling among sectors of the American economy constrained the ability to make profits in manufacturing industries and firms in those industries used their boards of directors to create cooptive relations through which the constraints could be circumvented. A mathematical model of constraint was adapted to the substantive area of organizations and markets. Hypotheses derived from the model were tested with data on corporate profits and directorate ties in the 1967 economy. The conclusions drawn in support of those hypotheses extend across time periods in the sense that the study is not a list of empirical generalizations so much as it is a theoretical argument tested with available data. To the extent that the sociological principles used to define constraint are valid, data on buying and selling observed in any time period could be fed into the model to determine market constraints during that time period.

Although the theory might live forever, the data only represent a specific time and place. This is especially salient to the analysis in Chapter 4 of the form of the association between market constraint and directorate ties. The form of this association is not defined in theory so much as some significant association is expected. The kinked association observed within industries, the linear association observed between industries, and the lack of an association between successful cooptation and profits (once market constraints were held constant) are clearly "empirical findings" rather than "validated hypotheses" and so need not generalize beyond the temporal confines of the late 1960s. Are the results reported here idiosyncratic to that time period? Would the same conclusions be drawn from similar data on the American economy in the 1970s or 1980s?

Unfortunately, the data necessary for testing the market constraint hypotheses and describing the form of association between constraint and directorate ties will never be available on the current economy. The critical data are the dollar flow coefficients in the disaggregated input–output table. This table is released by the Bureau of Economic Analysis (Department of Commerce) at irregular intervals. There is a disaggregated table available for the economy in 1963, 1967, and 1972. When this study was conducted, the 1967 data were the most recent available. The 1972 data became available after the project was underway. A 1977 table is scheduled to be released in 1983. In other words, there is a long lag between analyses of market constraints and the availability of data on buying and selling between narrowly defined sectors of the American economy. Studies of the directorate tie market will always be forced to rely on data that are much older than the survey or experiment data typically analyzed in the behavioral sciences. This state of affairs only highlights the importance of testing hypotheses in research on the directorate tie market rather than reporting empirical generalizations.

Looking toward the specification of hypotheses, it is possible to make some inferences about the directorate tie market over time—given the demonstrated validity of the constraint model. The model takes two items as exogenous determinants of market constraint: sector oligopoly (measured with concentration data) and patterns of buying and selling among sectors. First, there is evidence of increasing concentration in highly competitive industries from the mid-1950s through the early 1970s (Mueller & Hamm, 1974; Caves & Porter, 1980). In other words, industries became more homogeneous with respect to low intraindustry competition. Second, this homogeneity has implications for the stability of market constraints from industry suppliers and consumers. An assumption in input–output analysis is that proportionate inputs (direct requirements) are stable as long as production technology is stable, e.g., as long as cars are constructed more from steel than from glass or rubber, as long as books are printed on paper, as long as apparel is constructed from textiles. These production requirements change with changing technology, and it is difficult to track those changes over time given the changing definitions of input–output categories. Still, there is evidence of stability from the late 1940s to the early 1960s in intermediate input requirements for production in highly aggregated categories. There were systematic changes (especially in requirements for labor), and change became more obvious as well as more complex for more narrowly defined sectors (Carter, 1967, 1970; Vaccara, 1970; cf., Sevaldson, 1970). Focusing on the largest transactions, however, suppose that proportionate market transactions have been—in the main—stable over a long period of time. With decreasing variation in sector oligopoly and stable patterns of buying and selling, differences in industry profit margins would be determined more by differences in the structure of industry buying and selling, determined less by differences in industry concentration. Over time, market constraints in the American economy would be expected to increase in magnitude and variance reflecting increasingly severe extraindustry market constraints on profits. This in turn would increase the cooptive response of strategy-minded management, which means that the results obtained in 1967 should be stronger with the passage of time (assuming that firms continue to be as effective in coopting sources of constraint as they were in 1967). This inference is based on bold assumption and is accordingly weak. In the absence of research on the topic, however, it is a plausible null hypothesis to be tested in future research. That research can be guided in still finer detail.

Although there is reason to expect a stable—if not stronger—aggregate association between market constraint and directorate ties over time, there is also reason to expect predictable variation in the extent to which specific market constraint relations occur with strong directorate tie relations. The concept of market constraint contains an implicit assumption of stability over time. This point has been argued with respect to monopoly power (e.g., Grossack, 1972) and extends in an obvious way to market constraint generally. If a severe market constraint is a short-term event, then establishments constrained by it need only wait until it passes before getting on with their unconstrained activities. If the constraint is a stable feature of producing a particular commodity, on the other hand, then establishments producing the commodity can be expected to maintain cooptive relations to the source of constraint. In the same sense that market constraint would be severe as a function of intensity over time, directorate ties would be more obviously cooptive to the extent that they were stable over time. There are arguments stressing stability over time as an essential feature of the cooptive component in directorate ties (e.g., Koenig *et al.,* 1979; Ornstein, 1982; Palmer, 1983). What is more, there are the opportunities stable market conditions create for the development and implementation of cooptive strategies. Based on these considerations, it seems likely that the strongest association between market constraint and directorate ties should occur in the case of those constraints that are stable over time: Stable, intense constraints should occur with stable, multiplex directorate ties. Stable, negligible constraints should occur with the complete absence of directorate ties.

Note that time per se is not a causal variable. It is merely a medium through which ongoing processes operate. The passage of time itself does not make severe a market constraint that is stable over the passage. Rather, the perception by management that a market constraint has been—and can be expected to continue to be—severe over time makes time an important consideration in cooptive strategies. In contrast to time being a causal variable, it is a frame of reference within which management evaluates the severity of market constraint and alternative cooptive strategies.

Other Economic Systems

In addition to comparing different time periods, a comparison of different economic systems could reveal social processes maintaining a directorate tie market in the United States. Fennema and Schijf (1979) provide a review of directorate research with extensive reference to research on directorate structures in Europe. Consistent with tradition, very little of this work explicitly addresses the association between directorate ties and market constraint. Poensgen (1980) and Ziegler (1982) are obvious exceptions, Poensgen describing the situation in the Federal Republic of Germany, Ziegler describing the situation in Austria and Germany. In fact, Professor Ziegler reports an association between market constraints and directorate ties that is very similar to the one reported here.

There is the advantage of replication in comparative descriptions of directorate structures in different countries. The more varied the social circumstances in which directorate ties are demonstrated to be a function of market constraints, the more confidence one can have in the idea that directorate ties are cooptive relations.

But this does not exploit a deeper advantage to be obtained from comparative directorate research. If increasing variation in market conditions were the only goal of comparative research, then a comparison of different industries within the well-documented American economy might be as useful as any comparative research effort. Beyond mere variation, however, there are qualitative cultural and legal differences between economic actors in different countries that have the potential to reveal—as well as replicate—the association between directorate ties and market constraints within any one country better.

Corporate law in the Federal Republic of Germany, for example, defines two functionally distinct boards of directors. These two are combined within the one defined in American corporate laws. A German firm has a management board (*Vorstand*) responsible for running the firm and a supervisory board (*Aufsichtrat*) responsible for overseeing and electing persons on the management board. Members of either board can hold directorships in other firms, but no one can hold a seat on both boards within a single firm. As described by Poensgen (1980; cf., Bacon & Brown, 1977:27–37), "The supervisory board's duties go well beyond the rights of supervision. It is also charged with appointing and discharging the members of the managing board; it can stipulate, and usually does, that certain major decisions are not taken and transactions are not performed without its prior consent. It has an equal voice with management in determining dividend policy [p. 211]."

In other words, directorate ties in the German economy pose certain research advantages and disadvantages relative to the American economy. As a cost, the existence of two boards increases the complexity of directorate ties among establishments since ties could exist in different ways (as described in Chapter 3) between different types of boards (versus the one board in American firms). On the other hand, this complexity presents a research opportunity. The roles of different kinds of directors can be distinguished in cooptive direct interlocks between German firms. A firm can directly interlock with a second firm in either, or both, of two manners: A member of the managing board in the first firm could serve as a supervisory director in the second firm, and/or one person could serve as a supervisory director in both firms. If market constraint only predicted directorate ties between separate levels of boards (a single person being a supervisory director in one firm and a managing director in another), then corporate officers would be identified as a critical element in the use of directorate ties as cooptive relations. Such a finding would warrant analysis of American directorate ties in a way highlighting ties that involved corporate officers (e.g., Galaskiewicz & Wasserman, 1981; Mintz & Schwartz, 1981a; Mizruchi, 1982;

Palmer, 1983). If, on the other hand, market constraint only predicted directorate ties between supervisory boards, then third parties—rather than corporate officers—would be identified as a critical element in cooptive directorate ties. Financial institutions are the most likely candidate for this role of third party coordinating the activities of separate firms. Such a finding would warrant even more attention being given to the manner in which indirect financial interlocks integrate the activities of American firms.

Obviously, a great range of possible findings exist between these extremes of one type of direct interlock tie or the other being the only type associated with market constraint. The two-board directorate is found in countries other than the Federal Republic of Germany. However, a methodological point is clear from the example. The functional separation of director roles in interlock ties between German firms presents an opportunity to assess the relative importance of different roles in cooptive interlocking. More generally, cultural and legal differences between economic actors have the potential to highlight alternative strategies by which directorate ties could provide opportunities to circumvent market constraints. Leads for such research can be derived from the comparisons and brief summaries in Bacon and Brown (1977) of directorate practices in nine countries: Canada, the Federal Republic of Germany, France, Japan, Sweden, Turkey, the United Kingdom, the United States, and Venezuela.

DISAGGREGATING THE STUDY'S FINDINGS

In order to get on with the business of describing how directorate ties might be patterned by market constraints, I have ignored the unique qualities of components aggregated in a market constraint relation and a directorate tie. The documented association between market constraint and directorate ties could be greatly informed by a finer-grain analysis. Is the same association between directorate ties and market constraint observed when constraint and directorate ties are broken down into their social components of transactions, firms, and directors?

Market Constraint Components

The components in the aggregate constraint that a sector posed for an industry are (*a*) the extent to which the sector was an oligopoly, and (*b*) the extent to which the industry conducted the bulk of its market transactions with the sector. The analysis in Chapter 2 showed that industry profits in 1967 were constrained by having few separate supplier sectors and few oligopolistic consumer sectors (Tables 2.4 and 2.5). The combination of conditions constraining profits was then used to define the market constraint coefficients in Eq. (2.6) and assumed to determine directorate ties as a cooptive strategy to circumvent constraints. The components in market constraint were not analyzed in terms of their relative, direct association with directorate ties. In predicting directorate ties with market constraint relations, I have assumed that sector oligopoly had the same impact on extraindustry directorate ties that it had on industry profit margins. This need not have been true.

For example, it is possible that firms maintained directorate ties to all suppliers and consumers regardless of the extent to which suppliers or consumers were oligopolistic. There is a tradition of research termed "resource dependence" in which this is explicit. Firms are expected to create cooptive relations with organizations providing resources on which the firm's continued prosperity is dependent. The structural autonomy model is a special case of this perspective in the sense that it only predicts cooptive relations to a sector that is both a source of buying and selling *and* is relatively oligopolistic so as to pose a constraint on profits in industries buying or selling with it.

In Chapter 7, I compare the predictions of the structural autonomy model with those of the more general resource dependence perspective. Using the two-digit data, I show that buying and selling alone do not predict directorate ties as well as the interaction of exchange and sector oligopoly. As predicted by the structural autonomy model, directorate ties in 1967 tended to connect industry and sector to the extent that the sector was a principal trade partner for the industry *and* the sector was dominated by a small number of large firms so as to pose a constraint for industry profits.

Individual Firms

Perhaps the boldest assumptions have been made in order to compute the directorate tie relations. The partial exception of Chapter 3 notwithstanding, I have by and large ignored differences among corporations in order to get on with the direct comparison of market constraints with directorate ties. My concern has been with directorate ties among establishments at the expense of corporations as units of analysis. I have treated the firm less as the object of cooptation than as a medium for cooptation. Although acceptable as a temporary assumption for research, this assumption grossly oversimplifies a complex situation. The economic market does not create directorate ties, it only encourages them by providing a profit incentive for developing them in particular structural locations. The actual decision making entity that creates directorate ties is the firm.

In Chapter 8, I show that individual firms were a critical intervening variable in the association between market constraint intensity and directorate tie frequency. The association documented in Chapter 4 is principally a result of firms with extensive cooptive networks having ties to industries involved in severe market constraints in 1967. Differences in the range of cooptive networks were described in Chapter 3 as a function of differences in the size of, and distribution of control within, individual corporations. Building on these results and the results in Chapter 4 suggesting the existence of a directorate tie market, I specify a structural equation model in Chapter 8. The model defines parameters for research into the manner in which individual corporations could have been responsible for the directorate tie market observed in 1967. Eq. (8.6) defines an index of the extent to which a firm has been cooptively successful in the sense of developing directorate ties to sectors posing a constraint on profits in the industries where the firm operates its primary establishments. Figure 8.2 contains a specification of processes by which this condition could arise, contribute to corporate structural autonomy, and eventually affect the firm's success more generally. The firm's success in the directorate tie market combines with its freedom from constraint in the economic market of buying and selling to define the firm's structural autonomy as an expected profit margin [Eqs. (8.7) and (8.11)]. That defined ability to pursue interests without constraint in turn affects the firm's success in pursuing the more general corporate goals of profits and growth. The structural equation model in Figure 8.2 is specified to assess the extent to which a firm's cooptive success (i.e., its participation in a directorate tie market) has a direct effect on the firm's profitability and growth. To the extent that there is such an effect, individual firms have an incentive to maintain the association between directorate ties and market constraints that I have described as a directorate tie market.

Individual Directors

A second oversimplification I deliberately adopted in computing directorate ties concerns individual people. In order to get on with the comparison of directorate ties with market constraints, I have been concerned with the presence versus the absence of interlocking directorates between firms at the expense of concern with the people who constituted those ties. It is these people who defined the content of interlocking directorates, and I have assumed them all to be the same. Whoever he was, the person holding directorships in multiple firms has been viewed merely as a conduit for information, advice, and influence between the firms. This is obviously wrong. People differ in ways pertinent to the transfer of information, advice, and influence.

In the currency of interlocking directorates, in fact, people and firms are opposite sides of the same coin. A given directorate tie connects types of establishments through a type of person. In the same sense that there are significant differences between individual firms—differences that could underlie processes making individual firms responsible for the directorate tie market—there are differences between individual directors as people. Those differences too might underlie processes making individual people responsible for a directorate tie market.

For example, there is some empirical support for the idea that there exists a social class of persons who control the American economy in part through the many positions they hold as executives and directors of large American firms. In Chapter 9, I show that this perspective is inadequate to describe data on directors sampled from the boards of large manufacturing firms in 1967. Social prominence is independent of a director's executive role and the extent to which he held multiple directorships spanning severe market constraint. The association between executive role and providing constraint-spanning interlocks is more complex than the situation anticipated by the center–periphery metaphor advocated in class theory.

These results do not rule out the possiblity that directors—as individuals exploiting their positions in the economy—could have been responsible for the directorate tie market. Concluding Chapter 9, I specify a model for research into that possibility. Building on the idea that directors are stratified in part by their social and corporate prestige, I use the structural autonomy concept to capture the extent to which a director could have exploited his position in the economy to pursue his interests without constraint—creating a directorate tie market as a byproduct. Equations (9.2) and (9.3) define indices of the extent to which a director is integral to the ability of establishments to circumvent market constraint through directorate ties. These are measures of the director's participation in the successful cooptation generating a directorate tie market. Figure 9.2 contains a specification of processes by which this participation could arise, contribute to director structural autonomy, and eventually affect the director's success more generally. Participation in successful cooptation is attributed to differences in personal prestige and the extent to which a director is affiliated with a large, structurally autonomous firm controlled by diffuse interest groups. This participation, and the extent to which a director is primarily responsible for establishments free from market constraint, determines the director's structural autonomy as the maximum profit margin expected in firms for which he is an outside director [Eqs. (9.4) and (9.5)]. That defined ability to pursue interests without constraint in turn affects the director's success more generally in obtaining directorships in large, profitable firms. To the extent that there is such an effect, individual directors have an incentive to maintain the association between directorate ties and market constraints that I have described as a directorate tie market.

TURNING AN EYE TOWARD PUBLIC POLICY

The jump from scholarly conclusions to policy recommendations is typically bold and immodest. No such leap is proposed here. My concern in this study has been to describe organizational behavior in the aggregate. Public policy regarding corporate profits and cooptation, in contrast, is typically implemented through the courts on a case-by-case basis. Moreover, future research, perhaps in some of the directions outlined, is sure to refine the conclusions that I have drawn from the preceding analysis.

Then again, all research leaves room for refinement, and this study is not without its public policy implications. It seems fitting to close this chapter with some speculations—they are no more than that—about where this, and related, research on the directorate tie market would be most likely to inform public policy. The relevant policy, of course, is antitrust, two components of which require distinction here.

One component is made up of regulations defining illegal pricing behavior, behavior yielding excessive profits and constituting an abuse of autonomy in the market. Chief among these regulations are the articles of Section 1 in the Sherman Act and Sections 2 and 3 of the Clayton Act as amended. Section 1 of the Sherman Act prohibits pricing agreements among competitors allowing them to sell their product independently at an inflated price, and Section 3 of the Clayton Act prohibits pricing agreements between seller and buyer in which the buyer agrees not to deal with the seller's competitors (e.g., Neale, 1970:32–91, 203–224). Section 2 of the Clayton Act as amended by the Robinson–Patman Act prohibits price discrimination. For example, it is illegal—except in a great variety of provided-for circumstances—for a firm to offer different prices to different buyers or to offer rebates only to selected buyers (e.g., Neale, 1970:225–271). The reference to the turn-of-the-century price discrimination practices of Standard Oil in refining and transportation is obvious.

The second component of antitrust policy consists of regulations defining illegal efforts to acquire the ability to control prices. Where the first component defines and prohibits pricing behavior associated with excess profits, the second prohibits the intention to acquire the ability to obtain excess profits. Were I speaking of murder, the first component of antitrust would define a murder, and the second component would define conditions making it especially easy to commit murder. Chief among the regulations in this second antitrust component are the articles in Section 2 of the Sherman Act and Sections 7 and 8 of the Clayton Act as amended. Section 2 of the Sherman Act prohibits efforts to monopolize an industry so as to control pricing. The verb is important here. It is not monopoly per se that is prohibited (the first establishment in an industry by definition has a monopoly for some period of time); it is the effort to monopolize that is prohibited (e.g., Neale, 1970:92–125, 155–177). The Clayton Act was passed in 1914 to "arrest the creation of trusts, conspiracies and monopolies in their incipiency and before consummation." Section 7, as amended by the 1950 Celler–Kefauver Act, prohibits intraindustry and interindustry mergers that might enable a firm to control pricing (e.g., Neale, 1970:178–200). The revised wording reads as follows:

> No corporations engaged in commerce shall acquire, directly or indirectly, the whole or
> any part of the stock or other share capital and no corporation subject to the jurisdiction
> of the Federal Trade Commission shall acquire the whole or any part of the assets of
> another corporation engaged also in commerce, where, in any line of commerce in any
> section of the country, the effect of such acquisition may be substantially to lessen
> competition or to tend to create a monopoly.

This is a rather general prohibition and is followed by Section 8 in which interlocking directorates between competitors are prohibited. Putting interlocks with banks, communication firms, and transportation firms to one side as special considerations (because of other antitrust legislation solely concerned with such firms), the main provision of Section 8 reads as follows (quoted from Neale, 1970:201):

> no person at the same time shall be a director in any two or more corporations, any one of
> which has capital, surplus, and undivided profits aggregating more than $1 million,
> engaged in whole or in part in commerce . . . if such corporations are or shall have been
> theretofore, by virtue of their business or location or operation, competitors, so that the
> elimination of competition by agreement between them would constitute a violation of
> any of the provisions of any of the antitrust laws.

The implementation of Section 8 has been awkward. Officers of a firm are permitted to sit on the boards of a competitor, complaints are sometimes dismissed when the cited interlocks are dissolved, but other times not dismissed until cited firms can show that it would be reasonable to expect that the violation will not be repeated (Neale, 1970:201–202). In fact, the need to make the implementation of anti-interlock regulations less ambiguous was explicitly cited in a recent Senate report as a justification for the extreme policy of completely prohibiting interlocks between firms with assets or sales over a billion dollars (Turner, 1978:281). Given the enforcement ambiguity that exists, the lack of scholarly attention to interlocking as an antitrust violation is not surprising. Ambiguity does not encourage rigorous analysis. Neale (1970) mentions it as a footnote to his treatise on American antitrust law. Economic analyses typically ignore interlocking among industrials (e.g., Shepherd, 1975; Caves, 1982). Even Armentano's (1982, e.g., pp. 281–283) iconoclastic analysis deletes Section 8 from the significant portions of antitrust regulations discussed.

This study most clearly speaks to the second component of antitrust policy. It is the ability to obtain excess profits that has been addressed here rather than the pricing behaviors by which such profits have been obtained.

The results obtained here show no tendency for unusually high profits to be a direct consequence of cooptive directorate ties. Rather, profits and cooptive directorate ties were simultaneously determined by market constraints. Ties of diversification and interlocking directorates have the potential to, and were patterned to, facilitate necessary buying and selling within the economy—but the mere strategic placement of directorate ties had no direct effect on differences in industry profit margins above and beyond the effect of market constraint itself. Ostensible evidence of directorate ties increasing profit margins disappears when prediction equations correctly specify market constraints as a determinant of profits. One policy implication of this study for directorate ties, in sum, is that such ties should be left alone. This complements Armentano's (1982) provocative argument highlighting the inefficiency of antitrust action against firms simply because they were acquiring an ability to control pricing relative to the ability of other firms. I do not have the evidence to go as far as Armentano in pointing out the failures of antitrust as an incorrect policy. My evidence is merely that some aspects of antitrust policy would have been unnecessary in the late 1960s. Extensive involvement in directorate ties of diversification and interlocking (i.e., the ability to circumvent market constraint) is not in itself inefficient so as to constitute a violation of the pricing proscriptions of antitrust law.

However, this laissez faire implication should not be taken too far. There are documented instances of firms engaging in illegal pricing behavior. A second implication of this study concerns the detection of such behavior.

The implementation of antitrust policy focuses on intraindustry violations. This focus is consistent with the atomistic theory of competition underlying antitrust legislation. Neale (1970:373–400), Shepherd (1975; Chaps. 5, 7, 8), and Armentano (1982) offer insights into the bureaucratic implementation of antitrust policy, Shepherd and Armentano giving special attention to the theory of competition that is invoked to guide and legitimate policy (see especially Shepherd, 1975:38–61; Armentano, 1982:5–41). Even interindustry mergers and interlocks, so-called vertical integration, are evaluated in terms of their intraindustry impact.

The network approach taken in this study describes intraindustry pricing as an aggregate of many separate price agreements with suppliers and consumers. Antitrust implementation within this approach would search for violations in each class of transactions a firm has with its suppliers and consumers (where a class corresponds to a cell in the input–output table). This is not a new idea. For example, Shepherd (1975:2) calls attention to the need for antitrust regulation to consider the firm in the "context" of its input and output markets. Although antitrust case descriptions seem to me to indicate sensitivity to this issue, there is at least a theoretical problem and a logistic problem inherent in bringing antitrust pricing regulations to bear on interindustry transactions.

The theoretical problem is one of specifying a valid theory of competition that defines interindustry market constraint. Atomistic theory attends to competition between establishments producing the same product. Competition theory in structural sociology, notably the network model of structural autonomy that I have used in this study, is specified explicitly to describe competition between establishments producing different products but obliged to conduct business with one another as suppliers and consumers. I have gone beyond Shepherd's (1975:24–31, 88–91) treatment of context as ties to the finance sector, for example, to treat context as the entire pattern of an industry's buying and selling with each sector of the economy as a supplier or consumer. The market constraint coefficients predicting variation in profits and cooptation are the net result.

Monitoring all of these transactions, however, constitutes an overwhelming logistic problem. The task of monitoring market transactions so as to regulate interindustry directorate ties of diversification and interlocking would be quite simply impossible. Here is another point at which this study could inform public policy. It could do so by highlighting places in the economy where illegal pricing behavior would be especially profitable. These are the places of severe market constraint. Of the 880 extraindustry transactions involving two-digit manufacturing industries in 1967, slightly more than 10% (88) were places of severe market constraint. Of 129,122 such transactions involving four-digit industries, slightly more than 2% (3038) were places of severe constraint. (This ignores the negligible, but important to be monitored, market transactions with the finance sector; see Table 4.1.) As described in Chapter 2, the greatest profits are to be had in exploiting transactions in these places of severe market constraint. As described in Chapter 4, potentially cooptive directorate ties of ownership and interlocking are especially dense in these places. They accordingly constitute a logical focus for antitrust monitoring. A small class of market transactions and directorate ties can be more closely monitored than can all classes, and the savings here are nonnegligible: 90% at the level of two-digit industries, 98% at the level of four-digit industries. Of course, these figures refer to numbers of transactions in an input–output table and so do not reflect the individual establishment-to-establishment transactions to be monitored for antitrust violation.

In sum, I offer three public policy speculations. One concerns a restriction on the policy informed. This study does not speak to the actual pricing behaviors proscribed as violations of antitrust law so much as it informs the implementation of regulations prohibiting the acquisition of certain abilities to control prices. The second concerns restrictions on a firm's ability to circumvent market constraints through directorate ties. The lack of a unique effect on profit variation from cooptive success offers no encouragement for rigorous antitrust opposition to extensive directorate ties per se in the form of diversification and interlocking. The third concerns the efficiency of implementing policy. The definition of market constraints as places where it would be most profitable to engage in illegal pricing behavior encourages a greater efficiency in monitoring organizational behavior for antitrust violations. That greater efficiency would be obtained by focusing antitrust attention on the 2–10% of transactions where market constraint is defined to be especially severe.

PART II
NEW DIRECTIONS

6

A Note on Corporate Philanthropy[*]

In the context of the often strained relation between people and corporations as classes of actors in American society, corporate philanthropy offers a dual satisfaction. Corporate philanthropy, that is, tax-deductible gifts from corporations to charitable activities, provides the direct material benefit of improved public health, education, and welfare. It is a further satisfaction to know that corporate actors, as preeminently rational, profit-seeking bastions of power, have acted in the interests of persons rather than themselves. To be sure, corporate philanthropy is a cost-effective allocation of corporate income. But it is also a social setting in which the interests of persons and corporate actors come together in an intimate way. Accordingly, the corporate decision to make charitable donations provides a convenient laboratory for studying the nature of the relation from corporate actors to persons. I propose to analyze corporate philanthropy as a cooptive relation, akin to advertising, directed at persons collectively as a con-

*This analysis was a reaction to several microeconomic analyses of philanthropy appearing in the journal *Public Choice* (Levy & Shatto, 1978; Bennett & Johnson, 1980; Keim *et al.*, 1980) and was presented in 1981 at the "Albany Conference on Contributions of Network Analysis to Structural Sociology" held at the State University of New York, Albany. Portions of this chapter are reprinted from an article (Burt, 1983b) with the permission of *Social Forces*.

sumer sector of the economy.[1] The strength of this cooptive relation is predicted from a network definition of the extent to which corporations in an economic sector have a market incentive to institutionalize relations with people as consumers. As predicted, the portion of corporate net income donated to charity covaries with the extent to which firms in a sector are dependent on consumption by people and able to do something about eliminating uncertainty in the demand for their product. Methodologically, the discussion illustrates a problem often tackled in network analysis: Social context constraints on an actor are captured in a network model of the context and specified as parameters in a microeconomic decision model.

A MICROECONOMIC MODEL: PHILANTHROPY AS A COST-EFFICIENT EXPENDITURE

First and foremost, corporate philanthropy is to be understood as a rational decision made by a profit-oriented bureaucracy, an efficient allocation of income at a known price. Both personal (e.g., Feldstein & Clotfelter, 1976; Feldstein & Taylor, 1976) and corporate (e.g., Schwartz, 1966; Nelson, 1970) philanthropy can be viewed as an outcome from a microeconomic decision process. The level of giving by actor j, g_j, is determined in a constant elasticity equation by the unit cost, or price, of giving for the actor, c_j, and the level of income available for him to donate, i_j:

$$g_j = \beta(c_j)^{\beta_c}(i_j)^{\beta_i}(e_j), \tag{6.1}$$

where β, β_c, and β_i are effects to be estimated, e_j is an error term, and the price of giving, c_j, is the complement of actor j's tax rate. For example, if a corporation has a tax rate of 45%, then a dollar donated to charity costs the corporation only 55¢; the remaining 45¢ would have been lost to taxes anyway and so lost to the firm. In the absence of data on individual firms in a representative sample, data aggregated by the Internal Revenue Service from corporate tax returns for

---

[1]This concern with the decision to make charitable donations deserves emphasis since it excludes a concern with the manner in which donations actually reach the public. Like advertising agencies—brokers in the flow of corporate advertising expenditures to the public—there are organizations brokering the flow of philanthropic funds to the public. Funds come from corporate donors to philanthropic organizations of various kinds and from there are distributed to the public. The intervening philanthropic organizations range from divisions within profit-making corporations to more independent foundations, and the cooptive networks of these nonprofit brokers are an interesting topic in their own right. For example, Galaskiewicz (1982) offers an interesting perspective on the conditions under which patronage, hierarchy, and information in the cooptive networks of nonprofit organizations would be helpful to an organization seeking donations. For the purposes here, I am ignoring the nonprofit organizations brokering the flow of philanthropy funds and focusing on the market incentives for corporate actors to contribute to the flow.

economic sectors as a whole have been used to estimate price and income effects. This research has shown that dollars of donations by firms in sector j are positively associated with the dollars of net income they report (interpreted estimates of β_i ranging from .5 to 1.0) and negatively associated with the price of giving (interpreted estimates of β_c ranging from $-.9$ to -2.5), which is to say, positively associated with the tax rate in sector j (Schwartz, 1966; Nelson, 1970; Levy & Shatto, 1978; Bennett & Johnson, 1980).[2] In other (more economic) words, corporate philanthropy appears to be price elastic; β_c less than -1.0 means that a percentage decrease in the price of giving is associated with a larger percentage increase in giving. It yields more in additional gifts than is lost in potential additional tax revenue. These results could be used to recommend the manipulation of tax incentives as a strategy for increasing corporate philanthropy.[3] Such a judgment seems premature.

First, there is the question of evidence. Since 1936, the first year following the 1935 amendment allowing corporations to deduct charitable contributions from their taxable income, there has been an increase in corporate giving within the United States. Nelson (1970) reports the increase in dollars of gifts as one of three principal effects in his 1936–1963 time series, the other two being price and income effects. There has also been an increase in the percentage of net income donated. However, the percentaged donations have remained relatively stable at approximately 1% since the late 1950s, with the bulk of donations going to health and welfare (about 40%) and education (also about 40%). A smaller, but increasing, share has gone to cultural and civic activities, a share approaching 20% in the mid 1970s (e.g., see Watson, 1972; Klepper, 1977; Vasquez, 1977). This is well below the 5% maximum deduction allowed to corporations. In fact, the Commission on Private Philanthropy and Public Needs, a group of privately-funded experts drawn from academia, research organizations, and the business community, thought it prudent in 1975 merely to recommend that corporations increase their percentage contributions to 2% by 1980 (Commission, 1977:Vol. I). Further, only 53% of 408 chairmen and presidents of large

[2]Schwartz (1966) and Nelson (1970) offer the most carefully worked-out microeconomic analyses, with Nelson (1970:107–110) providing useful comments on why he and Schwartz obtain different estimates of price and income elasticities. Keim *et al.* (1980) discuss some difficulties in interpreting the parameter estimates presented by Levy and Shatto (1978).

[3]Harriss (1977) discusses modifications of the tax incentive for corporations. Reacting to a voluntaristic call for increased rates of corporate giving, members of the Donee Group within the Commission on Private Philanthropy and Public Needs recommended instead an increased tax rate (2% in addition to the current tax rate) that a firm could only avoid by making charitable contributions. To use the group's own words (Commission, 1977), "This proposal would guarantee an increase in corporate giving." The Donee Group felt that "Employing exhortation to increase corporate gifts to charity is a futile exercise. The Commission's own research and even corporate members of the Commission acknowledged that mere talk has not and will not increase corporate contributions [p. 75, Vol. I]."

American firms surveyed in 1975 said that increased tax incentives would result in their firms increasing charitable donations by even one-half within 2 to 5 years.[4] Beyond the weakness of evidence supporting tax incentives, there is the question of corporate social context.

The corporate decision to make a donation is not reached by an isolated actor. It is reached within a social context defined by interorganizational relations with competitors, suppliers, and consumers as well as relations with persons, persons in the communities where a firm owns establishments and persons collectively as an economic sector of consumers determining, in part, demand for the firm's product.

In one sense, corporate actors and persons can be viewed as two types of citizens living in the same society and accordingly benefiting from an improved society. For example, among other results from their survey of large American corporations, Harris and Klepper (1976) report some remarks made by the president of a major communications firm in justification of corporate philanthropy:

> A corporation exists in a community—local, regional, national even worldwide. It must be concerned with the condition of that community, with the development of the best and broadest possible base of talents, and with the quality of life. The corporate citizen, like the individual citizen, benefits from a healthy community and should encourage efforts to make the community better [p. 18].

Sentiments such as these are timely, but they are neither novel nor unique to corporate philanthropy. For example, similar sentiments were expressed by executives attending a 1955 conference on corporate charity policies (National Industrial Conference Board, 1956). More generally, there are so many expressions of the need for corporate citizenship by scholars and business practitioners that such sentiments have the omnipresence of a norm for corporate executives (see Moch and Seashore, 1981, for a review of work on the corporate norms theme).

Most importantly, these sentiments are not analytically informative with respect to variation in corporate philanthropy. All corporations are corporate cit-

---

[4]Responses were solicited from heads of all 1300 of the largest American firms listed in *Fortune*'s 1974 compilation (see Harris & Klepper, 1976). The low response rate (35%) means that the results cannot be generalized to the population of large firms; however, comments on the returned questionnaires are illustrative. Moreover, these data were sufficient for an 11-member Business Advisory Group, formed for the Commission on Private Philanthropy and Public Needs, to recommend (Commission, 1977) "that, except for equitable treatment, no additional tax incentives are needed— including the concept of more than 100 percent of contributions as a deductible expense, or providing a tax credit that would result in a lower 'after-tax cost' than the present 100 percent deductibility. . . . That there be neither a minimum tax floor before any contributions are deductible nor ceilings on corporate contributions. The first, according to The Conference Board survey, would have a major depressant effect upon contributions giving; the latter would have a minor effect upon major corporations [p. 1782, Vol. III]."

izens, but corporations differ extensively in the extent to which they are involved in philanthropic activities. Therefore, one is left with the microeconomic concepts of price and income as the principal, theoretically-defined variables available to explain observed differences in corporate philanthropy. What is needed is a concept capturing differences in contextual forces on specific corporations, or classes of corporations, differences that covary with differences in corporate philanthropy.[5]

A SOCIOLOGICAL MODEL: PHILANTHROPY AS A COOPTIVE RELATION

At this point it is useful to consider the pattern of relations defining a corporation's network position in the economy. Market relations among corporate actors and persons in the economy can be represented by an input–output table, where cell (j, i) of the table is the dollars of sales by establishments in sector j to those in sector i. As characterized in Figure 2.1, the firm operating in sector j occupies a network position defined by purchases from other sectors (column j elements) and sales to other sectors (row j elements). I can speak of a corporation's position because tax return data on corporate philanthropy force a whole corporation into a single economic sector (as I shall discuss in the following). This relational pattern of buying and selling provides an analytical handle on the social context in which the decision to make a donation is reached.

[5]For the individual committed to corporate attitudes as an explanation of corporate behavior, this problem is easily solved by claiming that different firms, or classes of firms, hold different attitudes as behavioral norms. There are two reasons why such a claim does not seem fruitful relative to the network approach to be presented in the text. First, it is difficult, if not impossible, to obtain *reliable* data *representative* of attitudes of corporate executives within a sector of the economy so as to measure differences across sectors. Seider (1974) provides an instructive attempt to obtain such data. In contrast, the census data on market structure in the American economy are quite good. Second, there is every reason to suspect that attitudes expressed by executives within a sector reflect the market conditions within which executive attitudes are formed. To the extent that an industry (as an executive's social context in the economy) provides a high market incentive for corporate philanthropy, executives employed within that industry would be expected to express attitudes emphasizing the importance of corporate philanthropy. In other words, some score x_j measuring the relative tendency for executives in an industry to express attitudes stressing the importance of corporate philanthropy should be correlated positively with the market incentive the industry provides or corporate philanthropy [m_j in Eq. (6.2)]. To the extent that executive attitudes are merely a reflection of the market conditions in which they operate, a regression equation in which levels of corporate giving, g_j, are predicted from x_j and m_j should reveal a strong positive effect from the market incentive and a negligible effect for executive attitudes (assuming that x_j is based more on sample data than the typically census-based m_j). Unfortunately, data on x_j are not available at an acceptable level of reliability and representativeness to empirically test this intuition. In the interim, I focus on what I believe to be the more fundamental causal element—the structural market incentive m_j defined in Eq. (6.2).

It provides an analytical handle by indicating the nature and intensity of market constraints on the sector in which the philanthropy decision is reached. More specifically, the relational pattern can be used to define the structural autonomy of sector establishments (their ability to act without constraint relative to establishments in other sectors) and the constraint each other sector poses for that autonomy. Establishments in sector j have high structural autonomy, $\mathbf{a}_j$, to the extent that there is low competition within the sector and high competition among sector suppliers and consumers. As defined in Chapter 2, the structural autonomy score $\mathbf{a}_j$ varies from zero to one as the profit margin expected in sector j given the market constraints on the sector. In 1967, low market constraint translated into high profits. To the extent that a corporation operates in a sector providing high structural autonomy, the firm is comparatively free from the market constraints of competitors, suppliers, and consumers.

More to the point of this chapter, profits in sector j are constrained by establishments in consumer sector i to the extent that two market conditions simultaneously characterize buying and selling between the sectors: (a) a dominant proportion of all sales by sector j are made to establishments in sector i, and (b) organizations within sector i are coordinated so as to form an oligopoly. The specific market constraint coefficient $\mathbf{a}_{ji}$ can be interpreted as the profit margin forgone in sector j by failing to coopt sector i as a source of market constraint [see Eqs. (2.10)ff]. In other words, the market constraint coefficient $\mathbf{a}_{ji}$ measures the market incentive firms in sector j have to develop cooptive relations to sector i. As might be expected from corporations as purposive actors, establishments in sectors i and j tended to be connected in 1967 by extensive and coordinated ties through corporate boards of directors to the extent that $\mathbf{a}_{ji}$ was strong. Through these cooptive directorate ties, market constraints could have been circumvented. These points are the focus of attention in Chapters 3 and 4.

People as consumers in the household sector of the economy pose no such constraint for corporate profits. The relational pattern of buying and selling characteristic of a firm's sector defines the extent to which demand for sector product is dependent on consumption by persons. Sectors do differ in the extent to which total demand for their product is a result of consumption by individuals in the household sector. For example, the ratio of dollars of final demand from individual households over total dollars of demand as reported in the 1967 input–output table (U.S. Department of Commerce, 1974) is .6816 for establishments manufacturing food products but only .0004 for those manufacturing primary metals products. Ceteris paribus, food firms would have a higher market incentive to coopt the household sector than would primary metals firms. But this inference ignores the extent to which buyers in the household sector are organized so as to form an oligopolistic consumer. Regardless of the extent to which demand for a sector's product is dependent on consumption by persons, people are so independent as buyers that together in the household sector they do not constitute an oligopoly. The market constraint coefficient a_{ji} for household sector i is negligible for all sectors j.[6]

This negligible market constraint posed by the household sector suggests that the sector would be ignored in the cooptive strategies of large corporations. There is evidence of cooptive relations occurring as a function of the amount of buying and selling between economic sectors in 1967; however, when sector oligopoly is held constant, it is clear that cooptive relations were directed to oligopolistic sectors with which extensive buying and selling was transacted. Cooptive relations were not directed to competitive sectors—regardless of the amount of buying and selling transacted with the sector. This topic is discussed further in Chapter 7.

Nevertheless, there is variation in the market incentive firms in different economic sectors have to coopt the household sector as a secondary source of market constraint. Consider the firm operating in a sector providing high structural autonomy but at the same time subjecting it to a reliance on consumption by people in order to maintain demand for its product. It is in the firm's self-interest to actively court the affections of people as consumers since that affection translates into stimulated demand for the firm's product. Moreover, the structurally autonomous firm is in a position to realize this particular self-interest since it is relatively free from threats to its profits from corporate consumers, suppliers, and competitors. If a firm cannot manufacture some product with a comfortable profit margin, then the extent to which it would depend on public consumption if it could manufacture with a profit is of little importance.[7] In other words, people as consumers in the household sector constitute a market constraint of secondary importance. Unlike the constraints captured in the structural autonomy model and analyzed in Chapters 2 and 4, constraint from the household sector does not pose an immediate threat to profits. But in the absence of more immediate threats—that is, for the structurally autonomous firm—it is an eminently strategic action for the firm to move to eliminate uncertainty in its profits by coopting the source of even secondary constraint (e.g., people in the household sector of the economy).

This means that the network position a firm occupies within the economy can be used to define a market incentive for the firm to coopt the household sector in the sense of institutionalizing its relations with people as consumers. For the firm

---

[6]More specifically, y_i in Table 2.4 is zero, so the component of the consumer constraint index, y_{j3}, expressing the constraint from the household sector i is also zero by multiplication ($y_i c_{ji}^2 = 0$).

[7]As a manufacturing corporation president explained his lack of interest in corporate philanthropy for the Harris and Klepper (1976) survey, "We must keep primary the role of making a profit so as to continue operating in order to supply jobs. Without profit, there will be nothing."

operating in sector j, that market incentive m_j is defined simultaneously by the structural autonomy of sector j and the extent to which consumption by persons determines demand for sector product:

$$m_j = \mathbf{a}_j(PD_j/TD_j), \tag{6.2}$$

where $\mathbf{a}_j$ is the structural autonomy provided by sector j [Eq. (2.5)], PD_j is the dollars of final demand for that sector's product from the household sector, and TD_j is the dollars of total demand for that sector's product. In terms of the analysis in Chapter 2, PD_j corresponds to the dollars of sales from sector j to the household sector, and TD_j corresponds to the total volume of sales by the sector.[8] The market incentive varies from zero to one. A firm will have a high market incentive to coopt the household sector to the extent that the sector in which the firm operates depends on consumption by people to maintain demand for its product and provides structural autonomy enabling the firm to do something about institutionalizing that demand so as to eliminate a source of uncertainty in its profits.

Corporate philanthropy can be viewed as serving a dual function for firms responding to a high market incentive to coopt the household sector. First, philanthropy legitimates the firm to the public as a protector of the public interest. This in turn can be expected to channel public buying toward commodities that the firm has had a hand in producing. Second, philanthropy can provide a further stimulus to demand by improving the ability of specific classes of individuals to purchase the firm's product.[9] There is some evidence of these functions in the survey results Harris and Klepper (1976) present. Of the chairmen and presidents giving reasons for company public service activities, 49% cite "self-interest" consisting of public services necessary for long-term survival.

With these functions in mind, corporations can be expected to allocate funds to

---

[8]I should stress here that the ratio *PD/TD* will typically vary from zero to one as the *extent* to which persons are responsible for the demand for a sector's product. It need not be the *proportion* of total demand represented by household consumption since extensive sales from inventories or from foreign firms could lower demand for a new domestic product. For the two-digit SIC manufacturing industries in 1967, however, this is a negligible consideration since there were few negative coefficients of final demand (see U.S. Department of Commerce, 1974:43).

[9]For example, Fischler (1980) draws on case studies by Emmet and Jeuck (1950) and Kile (1948) to describe the self-interested nature of early philanthropic activities by Sears, Roebuck and Company. Sears controlled a large share of the mail-order market just before World War I. During 1912 and 1913, it made extensive donations to institutionalize the county agents and local farm bureaus within the American Farm Bureau Federation. The Federation's purpose, a purpose successfully realized, was to improve the well-being of American farmers, in part by training them in better ways of farming through county agents. Conveniently for Sears, the bulk of the mail-order business came from farmers. In a postwar presentation for the Federation, the president of Sears remarked on the stimulated demand occasioned by improved farmer income: "As the farmer prospers so we do prosper . . . and as his income falls, so does ours."

improve the well-being of persons *ostentatiously* to the extent that they have the previously defined market incentive to coopt the household sector. Philanthropic activities would be pursued for the same reason that firms merge with establishments operating in sectors constraining a firm's profits and cultivate ties through boards of directors to firms operating in those sectors. In this sense of being an effort to eliminate uncertainty in profits, corporate philanthropy constitutes a cooptive relation from the corporate actor to people collective as consumers in the household sector. More specifically, the level of philanthropy predicted by the microeconomic model in Eq. (6.1) can be expected to increase in a systematic way with increasing values of m_j. Extending Eq. (6.1) to include a market incentive effect, β_m, the following sociological model results:

$$g_j = \beta(c_j)^{\beta_c}(i_j)^{\beta_i}(m_j)^{\beta_m}(r_j), \tag{6.3}$$

where r_j is a residual term and the market incentive effect should be significantly greater than zero with price and income effects on philanthropy expenditures held constant.

I shall take this argument one step further. Confidence in the proposed understanding of philanthropy as a cooptive relation can be increased with evidence on its concomitants. By this I mean that the construct validity of the argument would be more strongly established if, in addition to showing that philanthropy is generated by a market incentive for cooptive relations to the household sector, I could also show that involvement in philanthropy covaried with involvement in a blatantly cooptive relation to people, a relation simultaneously generated by the market incentive for cooptive relations to the household sector. Such evidence would support an understanding of corporate philanthropy as a cooptive relation both in terms of its etiology and its concomitants. Readily available data make this extension of the argument feasible.

Corporate advertising is the blatantly cooptive relation I have in mind. Advertising expenditures are reported to the Internal Revenue Service along with philanthropy expenditures. Both advertising and donations are tax deductible and so encouraged by the same tax incentive. Both can increase to the extent that income is available. Most important for this discussion, both cultivate a favorable impression of the firm in the public eye. Although advertising is a more malleable and direct form of reaching people, it is typically received with suspicion. This is less true of donations. Used together, advertising and philanthropy should be nicely able to realize the two market functions of philanthropy described earlier, and so should be pursued simultaneously by firms exposed to a high market incentive to coopt the household sector. Philanthropy and advertising are not the same thing, nor do they operate in the same manner. However, they serve very similar functions with respect to the market incentive to coopt the household sector. Holding price and income constant, the firms most involved in philanthropy should be the firms most involved in advertising as a complement to philanthropy and should be those firms operating in sectors giving them a high market incentive to coopt the household sector.

ANALYSIS

I propose to assess this line of reasoning with expenditure data reported to the Internal Revenue Service by firms in American manufacturing industries. Dollars of expenditures are reported by economic sector, 20 of which correspond to the two-digit manufacturing industries analyzed in the preceding chapters. This is an unfortunately small number of observations; however, reliable data on donations are not available for the more narrowly-defined industries.[10] Using the tax return data compiled in the *Statistics of Income, Corporation Income Tax Returns* for firms showing a profit during 1967 (Internal Revenue Service, 1971), advertising and philanthropy expenditures have been computed as proportions of industry profit. The proportion of net income allocated to advertising is computed as the ratio of dollars of reported advertising over net income plus dollars of reported advertising. In accordance with the computation of the 5% limit on tax-deductible gifts, the proportion of profit allocated to philanthropy is computed as the dollars of reported contributions divided by net income plus dollars of contributions (Internal Revenue Service, 1971:187).

As expected, advertising and philanthropy expenditures have a positive correlation with one another, and both have a positive correlation with the market incentive for such expenditures. If the firms within an industry made extensive donations, they also allocated extensive funds to advertising. Log dollar expenditures on advertising are correlated .75 with log dollar expenditures on philanthropy. If those donations constituted a high proportion of their net income, a high proportion of net income was also allocated to advertising. Log proportionate expenditures have a .30 correlation with one another. The market incentive index in Eq. (6.2) has been computed for each industry as of 1967 using the structural autonomy scores in the Appendix and data on final demand in the aggregate input–output table (U.S. Department of Commerce, 1974). The natural logarithm of the market incentive m_j has strong, positive correlations with log proportionate expenditures, .75 for advertising and .39 for philanthropy. Table 6.1 reports mean expenditure data showing that these results were not idiosyncratic to 1967. The mean proportion of net income allocated to philanthropy in any one of the five years reported is correlated with the mean allocation to advertising, both means increasing toward the end of the 1960s ($r = .76$).

---

[10]Data could be compiled for the more narrowly-defined manufacturing industries; however, their reliability and accuracy would be suspect as I have explained in footnote 4 to Chapter 2. Johnson (1966:490–494) and Nelson (1970:107–110) provide informative discussion of issues in using these tax return data to analyze corporate giving.

TABLE 6.1
Corporate Philanthropy and Advertising from 1965 to 1969[a]

	1965	1966	1967	1968	1969
Mean percentage of profits spent on philanthropy by firms in					
Low incentive industries	.95%	.98%	.89%	1.10%	1.12%
All manufacturing industries	1.09%	1.03%	1.08%	1.26%	1.36%
High incentive industries	1.56%	1.49%	1.56%	1.53%	1.53%
Mean percentage of profits spent on advertising by firms in					
Low incentive industries	7.01%	6.69%	7.31%	7.09%	7.51%
All manufacturing industries	14.70%	14.52%	15.81%	15.27%	16.62%
High incentive industries	22.18%	20.92%	21.22%	20.89%	22.28%

[a]Ratios are based on data presented in the *Statistics of Income* series (e.g., Internal Revenue Service, 1971). Ratios for all manufacturing industries are based on the "total manufacturing" data in the series. Ratios for low market incentive industries are the means for five industries (lumber, stone–clay–glass, primary metals, fabricated metals, mechanical machinery). Ratios for high incentive industries are the means for five industries (food, apparel, furniture, leather, miscellaneous).

Annual time series on the market incentive m_j are not available since it is based on input–output data, so I have only drawn a crude distinction between the five industries in which there was a low market incentive in 1967 to coopt people versus five industries in which there was a high incentive. The five lowest industries stand apart in the distribution of m_j for all 20 industries, and the mean m_j for them is well below the mean for all industries (.005 versus .071, respectively). Firms in these industries (the lumber industry; the stone, clay, and glass industry; the primary metals industry; the fabricated metals industry; and the mechanical machines industry) had little to gain by improving the well-being of people, and their expenditures show it. On average, they allocated 0.89% of their net income to philanthropy and allocated 7.31% to advertising. Both allocations were well below the 1967 averages for all industries reported in Table 6.1. Six industries clearly stand apart as high market incentive industries in 1967, and the mean m_j for them is well above the mean for all industries (.166 versus .071, respectively). Firms in these industries (the food industry, the tobacco industry, the apparel industry, the furniture industry, the leather industry, and the diverse subsectors known as the miscellaneous industry) had a great deal to gain by acquiring recognition as contributors to the well-being of people. Putting aside the tobacco industry for reasons that will be clear shortly, the remaining five high incentive industries made above-average allocations in 1967 to philanthropy and advertising. On average, they allocated 1.56% of their net income to philanthropy and 21.22% to advertising. These differences between low and high market incentive industries in 1967 were characteristic of the late 1960s. From

1965 to 1969, the mean proportion of profits allocated to philanthropy by firms in the low incentive industries was consistently lower than that given by firms in the high incentive industries. The same is true for the mean proportion of profits allocated to advertising. Further, these two types of expenditures were consistently lower in the low incentive industries than they were for manufacturing as a whole. They were consistently higher in the high incentive industries than they were for manufacturing as a whole.

These results ignore industry differences in the cost of philanthropy or advertising and differences in the profit typically available to be allocated to such expenditures. Along with the market incentive, these differences could be responsible for industry differences in expenditures. The profit margin typical of industry j in 1967 has been computed as p_j in Chapter 2. This is the proportion of sales that is profit and so available to be allocated to nondirect cost activities such as advertising or philanthropy. The unit cost, or price, of advertising and philanthropy for firms in industry j, c_j, is the complement of the industry tax rate which is taken from the 1967 tax return data in the *Statistics of Income*.[11] Given a price C, an income available as profit P, and a market incentive M for an industry, the industry expenditures E on advertising and philanthropy should be determined by the following equation [cf. Eq. (6.3)]:

$$E = b(C)^{b_c}(P)^{b_i}(M)^{b_m}(R),$$

which can be estimated with ordinary-least squares after taking the natural logarithm of both sides of the equation:

$$\ln E = \ln b + b_c(\ln C) + b_i(\ln P) + b_m(\ln M) + \ln R. \qquad (6.4)$$

I shall use this regression equation to describe unconstrained price (b_c), income (b_i), and market incentive (b_m) effects on philanthropy and advertising expenditures in 1967. Tables 6.2 and 6.3 contain estimates of the effects.

Point estimates of the effects are presented in Table 6.2 with two different specifications of the residual term R in Eq. (6.4). Let e be a random error with $\ln e$ having the usual properties of an error term in least-squares estimation. The

---

[11]More specifically, c_j is defined as one minus the ratio of industry tax due over industry taxable income: $c_j = 1 - $ (industry tax due)/(industry taxable income). In computing the price of philanthropy for persons, Feldstein and Taylor (1976:1202, 1207–1208) point out that price must be computed from tax rates that consider the added income a person would have had if no donations were made. Since personal tax rates are progressive, the added income forgone in donations could easily put him into a higher tax bracket, which would lessen the price of making donations and so strengthen the price effect on making donations. Corporate tax rates, however, are far less progressive than those for persons. In 1967, corporate tax was computed as 22% of taxable income plus 26% of taxable income exceeding a surtax exemption, the exemption having a maximum of $25,000 (Internal Revenue Service, 1971:182ff). This comparatively flat tax rate for the added income that philanthropy would generate and the fact that a whole industry is being characterized by a single tax rate suggest the simple ratio of tax due over taxable income as an adequate measure of industry tax rate.

TABLE 6.2
Price, Income, and Market Incentive Effects in 1967[a]

	b	Market incentive b_m	Price b_c	Income b_i	b_d	Multiple correlation
Proportion of profits spent on philanthropy given						
$R = e$	.04	.11	.86	.15	−.80	.79
	(3.4)	(0.7)	(0.6)	(4.0)		
$R = e(D^{b_d})$	.07	.08	1.97	.19	—	.48
	(1.9)	(1.2)	(0.6)			
Proportion of profits spent on advertising given						
$R = e$	.38	.21	−.89	.64	−.04	.82
	(4.4)	(0.5)	(1.8)	(0.2)		
$R = e(D^{b_d})$	.39	.21	−.83	.64	—	.82
	(4.6)	(0.5)	(1.9)			

[a] Ordinary least-squares regression estimates of the parameters in Eq. (6.4) are presented with t-tests given in parentheses. Estimates are based on the 20 two-digit industries, and b_d is the amount by which log expenditures in the tobacco and transportation equipment industries must be adjusted in order for them to match the expenditures expected as a result of price, income, and market incentive effects for industries generally.

residual term R is first treated in Table 6.2 as equivalent to e and then treated as a product of e and (D^{b_d}), the latter expressing a systematic tendency for the tobacco and transportation equipment industries to give less to charity than would have been expected from the market incentive, price, and income conditions in the two industries. The dummy variable D equals one for all industries except tobacco and transportation equipment, for which it equals 2.7183, the natural logarithm base. Under this second specification of the residual in Eq. (6.4), R equals $e(D^{b_d})$ and the natural logarithm of R, ln R, equals ln $e + b_d(\ln D)$, which means that the log dummy variable is the usual zero–one dummy variable in the estimation equation and b_d is the adjustment in log expenditures required in order to predict spending by firms in the tobacco and transportation equipment industries. An examination of the residuals when R is assumed to equal the random error e suggested the adjustment for tobacco and transportation equipment expenditures. The distribution of the (ln e) residuals when R equals $e(D^{b_d})$ does not suggest a respecification of the equation, and a linear functional form yields squared multiple correlations lower than those obtained with the multiplicative model.

In order to demonstrate the stability of the market incentive effect across different measures of philanthropy expenditures and profit, interval estimates of price, income, and market incentive effects on philanthropy are presented in

Table 6.3 for three expenditure measures and two income measures. As is clear
from the interval estimates of the tobacco–transportation adjustment, b_d, in the
table, these estimates have been obtained from Eq. (6.4) when the residual term
is specified as $e(D^{b_d})$. The three expenditure measures are (a) total dollars of
contributions from an industry (e.g., Nelson, 1970), (b) per capita dollars of
contributions [computed as the total dollars divided by the number of tax returns
submitted with net income, e.g., Schwartz (1966)], and (c) the proportion of
profit measure used in Table 6.2 (e.g., Johnson, 1966). Different income measures are appropriate for predicting the three expenditure measures. Using the
1967 tax return data, (a) a total income measure has been coded as the dollars of
net income reported plus the dollars spent on contributions, (b) a per capita
income measure has been computed as total income divided by the number of
industry tax returns submitted with net income, and (c) a profit margin measure
has been computed as the ratio of total net income (after taxes) divided by total
receipts. Unfortunately, these tax return measures contain the same sampling–coding problems contained in the expenditure measures and so constitute
stochastic rather than true predictors of the expenditures. In response to this
problem, I have also measured industry income with the *Census of Manufactures*
data for 1967. These are population data and do not force all of a firm's holdings
into a single industry (see footnote 4 to Chapter 2). Census income measures
correspond to the tax return income measures: (a) total income being the dollars
by which value added for an industry exceeded labor costs (correlated .90 with
the tax return measure), (b) per capita income being the ratio of dollars of total
income over the number of companies in an industry (correlated .94 with the tax
return measure), and (c) profit margin being the corrected price–cost margins,
p_j, used to estimate effects in Table 6.2 (correlated .77 with the tax return
measure of industry profit margin). If nothing were known about the direction of
the effects in Eq. (6.4) and repeated samples were drawn to replicate the data
used here, one could expect the parameter estimates for Eq. (6.4) estimated in
four out of five repeated samples to lie within the intervals given in Table 6.3.[12]

---

[12]In fact, these interval estimates are likely to have a higher than .80 probability of containing
estimates in replicate samples. The intervals are computed (see footnote a of Table 6.3) under the
assumption of independent replicate samples; however, only expenditures by small firms are projec-
tions from sample data (see footnote 4 to Chapter 2). All firms with assets over $10 million are
tabulated in the expenditure measures. Since these large firms are responsible for a disproportionately
large share of expenditures, replicate samples are likely to yield expenditure estimates similar to
those published by the Internal Revenue Service. Not only would replicate samples generate interdependent estimates because of all large firms appearing in each sample, all 20 two-digit industries have
been used to estimate Eq. (6.4). Because the standard errors used to compute interval estimates for
Table 6.3 are based on observed variance and much of that variance would be stable across replicate
samples, the intervals in Table 6.3 probably have a higher than .80 probability of containing estimates in replicate samples. I have presented them, nevertheless, as illustration of the stability of the
market incentive effect. This robustness merits attention given the small number of industries and the
policy relevance of the effects estimated.

TABLE 6.3

Interval Estimates of Effects on Corporate Philanthropy in 1967[a]

	Market incentive b_m	Price b_c	Income (b_i)		b_d	Multiple correlation
			Tax returns	Census		
Proportion of profits spent on philanthropy	0.07 to 0.16	−0.94 to 2.28	−0.28 to 0.33	—	−1.09 to −0.53	.78
	0.07 to 0.16	−0.76 to 2.48	—	−0.18 to 0.48	−1.07 to −0.53	.79
Per capita dollars spent on philanthropy	0.03 to 0.12	−1.82 to 1.76	0.81 to 0.98	—	−0.93 to −0.26	.98
	0.02 to 0.17	1.02 to 7.90	—	0.85 to 1.20	−0.68 to 0.37	.94
Total dollars spent on philanthropy	0.02 to 0.11	−1.76 to 1.96	0.79 to 1.00	—	−1.09 to −0.53	.96
	0.01 to 0.15	−4.64 to 0.48	—	0.71 to 1.05	−0.87 to −0.06	.91

[a]These are 80%, two-tail confidence intervals defined as $b \pm 1.34(SE)$, where SE is the standard error of the estimate b (but see footnote 12 for further interpretation). The alternative income measures are computed from tax return data versus census data as explained in the text. The intervals for proportionate philanthropy are interval estimates of the parameters expressed as point estimates in Table 6.2. The parameters estimated are specified in Eq. (6.4).

I draw three conclusions from the estimates in Tables 6.2 and 6.3 in regard to the connection between corporate philanthropy and the market incentive to coopt the household sector.

First, there is evidence of a strong market incentive effect. In all four equations reported in Table 6.2, the market incentive effect on philanthropy and advertising is significantly greater than zero. With the adjustment for tobacco and transportation equipment, the market incentive effect for both expenditures is significantly greater than zero at beyond the .001 level of confidence. Without the adjustment, the effect on philanthropic expenditures is lower but still significantly greater than zero beyond the .05 level of confidence. The standardized estimates of the effects for philanthropy and advertising are .56 and .69, respectively, with the adjustment for tobacco–transportation, and .42 and .68, respectively, without the adjustment. The metric estimate of the market incentive effect on philanthropy is a small fraction. In four out of five repeated samples, one could expect estimates of the market incentive effect on philanthropy [b_m in Eq. (6.4)] to be a positive, but very small, fraction contained within intervals ranging from a minimum of .01 up to .17 as a maximum (see footnote 12). In terms of the absolute magnitude of this coefficient, very similar estimates are reported in Table 6.3 for each of the three types of expenditure measures: total dollars of philanthropy, per capita dollars, and proportion of profits. This means that the market incentive had its most dramatic effect in industries providing a low incentive to coopt the household sector. I shall return to the metric of the market incentive effect in a moment. For now, it is clear that the firms increased their philanthropy and advertising expenditures to the extent that their network positions in the economy gave them a market incentive to coopt the household sector.

Second, the proportion of profits allocated to philanthropy and advertising is much more determined by the market incentive than it is by price or income. Two conclusions summarize price and income effects: (a) The level of expenditures on philanthropy and advertising is strongly associated with the level of net income as profits; however, the rate of expenditures is not. (b) The price of advertising and making donations—in terms of the tax advantages of such expenditures—had no effect on expenditures.

Income is positively associated with philanthropy and advertising. The estimates of b_i in Table 6.2 are positive, and those for advertising are significantly greater than zero at a .05 level of confidence. All income effects in the table, however, are less significantly different from zero than corresponding market incentive effects. Switching from the rate of giving to the amount given, there is evidence of a strong income effect. The association between dollars (per capita dollars) of profit and dollars (per capita dollars) of philanthropy and advertising in an industry is significantly greater than zero beyond the .001 level of confidence. As could be expected from past research, estimates of this income effect, b_i, are equal to or slightly less than 1.0 (see Table 6.3). This association in raw dollars does not mean that industries with a high volume of business had a high rate of giving. The proportion of net income allocated to philanthropy is not contingent on the proportion of sales that was net income as reported in Table 6.2. Not reported are regression equations in which dollars of net income and per capita dollars of net income also fail to predict the proportion of profit allocated to philanthropy.

Turning to the price effect columns in Tables 6.2 and 6.3, skepticism over tax incentives for corporate philanthropy certainly seems justified. Price had no unique effect on the level or rate of corporate philanthropy expenditures in 1967. Typically, the interval estimates of the price effect contain negative values; however, point estimates cannot be interpreted with confidence. In four out of five repeated samples, the price effect on philanthropy [b_c in Eq. (6.4)] could range from -4.64 to 7.90. Price is not a determinant of dollar expenditures because of the close association between income and price. The correlation between log scores of price and dollar expenditures for philanthropy and advertising are negative and quite strong: $-.40$ and $-.57$, respectively, for total dollars of expenditures and $-.52$ and $-.56$, respectively, for per capita dollars. However, industries with a high tax rate (and therefore low price) were industries with extensive net income as profits. This creates a strong negative correlation between dollars of income and price that (given the very strong association between dollars of income and dollars of expenditures) results in price having no direct effect on 1967 expenditures when income is held constant. Price does not have even a zero-order association with the proportion of net income allocated to philanthropy or advertising.

My third conclusion is that the market incentive effect was more likely to result in advertising than in philanthropy. To some extent, this is demonstrated by the means in Table 6.1, advertising being allocated a mean 15.81% of industry profits whereas philanthropy was allocated only 1.08%. Further, advertising expenditures are more accurately predicted than philanthropy expenditures by the market incentive index. Standardized estimates of b_m are larger and more significantly different from zero for advertising than they are for philanthropy. Further still, the metric estimates of b_m are higher for advertising than for philanthropy. This difference reflects the tendency for advertising expenditures to have increased more quickly than philanthropy expenditures with increasing market incentive to coopt the household sector. Finally, philanthropy expenditures require a special downward adjustment not necessary for advertising expenditures. The adjustment for spending by firms in the tobacco and transportation equipment industries, $\hat{b}_q$, is negative for both types of expenditures. However, it is significantly negative only for philanthropy expenditures. An analysis of intraindustry directorate ties vis-à-vis industry concentration showed that the tobacco and transportation equipment industries were clear outliers from an otherwise positive, monotonic association between the frequency of intraindustry ties and the level of industry concentration (Burt, 1980c). Firms in these industries were argued to have no special need for directorate ties. They were capable of coordi-

nating their actions without actually sharing members of their respective directorates. This point is argued in the more general context of four-digit industries in
Chapter 4. The point here is that firms in the tobacco and transportation equipment industries in 1967 could look forward to stable profits. They had no special
need to coopt people as a consumer sector. Although these industries did not
provide equal market incentive to institutionalize relations with people, firms in
both industries had equally unexpectedly low involvement in philanthropic activities. Thus the strongly negative adjustment $\hat{b}_d$ for philanthropy expenditures.
No such adjustment was necessary for advertising expenditures. In short, firms
within these industries did not choose to contribute a proportion of their profits to
philanthropy as would have been expected from their market incentive to do so—
but they did allocate profits to advertising in proportion to that market incentive.
This situation might be different at later points in time, given the increasing
federal regulation of these industries and the public displeasure with the efficiency of Detroit automobiles and the cancer connection with smoking, but the
dominant feature of relations with people in 1967 was an asymmetric flow of
information in the form of advertising to people from tobacco and transportation
equipment firms.[13]

[13]The significance of the tobacco and transportation equipment spending adjustment suggests a
negative relation between concentration within an industry and philanthropy. Johnson (1966:495)
presents a graph showing a negative correlation between the percentage of profits allocated to
philanthropy and industry concentration. Bennett and Johnson (1980:140–141) show that this negative association remains significant when various other industry characteristics are held constant.
Since concentration ratios are a component in industry structural autonomy, which in turn produces
the market incentive for philanthropy in Eq. (5.2), the negative association between concentration
and philanthropy suggests that the negative effect of concentration has been obscured by aggregating
it into structural autonomy. There is a negative correlation between the proportion of profits allocated
to philanthropy within the two-digit industries considered here and the typical four-firm concentration
ratio for four-digit subsectors of the industry ($r = -.60$, using logarithms of 1967 data). This
warranted constructing a new measure of market incentive in which the aggregate concentration in
two-digit industries was used in place of structural autonomy in Eq. (6.2). Reestimating Eq. (6.4) in
log form with this alternative measure yields the same, but weaker, results discussed in the text. The
proportion of profits given to philanthropy is predicted by the concentration measure of market
incentive (mc_j) as:

$$\ln g_j = -2.98 + .11(\ln mc_j) + 1.34(\ln c_j) + .17(\ln p_j) - .86 (\ln d_j) + \ln e_j,$$
$$\qquad\qquad\quad (3.1)\qquad\qquad (1.0)\qquad\quad (0.7)\qquad\quad (4.0)$$

where the t-tests in parentheses are not much different from those reported in Table 6.2. The results
for predicting advertising are stronger, yielding a 4.2 T-test of the concentration-based market
incentive effect. In short, the market incentive effect discussed here refers to the interaction effect of
firms having an advantage in coopting people and having the market freedom to be able to do so.
These slightly weaker results for concentration alone are to be expected since concentration is only a
part of the equation defining the market freedom of firms. Concentration alone does not consider
constraint from suppliers and consumers. Structural autonomy does, so stronger market incentive
effects should be obtained when structural autonomy is used to measure the market incentive in Eq.
(6.2), and they are. Of course, these are two-digit data, and market effects are difficult to observe at
this level of aggregation. Much more significant market effects are obtained for the four-digit data in

This third inference from the results in Table 6.2 raises a question. To what extent are the different price, income, and market incentive effects on advertising versus philanthropy a result of the smaller scale of philanthropy expenditures? They could be a result of nonnegligible differences in the processes generating these expenditures. Income is more important to advertising than it is to philanthropy. The market incentive has a stronger effect on advertising than it does on philanthropy. On the other hand, the observed differences could merely be a result of the broader range of advertising expenditures in the sense that the amount of advertising expected from an industry is a single parameter transformation increasing the amount of philanthropy expected from the industry.

This question can be addressed by constraining price, income, and market incentive effects to be identical for the two types of expenditures and allowing for a broader range of advertising expenditures. Let g_j be a true proportion of profits expected to be allocated to philanthropy within industry j as a consequence of price, income, and market incentive effects [cf. Eq. (6.3)]:

$$\mathbf{g}_j = \beta(m_j)^{\beta_m}(c_j)^{\beta_c}(p_j)^{\beta_i}. \tag{6.5}$$

Actual philanthropy expenditures equal this expected proportion weighted by a residual term for philanthropy, r_{jg}:

$$g_j = (\mathbf{g}_j)(r_{jg}). \tag{6.6a}$$

Actual advertising expenditures equal the expected philanthropy expenditure weighted to reflect the higher level of advertising expenditures (α), the resulting higher variation in advertising expenditures (γ), and a residual term for advertising, r_{jv}:

$$v_j = \alpha(\mathbf{g}_j)^\gamma(r_{jv}), \tag{6.6b}$$

where v_j is the proportion of industry net income allocated to advertising. If the adjustment for tobacco and transportation equipment industries is to be made, the residual terms in Eqs. (6.6) are products of a random error (e) and underspending by firms in the tobacco and transportation equipment industries measured by an exponent to the dummy variable d_j:

$$g_j = (\mathbf{g}_j)(d_j)^{\gamma_g}(e_{jg}), \tag{6.7a}$$

$$v_j = \alpha(\mathbf{g}_j)^\gamma(d_j)^{\gamma_v}(e_{jv}). \tag{6.7b}$$

These models can be treated as examples of the canonical correlation class of covariance structures. Eqs. (6.5)–(6.7) are linear and additive when expressed in terms of natural logarithms. The path diagrams representing them (ignoring the

---

Chapter 2, so differences between market incentive effects based on structural autonomy versus concentration alone should be more significant at the four-digit level than they are here—if philanthropy data could be obtained at the more detailed level.

level effects β and α) are presented in Figure 6.1, Eqs. (6.6) represented by the upper diagram and Eqs. (6.7) represented by the lower diagram. The important feature of these diagrams for this discussion is the single dimension of corporate giving determined by a price effect, an income effect, and a market incentive effect. This specification says that the two price effects would be observed for philanthropy and advertising separately, but the underlying effect would be a price effect for philanthropy, β_c, and an identical price effect for advertising but increased to express the broader range of advertising expenditures, $\beta_c\gamma$. Similarly, there is a single market incentive effect for philanthropy, β_m. There is an identical market incentive effect for advertising, but it is increased to express the broader range of advertising expenditures, $\beta_m\gamma$. The model specified in Eqs. (6.5) and (6.6), the model diagrammed at the top of Figure 6.1, is a canonical correlation model relating m_j, c_j, p_j with g_j, v_j and setting the variation of the canonical variate $\mathbf{g}_j$ equal to the variation in corporate giving, g_j, that is predicted by price, income, and market incentive effects.[14] The model specified in Eqs.

---

[14]It is useful to make this analogy explicit even though the computations are readily available in the published literature (e.g., Hauser and Goldberger, 1971). It is useful to give details on this comparatively simple model because the same computations are necessary in the slightly more complicated model of interest here. There are four steps to estimating effects in the model at the top of Figure 6.1. (a) Routine canonical correlation results are obtained relating m_j, c_j, p_j with the two expenditure variables g_j and v_j. Let x_m, x_c, and x_i be the canonical weights for m_j, c_j, and p_j, respectively, on the largest canonical correlation. Let y_g and y_v be the corresponding canonical weights for g_j and v_j, respectively. Let λ be that largest canonical correlation. As indicated in Figure 6.1, all scores should be expressed as log scores. I am not writing ln in front of each variable here merely in order to simplify the presentation. (b) The correlations between the canonical variate predicted by price, income, and market incentive and the two expenditure variables are obtained. Let R_y be the (2,1) vector containing these correlations and R_{yy} be the (2,2) correlation matrix among the two log expenditure measures. The two canonical weights y_g and y_v form a (2,1) vector Y corresponding to R_y. With canonical weights based on correlations among the observed variables, the desired correlations are given as $R_y = \lambda R_{yy}Y$. (c) The predicted variance in philanthropy is obtained. Given r_g as the correlation between the price–income–market-incentive canonical variate and observed philanthropy, the variance in philanthropy predicted by the three market variables is the product of the correlation r_g squared and the observed variance in philanthropy: $r_g^2 s_g^2$, where s_g is the observed standard deviation in philanthropy. (d) Standardized effects are transformed to metric estimates. With the canonical weights based on correlations among the observed variables, the canonical weights for price, income, and market incentive are standardized estimates of price, income, and market incentive effects. The standard deviation of $\mathbf{g}_j$ is the predicted standard deviation in observed philanthropy: $s_{\mathbf{g}} = r_g s_g$. Metric estimates of the price, income, and market incentive effects are therefore given as $\hat{\beta}_m = x_m s_{\mathbf{g}}/s_m$, $\hat{\beta}_c = x_c s_{\mathbf{g}}/s_c$, and $\hat{\beta}_i = x_i s_{\mathbf{g}}/s_i$, where s_m, s_c, and s_i are standard deviations of log scores for m_j, c_j, and p_j, respectively. The adjustment for the broader range of advertising expenditures is similarly given as $\hat{\gamma} = r_v s_v/s_{\mathbf{g}}$. The path leading from $\mathbf{g}_j$ to observed donations, g_j, equals $r_g s_g/s_{\mathbf{g}}$, which is equal to one since $s_{\mathbf{g}}$ has been set equal to $r_g s_g$. A fifth computational step would be needed in order to obtain the two intercept terms. The philanthropy intercept is given as ln $\hat{\beta} = \bar{g} - \hat{\beta}_m\bar{m} - \hat{\beta}_c\bar{c} - \hat{\beta}_i\bar{p}$, where $\bar{g}$, $\bar{m}$, $\bar{c}$, and $\bar{p}$ are means. The increased intercept for advertising is the product $\alpha\beta^\gamma$, where the component α is specified in Eq. (6.6b) and given as ln $\hat{\alpha} = (\bar{v} - \hat{\gamma}\hat{\beta}_m\bar{m} - \hat{\gamma}\hat{\beta}_c\bar{c} - \hat{\gamma}\hat{\beta}_i\bar{p}) - \hat{\gamma}(\ln \hat{\beta})$ in which $\bar{v}$ is the mean advertising expenditure. Means here are all geometric means since the variables have been measured as log scores.

TABLE 6.4

Constrained Price, Income, and Market Incentive Effects (cf. Table 6.2)[a]

	Intercept	Market incentive	Price	Income		Squared multiple correlation
Percentage of profits spent on philanthropy	$\hat{\beta}$	$\hat{\beta}_m$	$\hat{\beta}_c$	$\hat{\beta}_i$	$\hat{\gamma}_g$	
Eq. (6.6a)	.02	.09	-.02	.24	-.66	.51
Eq. (6.5a)	.02	.07	-.07	.20		.15
Percentage of profits spent on advertising	$\hat{\alpha}\hat{\beta}\hat{\gamma}$	$\hat{\gamma}\hat{\beta}_m$	$\hat{\gamma}\hat{\beta}_c$	$\hat{\gamma}\hat{\beta}_i$	$\hat{\gamma}_v$	
Eq. (6.6b)	.51	.20	-.04	.51	.36	.64
Eq. (6.5b)	.57	.21	-.22	.64		.66

[a] Effects are specified in Eqs. (6.5)–(6.7) and diagrammed in Figure 6.1. Estimates unadjusted for low spending by tobacco and transportation equipment firms are specified in Eqs. (6.6), diagrammed at the top of Figure 6.1, and correspond to rows 2 and 4 in Table 6.2. Estimation is explained in Footnote 14. Adjusted estimates are specified in Eqs. (6.7), diagrammed at the bottom of Figure 6.1, and correspond to rows 1 and 3 in Table 6.2. Estimation is explained in footnote 15.

(6.5) and (6.7), the model diagrammed at the bottom of Figure 6.1, is slightly more complicated since it contains an adjustment for the tobacco and transportation equipment industries; however, it too is no more than a variation on the canonical correlation model.[15] This connection with the canonical correlation model means that estimates of the unknown parameters are easily available and there is a routine test statistic for the hypothesis that there is only a single price effect, income effect, and market incentive effect determining both advertising and philanthropy expenditures. Table 6.4 reports estimates of the unknown parameters in Figure 6.1. The table corresponds to Table 6.2 in which unconstrained estimates are presented. If the observed price, income, and market

---

[15]The variation is that canonical weights are computed from partial correlations rather than zero-order correlations. A detailed discussion of the computations is available elsewhere (Hauser, 1972, esp. the Appendix). All five log variables in the diagram at the top of Figure 6.1 (i.e., m_j, c_j, p_j, v_j, and g_j) are regressed over the dummy variable d_j, and the residuals from this regression are the scores input to a routine canonical correlation estimation relating the three residual market variables with the two residual expenditure variables. This provides canonical weights for the three market variables (x_m, x_c, x_i), canonical weights for the two expenditure variables (y_v, y_g), and a partial canonical correlation λ, a canonical correlation expressing the maximum correlation between the three market variables and expenditures adjusted for low spending by firms in the tobacco and transportation equipment industries. With these results in hand, computations can proceed as described in steps b through d in footnote 14. A fifth computational step is needed in order to obtain the two intercept terms. The philanthropy intercept can be computed as $\ln \hat{\beta} = \bar{g} - \hat{\beta}_m \bar{m} - \hat{\beta}_c \bar{c} - \hat{\beta}_i \bar{p} - \hat{\gamma}_g \bar{d}$, where $\bar{g}$, $\bar{m}$, $\bar{c}$, $\bar{p}$, and $\bar{d}$ are mean log scores. I have included the intercept component for the dummy variable d_j even though it does not appear in Eq. (6.5). So computed, β is the intercept term for the full equation determining observed giving in Eq. (6.7a). The increased intercept for advertising is the product $\alpha\beta^\gamma$, where the component α is specified in (6.7b) and given as $\ln \hat{\alpha} = \bar{v} - \hat{\gamma}\hat{\beta}_m \bar{m} - \hat{\gamma}\hat{\beta}_c \bar{c} - \hat{\gamma}\hat{\beta}_i \bar{p} - \hat{\gamma}_v \bar{d} - \hat{\gamma}(\ln \hat{\beta})$ in which $\bar{v}$ is the mean log advertising expenditure. A final note concerns the adjustment effects, γ_v and γ_g. This procedure for estimating constrained effects completely eliminates the effect of d_j from the associations between the market variables and expenditure variables. The effects constrained here are only the direct effects of the three market variables. Direct and indirect (through the market variables) effects of the dummy variable d_j are aggregated into the direct effects of d_j in the constrained model. In other words, the constrained model is a conservative representation of price, income, and market incentive effects. The direct effect of adjustment for philanthropy expenditures is the estimated value of b_d for g_j in Table 6.2 ($\hat{b}_{d(g)} = -.80$). The direct adjustment for philanthropy expenditures in the constrained model, γ_g, is a sum of this unconstrained direct effect and unconstrained indirect effects through the market variables. That sum is simply that regression of giving, g_j, over the dummy variable d_j, ignoring the three market variables; that is, $\hat{\gamma}_g = \hat{b}_{d(g)} + (\hat{b}_m\hat{b}_{md} + \hat{b}_c\hat{b}_{cd} + \hat{b}_i\hat{b}_{pd}) = r_{gd}s_g/s_d$, where the parenthetical expression is the sum of indirect effects on giving from the dummy variable, the unconstrained market variable effects are given in row 1 of Table 6.2 ($\hat{b}_m$, $\hat{b}_c$, $\hat{b}_i$), the regression coefficients leading to these variables from the dummy are $\hat{b}_{md}$, $\hat{b}_{cd}$, and $\hat{b}_{pd}$, respectively, and r_{gd} is the zero-order correlation between the dummy variable d_j and corporate philanthropy g_j. The adjustment for advertising expenditures in the constrained model is similarly computed as the zero-order direct effect of d_j on v_j: $\hat{\gamma}_v = r_{vd}s_v/s_d$, where r_{vd} is the correlation between v_j and d_j, s_v is the standard deviation of v_j, and s_d is the standard deviation of d_j, all variables expressed as log scores. This summing of direct and indirect effects in the constrained model is apparent from a comparison of Tables 6.4 and 6.2. The adjustments $\hat{\gamma}_v$ and $\hat{\gamma}_g$ in Table 6.4 are more positive than their corresponding estimates under b_d in Table 6.2.

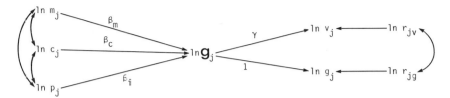

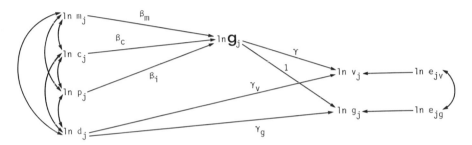

Figure 6.1. Path diagrams of the effects among log scores specified in Eqs. (6.5)–(6.7). The top diagram contains the parameters reported in Table 6.3 as unadjusted estimates, and the bottom diagram contains those reported as adjusted estimates.

incentive effects on philanthropy and advertising were in fact generated by a single underlying process—allowing for the broader range of advertising expenditures—then the estimates in Tables 6.2 and 6.4 would be identical.[16]

There is evidence of a single process of price, income, and market incentive effects generating the two types of expenditures. The estimates in Tables 6.2 and 6.4 are not identical, but the differences between them are statistically trivial.

[16]There are a great variety of methods by which the effects of the three market variables could be constrained to reflect a single underlying process generating the expenditure data. The method adopted here based on canonical correlation has the advantage of being well understood and easily available. For the reader interested in alternative specifications, however, the moments from which effects have been computed are listed below as a correlation matrix with standard deviations in the diagonal:

$$
\begin{array}{lcccccc}
\ln m_j & (1.8536) \\
\ln c_j & -.1825 & (.0524) \\
\ln p_j & .1954 & -.3067 & (.2514) \\
\ln d_j & .2515 & -.2645 & .0785 & (.3078) \\
\ln g_j & .3942 & .1643 & .1247 & -.5521 & (.3689) \\
\ln v_j & .7547 & -.2899 & .4438 & .1934 & .2990 & (.5643)
\end{array}
$$

Assume, for a moment, that the residual terms r_{jg} and r_{jv} are random errors so that effects can be estimated directly from Eqs. (6.5) and (6.6), the model diagrammed at the top of Figure 6.1. The canonical variate $\mathbf{g}_j$ in this model is that combination of price, income, and market incentive that is maximally correlated with observed expenditures. That maximum correlation (the canonical correlation associated with $\mathbf{g}_j$) is .83 and is significantly greater than zero at the .002 level of confidence. The likelihood ratio χ^2 for the null hypothesis is 20.82 with 6 degrees of freedom. This one canonical variate is sufficient to describe covariation with both types of expenditures, given the fact that the second canonical correlation is not significantly different from zero (χ^2 of 1.85 with 2 degrees of freedom, $p = .40$). Even without an adjustment for the tobacco and transportation equipment industries, in other words, philanthropy and advertising expenditures can be interpreted as outcomes of identical price, income, and market incentive effects—allowing for the broader range of advertising expenditures. (The estimated adjustment for that broader range is well above one: $\hat{\gamma} = 3.28$.) It is no surprise, therefore, to find that identical price, income, and market incentive effects generate both types of expenditures adjusted for low spending by firms in the tobacco and transportation equipment industries. The canonical variate $\mathbf{g}_j$ generated by Eqs. (6.5) and (6.7) is that combination of price, income, and market incentive that is maximally correlated with expenditures adjusted for spending by tobacco and transportation equipment firms. This maximum correlation, a partial canonical correlation holding constant spending by tobacco and transportation equipment firms, is .85 and is significantly greater than zero at the .001 level of confidence ($\chi^2 = 23.05$ with 6 degrees of freedom). A second canonical variate would be needed in order to describe observed covariation with expenditures adequately if there were significant differences between price, or income, or market incentive effects on philanthropy versus advertising—differences beyond the adjustment γ for the broader range of advertising expenditures. However, the covariation unexplained by the one variate $\mathbf{g}_j$ in Eqs. (6.6) is trivial (χ^2 of 1.41 with 2 degrees of freedom, $p = .49$).[17] In short, the estimated

[17]The χ^2 tests reported here are large-sample approximations and so are hardly exact when applied to data on the 20 two-digit industries. For both models in Figure 6.1, however, the second canonical correlation is so negligible relative to the first and so negligible in terms of the small χ^2 statistic it generates that the large-sample test statistics are used here more as a routine report of significance than as an actual decision criterion. Small-sample corrections to the χ^2 statistics would not increase them sufficiently to reject the null hypothesis regarding the second canonical correlation. More descriptively, the first canonical variate describes almost all of the covariation available to be explained in each model: 87% of the covariation in the model at the top of Figure 6.1 and 90% of the covariation in the model at the bottom of the figure. The total covariation available to be explained is indexed by the sum of the two canonical correlations squared, and these percentages are the ratio of the first canonical correlation squared over the relevant total. If the price, income, and market incentive effects for philanthropy versus advertising were identical, these percentages would be 100%. They are very close to that ideal.

price effect ($\hat{\beta}_c$), income effect ($\hat{\beta}_i$), and market incentive effect ($\hat{\beta}_m$) reported in Table 6.4 underlie both corporate philanthropy and corporate advertising. The price effect is a small negative fraction, the income effect is a much larger positive fraction, and the market incentive effect is a small positive fraction.

The small positive fraction estimated as a market incentive effect implies that the market incentive had its most dramatic effects on expenditures in low incentive industries. This point is easily demonstrated by tracing the changes in philanthropy and advertising expected across different levels of market incentive. Consider the hypothetical example of a diversified corporation shifting its principal manufacturing activities from one industry into another perceived to have more stable future profits. If this shift took the firm from an industry providing a low incentive to coopt people into one providing a high incentive, then a drastic marginal increase in the firm's philanthropic and advertising expenditures would have occurred—ceteris paribus. The expected changes are graphed in Figure 6.2.[18] Reading from the graph, and realizing that this is merely a heuristic device, suppose that the firm had moved from the primary metals industry (for which m_j is .0001, a minimal incentive to the far left of the graph) into the chemicals industry (for which m_j is a slightly higher .0495 to the right of the primary metals industry). Following the curve of expected philanthropy, the firm would be expected to have increased its charitable donations from 0.67% of its profits up to 1.21% of its profits, almost twice what it was previously donating. These two points are marked A and B on the philanthropy graph. Firms more accustomed to the market incentive would not have reacted so drastically. A firm that shifted its principal operations from the chemical industry into the food industry (for which m_j is still further to the right in Figure 6.2 at a value of .1874) would be expected to have increased its charitable donations from 1.21% of its profits up to 1.36% of its profits, a miserly 1.1 times what it was donating before. This point is marked C on the philanthropy graph. In short, it would seem that the most critical contact with people for generating corporate philanthropy occurred with initial contact. Firms in industries subject to severe

---

[18]I have taken the ceteris paribus conditions to mean that the hypothetical firm is operating in industry j, an industry with an average tax rate and an average profit margin. The proportion of profits expected to be spent on philanthropy, $\hat{g}_j$, is then given by Eq. (6.7a) as

$$\hat{g}_j = [\beta(\bar{c})^{\beta_c}(\bar{p})^{\beta_i}](m_j)^{\beta_m} = .016(m_j)^{.094},$$

where $\bar{c}$ and $\bar{p}$ are the geometric mean values of c_j and p_j across all 20 industries. If the firm shifted its principal operations into the tobacco or transportation equipment industries, this equation would have to include the adjustment for spending in these industries ($d^{\gamma g}$ would be included in the bracketed term). The proportion of profits expected to be spent on advertising, $\hat{v}_j$, is similarly defined by Eq. (6.7b) as

$$\hat{v} = [\alpha\beta^{\gamma}(\bar{c})^{\gamma\beta_c}(\bar{p})^{\gamma\beta_i}](m_j)^{\beta_m} = .256(m_j)^{.201}.$$

Observed values of m_j range from .0001 in primary metals to .2125 in the tobacco industry.

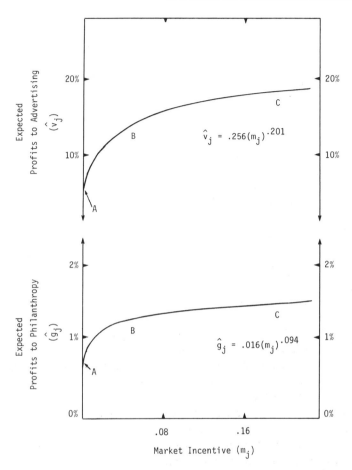

Figure 6.2. Philanthropy and advertising expenditures by market incentive to institutionalize coop-tive relations with people as consumers (note the different scales for philanthropy and advertising).

market constraint and having no direct contact with people as consumers (low market incentive industries) engaged in minimal philanthropy. With very small increases in sales to people and freedom from market constraint, dramatic increases in philanthropy occurred. Moderate and high incentives to coopt people did not greatly affect philanthropy in the sense that the philanthropy curve in Figure 6.2 is relatively flat at the geometric mean market incentive ($\bar{m} = .030$) and continues so with increasing values of the market incentive to the right of the graph. The same pattern of expected changes was typical of advertising expenditures except that a higher proportion of profits was allocated to advertising in every industry and the advertising curve in Figure 6.2 does not flatten out as quickly with market incentives beyond a moderate level. Points A, B, and C on the advertising graph correspond to the A, B, and C points on the philanthropy graph. A firm moving from the primary metals industry to the chemicals industry (point A to point B) would be expected to have increased its advertising expenditures from 4.02% of its profits up to 13.99% of its profits. Movement from the chemicals industry to the food industry (point B to point C) would be expected to have resulted in an increase from 13.99% of the firm's profits up to 18.28%. The first shift between industries would have increased advertising to three-and-a-half times the initial level, but the second shift would have resulted in a much smaller increase of one-and-a-third times the initial level (13.99/4.02 versus 18.28/13.99).

CONCLUSION

In summary, the analysis of corporate philanthropy data has been fruitfully informed by including in the analysis an explicit consideration of a firm's network position within the economy. I have argued that the relational pattern defining a firm's position also defines a market incentive for the firm to coopt the houshold sector—to institutionalize its relations with people as consumers so as to coopt a source of uncertainty in its profits. The market incentive is high to the extent that consumption by people is a major determinant of the demand for a firm's product, and the economic sector within which it operates offers high structural autonomy, i.e., offers comparative freedom from market constraints on the firm's profits. It is in the self-interest of such a firm to court the affections of people actively since that affection translates into stimulated demand for the firm's product. Corporate philanthropy can both legitimate the firm to the public as a protector of the public interest, which can be expected to channel public buying toward commodities in which the firm has had a hand in producing, and provide a further stimulus to demand by improving the ability of specific classes of consumers to purchase the firm's product. Moreover, the structurally autonomous firm is in a position to realize these self-interests since it is comparatively free of market constraints on its profits from corporate competitors, suppliers, and consumers. In this sense of being an effort to eliminate uncertainty in profits, corporate philanthropy constitutes a cooptive relation from the corporate actor to people collectively as consumers. A firm can be expected to indulge in philanthropy for the same reasons that firms generally have cooptive relations with establishments in sectors constraining their profits. Unlike the constraints described in the preceding chapters, people do not constitute an immediate threat to profits because they are not organized as consumers. In the absence of more immediate threats from corporate actors, however, it is an eminently strategic action for a firm to move to eliminate uncertainty by coopting the source of even secondary constraint (i.e., people). Further, I have argued that the understanding of philanthropy as a cooptive relation can be enriched by analyzing philanthropy as a concomitant of a blatantly cooptive relation, advertising. Advertising and philanthropy are complementary allocations to the same task of coopting the household sector, and so both should be generated by the market incentive to coopt the household sector. Holding constant price and income, the firms most involved in advertising and philanthropy should be those operating in sectors giving them a high market incentive to coopt the household sector by institutionalizing their relations with people.

Not only is this the case for the two-digit manufacturing industries in 1967, the market incentive effect is stronger than either price or income effects in determining the proportion of net income allocated to corporate philanthropy. In fact, there is no evidence of a price effect. The tax incentive for philanthropy or advertising expenditures had no unique association with expenditures actually made after income and market incentive are held constant.

The market incentive effect observed in 1967 is a marginally decreasing effect. The proportion of profits allocated to philanthropy and advertising is determined by a constant times the market incentive raised to a power, β_m, where the market incentive effect β_m is estimated to have been .1 for philanthropy and .2 for advertising. As illustrated in Figure 6.2, this means that the market incentive effect had its most dramatic effects across industries providing comparatively low market incentive. At moderate and high levels of market incentives, differences in contributions to philanthropy with changes in market incentive to coopt the household sector were small.

These results carry a number of policy implications (bearing in mind the limited data base available for analysis), one of which concerns the manipulation of tax incentives for philanthropy. The comparatively nonprogressive nature of corporate tax rates together with the near random association between differences in philanthropy and differences in tax rates implies that such a policy would not be effective. Corporate position in the economy is much more a determinant of corporate philanthropy than is its tax rate. The results of this analysis corroborate the recommendation by the Business Advisory Group of the Commission on Private Philanthropy and Public Needs against manipulation of tax incentives as a method for encouraging donations from large American corporations (see the quote in footnote 4).

A second policy implication concerns what might be termed the morality of corporate philanthropy. The observed market incentive effect does not reveal an insidious component to corporate philanthropy, a component that might be taken as contrary to the public good. Rather, the effect reveals a rational basis for ostensible altruism by corporations as self-interested profit-seeking bureaucracies. Any advance in understanding economic or sociological motives for corporate philanthropy seems to me to advance our ability to design government policy—policy for more effectively encouraging corporate philanthropy while safeguarding against tax-deductible donations that further the well-being of corporate actors at the expense of people.

As a closing note, let me once again stress the purpose of this chapter. My purpose has been to illustrate the use of the structural autonomy model in analyses of corporate behavior beyond involvement in directorate ties. Much of this chapter is given to extending a microeconomic model of corporate philanthropy to a sociological model in which philanthropy is understood to be a type of cooptive relation. The strength of the substantive results obtained, especially the strength of the market incentive effect relative to price and income effects in the microeconomic model, buttresses my conviction that the network model used in the preceding chapters is not without value in suggesting hypotheses for empirical research well beyond the scope of this book.

7

A Note on Cooptation and
Definitions of Constraint *

In contrast to much research on organizations and markets, research in which constraints are defined by the intensity of buying and selling between industry and sector, the proposed understanding of constraint in terms of structural autonomy focuses attention on the structure of market relations. My purpose in this chapter is to show how this proposed concept of constraint is a more accurate predictor of cooptive directorate ties.

To begin with, this whole chapter concerns a refinement within the general resource dependence perspective on organizational behavior. From this perspective, corporate actors are viewed as being dependent on resources provided by other actors, or classes of actors, in an organizational environment. This dependence poses a constraint on the freedom corporate actors have to pursue their organization-specific interests. At the same time, however, corporate actors are understood to be purposive in the sense that they can adapt to these constraints

*The idea for this chapter was stimulated by an analysis of market constraint and directorate ties in Germany and Austria that was conducted under Rolf Ziegler's direction at the University of Munich. This chapter resulted from my discussions with Professor Ziegler and his colleagues during an evaluative network conference held in 1981 at Schloss Reisensburg, West Germany. Portions of this chapter were presented at the 1982 annual meetings of the American Sociological Association and are reprinted from *Social Structure and Network Analysis,* edited by P. V. Marsden and N. Lin (Burt, 1982b).

and manage their access to needed resources. In a review of the sociology of organizational environments, Aldrich and Pfeffer (1976) succinctly summarize the principal theme of the resource dependence perspective:

> Administrators manage their environments as well as their organizations, and the former activity may be as important, or even more important, than the latter. The presumed end result of such strategies is the acquisition of resources and the survival of the organization, as well as the stabilization of relationships with environmental elements. . . . The resource dependence model calls attention to the importance of environmental contingencies and constraints, at the same time leaving room for the operation of strategic choice on the part of organizational members as they maneuver through known and unknown contexts [pp. 83–84].

The concepts of constraint and cooptive strategies for circumventing or managing constraint are clearly central issues in the resource dependence perspective.

When translated into empirical research on relations among organizations, the resource dependence perspective is typically translated into a concern with the strength of resource and cooptive relations. To the extent that some organization A obtains a large proportion of its resources from some other organization, or class of organizations, B, organization A is expected to have cooptive relations to B in order to manage its access to needed resources. The more intense, the stronger, the flow of resources from B to A, in other words, the more likely are cooptive relations between B and A. Empirical research is used to show that interorganizational cooptive relations of various types are predicted by interorganizational resource relations. An illustrative example would be helpful here. There are many studies adopting a resource dependence perspective, but those by Jeffrey Pfeffer with several colleagues are particularly well-known and have been conveniently assembled in a book on organizational environments by Pfeffer and Salancik (1978). An extensive review of this and related research through the mid-1970s can be obtained from chapters in the Nystrom and Starbuck (1981) handbook on adapting organizations to their environments.

A resource dependence measure Pfeffer and his colleagues have found useful is the proportion of all sales and purchases by organizations in some sector j of the American economy that is transacted with organizations in some other sector i. Let pz_{ji} refer to the proportion of extraindustry buying and selling that is transacted with sector i. To the extent that pz_{ji} is high, organizations in industry j obtain a large proportion of their resources from organizations in sector i, which means that organizations in the two sectors should be connected by cooptive relations in order to manage the flow of resources between them. Mergers and joint ventures are explicitly cooptive relations. An organization could coopt another by buying it outright (merger) or agreeing to pool resources with it for a specific project (joint venture). The frequency and strength of these two relations between organizations in separate sectors of the economy increase with the intensity of buying and selling between them, i.e., in proportion to pz_{ji} for sectors i and j (Pfeffer and Salancik, 1978:114ff, 157ff).

Given the increasing popularity of network analysis as a strategy for representing organizational environments, it seems likely that the prediction of cooptive relations from the strength of resource relations will become even more common in future research on organizational behavior. As in past research, there is likely to be a positive association between the strengths of corresponding resource and cooptive relations.

Network analysis brings with it, however, an emphasis on the conceptualization of constraint in the organizational environment. This emphasis goes well beyond a concern with the mere strength of relations. At issue is the structure of relations to actors providing resources and the manner in which those actors themselves are structured. Here again, an illustrative example would be helpful. Such an example is provided by the structural autonomy model.

The market constraint a_{ji} is derived from the structural autonomy model as the contribution to profits in industry j that can be attributed to industry purchases and sales with establishments in sector i. Establishments in sector i pose a severe market constraint for those in industry j to the extent that two conditions occur simultaneously: (a) the sector is the sole source of buying and selling for the industry, and (b) organizations within the sector are coordinated to form an oligopoly. In other words, the structure of relations is emphasized over the strength of a relation. It is not the mere obtaining of resources from the sector that makes it a constraint for the industry so much as it is the lack of alternatives. Industry establishments have alternative actors from whom they can obtain needed resources to the extent that they buy and sell with many different sectors and to the extent that each sector contains many organizations competing with one another to provide the industry its needed resources—needed in the sense of a low price for supplies purchased from the sector, and needed in the sense of a high price charged for industry output sold to the sector. To the extent that a sector is the principal source of the industry's resources and sector organizations are coordinated to negotiate as a single actor, these alternatives are absent, and the sector poses a constraint on industry profits.

This understanding of market constraint is obviously consistent with the resource dependence perspective. As would be expected, cooptive interorganizational relations are predicted by market constraint so conceived. To the extent that sector i posed a market constraint for obtaining profits in manufacturing sector j, organizations in the two sectors tended to be connected by ownership ties, direct interlock ties, and indirect financial interlock ties. These three types of interorganizational relations through corporate boards of directors have the potential to coopt sources of market constraint (Chapter 3). The fact that they tended to occur together with the most severe market constraints on corporate profits certainly gives them the appearance of being used with cooptive intent (Chapter 4).

The empirical adequacy of alternative concepts of constraint poses a basic question for the resource dependence perspective on organizational behavior: How important is it to understand constraint in terms of the structure of resource relations rather than equating constraint with the strength of a resource relation?

The structure of resource relations is emphasized in the network model of structural autonomy and the concept of constraint in this model has some appealing features. When applied to organizations and markets, the constraint posed by sector i for sector j is the profit margin in sector j attributable to buying and selling with sector i. It is also the profit margin forgone in sector j by failing to coopt sector i. In other words, market constraint defined by the $\mathbf{a}_{ji}$ has a precise theoretical meaning [Eq. (2.10)ff]. Moreover, this theoretical meaning has substantive merit in the sense that low profit margins in fact occur in industries confronted with severe market constraint as defined by the model and in the sense that cooptive directorate ties occur as a function of severe market constraint defined by the model.

This does not mean that the persons responsible for creating and maintaining cooptive relations are accurate in perceiving the market constraints confronting them. It is much simpler to understand constraint solely in terms of a resource relation's strength, and empirical evidence can be mustered to advocate such an understanding. Available research within the resource dependence perspective shows that the likelihood of cooptive relations between two corporate actors increases with the strength of the resource relations between them. If relational strength alone predicts cooptive relations, then perhaps relational strength alone defines constraint as perceived and that perception is the stimulus for cooptive relations. The directors of an organization operating within a highly competitive market might be so insecure about their survival that they strive to coopt all of their suppliers and consumers in order to reduce some of the uncertainty in their profits. It is not impossible, in other words, to envision cooptive relations being maintained solely as a function of resource relation strength—regardless of actual constraints on profits. Further, it is not impossible that the success in predicting cooptive directorate ties from the $\mathbf{a}_{ji}$ as market constraints merely reflects the fact that the intensity of buying and selling between industry j and sector i is a component in the market constraint $\mathbf{a}_{ji}$.

Data on the two-digit industries can be used to show that this possibility did not occur in fact—at least not in 1967. The persons responsible for cooptive directorate ties among large American firms in 1967 were quite accurate in perceiving sources of market constraint on their profits. The likelihood of directorate ties increased in a systematic way with the market conditions proposed in the structural autonomy model to be conditions of constraint, conditions demonstrated to have had a negative effect on profits.

Three types of data are required in order to demonstrate this point: data on the strength of resource relations, data on sector oligopoly, and data on cooptive relations. All three types of data have been introduced in the preceding chapters. The proportion of extraindustry buying and selling that establishments in two-digit industry j transacted in 1967 with establishments in sector i has been referenced as pz_{ji}. In other words, pz_{ji} varies from 0.0 to 1.0 as the extent to which industry establishments transacted all of their extraindustry buying and selling with establishments in sector i. Data for computing these proportion relations are given in Table A.1 of the Appendix. Also given there are measures of the extent to which sector i was dominated in 1967 by a small number of large firms so as to constitute an oligopoly. The score y_i for sector i is discussed in Chapter 2 (e.g., Table 2.4) as an aggregate concentration ratio or an approximation to such a ratio. For the purposes here, I make a crude distinction between sectors that were relatively competitive (y_i low) versus those that were relatively oligopolistic (y_i high). The criterion level of y_i used to dichotomize sectors is based on the analysis of intraindustry directorate ties in Chapter 4 and intended to treat all but highly competitive sectors as oligopolies.[1] Finally, the two-digit sample of large American firms involved in manufacturing provides directorate tie frequencies between sectors. Let w_{ji} be the number of establishments in industry j connected to sector i, where each industry establishment had an ownership tie, direct interlock ties, and indirect financial interlock ties to sector establishment(s). Given establishments in 20 industries buying and selling with establishments in 43 other nonfinancial sectors, there are 860 transactions defined by these data. For each transaction, there is a resource relation (pz_{ji}, the proportion of extraindustry sales and purchases transacted with sector i), sector oligopoly

---

[1]This liberal definition of oligopoly weakens empirical support for the market constraint effect implied by the structural autonomy model since relatively competitive sectors are being treated as if they were oligopolies. In other words, sectors that could not impose a constraint on industry profits are being treated as if they could. Of 44 nonfinancial sectors, 18 (or 41%) are coded as oligopolistic and accordingly have the potential to be sources of severe market constraint on industry profits. The criterion level of y_i used to dichotomize sectors as competitive versus oligopolistic is based on the distribution of the y_i across different sectors and the distribution of directorate ties among competitors within manufacturing industries. The mean value of y_i across the 44 nonfinancial sectors considered is .22, but industries with higher scores than this contained very few interlock ties among competitors—giving them the appearance of being highly competitive. The highest frequencies of intraindustry directorate ties were observed in industries with values of y_i greater than .28, so sectors over this criterion are coded as relatively oligopolistic in order to illustrate the market constraint effect on directorate ties. Not all sectors over this criterion had extensive directorate ties—as is clear from the analysis—but the most frequent ties occurred in industries over this criterion (cf. Figure 4.3 and the listing of y_i by sector names in Table A.1 of the Appendix).

(y_i, competitive versus oligopolistic, zero versus one, respectively), and a cooptive relation (w_{ji}, the number of sampled establishments in industry j that had all
three types of directorate ties to sector i).[2]

The structural autonomy concept of constraint predicts that the likelihood of
cooptive directorate ties between industry j and sector i increases to the extent
that two market conditions simultaneously characterize buying and selling between industry and sector establishments: (a) a high proportion of industry buying and selling is transacted with the sector (i.e., pz_{ji} is high), and (b) the sector
is oligopolistic in the sense of being dominated by a small number of large firms
(i.e., y_i equals one rather than zero). To the extent that pz_{ji} and y_i are high
simultaneously, sector i posed a severe market constraint in 1967 for profits in
industry j, and cooptive directorate ties are expected between industry and sector
establishments.[3] Put in another way, highly competitive sectors (y_i equal to zero)
posed no constraint for profits and so should not have been the object of competitive directorate ties—regardless of the extent to which they were a source of
industry sales and purchases. This is precisely what occurred.

One illustration of this point is obtained by regressing the strength of cooptive
relations over the strength of corresponding resource relations—holding constant
differences in sector oligopoly. The following results are obtained across all 860
transactions when w_{ji} is regressed over pz_{ji}, y_i, and their interaction (routine t-
tests for null hypotheses are presented in parentheses):

$$\hat{w}_{ji} = .23 + .94(pz_{ji}) + .47(y_i) + 14.36(pz_{ji}y_i),$$
$$\quad\quad (1.1) \quad\quad (6.1) \quad\quad (10.2)$$

which accounts for 28% of the variation in ODI multiplex directorate ties (i.e.,
$R^2 = .28$). Similar results are obtained if the cooptive relation is measured as the

---

[2]The conclusions reached here with ODI multiplex directorate ties are also reached if cooptive
relations are measured in terms of each type of directorate tie. For the purposes of this chapter, I have
only presented results for the strongest of cooptive directorate ties, the ODI multiplex.

[3]These conditions are most similar to the initial measure of constraint, given on p. 37, which is
summed across sectors i to obtain the aggregate index of extraindustry constraint, y_{j2} in Eq. (2.3). As
was true of the two-digit computations in Chapter 2, intraindustry buying and selling is deleted from
the proportionate purchase and sales measure pz_{ji} (see footnote 19 to Chapter 2). The two market
conditions pz_{ji} and y_i combined do not equal the market constraint coefficient $\mathbf{a}_{ji}$, both because the
market constraint coefficient contains an adjustment for the level of oligopoly within industry j and
because the market constraint coefficient contains a distinction between supplier constraint and
consumer constraint [see Eqs. (2.5) and (2.6)]. These refinements are not directly pertinent to my
argument in this chapter that the structure, rather than the strength, of market relations is the key to
market constraint. I have therefore simplified the argument by focusing on the aggregate components
of market constraint, pz_{ji} and y_i. At the same time, these two components alone capture the severe
market constraints analyzed in Chapter 4. Of the 88 severe market constraints identified in Chapter 4,
73 (83%) are $\mathbf{a}_{ji}$ for which sector i is coded here as an oligopoly and/or sector i is the source for 10%
or more of extraindustry sales and purchases for industry j.

proportion of sampled industry establishments with ODI multiplex ties to sector i:

$$\widehat{w_{ji}/n_j} = .02 + .10(pz_{ji}) + .05(y_i) + 1.08(pz_{ji}y_i),$$
$$\quad\quad\quad (1.3) \quad\quad\quad (7.4) \quad\quad (8.1)$$

where n_j is the number of establishments sampled from industry j and routine t-tests are given in parentheses.[4] This second equation accounts for 25% of the variation in proportionate ODI multiplex directorate ties ($R^2 = .25$ for the dependent variable w_{ji}/n_j).

From these results, I infer a strong interaction effect between resource relation strength (z_{ji}) and sector oligopoly (y_i) in determining cooptive relations between industry and sector. The direct effect of extensive buying and selling with a sector (the effect of transactions with a nonoligopoly) was negligible as indicated by the respective t-tests of 1.1 and 1.3, which provide no basis for rejecting the null hypothesis. In other words, the expected number of multiplex directorate ties between industry j and sector i when sector i is highly competitive is .23 + .94(pz_{ji}), and the proportion of industry establishments with such ties to the competitive sector is .02 + .10(pz_{ji}). The likelihood of cooptive directorate ties between industry and sector increases with the intensity of buying and selling between industry and sector; however, the increase can be attributed to random error in sampling directorate ties. In contrast, the expected number of ODI multiplex ties when sector i is oligopolistic is .70 + 15.30(pz_{ji}), and the proportion of industry establishments with such ties to the oligopolistic sector is .07 + 1.18(pz_{ji}).[5] The likelihood of cooptive directorate ties increased significantly with sales and purchases with oligopolistic sectors. The t-tests for sector oligopoly effects in the preceding regression equations are significant at well

---

[4]I have presented the proportion measure w_{ji}/n_j in the text because it is easily interpreted. This proportion does not consider the number of establishments sampled from sector i for two reasons: (a) The sample was drawn to represent the manner in which firms in manufacturing industries reached across economic sectors generally with directorate ties, and (b) an industry establishment need not have coopted every sector establishment in order to have circumvented market constraint from the sector. All that would have been needed were ties to selected trade partners in the sector to ensure access to sales and purchase transactions, and access to information on business activities within the sector. These points are elaborated in Chapter 3.

[5]The effects in these equations are summed coefficients in the preceding ordinary least-squares regression equations. If sector i is an oligopoly, y_i equals one and the regression equations can be stated as

$$\widehat{w_{ji}} = .23 + .94(pz_{ji}) + 47 + 14.36(pz_{ji}),$$
$$\widehat{w_{ji}/n_j} = .02 + .10(pz_{ji}) + 05 + 1.08(pz_{ji}),$$

and summing effects in these equations gives the relation between cooptive relations and pz_{ji} reported in the text for oligopolistic sectors.

beyond the .001 level of confidence.[6] It was when an industry relied on a sector for extensive sales and purchases *and* the sector was oligopolistic that cooptive directorate ties were most likely between industry and sector.[7]

A more intimate feel for the interaction effect can be obtained from Figure 7.1, where bar graphs indicate the strength of cooptive relations typical of different combinations of market conditions. The height of each bar in Figure 7.1 indicates the percentage of sampled establishments in industry j that had ODI multiplex ties to sector i (i.e., 100 times w_{ji}/n_j in the second regression equation) for specified market conditions. Market conditions are distinguished in terms of sector oligopoly (y_i low versus high) and five categories of resource relation strength (pz_{ji} equal to .00, .01, .02–.04, .05–.09, and .10 or more).[8]

The observed association between resource relation strength and cooptive

[6]More important than the absolute significance of these effects is their significance relative to the significance of the direct effect of pz_{ji} on cooptive directorate ties. The direct effect of pz_{ji} is negligible, whereas the direct and interaction effects of sector oligopoly are quite strong. The significance of both effects is probably overstated by routine statistical inference, however, because the w_{ji} do not constitute 860 independent observations (see footnote 9 to Chapter 4). They are based on a much smaller number of firms and establishments. In the absence of appropriate test statistics here, I have reported routine statistical tests. This means that the relative significance of effects is much more meaningful than their absolute significance.

[7]It is worth noting that this conclusion is true if effects are limited to relations among manufacturing industries alone. Of the 44 nonfinancial sectors being considered, 21 are manufacturing industries. Since large firms involved in manufacturing have been sampled and since oligopoly tended to be higher in manufacturing industries than in nonmanufacturing sectors, it might seem that the results in the text merely reflect a separation between manufacturing and nonmanufacturing sectors. This is not the case. If the two regression equations in the text are estimated from only the 400 transactions between manufacturing industries, the direct effect of resource relation strength is negligible (t-tests of .04 and .05, respectively, for direct effect of pz_{ji} on w_{ji} and w_{ji}/n_j). The effects of sector oligopoly are quite strong. The effects of the dummy variable y_i on w_{ji} and w_{ji}/n_j have t-tests of 4.4 and 5.8, respectively. The interaction effects of $pz_{ji}y_i$ on the same two measures of cooptive relation strength have t-tests of 4.5 and 3.6, respectively. Sector oligopoly cannot be ignored as a determinant of cooptive directorate ties.

[8]Distinctions among categories of pz_{ji} are based on substantive and/or analytical considerations. There is a qualitative difference between the complete absence of buying and selling (pz_{ji} equal to zero) and a very small amount of buying and selling (pz_{ji} nonzero). Cooptive relations were more frequent when pz_{ji} equals a mere .01 than when it is zero (see Figure 7.1). I have distinguished a category of no buying and selling (pz_{ji} equal to zero) from a category of very little buying and selling (pz_{ji} greater than zero but less than .015 defines the .01 category in Figure 7.1). Although it would be analytically advantageous to have many categories across increasing values of pz_{ji}, few relations are available. Values of pz_{ji} range from zero to .56; however, the distribution is highly skewed with many industries having no transactions with many sectors and very few having extensive transactions with a single sector (note the N under the dotted bars in Figure 7.1). All values of pz_{ji} greater than .09 have been grouped together as a category of strong resource relations because (a) there are very few relations within small intervals of pz_{ji} greater than .09, (b) the frequency of cooptive relations was consistently high past the .09 criterion for pz_{ji}, and (c) all pz_{ji} greater than .09 correspond to the severe market constraints identified in Chapter 4.

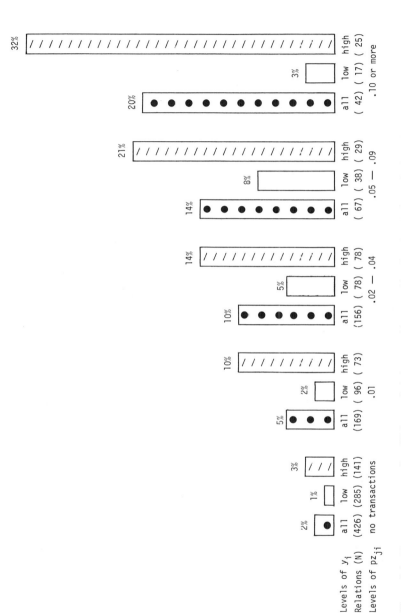

Figure 7.1. Mean percentages of establishments in industry j with ownership, direct interlock, and indirect financial interlock ties simultaneously to sector i under varying combinations of market conditions.

relation strength is illustrated by the dotted bars. They show that cooptive directorate ties were increasingly likely with increasingly intense buying and selling
between industry and sector. About 2% of industry establishments had ODI
multiplex ties to sectors in which they conducted no buying and selling. With a
mere 1% of their extraindustry buying and selling being transacted with a sector,
the mean percentage with ODI ties to the sector increases to 5%. The mean
percentage of industry establishments with ODI multiplex ties to a sector increases further to 10%, 14%, and 20% with increasingly strong resource relations to the sector (.02–.04, .05–.09, and .10 or more, respectively). In short,
the often-reported association between resource relation strength and cooptive
relation strength is apparent in these data.

The importance of sector oligopoly is illustrated by the white and striped bars
in Figure 7.1. The white bars refer to relatively competitive sectors, and the
striped bars refer to relatively oligopolistic sectors. Note that within each category of buying and selling intensity, the striped bar is higher than the white bar.
The difference is small when there is no buying and selling between industry and
sector: 1% of industry establishments had ODI multiplex ties to competitive
sectors, and 3% had such ties to oligopolistic sectors. The difference between
competitive and oligopolistic sectors increases quickly after that. With the smallest fraction of extraindustry buying and selling being transacted with some sector
$(.00 < pz_{ji} < .015)$, 2% of industry establishments on average had ODI multiplex ties to the sector if it was competitive, and 10% had such ties if the sector
was oligopolistic. These respective percentages increase to 5% and 14% if 2–4%
of extraindustry transactions were conducted with the sector $(.015 \leq pz_{ji}$
$< .045)$ and to 8% and 21% if 5–9% of extraindustry transactions were conducted with the sector $(.045 \leq pz_{ji} < .095)$. When pz_{ji} was .10 or more, 3% of
industry establishments on average had ODI multiplex ties to sector i if the sector
was competitive, and 32% had such ties to the sector if it was oligopolistic. In
short, there is a clear tendency for industry establishments to have had ownership, direct interlock, and indirect financial interlock ties simultaneously to
oligopolistic sectors with which they conducted an extensive proportion of extraindustry buying and selling. In comparison, competitive sectors were all but
ignored regardless of the extent to which they were sources of industry sales and
purchases.

The point illustrated with Figure 7.1 can be made more formally with the
frequencies in Table 7.1. Here rows distinguish the market conditions distinguished in Figure 7.1. Columns distinguish three categories of cooptive relation strength between industry j and sector i: null relations (the complete absence
of all three types of directorate ties between industry and sector), mixed relations
(the presence of one or two types of directorate ties, but not all three), and ODI
multiplex (the presence of all three types of directorate ties between industry and
sector).

TABLE 7.1

Cooptive Directorate Ties Observed under Different Combinations of Market Conditions[a]

Market conditions		Cooptive directorate ties		
Proportion of extraindustry buying/selling with sector	Sector oligopoly	Null	Mixed	ODI multiplex
no transactions	low	101	113	71
	high	19	71	51
.01	low	10	29	57
	high	0	11	62
.02–.04	low	5	26	47
	high	1	11	66
.05–.09	low	4	9	25
	high	0	0	29
.10 or more	low	3	6	8
	high	0	1	24

[a]The three categories of cooptive directorate ties refer to the complete absence of all three types of ties (null), the occurrence of one or two—but not all three—types of ties (mixed), and the occurrence of all three types of ties (ODI multiplex). The varying market conditions are distinguished in Figure 7.1 and discussed in the text.

These three categories of cooptive directorate ties are strongly contingent on market constraint severity. Null relations refer to row 1 of Table 4.1, mixed relations to rows 2–7, and ODI multiplex relations to row 8. The 88 severe market constraints identified in Chapter 4 have the following distribution across the three columns of Table 7.1: 5, 11, and 72, respectively. The 772 negligible constraints from nonfinancial sectors have the following distribution: 138, 266, and 368, respectively. Severe market constraint tended to occur with ODI multiplex ties, and negligible market constraint tended to occur with the absence of directorate ties. The null hypothesis that constraint severity (negligible versus severe) is independent of the three cooptive relation categories can be rejected at well beyond the .001 level of confidence (likelihood-ratio χ^2 of 39.8 with 2 degrees of fredom). This significant contingency—documented in detail in Chapter 4—reflects both the intensity of buying and selling between an industry and a sector (pz_{ji}) as well as the extent to which the sector is oligopolistic (y_i).

The categories of cooptive relation strength are contingent on both resource relation strength and sector oligopoly in Table 7.1. The null hypothesis that the five categories of buying and selling and the two categories of sector oligopoly are independent of the three cooptive relation categories can be rejected at well beyond the .001 level of confidence (with a χ^2 of 286 with 18 degrees of freedom).

Neither sector oligopoly nor the extent of extraindustry buying and selling with the sector can be ignored. The null hypothesis that the three cooptive relation categories are independent of sector oligopoly—given the five categories of buying and selling—can be rejected at well beyond the .001 level of confidence (with a χ^2 of 88.6 and 10 degrees of freedom). Similarly, the null hypothesis that the three cooptive relation categories are independent of the five categories of buying and selling—given sector oligopoly—can be rejected at well beyond the .001 level of confidence (with a χ^2 of 207.0 and 16 degrees of freedom). Finally, the null hypothesis that there are no three-way interactions among categories of cooptive directorate ties, sector oligopoly, and buying and selling can be rejected at the .001 level of confidence (with a χ^2 of 26.4 and 8 degrees of freedom).

More specifically, cooptive relations were more likely with oligopolistic sectors than with competitive sectors. The observed number of ODI multiplex relations to competitive sectors is, on average, half the number expected from extraindustry buying and selling. The observed number to oligopolistic sectors is, on average, twice the number expected from extraindustry buying and selling with the sector. This tendency is significant at well beyond the .001 level of confidence given its 5.6 unit normal test statistic.[9] The tendency is illustrated in Figure 7.1 by the fact that within each category of buying and selling with a

[9]This effect, and the χ^2 statistics discussed in the preceding paragraph, is based on models of the frequencies in Table 7.1. Where f_{ijk}^{ZYW} is the observed number of industry sector relations at level i of buying and selling (i equal to one of the five categories of pz_{ji}), level j of sector oligopoly (j equal to competitive or oligopolistic), and level k of the three-category cooptive relations (k equal to null, mixed, or ODI multiplex), four marginal effects and four interaction effects are defined by the table (e.g., Goodman, 1970):

$$f_{ijk}^{ZYW} = [\gamma \ \gamma_i^Z \ \gamma_j^Y \ \gamma_k^W] \ \gamma_{ij}^{ZY} \ \gamma_{ik}^{ZW} \ \gamma_{jk}^{YW} \ \gamma_{ijk}^{ZYW},$$

where marginal effects are in brackets and the tendency for complete multiplex directorate ties to have occurred with oligopolistic sectors—holding constant the intensity of buying and selling with the sectors—is given by γ_{23}^{YW}. After adding .5 to the tabulated frequencies in order to eliminate zeros, γ_{23}^{YW} has an estimated value of 1.91 with a unit normal test statistic of 5.58. This means that there was a .52 tendency for complete multiplex ties to have occurred with competitive sectors ($1/\gamma_{23}^{YW}$)— holding constant the intensity of buying and selling with the sectors.

The likelihood-ratio χ^2 statistics have been generated by forcing specific effects to be negligible (equal to one) and attempting to describe the frequencies in Table 7.1 with the simplified model. The null hypothesis that cooptive relations were independent of sector oligopoly and buying/selling assesses the fit of the marginal parameters (in brackets) and γ_{ij}^{ZY}. In other words, γ_{ik}^{ZW}, γ_{jk}^{YW}, and γ_{ijk}^{ZYW} are forced to equal one. The null hypothesis that sector oligopoly is independent of cooptive relations given buying/selling was tested by forcing γ_{jk}^{YW} and γ_{ijk}^{ZYW} to equal one. The null hypothesis that buying/selling is independent of cooptive relations given sector oligopoly was tested by forcing γ_{ik}^{ZW} and γ_{ijk}^{ZYW} to equal one. Finally, the null hypothesis of no third-order interactions was tested by forcing the γ_{ijk}^{ZYW} effects to equal one. As discussed in the text, all of these null hypotheses are rejected.

sector, the white bar (competitive sectors) is lower than the dotted bar (sectors on average), which is lower than the striped bar (oligopolistic sectors).

In conclusion, these results have a clear implication for organizational research within the resource dependence perspective. The constraints organizations strategically manage are defined more by the structure of resource relations in their environment than the strength of their resource relations to specific actors in the environment. Systematic errors in predicting cooptive relations can be expected if constraint is equated with the strength of a resource relation. Cooptive directorate ties between sectors of the 1967 American economy did increase with the intensity of buying and selling between the sectors. However, the frequency of directorate ties expected from buying and selling alone is consistently greater than the observed frequency of ties to competitive sectors (dotted versus white bars in Figure 7.1) and consistently less than the observed frequency of ties to oligopolistic sectors (dotted versus striped bars in Figure 7.1). In other words, the market constraints that cooptive directorate ties were patterned to manage are the constraints defined by the structural autonomy model and demonstrated to have had a negative effect on corporate profits. Competitive suppliers and consumers posed no threat to a firm's profits and were not the object of cooptive directorate ties. Oligopolistic suppliers and consumers could have posed a threat and were the object of cooptive ties. The bottom line here is that across varying intensities of resource dependence, cooptive relations can be expected to occur as a function of both the intensity of resource exchange and the structure of relations among the actors with whom resources are exchanged.

8

Corporations in the
Directorate Tie Market*

In presenting evidence of a social market of directorate ties patterned by market constraints in 1967, I have ignored a crucial actor. Market constraint does not create directorate ties as cooptive relations. It only encourages them by providing a profit incentive for developing and maintaining them in particular structural locations. The actual decision-making actor that creates directorate ties is the firm. In this chapter, I specify a model of processes by which individual firms could have been responsible for, and differentially successful in, the social market of directorate ties.

THE FIRM AS AN INTERVENING VARIABLE

The significance of the individual firm in the creation of this social market can be demonstrated with a brief reconsideration of industry-to-sector directorate ties. The association between w_{ji} and $\mathbf{a}_{ji}$ described in Chapter 4 has been described as a direct effect of market constraint on cooptive relations. However, the

*This chapter was a component in a 1981 research proposal submitted to the National Science Foundation. The research is currently in progress at the Center for the Social Sciences, Columbia University, New York.

association could also have been a result of at least two indirect processes involving individual firms operating in industry j and sector i.[1]

The association could have resulted from the *number* of firms operating in industry and sector. There had to be firms in industry j and sector i in order for directorate ties to occur between the two. If there were only a few firms owning establishments in the sector and a few in the industry, then there could only be a few directorate ties between industry and sector. The more firms that owned establishments in the industry and the more that owned establishments in the sector, the more directorate ties there could have been between industry and sector. Let n_{ji} be the number of different firms owning establishments in industry j and sector i.[2] With increasing numbers of firms in the industry and sector, increasingly frequent directorate ties could be expected, so n_{ji} should have a positive correlation with directorate tie frequency, w_{ji}. If high levels of market constraint from sector i on industry j attract large numbers of firms to the sector or the industry (i.e., if $\mathbf{a}_{ji}$ has a negative association with n_{ji}), then a negative association could be expected between $\mathbf{a}_{ji}$ and w_{ji} simply because more firms were available in sectors involved in market constraint so that more directorate ties appeared between such sectors.

Alternatively, the observed association between market constraint and directorate ties could have been an indirect result of the *nature* of firms operating in separate sectors. Given the different tendencies for different types of firms to have extensive cooptive networks (the most extensive networks being associated with large firms controlled by diffuse interest groups as described in Chapter 3), a few large firms controlled by diffuse interest groups could have been responsible for a high frequency of directorate ties. If only small, family-dominated firms operated in industry j and sector i, on the other hand, then a low frequency of directorate ties could be expected between industry and sector. Therefore, a second explanation for the observed association between $\mathbf{a}_{ji}$ and w_{ji} is indirect through the typical range of cooptive networks of firms operating in industry j and those operating in sector i. If firms reacted to market constraint by developing extensive networks of directorate ties to all sectors of the economy, then a negative association would be expected between $\mathbf{a}_{ji}$ and w_{ji} simply because the types of firms operating in sectors involved in market constraint were firms with extensive cooptive networks.

---

[1]Intraindustry ties are considered in a more detailed discussion given elsewhere (Burt, 1980c). The same conclusion reached here for industry-to-sector ties holds for intraindustry ties, so a reanalysis of intraindustry ties here would only add more details to my demonstration of the importance of the firm as an intervening variable.

[2]This is the number of firms owning establishments in industry j plus the number owning establishments in sector i minus the number owning establishments in both. When predicting ownership ties between industry and sector, the number of nonmanufacturing firms in sector i is subtracted from n_{ji} since ownership ties only involve the positional sample of manufacturing firms [see the definition of $w_{ji(o)}$ in Eq. (3.1)].

In order to assess this second possibility, I computed the per capita number of directorate ties between industry j and sector i to be expected from the typical cooptive network range of firms operating in the industry and sector. This average number of ties per firm, r_{ji} is computed as

$$r_{ji} = E(w_{ji})/n_{ji}.$$

$E(w_{ji})$ is the value of w_{ji} expected from the number of establishments represented on the boards of firms in industry j where number of establishments N_j is the sum,

$$N_j = \sum_i w_{ji},$$

the number of establishments represented on the boards of firms in sector i where the number of establishments N_i is the sum,

$$N_i = \sum_j w_{ji},$$

and the number of establishments being considered in all economic sectors,

$$N = \sum_i \sum_j w_{ji},$$

so that the expected cooptive network range of firms in the industry and sector is given as an expected number of establishments[3]:

$$E(w_{ji}) = N_i N_j / N.$$

Note that r_{ji} is based on the observed ranges of cooptive networks rather than the factors (such as size, family control, or management control) that have been used to explain involvement in directorate ties. It therefore takes into account not only the factors known to predict extensive involvement in directorate ties but unknown factors as well.

These three alternative explanations for the observed association between market constraint and directorate ties are brought together in three equations shown in Figure 8.1 as a path diagram. The three regression equations specified in the diagram predict per capita range from market constraint,

$$r_{ji} = \beta_{ra}\mathbf{a}_{ji} + e_{ji(r)}, \tag{8.1}$$

where $e_{ji(r)}$ is a residual term incorporating the regression intercept; predict number of firms in industry and sector from market constraint,

$$n_{ji} = \beta_{na}\mathbf{a}_{ji} + e_{ji(n)}, \tag{8.2}$$

---

[3]Numerical illustration of the computation of the expected values of w_{ji} is given elsewhere (Burt, 1979b).

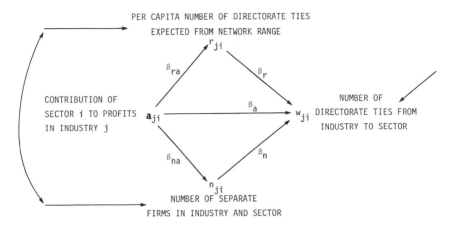

Figure 8.1. Three paths for the market constraint effect on directorate tie frequency.

where $e_{ji(n)}$ is again a residual term; and predict industry to sector directorate tie frequency from market constraint (β_a), number of firms (β_n), and cooptive network range (β_r),

$$w_{ji} = \beta_a \mathbf{a}_{ji} + \beta_n n_{ji} + \beta_r r_{ji} + e_{ji}. \qquad (8.3)$$

The total observed association between market constraint and directorate ties is given by the regression coefficient β in Eq. (4.4). The model diagrammed in Figure 8.1 disaggregates this total association into three components corresponding to the three explanations for the observed association.

Most simply, market constraint could be directly responsible for directorate ties. To the extent that β_a in Figure 8.1 equals β in Eq. (4.4), market constraint directly determined directorate tie frequencies regardless of the number of firms available to create those ties and regardless of the range of their cooptive networks.

Constraint could be spuriously associated with directorate ties as a result of large numbers of sampled firms operating in sectors involved in severe market constraint. In this case market constraint would appear to have had its effect on directorate ties indirectly through the number of sampled establishments between which ties could occur. This indirect effect is given by the compound path coefficient through n_{ji}, $\beta_n \beta_{na}$. To the extent that the observed association is completely a result of this indirect effect, this compound coefficient will equal the aggregate coefficient β.

Finally, market constraint could be responsible for directorate ties indirectly in the sense that firms tended to be involved extensively in such ties when they operated in industries severely constrained by, or constraining, other economic sectors. In this case, market constraint would appear to have had its effect indirectly through the expected per capita directorate tie frequencies. The indirect effect is given by the compound path coefficient through r_{ji}, $\beta_r \beta_{ra}$. To the extent that the observed association between market constraint and directorate ties is completely a result of this indirect effect, the compound coefficient $\beta_r \beta_{ra}$ will equal the aggregate coefficient β.

Taken together, these three effects sum to the aggregate association described in Chapter 4. The aggregate coefficient β, in other words, is the sum of the three effects:

$$\beta = \beta_a + \beta_n \beta_{na} - \beta_r \beta_{ra}.$$

The empirical problem is to assess the extent to which any one of these effects is principally responsible for the observed association between market constraint intensity and directorate tie frequency.

Table 8.1 presents ordinary least-squares estimates of these three effects for the two classes of relations described in Table 4.6 of Chapter 4, 855 relations with nonfinancial sectors and 83 relations with sources of severe constraint. The standardized estimate of β is presented from Table 4.6, and the three component effects that sum to β are then presented. Reading across the first row, for example, a_{ji} has a $-.438$ correlation with $w_{ji(o)}$. This zero-order correlation is the sum of a direct effect of market constraint on ownership ties (standardized $\hat{\beta}_a$ is $-.145$), an indirect effect of market constraint through the number of firms

TABLE 8.1
Disaggregating Components in the Market Constraint Effect on Extraindustry Directorate Ties[a]

	Total effect (β)	Direct effect (β_a)	Spurious effect due to number of available firms ($\beta_n \beta_{na}$)	Indirect effect through network range ($\beta_r \beta_{ra}$)
Nonfinancial sectors ($N = 855$)				
Owned establishments	$-.438$	$-.145$	$-.003$	$-.290$
Direct interlock ties	$-.222$	$.060$	$-.043$	$-.239$
Indirect financial interlock ties	$-.277$	$.033$	$-.038$	$-.272$
Sources of severe market constraint ($N = 83$)				
Owned establishments	$-.440$	$-.095$	$-.002$	$-.343$
Direct interlock ties	$-.372$	$.002$	$-.034$	$-.340$
Indirect financial interlock ties	$-.381$	$.010$	$-.028$	$-.363$

[a]Standardized estimates of ordinary-least-squares estimates are presented. Parameters are specified in Eqs. (8.1)–(8.3). The three partial effects to the right sum to the zero-order correlation β. Estimates have been computed from the two-digit data used to estimate effects in Table 4.6.

available to create ownership ties (standardized $\hat{\beta}_n\hat{\beta}_{na}$ is $-.003$), and an indirect effect of market constraint through the range of ownership ties in cooptive networks (standardized $\hat{\beta}_r\hat{\beta}_{ra}$ is $-.290$).[4]

The largest component in the observed association between market constraint and directorate ties is clearly the indirect effect through cooptive network range. In comparison to the direct effect of market constraint (β_a) or the possibility of a spurious association resulting from the number of establishments available for directorate ties ($\beta_n\beta_{na}$), the consistently dominant effect in the table is the tendency for constraint to operate indirectly through cooptive network range ($\beta_r\beta_{ra}$). For severe and negligible market constraint and for each type of directorate tie (ownership, direct interlock, or indirect financial interlock), the compound coefficient $\beta_r\beta_{ra}$ is much more negative and close to the total effect β than is β_a or $\beta_n\beta_{na}$.

In other words, market constraint resulted in directorate ties by determining the range of directorate ties in which firms were involved. The greater the constraint in which a firm's establishments were involved, the more the firm tended to own establishments in many sectors and share its directors with firms operating in other sectors. The analysis in Chapter 4 makes it clear that one need not take individual firms as units of analysis in order to demonstrate a significant association between market constraint and directorate ties. The results in Table 8.1 make it equally clear that the firm is an important intervening actor that translates market constraint into directorate ties. These results suggest that the firm could be an informative unit of analysis for research focused on understanding how a social market of directorate ties might arise through individual firms from the economic market of sales and purchases.

CORPORATE STRUCTURAL AUTONOMY

The network model of structural autonomy can be adapted to provide a guide for such research. A firm's structural autonomy would be determined in part by its pattern of sales and purchase transactions within the economic market as well as its relational pattern within the social market of directorate ties. These considerations come together in an index of corporate structural autonomy: the extent to which a firm is free from, and able to circumvent, market constraints on its pricing discretion.

[4]I have only presented standardized effects in order to compare the relative magnitudes of the effects more clearly. Metric effects are readily available from the standard deviations reported in Table 4.6. Given a standardized effect p_{ij} from variable j to variable i in Table 8.1, and the standard deviations for these variables in Table 4.6 (s_j and s_i, respectively), the metric effect b_{ij} equals $p_{ij}s_i/s_j$.

The firm would be free from market constraint to the extent that its establishments operated in industries providing high structural autonomy. Given market constraints defined at the establishment level of organization, market constraint on a firm can be obtained by aggregating the constraints on its establishment. Unfortunately, a large firm's establishments are likely to vary in their centrality within the firm's economic activities. At the core of a firm's economic activities is a set of establishments critical for the firm's production in general and responsible for a large proportion of the firm's total volume of business. These are the firm's primary establishments (cf. Thompson's, 1967:19–23, discussion of a firm's "core technology"). Market constraints on their pricing discretion are a direct threat to the firm's continued profitability and growth. These are the establishments that a firm would be most likely to protect with cooptive relations if any of its establishments were to be protected in such a manner. Establishments producing commodities peripheral to the firm's general economic activities and contributing a small proportion of the firm's total volume of business can be treated as secondary establishments. While quantitative data are typically not available on the extent to which each of a firm's establishments contributes to the firm's total volume of business, data are available to make some crude distinctions between primary and secondary establishments. The data are available in annual reports and Form 10-K reports. All large, publicly-owned firms are required to file Form 10-K reports at the end of each fiscal year with the Securities and Exchange Commission in accordance with the Securities Exchange Act of 1934. Among other items in this report, the filing corporation must provide a description of the principal lines of business in which it has been involved. Lines of business are not strictly defined by any systematic categories; input–output sectors, Standard Enterprise Classification, or Standard Industrial Classification. They are described in sufficient detail, however, to identify the three-digit SIC industry in which the largest proportion of the typical firm's activities were conducted. Such a coding has been carried out for the last twenty years and published in *News Front* compilations of the "Leading U.S. Corporations" (e.g., the compilation published in 1970 reports data on the 25,000 leading firms during 1967, and the compilation published in 1980 reports data on the 50,000 leading firms during 1977). Each firm is assigned—based on its annual report and Form 10-K report (available for large, publicly-owned firms)—to the three-digit SIC industry in which the bulk of the firm's activities are conducted. This assignment, and other accounting data coded on the firm, is then checked with a letter to the firm asking for confirmation of the coding. With the more detailed financial data requested in 10-K reports during the 1970s, the *News Front* compilations report a single four-digit SIC category in which the largest proportion of a firm's activities are conducted—even though the whole of the typical large firm's activities could not be assigned to such a narrowly-defined economic sector.[5] *Poor's* reports the four-digit SIC categories in which a firm operates. These reports were used in the preceding chapters to define establishments within input–output categories. Of all a firm's four-digit establishments, those falling within the three-digit industry coded by *News Front* as the principal context for the firm's operations can be treated as the firm's primary establishments. All others could then be treated as secondary establishments within the firm.

The firm's structural autonomy within the economic market can now be defined by the structural autonomy of its primary establishments.[6] The structural

[5]Although current SEC guidelines discuss lines of business in terms of industry segments in which a firm operates, "industry" is not defined as a category in the Standard Enterprise Classification or Standard Industrial Classification. Helpful information for using the Form 10-K report as a data source can be found in the guides written to help corporations in filling them out. Beresford *et al.* (1978:Chap. 2) offer an informative overview. Providing more specific explanation of industry segments, the SEC issued an interpretation release in 1978 to guide firms in identifying the industry segments in which they owned establishments. The release is available from the SEC Division of Corporation Finance (Release No. 14523 on the Securities Exchange Act of 1934). Unfortunately, the guides are not only ambiguous, they explicitly acknowledge the legitimacy of different firms using different definitions of industry segment. Moreover, these relatively stringent definitions only took effect in fiscal years beginning in 1977. Firms were required after July, 1969 to include information about lines of business in the business description; however, no such information was required in the financial statements until the Financial Accounting Standards Board issued its Statement of Financial Accounting Standards No. 14 in December, 1976. Data such as those available in annual reports or 10-K reports clearly could not be used to identify establishments with the precision possible in the census data; however, they should be adequate to the task of identifying the principal economic sector in which a firm operates. Mr. Baldwin H. Ward, publisher of the *News Front* compilations, described some of the methods his organization has adopted to deal with the problem of coding a whole firm into a single industry. The general procedure is to locate the one SIC category in which the highest proportion of a firm's sales occur. If a firm sold product in three industries, respectively accounting for 30%, 30%, and 40% of total sales, the last industry would be the one into which the firm would be coded. In other words, 60% of the firm's business would be ignored in favor of the modal 40%. Most firms can be coded without difficulty into three-digit SIC categories, according to Mr. Ward; however, it is difficult to represent the activities of a large firm with a single four-digit category. This problem has been met in two ways in the *News Front* compilations. First, multiple four-digit SIC categories are available in a computer tape. Instead of coding a firm into a single four-digit SIC category, its activities are coded into one, two or three categories, depending on its diversification. The above 30–30–40 firm, for example, would be coded into three SIC categories. Second, firms that are too highly diversified to be coded into a small number of four-digit SIC categories are assigned to a category set aside for "diversified/conglomerate" firms ("3999" in the 1967 data, "398" in the 1977 data). In sum, the *News Front* coding of annual reports seems to be a very useful reference for identifying, among other data, the primary establishments of firms.

[6]Of course, a firm's structural autonomy could easily be defined in terms of its primary and secondary establishments merely by extending the equations given here for primary establishments [Eqs. (8.4) and (8.6)]. To the extent that a firm is engaged in any cooptive strategy, however, that strategy would be most likely intended to protect the firm's primary establishments rather than every establishment the firm owned. I have focused on primary establishments because I believe that the

autonomy of establishments within industry j has been defined in Eq. (2.5) as $\mathbf{a}_j$, the typical industry profit margin to be expected from the industry's pattern of sales and purchases with all sectors of the economy. Therefore, a firm's structural autonomy in the economic market could be defined as a weighted average of the structural autonomy provided by the industries in which the firm operates its primary establishment(s). The structural autonomy of firm k, α_{k1}, operating primary establishments in industries j, would be given by the following equation:

$$\alpha_{k1} = \sum_j \delta_{kj} \mathbf{a}_j, \tag{8.4}$$

where summation is across all four-digit SIC categories j within the three-digit SIC industry listed by *News Front* as firm k's principal context of operations, and δ_{kj} is a proportion indicating the extent to which establishment j is central in firm k's economic activities (i.e., $\sum_j \delta_{kj} = 1$).[7] The index α_{k1} will vary from zero to one as the profit margin to be expected in firm k's primary establishments as a result of the patterns of buying and selling typical of the industries in which the establishments operate. Firm k is free from market constraint on its pricing decisions to the extent that α_{k1} equals one.

Position in the directorate tie market also affects corporate structural autonomy. A firm with strong directorate ties to sources of market constraint on its primary establishments is in a position to circumvent those constraints on its pricing decisions. For the purposes here, consider only the strongest of directorate ties—the simultaneous presence of ownership, direct interlock, and indirect financial interlock ties to a sector. Let w_{ki} be a binary variable equal to zero unless firm k owns an establishment in sector i and has one or more direct

clearest market effects will be observed for them. If the analysis of corporate structural autonomy turned out to be substantively informative when stated in terms of primary establishments alone, then an extension to primary and secondary establishments would be warranted.

[7] Three ways of measuring the proportional weight δ_{kj} seem reasonable, but selecting a particular measure would depend on the purpose of a specific research effort. Most simple of all, δ_{kj} could be binary: zero for all establishments except the largest of firm k's establishments. The index α_{k1} would then measure the structural autonomy of the firm's largest primary establishment. The larger the firm, the more likely that this focus on a single establishment would be misleading (see footnote 5). Second, δ_{kj} could be equal to one over the number of four-digit establishments j that firm k operates within the three-digit industry into which firm k has been coded. The index α_{k1} would then refer to the average structural autonomy of the firm's primary establishments. The more unequal the size of the firm's primary establishments, the more misleading this equal weighting assumption would be. Third, δ_{kj} could be a variable proportion roughly determined from the relative size of firm k's primary establishments according to the firm's annual report or 10-K report. Differences in criteria for distinguishing industry segments in these reports filed by separate firms, however, mean that this third operationalization of δ_{kj} is likely to have low reliability. None of the three operationalizations is without serious drawbacks as a general strategy, so selections among them would have to be made with respect to the specific study under consideration.

interlock ties to other firms owning establishments in sector i, and has one or more indirect interlock ties to such firms through intermediary financial institutions. If all three types of ties exist simultaneously, the firm has an ODI multiplex tie to the sector, and w_{ki} equals one. This binary variable is a crude measure of the extent to which firm k can use directorate ties to circumvent market constraint from sector i. The market coefficient $\mathbf{a}_{ji}$ expresses the intensity of market constraint sector i poses for industry j, and negative two times the raw market constraint times a binary variable w_{ji} equaling one if the industry has a cooptive relation to the sector (i.e., $-2a_{ji}^{*}w_{ji}$) is described in Chapter 4 as the profit margin increase in the industry to be expected from coopting the sector. Eq. (4.5) provides a measure $d(\mathbf{a}_j)$ of the overall increase to be expected by circumventing market constraints on industry j through directorate ties by summing these products across all sectors i constraining the industry (i.e., for which $\mathbf{a}_{ji}$ is negative). Therefore, a measure of the overall increase to be expected for firm k from being able to use directorate ties to circumvent market constraints on its primary establishments could be defined similarly by summing these products ($-2a_{ji}^{*}w_{ki}$) across all industries j in which the firm owns a primary establishment (i.e., for all j where $\delta_{kj} > 0$):

$$d(\alpha_{k1}) = \sum_j \delta_{kj} \left[\sum_i (-2a_{ji}^{*}w_{ki}) \right] \qquad \text{for all} \quad \mathbf{a}_{ji} < 0, \qquad (8.5)$$

where δ_{kj} is given in Eq. (8.4). The ratio of this weighted sum of coopted sources of constraint over the unweighted sum of constraint provides a measure of the proportion of market constraint on its primary establishments that firm k can circumvent through ODI multiplex directorate ties[8]:

[8]An alternative to this ratio measure is the absolute increase in industry profit margins defined in Eq. (8.5). The ratio measure seems preferable to me at this point because of the close association between market constraint and directorate ties documented in Chapter 4. Successful cooptation, a measure analogous to $d(\alpha_{k1})$ in Eq. (8.5), is much more strongly correlated with market constraint available to be coopted than with unexpected profit margins (see Table 4.8). All potential sources of market constraint tended to be the object of each type of directorate tie from industries as well as the object of all three types simultaneously. There is likely to be much more variability in $d(\alpha_{k1})$ as a measure of cooptive success across firms than there is variability in $d(\mathbf{a}_j)$ as a measure of industry cooptive success, given the tendency for extreme market conditions to be homogenized into average conditions with increasing aggregation at the industry level. However, it is also likely that large firms will have successfully developed directorate ties to most sectors posing severe constraint for their primary establishments given the close association between market constraints and directorate ties involving large firms as observed here. In other words, the ratio in Eq. (8.6) is likely to be well above zero for a thriving corporation. Since Eq. (8.4) measures the extent to which a firm's primary establishments are free from market constraint, I wished to have some measure of the extent to which its directorate ties could protect its primary establishments from whatever potential market constraint they confront—regardless of the absolute magnitude of that constraint. The ratio in Eq. (8.6) does this by holding constant (in the denominator) the absolute magnitude of potential market constraint confronting firm k's primary establishments.

$$\alpha_{k2} = [d(\alpha_{k1})] \Big/ \left\{ \sum_j \delta_{kj} \left[\sum_i (-2a_{ji}^*) \right] \right\} \qquad \text{for all} \quad \mathbf{a}_{ji} < 0. \quad (8.6)$$

The ratio in Eq. (8.6) is a measure of the extent to which firm k's pattern of relations in a social market of directorate ties could protect its primary establishments from the uncertainties of market constraint on industry profit margins. It will vary from zero to one as the extent to which firm k has ODI multiplex directorate ties to every sector potentially constraining profits in the industries in which it operates its primary establishments. The closer to one that α_{k2} is, the more that firm k's primary establishments could circumvent whatever market constraints might be imposed on them from suppliers and consumers.[9]

These two conditions come together to define a corporation's structural autonomy as the extent to which the firm's primary establishments are free from, and able to circumvent, market constraint. The extent to which those establishments are free from market constraint is given by the structural autonomy of firm k within the economic market of buying and selling, α_{k1} in Eq. (8.4). The extent to which those establishments are able to circumvent the market constraint they do face is given by the structural autonomy of firm k within the social market of directorate ties, α_{k2} in Eq. (8.6). The product of these two indices would vary from zero to one as the extent to which firm k derived autonomy from its relations in the economic market and its relations in the social market of directorate ties, $\alpha_{k1}\alpha_{k2}$. The extent to which these three variables are high simultaneously defines the structural autonomy of firm k, $\mathbf{a}_k$, as the extent to which the firm is able to pursue its interests without constraint:

$$\mathbf{a}_k = b + b_1\alpha_{k1} + b_2\alpha_{k2} + b_x\alpha_{k1}\alpha_{k2}, \qquad (8.7a)$$

where b is an arbitrary constant (arbitrary because the two indices α_{k1} and α_{k2} are not intended as measures of freedom from constraint in some absolute sense), and the remaining coefficients weight the relative importance of autonomy in the economic market, autonomy in the social market, and their interaction (b_1, b_2, and b_x, respectively) in determining the structural autonomy of individual firms. Given the interval, rather than ratio, measures of freedom from constraint, it is convenient to express $\mathbf{a}_k$ in the following form[10]:

---

[9]I am ignoring a host of issues that could be considered here, such as the effectiveness with which available directorate ties are used, the tractability of the establishments reached through those ties, and the scale of supply and consumption firm k's primary establishments require. The ratio α_{k2} only measures the opportunities those establishments have to circumvent the market constraints they face from suppliers and consumers.

[10]This alternative is needed because of the interaction term specified in the equation as explained in footnote 21 to Chapter 2. The weights in Eq. (8.7a) are immediately available from estimates of the effects in Eq. (8.7b): $b_1 = \beta_1 - \beta_x\bar{\alpha}_2$, $b_2 = \beta_2 - \beta_x\bar{\alpha}_1$, and $b_x = \beta_x$.

$$\mathbf{a}_k = \beta + \beta_1 \alpha_{k1} + \beta_2 \alpha_{k2} + \beta_x (\alpha_{k1} - \bar{\alpha}_1)(\alpha_{k2} - \bar{\alpha}_2), \qquad (8.7b)$$

in which the positive effect of structural autonomy within the economic market is given by β_1, the positive effect of structural autonomy within the social market of directorate ties is given by β_2, and the positive effect of simultaneously being autonomous in both markets is given by β_x. The terms $\bar{\alpha}_1$ and $\bar{\alpha}_2$ are the mean values of α_{k1} and α_{k2}, respectively, within a sample of firms for which effects are being estimated.

ANALYZING CORPORATE STRUCTURAL AUTONOMY

In the same way that the structural autonomy model specified in Eq. (2.4) was an initial model for the analysis of market constraint, the model specified in Eq. (8.7) is an initial model for the analysis of processes by which individual corporations are responsible for a social market of directorate ties. More specifically, it highlights processes determining and resulting from a firm's structural autonomy. Some initial lines of inquiry can be drawn from the preceding chapters. There is little value in discussing these lines of inquiry in too-great detail in the absence of data, but some general remarks are in order to outline research directions. Figure 8.2 presents a path diagram of effects in the processes I shall outline. From this point on, variables are assumed to be deviations from their mean values. This will spare the discussion from the (for the moment) uninformative detail of considering regression intercept terms.

There is, first, the question of how different types of corporations are distributed across sectors of the economy. Types of firms are reviewed in Chapter 3 as they have appeared in directorate research. The results obtained in that analysis documented the importance of corporate size and the lack of a single dominant group in the directorate, a kinship group or management as a group. Large firms not dominated by a single group tended to be involved extensively in multiplex directorate ties. Let s_k refer to the size of firm k. Let c_k refer to the concentration of control over firm k, c_k being high to the extent that the firm is dominated by a single group. There are many other characteristics of firms which might be considered. If nothing else, the control variable could be disaggregated to distinguish control by kinship, management, or a financial group. For the purposes here, however, I propose the two general variables s_k and c_k as research-proven, initial variables representative of corporate characteristics significantly associated with involvement in directorate ties.

Given the results in Chapters 2 and 3, it seems likely that these two variables are associated with a firm's structural autonomy within the economic market of buying and selling. For one thing, industry concentration is a factor determining

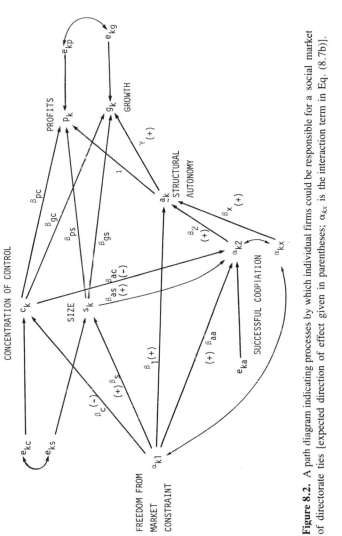

Figure 8.2. A path diagram indicating processes by which individual firms could be responsible for a social market of directorate ties [expected direction of effect given in parentheses; α_{kx} is the interaction term in Eq. (8.7b)].

industry autonomy so that large firms would be expected to own primary establishments within highly autonomous industries. More generally, freedom from market constraint would give a firm special opportunities to expand its holdings so that large firms would be expected to own primary establishments in autonomous industries. In other words, β_s in the following regression equation would be positive, where e_{ks} is a standard error term:

$$s_k = \beta_s \alpha_{k1} + e_{ks}. \tag{8.8}$$

At the same time, the freedom to pursue diverse corporate goals, a freedom ensured by industry structural autonomy, would facilitate the emergence of diverse interest groups within the corporation. This implies that firms dominated by a single interest group would be unlikely to own a primary establishment in an industry to the extent that the industry provided a high level of structural autonomy. In other words, β_c in the following regression equation would be negative, where e_{kc} is a standard error term:

$$c_k = \beta_c \alpha_{k1} + e_{kc}. \tag{8.9}$$

Given the results in Chapters 3 and 4, these considerations affect a firm's success in developing cooptive directorate ties to sectors potentially constraining industry profits for their primary establishments. Based on the results in Chapter 3, large firms not dominated by a single interest group would be most extensively involved in multiplex directorate ties so that, ceteris paribus, these would be the firms most likely to have developed such ties to sources of market constraint. At the same time, this cooptive success is accomplished in the context of sales and purchase transactions potentially constraining the firm's control over its profits. It seems likely that firms operating in structurally autonomous industries would have an easier time coopting sources of constraint than would firms operating in severely constrained industries. In other words, cooptively successful firms (a firm k with a value of α_{k2} close to one) should be large, not dominated by a single interest group, and have primary establishments in structurally autonomous industries. This means that in the regression equation predicting cooptive success,

$$\alpha_{k2} = \beta_{as} s_k + \beta_{ac} c_k + \beta_{aa} \alpha_{k1} + e_{ka}, \tag{8.10}$$

the effect of increasing size should be positive (β_{as}), the effect of increasing concentration of control within the firm should be negative (β_{ac}), and the effect of freedom from market constraint should be positive (β_{aa}). The term e_{ka} is once again a standard error term in ordinary least-squares regression.

These direct effects combine in two indirect processes by which owning primary establishments in structurally autonomous industries could result in a firm successfully coopting sources of market constraint on its primary establishments. First, there is the ability of firms to grow large within industries free from market constraint ($\beta_s > 0$) and the tendency for large firms to be involved extensively in directorate ties ($\beta_{as} > 0$) so that a positive indirect effect results, $\beta_s \beta_{as}$. Second, there is the facilitating effect freedom from market constraint could have on the segregation of interest groups within a firm each with partial control over its directorate ($\beta_c < 0$), and the tendency for firms not dominated by a single interest group to be involved extensively in directorate ties ($\beta_{ac} < 0$) so that a positive indirect effect results, $\beta_c \beta_{ac}$.

In other words, Figure 8.2 distinguishes three processes through which individual firms could become cooptively successful: (a) Success could result directly from a firm's primary establishments operating within industries free from market constraint. This effect is captured by β_{aa}. (b) Success could result directly from the size and distribution of control within a firm. These effects are captured by β_{as} and β_{ac}. (c) Finally, success could result indirectly by specific types of firms being extensively involved in directorate ties and those types of firms tending to operate their primary establishments in industries free from market constraint. This effect is captured by the sum of effects $\beta_s \beta_{as} + \beta_c \beta_{ac}$. The relative magnitudes of these effects will indicate the relative extent to which each process is responsible for the documented association between market constraint and directorate ties.[11]

Given these general determinants of cooptive success, there is the question of how corporate structural autonomy affects corporate success more generally. The higher a firm's structural autonomy, the greater the ability of its directors to

---

[11]Although clear effects are particularly likely to result from an analysis of cooptive directorate ties in terms of ODI multiplex ties, an analysis of individual types of ties could prove informative. For example, values of α_{k2} could be computed using ownership ties to construct the binary variable w_{ki} [d_{ki} in Eq. (3.1) would equal w_{ki}]. The index α_{k2} would then measure the extent to which firm k owned an establishment in every sector posing a constraint for profits in the industries where it owned a primary establishment. The betas in Eq. (8.10) when this measure is predicted would indicate the relative importance of size, control, and a lack of market constraint for the successful diversification of firms. Alternatively, α_{k2} could be computed from direct interlock ties so that it would measure the extent to which firm k interlocked with other firms owning establishments in sectors posing a constraint for its primary establishments. If this measure were predicted by Eq. (8.10), the estimated betas would indicate the relative importance of size, control, and a lack of market constraint for cooptively successful interlocking. Differences in corresponding betas obtained when different types of directorate ties were used to operationalize cooptive success as α_{k2} would indicate different processes by which firms became involved in the social market of directorate ties—given the economic contexts in which they operated. For example, if a higher value of β_{ac} were obtained when α_{k2} is computed using ownership ties than the value obtained when α_{k2} is computed using direct interlock ties, then it could be argued that firms dominated by a single interest group use ownership ties rather than direct interlock ties in order to coopt potential sources of constraint. If a higher value of β_{aa} were obtained when α_{k2} is computed using ownership ties, then it could be argued that the lack of market constraint on a firm more directly facilitates the successful development of cooptive ownership ties than the similar development of cooptive interlock ties. There is evidence to suggest that this is true (Burt, 1980c:172ff).

pursue goals without constraint. The freer they are to plan and pursue goals—
ceteris paribus—the greater the likelihood that their firm will be successful. This
assumes that high quality executives are available to serve on the board and that
firms can expand or scale down their establishments to meet corporate needs
efficiently. This is not to say that these assumptions hold true for every firm at all
times so much as it is to say that they hold on average across firms. Without
attempting to cover the many components shaded by the umbrella concept of
organizational effectiveness in pursuing goals, I shall specify a corporation's
profits and growth as commonsensical, initial indicators representing corporate
success.[12] Let p_k be some measure of firm k's profit margin such as the ratio of
net income over total sales. Let g_k be some measure of the firm's growth such as
the average annual increase in sales or assets over the course of several preceding
years.[13] These indicators should have a positive association with corporate structural autonomy.

Several processes are distinguished in Figure 8.2 as components in the association between corporate success and structural autonomy. The profit margin
observed for firm k is defined as an aggregate of four components: a random
error of observation (e_{kp}), an adjustment for the size of the firm ($\beta_{ps}s_k$), an
adjustment for the concentration of control within the firm's directorate ($\beta_{pc}c_k$),
and the firm's structural autonomy ($\mathbf{a}_k$):

$$p_k = [\mathbf{a}_k] + \beta_{ps}s_k + \beta_{pc}c_k + e_{kp}. \tag{8.11}$$

In Chapter 2, an industry's structural autonomy is the profit margin it is predicted
to have as a consequence of market constraints implied by its pattern of buying
and selling transactions. In keeping with that analysis, Eq. (8.11) defines a
corporation's structural autonomy as the profit margin it is expected to have as a

---

[12]Just as corporate size and concentration of control would be initial characteristics of firms, a set
of variables to be expanded to include other characteristics in an actual data analysis, so profit and
growth indices would be expanded to include multiple indicators of corporate success. Goodman and
Pennings (1977) provide a collection of papers describing a broad range of considerations for
selecting such indicators. Galbraith (1973:Chap. 11) provides a detailed discussion of corporate
growth as the principal goal pursued by large firms once they have brought uncertainty in profits
under control. Control over profit uncertainties here is captured by the cooptive success index in Eq.
(8.6), and, in complete agreement with Mr. Galbraith's argument, I believe that it is positively
associated with corporate profits and growth as specified in Figure 8.2.

[13]Other measures of corporate profits and growth should be considered in an actual data analysis to
ensure the generality of inferences. For example, there is the question of whether growth should be
measured in absolute dollars as given in the text or marginally as the ratio of increased sales or assets
over previous sales or assets. More importantly, there is the question of whether firms pursue profits
and growth on a continuous scale or merely strive to avoid losses. If firms merely sought to avoid
losses, then dichotomous measures of profit and growth might be considered, p_k being zero unless
firm k increased its profits over the previous year, whereupon it would equal one, and g_k being zero
unless the firm expanded its sales or assets over previous sales or assets, whereupon it would equal
one.

consequence of its freedom from market constraint and its ability to circumvent through directorate ties the constraint it does confront—holding constant differences in profit margins resulting from differences in the size of firms and differences in the distribution of control within them [cf. Eq. (2.5)]. The growth of firm k is defined in Figure 8.1 by the same determinants, but the firm's structural autonomy is allowed to exercise a stronger or weaker effect on growth than it does on profits:

$$g_k = \gamma[\mathbf{a}_k] + \beta_{gs}s_k + \beta_{gc}c_k + e_{kg}, \qquad (8.12)$$

where γ expresses the positive effect of structural autonomy on growth. Estimates of the effects in Eqs. (8.11) and (8.12) and those defining structural autonomy in Eq. (8.7) can be obtained in a canonical correlation analysis similar to the analysis used in Chapter 6 to describe the association between market variables and corporate philanthropy.[14] Corporate structural autonomy will be that weighted sum of α_{k1}, α_{k2}, and their interaction that is maximally correlated with corporate profits and growth—holding constant differences in corporate size and distribution of control.

The relative effects of specific processes by which corporate success results from structural autonomy are apparent when structural autonomy in Eqs. (8.11) and (8.12) is replaced with its definition in Eq. (8.7b):

$$p_k = [\beta_1\alpha_{k1} - \beta_2\alpha_{k2} + \beta_x\alpha_{kx}] + \beta_{ps}s_k + \beta_{pc}c_k + e_{kp}, \qquad (8.13a)$$

$$g_k = \gamma[\beta_1\alpha_{k1} + \beta_2\alpha_{k2} + \beta_x\alpha_{kx}] + \beta_{gs}s_k + \beta_{gc}c_k + e_{kg}, \qquad (8.13b)$$

where the intercept term β is deleted because I am focusing on deviations from means here, and α_{kx} is the interaction term in Eq. (8.7b). In other words, the effects determining a firm's structural autonomy are effects on the firm's profit margin: β_1, β_2, and β_x, respectively, express the profit margin increase expected from structural autonomy within the economic market of buying and selling (α_{k1}), the profit margin increase expected from cooptive success as the ability to circumvent through directorate ties the market constraint the firm does confront (α_{k2}), and the profit margin increase expected from simultaneous freedom from constraint and cooptive success (α_{kx}). The three parameters multiplied by γ ($\gamma\beta_1$, $\gamma\beta_2$, and $\gamma\beta_x$, respectively) express the corporate growth expected with increases in these three predictors. Parameter β_2 is the key to assessing the importance of cooptive success for corporate success more generally. To the

[14]These coefficients can be computed from ordinary least-squares regression coefficients in the reduced-form equations predicting corporate success, or they can be computed from partial correlations between the indices combined in structural autonomy [α_{k1}, α_{k2}, and their interaction in Eq. (8.7b)] and profits and growth after the corporate characteristics s_k and c_k are held constant. Computation details are given in footnotes 14 and 15 to Chapter 6 for the model diagrammed in Figure 6.1.

extent that β_2 is significantly positive, successful cooptation through directorate ties has a unique effect on corporate profits and growth above and beyond the effect of freedom from market constraint (α_{k1}) and across different types of firms (s_k and c_k).[15] Even if this turns out to be true, of course, it would be possible for market constraint and distinctions among types of firms to have a substantial indirect effect, through cooptive success, on corporate profits and growth because they jointly determine cooptive success in Eq. (8.10). These effects are apparent when cooptive success in Eq. (8.13) is replaced with its determinants in Eq. (8.10).[16]

---

[15]Two studies present evidence related to this effect, but distinct from it. Pfeffer (1972a; Pfeffer & Salancik, 1978:169–170) presents some related evidence. Profit margins for 80 firms are correlated with the absolute values of residuals from a regression equation predicting the proportion of the firm's directors who were current or previous managers in the firm from four predictors: firm size, debt-to-equity ratio, and two dummy variables indicating whether the firm was subject to national or local regulation. A strong deviation from the proportion of inside directors to be expected from this equation indicates that a firm had an unusually high or low proportion of management directors on its board. Pfeffer argues that this should be negatively associated with the firm's profit margin. There is no more than a random association between profit margins and the deviation scores. However, when profit margins are measured as the extent to which a firm's profit margin exceeded the normal profit margin for its industry, the expected negative correlation is obtained. Holding industry profit differences and relevant corporate characteristics constant, in other words, Pfeffer shows that a firm's profit margin is correlated with the extent to which it has a "correct" proportion of inside directors on its board. Pennings (1980:135–187) offers an extensive description of the connection between corporate effectiveness and involvement in directorate ties. He (1980:148) shows that a firm's profit margin (income over sales) is strongly correlated with the number of interlocks connecting the firm to other firms ($r = .28$ across 634 firms). Since large firms are profitable and tend to be extensively involved in directorate ties, it seems likely that this positive correlation is in part a result of the types of firms simultaneously determining the correlated variables. Moreover, there is the question of industry differences. Those firms operating in structurally autonomous industries will be making high profits, and such industries will facilitate the development of directorate ties. In fact, when Pennings (1980:158–159) holds constant some interindustry differences, the previously significant association between profit margins and interlocks dissolves before strong industry effects. Both of these studies hold out the promise that cooptive success could be a significant determinant of corporate success more generally, and both highlight the importance of holding constant differences in market position and corporate attributes when assessing the strength of that determination. As is explicitly stated in Figure 8.2, corporate success in obtaining profits and expanding its holdings is a result of differences in types of firms (s_k, c_k), differences in corporate freedom from market constraint (α_{k1}), and differences in successful cooptation through directorate ties (α_{k2}).

[16]These indirect effects are complicated by the interaction term in the definition of structural autonomy and of secondary interest for the purposes of this chapter, so I have not defined them in the text. Their complexity notwithstanding, they are quite clearly defined. The effects on profits and growth are obvious once the effects on structural autonomy are defined. Substituting (8.10) into (8.7a) shows that the indirect effect of corporate size, s_k, on corporate structural autonomy equals $b_2\beta_{as} + b_x\beta_{as}\alpha_{k1}$. The same substitution shows that the indirect effect of control concentration, c_k, on corporate structural autonomy equals $b_2\beta_{ac} + b_x\beta_{ac}\alpha_{k1}$. These are the respective indirect effects of size and control concentration on corporate profit margin [Eq. (8.11)] and the indirect effects on corporate growth when multiplied by γ [Eq. (8.12)]. The interaction between freedom from market

In summary, the network model of structural autonomy provides a succinct and rigorous guide for empirical research on processes by which individual corporations could have been responsible for the social market of directorate ties inferred from the analysis in Chapters 2–4. The results in Table 8.1 illustrate the importance of the individual firm as an intervening variable in the documented association between market constraint intensity and directorate tie frequency. Eq. (8.6) defines an index of the extent to which a firm has been cooptively successful in the sense of developing directorate ties to sectors posing a constraint on profits in the industries where it operates its primary establishments. Figure 8.2 specifies processes by which this condition could arise, contribute to corporate structural autonomy, and eventually affect the firm's success more generally. The firm's cooptive success in the social market of directorate ties combines with its freedom from constraint in the economic market of buying and selling to define the firm's structural autonomy as an expected profit margin [a_k in Eqs. (8.7) and (8.11)]. That defined ability to pursue interests without constraint in turn affects the firm's success in pursuing the more general corporate goals of profits and growth.

---

constraint, α_{k1}, and cooptive success, α_{k2}, means that the indirect effect of freedom from market constraint on structural autonomy through cooptive success increases with increasing freedom from market constraint. Substituting Eqs. (8.8) and (8.9) into Eq. (8.10) and then substituting the resulting equation into Eq. (8.7a) shows that the indirect effect of α_{k1} on corporate structural autonomy through α_{k2} equals the following sum of compound effects: $b_2(\beta_{as}\beta_s + \beta_{ac}\beta_c + \beta_{aa}) + b_x\alpha_{k1}(\beta_{as}\beta_s + \beta_{ac}\beta_c + \beta_{aa})$. This is the indirect effect on corporate profit margin and, when multiplied by γ, equals the indirect effect on corporate growth.

9

Directors in the Directorate Tie Market[*]

Throughout the preceding chapters, I have ignored a crucial component in directorate ties. I have been concerned with the existence of ties at the expense of concern with the people who constitute those ties. It is these people who define the content of interlocking directorates, and I have assumed them all to be the same. Whoever he was, the person holding directorships in multiple firms has been viewed merely as a conduit for information, advice, and influence between the firms. But people differ, and some of those differences could underly processes making individual people differentially responsible for a social market of directorate ties. In this chapter, I specify a model of processes by which individual directors could have been responsible for, and differentially successful in, the social market of directorate ties.

THE SOCIAL STRATIFICATION OF DIRECTORS

To the extent that director differences have been researched by sociologists, they have been researched in terms of social class. There is a considerable constituency of sophisticated researchers for the idea that there exists a class of

[*]This chapter was a component in a 1981 research proposal submitted to the National Science Foundation. The research is currently in progress at the Center for the Social Sciences, Columbia University, New York.

persons who control the American economy in part through the many positions they hold as executives and directors in large American firms. Mills (1956) called attention to the possibility that a concentration of capital in large corporations and the diverse holdings of those corporations would encourage their executives to pursue corporate interests generally rather than interests somehow peculiar to individual firms. In his own popular rendition of the class theme, Domhoff (1967) stresses the importance of interlocking directorates as a mechanism integrating an American upper class. Useem (1980, 1982) offers detailed discussion of the class perspective focusing particularly on that segment, the corporate elite, controlling large American corporations as owners, directors, and/or executives. He argues that social and political cohesion within this corporate elite arises through interlocking directorates and exchanges of executives between firms; through various formal groups such as cultural, social, and business associations; through exclusive schooling; and through extended kinship. Cleavages in the economy between business sectors pose an especially dangerous threat to the cohesion of this corporate elite, so interlocking directorates spanning potentially conflicting sectors of the economy are crucial to the stability of the elite.

This class perspective is not without empirical support. Studies of American firms during the first half of this century report slightly less than half of a corporate elite coming from well-to-do families. For example, there is the 44% reported by Taussig and Joslyn (1932:82ff, 237) in their description of mail-survey data obtained from over 8000 directors (58% response rate) sampled from the 1928 edition of *Poor's Register of Directors.* There are the 46%, 39%, and 39% reported for 1900, 1925, and 1950, respectively, by Newcomer (1955:63) in her description of archival data on slightly more than 1400 presidents and board chairmen in large industrial firms. Attending more specifically to the sociological meaning of an upper class, Domhoff (1967:51–52) reports that 53% of the directors in 50 of the largest American firms in 1963 were members of an American upper class defined by (a) listings in the *Social Register,* (b) attendance at exclusive private schools, and (c) memberships in exclusive social clubs. The remaining 47% were types of persons who would depend on large institutions, ostensibly controlled by members of the upper class (senior corporate officers, technical experts relevant to a firm's operations, college presidents, former military men, corporate lawyers, and foundation presidents) and a negligible number of types of persons perhaps unassimilated into the upper class (local businessmen, members of a "Jewish upper class," and foreign nationals). Using data on a random sample of directors in the largest American manufacturing firms as of 1969 in order to build on Domhoff's study, Soref (1976) shows that 32% of the directors could be interpreted to be members of an upper class whose members are identified by listings in the *Social Register,* attendence at exclusive schools, and membership in exclusive social clubs. There is a significant tendency for members of this upper class to have held multiple directorships at the time. Using data on university and college trustees who were executives and/or directors of large corporations in 1968, Useem (1978) shows that persons holding multiple directorships tended to have high incomes and memberships in exclusive social clubs. Continuing with an analysis of directors in the 797 largest American firms as of 1969, Useem (1979) shows that persons holding multiple directorships tended to hold executive positions, to be involved in the governance of nonprofit private organizations, to be advisors to government agencies, and to be members of business policy associations.

In short, there is some reason to believe that directors could be distinguished in terms of their centrality within a corporate elite, an inner group within an American capitalist class. Those directors central in this elite would be persons holding multiple directorships in large firms, holding an executive position in a large firm, and having social prominence to the extent of being listed in the *Social Register*.[1] Those directors peripheral in this elite would hold a single directorship, hold no executive position, and have a social prominence ensuring absence from the *Social Register*.

This idea of a corporate elite provides a ready explanation for the social market of directorate ties. A close association between market constraints and directorate ties would be expected because it is precisely those transactions conducted in severe market constraint that most threaten the cohesion of a corporate elite. In the interest of most efficiently ensuring a stable economy, an economy free from conflict between large corporations, it would make sense for the corporate elite to ensure interlocks between firms whose establishments pose severe market constraint for one another, and not to bother maintaining such connections between firms not constraining one another. It is transactions conducted in highly competitive contexts posing market constraint that underlie the most serious cleavages in the economy and would therefore be the most likely to explode in corporate conflict. If it is true that a corporate elite exists in the class sense, then those directors most central in such an elite should be most likely to interlock firms whose establishments pose a serious market constraint for one or the other's profits.

But at the same time that there is empirical support for the class perspective on corporate directors, there is evidence limiting it. Multiple-seat directors tend to hold executive positions; however, they tend not to be involved in the administration of every firm in which they hold directorships. Soref (1976) shows that directors drawn from the upper class, the directors he also reports to be involved

---

[1]Domhoff (1967:13ff) prescribes listings in the *Social Register* as a basic indicator of social class; however, he augments this source with additional, alternative criteria such as attendance at exclusive schools and membership in exclusive social clubs. As both he and Soref emphasize, not all members of what they interpret to be an upper class will be listed in the *Social Register*. Domhoff (1967:15–16) discusses specific reasons for the *Social Register* being a conservative listing of an American upper class.

in multiple directorships, tend not to be members of the executive committee of a firm in which they are not officers. Allen (1978a) presents results that more seriously restrict the class perspective. Focusing exclusively on persons who held four or more directorships in 250 large American firms in 1935 and 1970, Allen reports that these "core corporate elite" tended not to come from an upper class (in the sense that they did not inherit great wealth, obtain exclusive schooling, hold membership in an exclusive social club, or merit mention in one of several earlier studies of the upper class)—18% were drawn from the upper class in 1935 and 14% were drawn from the upper class in 1970. Moreover, these core corporate elite tended not to have extensive personal assets, 28% being what Allen terms "super-rich" in 1935 (using a criterion of $2 million in personal assets) and 17% in 1970 (using a criterion of $10 million). Further, the majority of these elite directors evidenced careers as corporate executives, 55% in 1935 and 81% in 1970, rather than careers of inherited prominence or entrepreneurial action. Similarly, Newcomer's study of presidents and board chairmen showed decreasing evidence of the corporate elite being drawn from a social elite. For example, these senior roles in industrial firms were decreasingly (if often) filled with persons from wealthy families, 7.5% in 1900 versus 13.1% in 1950 were from poor families and 48.6% in 1900 versus 39.4% in 1950 were from wealthy families (Newcomer, 1955:63). Beyond reporting an increasing frequency of corporate elite drawn from poor and middle-class families, Newcomer emphasizes changes in the occupational careers leading to the position of president and board chairman. The most striking changes occurred with respect to entrepreneurial versus administrative backgrounds. The percentage of presidents and board chairmen with careers as professional administrators increased from 19.5% in 1900 to 41.1% in 1950. The percentage who had established and operated independent businesses at some time decreased from 31.0% in 1900 to 9.9% in 1950 (Newcomer, 1955:90). By 1950, the typical person filling the role of president or board chairman was a "bureaucrat" with nominal stock ownership in his firm (less than 1% of the voting stock, Newcomer, 1955:105, 149).

A further pall is drawn over the class perspective by reconsidering the attributes of directors analyzed in the preceding chapters. Of the 197 individuals who connected manufacturing firms in the two-digit sample with one or more of the other 151 firms in the sample, 80 spanned at least one severe market constraint. Each of these 80 persons spanned severe market constraint in the sense that one or more of the establishments owned by one firm in which he was a director operated in sector(s) posing severe market constraint for one or more of the establishments owned by another firm for which he was a director. I am using severe here in the sense described in Chapter 4, where market constraint is dichotomized into negligible versus severe. These 80 persons can be discussed as constraint directors. They would have been an important integrative element in the economy since they constituted a personal channel for advice, information, and influence between two or more firms engaged in the most intensely constrained economic transactions.[2] The other 117 directors who connected firms provided communication channels between firms posing negligible constraint for one another's profits. These 117 people can be discussed as nonconstraint directors. Even less integrative in terms of spanning cleavages in the economy are directors who only held a seat on the board of a single firm. A random sample of 80 such directors was drawn from the directorates of manufacturing firms. These 80 single-seat directors obviously could not have spanned severe market constraint between firms, so they too can be discussed as nonconstraint directors.

Figure 9.1 shows the strong tendency for those directors who held multiple directorships to interlock firms that posed severe market constraint for one or the other's profits. For individuals holding a specific number of directorships, the figure reports the percentage who were constraint directors in the sense of spanning one or more severe market constraints. The association between spanning severe constraint and holding multiple directorships is significant at well beyond the .001 level of confidence.[3] None of the single-seat directors spanned constraint, of course, but most of the directors who only connected two firms also failed to span severe constraint. Of the 107 two-seat directors, only 16% spanned at least one severe market constraint. With three or more seats, however, directors tended to span one or more severe constraints: 63% of these directors spanned market constraint on average, and 100% of those holding five or six directorships spanned one or more severe constraints. The likelihood of spanning at least one severe market constraint clearly increased with the number of directorships held, with a quantum leap in probability occurring when a person acquired a third directorship.

In one sense, these results are quite in keeping with the class perspective on a corporate elite. The research reviewed previously focuses on number of directorships held by an individual as an indicator of the extent to which he is central in a

[2]Constraint directors could be further distinguished in terms of the number of constraints they spanned. They spanned from one to six; however, it is difficult to give this number a substantive interpretation. Multiple constraints could have occurred between the same firms, two establishments of one constraining one or more of the other's establishments, or involved different firms. Further, constraints could have involved secondary or primary establishments. Rather than attempt a quantitative description of the level of constraint an individual spanned, my brief remarks here are concerned solely with the qualitative distinction between directors who connected firms in the absence of severe market constraint versus those who connected firms posing a threat for one or the other's profits. These results were made possible by the programming skills of Harold Kilburn with the facilities at the State University of New York at Albany. A more detailed analysis of the directors briefly described here is given elsewhere (Kilburn, 1981).

[3]The hypothesis of independence between number of directorships and spanning severe constraint is strongly rejected with a χ^2 statistic of 64.39 with 4 degrees of freedom. This statistic excludes the frequencies for single-seat directors since these directors could not span severe market constraint. Including them would only increase the χ^2 statistic.

corporate elite. Figure 9.1 shows that this also measures the likelihood of him spanning severe market constraint, thereby integrating the economy as would be expected of a corporate elite.

On the other hand, randomness could be at work here. The more firms a person connected, the more likely that he would have connected, at least once, two firms posing a severe market constraint for one or the other. If there were some given probability for any one interlocking directorate spanning severe market constraint, then the more such interlocks a person provided, the higher the number of market constraints he would have spanned. Accordingly, the possibility of a spurious association between constraint and multiple director-ships cannot be ruled out by the significant association between the number of severe constraints spanned and the number of directorships held.[4]

Whatever the reason for the association between these two variables, number of directorships and spanning severe constraint together define each director's market position. The bar graphs in Figure 9.1 show that it is important to distinguish single-seat directors from two-seat directors and to distinguish both from three-or-more-seat directors. However, the tendencies for directors holding three, four, five, or six seats to have spanned one or more severe market con-straints are so similar—relative to one- and two-seat directors—that I shall treat them aggregately as multiple-seat directors. There are then five qualitatively different director market positions: (*a*) single-seat directors who, of course, did not span any severe market constraints, (*b*) nonconstraint directors who held positions in two firms, (*c*) nonconstraint directors who held positions in three or four firms, (*d*) constraint directors who held positions in two firms, and (*e*) constraint directors who held positions in three, four, five, or six firms.

These five categories are weakly ordered indicators of the extent to which a sampled director occupied an integrative market position. They need not repre-sent equal intervals or even strictly ordered levels of such a condition. They merely represent increasingly integrative market positions from the minimum of a single-seat director to a maximum of a director who held multiple directorships in large firms and spanned severe market constraints between the firms. Con-straint directors who held positions on the boards of multiple firms were in the best market positions to manage corporate conflict. The key question now con-cerns the extent to which such directors evidence characteristics of being a corporate elite.

There is no tendency for a social elite to have filled the most integrative market positions any more than they filled the least integrative. A tabulation of the five

---

[4]Number of constraints spanned (0, 1, 2, 3, 4, 5+) and number of directorships held (2, 3, 4, 5, 6) are strongly associated at beyond the .001 level of confidence with a χ^2 statistic of 133.96 and 20 degrees of freedom for the null hypothesis of independence. As in footnote 3, the single-seat directors are excluded from the statistic because they would spuriously inflate it. Number of constraints spanned increases with number of directorships held.

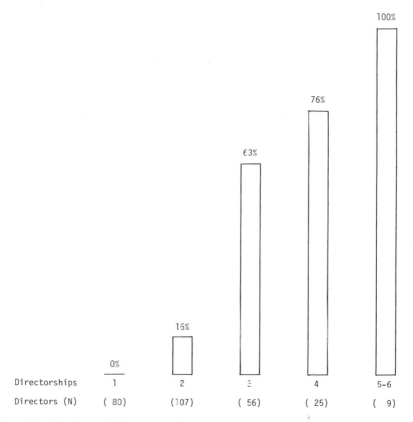

Figure 9.1. Percentage of directors spanning one or more severe market constraints by number of directorships held.

market position categories by listing in the *Social Register* is given in Table 9.1. About a quarter of all 277 sampled directors were listed there. This percentage varies little across the types of directors listed in the table. Of the constraint directors, 23% were listed in the *Social Register,* and 27% of the nonconstraint directors were listed. Of the persons who held three or more directorships, 26% were listed in the *Social Register,* and 26% of the one- and two-seat directors were listed. More specifically, there is no tendency for listing in the *Social Register* to be contingent on number of directorships held or number of severe market constraints spanned.[5] Although *Social Register* listings can be argued to be a conservative enumeration of socially elite people, these results show no systematic tendency for this conservative listing to represent directors in particu-

[5]The null hypothesis of independence is acceptable in both tabulations. With 5 degrees of freedom, the χ^2 statistic for number of directorships is 2.2 and the statistic for number of constraints spanned is 4.9.

TABLE 9.1

Director Social Class by Market Position[a]

Market position	N	Listing in *Social Register*	
		No	Yes
Nonconstraint directors			
One directorship	80	63	17
Two directorships	90	61	29
Three or four directorships	27	20	7
Constraint directors			
Two directorships	17	15	2
Three or more directorships	63	47	16
All directors	277	206	71

[a]Constraint directors connected firms, at least once, that posed a severe market constraint for one or the other's profits, and nonconstraint directors did not connect firms constraining one another. Listings have been taken from the 1965 *Social Register* and directorships refer to listings in the 1968 *Poor's* for the two-digit sample of firms. Pearson's χ^2 statistic for the null hypothesis of independence is an acceptable 4.6 with 4 degrees of freedom ($p = .33$).

larly integrative market positions over directors in minimally integrative positions. It could be true that socially-elite directors held positions in large firms but nonelites held positions in small (let us say nonconsequential) firms. However, the firms in the two-digit sample were quite large. There should have been a tendency for socially-elite persons to have held the most integrative market positions—if social and corporate elites were in fact the same elite group. They appear to have been distinct groups with a small overlap of about one in four sampled social elites being involved with large manufacturing corporations.

If not a social elite, the directors occupying the most integrative market positions did constitute an executive elite. Three inferences can be drawn from a consideration of tabulating executive roles with the five market position categories. Table 9.2 presents such a tabulation for the 277 directors taken from the boards of the 42 large manufacturing firms in the two-digit sample.[6]

[6]The table indicates the sample nature of the data being described. Note that some of the single-seat directors held executive positions, many senior, in other than the sampled manufacturing firms. This would have been impossible if they were in fact people who only held one directorship. It is possible here because the five-category market position variable is based only on the two-digit sample data. The single-seat directors holding executive positions in other firms are directors who represent interlock ties not captured in the sample data. By the same token, two-seat directors in Table 9.2 could have been three-seat directors, nonconstraint directors could have been constraint directors, three-seat directors could have been four-seat directors, and so on. (Of course, this does not work in reverse. Four-seat directors, for example, could not have actually been three-seat directors.) Clearly, inferences from the market position variable are only valid in terms of comparisons between categories rather than descriptions of directors within individual categories.

TABLE 9.2
Director Executive Roles by Market Position[a]

Market position	N	Executive in sampled manufacturing firm		Not an executive in sampled manufacturing firm		
		Nonsenior executive	Senior executive	Nowhere an executive	Nonsenior executive elsewhere	Senior executive elsewhere
Nonconstraint directors						
One directorship	80	31.3%	17.5%	33.8%	2.5%	15.0%
Two directorships	90	7.8%	22.2%	17.8%	10.0%	42.2%
Three or four directorships	27	0.0%	25.9%	11.1%	11 1%	51.9%
Constraint directors						
Two directorships	17	5.9%	17.6%	17.6%	17.6%	41.2%
Three or more directorships	63	1.6%	14.3%	12.7%	7.9%	63.5%
All directors	277	12.3%	19.1%	20.6%	7.9%	40.1%

[a]Executive roles are taken from the 1968 *Poor's* and *Who's Who*. Presidents and chairmen of the board are senior executives. The following roles are nonsenior: vice-chairman of the board, senior vice-president, executive vice-president, vice-president, chief executive officer, chief operating officer, secretary, treasurer, and general counsel.

The first inference to be drawn from Table 9.2 is the tendency for all directors to have been executives somewhere, especially those directors occupying the most integrative market positions. Four out of five sampled directors held executive positions in some firm according to *Poor's;* that is, 21% of them are reported in Table 9.2 as having held no executive positions. The tendency to be an executive varied systematically with market position. Among directors holding three or more directorships, 88% were executives somewhere. This percentage drops to 82% of directors holding two directorships and drops further to 65% of single-seat directors. Among constraint directors, 88% were executives somewhere, but only 77% of nonconstraint directors were executives. As might be expected from these percentages, the null hypothesis that market position and executive position (yes versus no) were independent can be rejected with confidence (Pearson χ^2 statistic of 14.4 with 4 degrees of freedom, $p = .006$). All percentages are high, showing that directors generally tended to be executives somewhere, but nonexecutives were more likely among single-seat directors than they were among constraint directors holding multiple directorships.

A second inference from Table 9.2 is that the sampled firms were not using their own executives as cooptive directorate ties to sources of market constraint. Directors have been sampled here from the boards of 42 large manufacturing firms. Executive roles are distinguished in Table 9.2 with respect to those firms. Among all 277 directors, 31% were executives in the sampled manufacturing firms (combine columns 3 and 4 of Table 9.2), 21% were not executives anywhere (column 5 of the table), and 48% were executives in firms other than the sampled manufacturing firms (combine columns 6 and 7 in the table). Not only are executives in the sampled manufacturing firms a minority in the sample (about one in three, 31%), there is a systematic tendency for them to have occupied the least integrative market positions and for executives from other firms to have occupied the most integrative. Being an executive in one of the sampled manufacturing firms is strongly contingent on market position (Pearson χ^2 of 19.2 with 4 degrees of freedom, $p = .001$); however, the likelihood of having been such an executive decreased across increasingly integrative market positions. About half of the single-seat directors were executives in the sampled manufacturing firms (49%). In contrast, 19% of the persons holding three or more directorships were executives in these firms. Moreover, 29% of the nonconstraint directors holding two or more directorships were executives in the sampled manufacturing firms, but only 16% of the constraint directors holding multiple directorships were executives in the firms. This decreasing percentage of executives is not true of firms outside the sampled manufacturing firms. The lowest percentage of outside executives occurs among single-seat directors (18%). This increases to 53% of directors who held two seats and increases still further to 69% of directors who held three or more seats. Similarly, nonconstraint directors were less often executives in firms other than the sampled manufacturing firms; 40% of the nonconstraint directors were outside executives, and 69% of the constraint directors were outside executives.

My third, and final, inference from Table 9.2 is that corporate presidents and chairmen of the board—the most senior of executives—were disproportionately likely to have occupied the most integrative market positions. Single-seat directors were equally likely to have been nonexecutives (33.8%), nonsenior executives (33.8%), or senior executives (32.5% were presidents or chairmen of the board). Nonexecutives and nonsenior executives were decreasingly likely in increasingly integrative market positions, however, and senior executives were increasingly likely. Among directors who held three or more directorships, 12% were nonexecutives, 10.0% were nonsenior executives, and 78% were senior executives. Among constraint directors, 14% were nonexecutives, 13% were nonsenior executives, and 74% were senior executives. This tendency for presidents and chairmen of the board to have held multiple directorships spanning severe market constraint illustrates the noted tendency for firms to recruit outside directors from the most senior positions in other firms. The executives treated as nonsenior here are at the top of corporate bureaucracies (see footnote a in Table 9.2); however, they do not hold the most senior title in their respective bureaucracies. As evidenced by the similarity of percentages for nonexecutives and nonsenior executives in Table 9.2 relative to senior executives, the title of president or chairman of the board was an important determinant of receiving a directorship offer from the large manufacturing firms considered here.[7]

It is difficult to assess the strength of these three inferences together because they come together in a complex way in observed percentages. For example, increasingly integrative market positions would be expected to contain increasing percentages of senior executives but decreasing percentages of executives from the sampled manufacturing firms. These two effects together show up in Table 9.2 as a low percentage of senior executives in the sampled manufacturing firms being in integrative market positions, but a percentage higher than the percentage of nonsenior executives. Comparing directors holding multiple directorships, the percentages in column 4 of Table 9.2 (senior executives in the sampled manufacturing firms) are higher than those for nonsenior executives (columns 3 and 6) but lower than those for senior executives in firms other than the sampled manufacturing firms (column 7). The complex intertwining of effects in Table

---

[7]In his description of American directors, Mace (1971) stresses the tendency for senior officers to receive directorship offers. As one corporate president stated the matter to Mace (1971),

> We have a standing rule that no one can be an outside director in our company who is not the top person in his organization. If he isn't, he can't be on our board. I don't care how able he is; our board as now constituted has top men as outsiders, so any replacements over the years have got to be their peers. You can't downgrade the prestige of our board membership by inviting, say, a promising vice president to serve as a board member [p. 87].

9.2 and the possible further complication of social class (e.g., senior executives occupying the most integrative market positions could have been drawn disproportionately from social elites) makes it analytically useful to express interactions among the categories of market position, executive role, and social class in a more rigorous way.

Table 9.3 presents a three-way tabulation of market position, social class, and executive roles for the two-digit sample of directors used in Tables 9.1 and 9.2. Let frequency f_{ijk} be the number of directors observed in the ith market position ($i = 1, 2, 3, 4,$ or 5 as the rows in Table 9.2), the jth social class ($j = 1$ or 2, corresponding to "no" and "yes" in Table 9.1), and the kth executive role ($k = 1, 2, 3, 4,$ or 5, corresponding to columns 3–7 in Table 9.2). For example, f_{111} is given in Table 9.3 as 20, f_{121} is 5, f_{525} is 11, and so on. These frequencies are described by the following model:

$$f_{ijk} = [\gamma \; \gamma_i^M \; \gamma_j^S \; \gamma_k^E] \; \gamma_{i\;k}^{ME},$$

where γ is an overall mean effect, γ_i^M is the tendency for directors to have occupied the ith market position, γ_j^S is the tendency for them to have been in the jth social class, γ_k^E is the tendency for them to have performed the kth executive

TABLE 9.3
Director Social Class, Executive Roles, and Market Position[a]

	Executive roles				
	1	2	3	4	5
Nonconstraint directors					
One directorship					
nonelite	20	12	22	2	7
social elite	5	2	5	0	5
Two directorships					
nonelite	7	16	9	5	24
social elite	0	4	7	4	14
Three or four directorships					
nonelite	0	5	3	2	10
social elite	0	2	0	1	4
Constraint directors					
Two directorships					
nonelite	1	3	3	2	6
social elite	0	0	0	1	1
Three or more directorships					
nonelite	1	6	8	3	29
social elite	0	3	0	2	11

[a]Categories are defined in Tables 9.1 and 9.2. Columns of Table 9.1 are referenced here as nonelite versus social elite (listed in *Social Register*).

role, and $\gamma_{i\,k}^{ME}$ is the tendency for directors to have been in the ith market position and the kth executive role simultaneously.

The significant point here is the lack of interaction terms required in order to describe the observed data accurately. Given the marginal tendencies for each category to have occurred (these are the terms in brackets), there is no differential tendency for types of executives to have been listed in the *Social Register* (there is no γ_{jk}^{SE} term), no differential tendency for directors in different market positions to have been listed in the *Social Register* (there is no $\gamma_{i\,j}^{MS}$ term), and no higher-order interactions among the market position, executive role, and social class categories (there is no $\gamma_{i\,j\,k}^{MSE}$ term).[8] With so many parameters deleted, it is not surprising to find that the model cannot perfectly describe the observed frequencies. Its inaccuracy, however, is statistically negligible. The likelihood ratio χ^2 for this restricted model is 28.6 with 23 degrees of freedom, which would have slightly less than a .24 probability of being obtained if market position and executive role were independent of being listed in the *Social Register*. This probability is well above .05, so the independence hypothesis seems quite adequate.[9]

---

[8]Negligible interactions with being listed in the *Social Register* are also obtained if market position is expressed only in terms of the number of directorships held ($\chi^2 = 22.5$ with 14 degrees of freedom, $p = .07$) or the constraint–nonconstraint director dichotomy ($\chi^2 = 15.0$ with 9 degrees of freedom, $p = .09$). Although negligible, these χ^2 statistics are much closer to significance than the χ^2 for the five-category market position variable discussed in the text. Nevertheless, there are no strong interactions with market position categories underlying this increased lack of fit. The strongest interaction with market position is with spanning severe constraint, but the null hypothesis of independence could only be rejected at a .40 level of confidence. The increased lack of fit comes from clearer negligible tendencies for outside executives to have been listed in the *Social Register*. In the notation of the restricted model in the text, parameters γ_{24}^{SE} and γ_{25}^{SE} would indicate the tendencies for outside nonsenior and senior executives, respectively, to have been listed in the *Social Register*. To the extent that they are greater than one, such executives tended to be *Social Register* listees. When estimated with the five-category market position variable, the parameters have estimated values of 1.28 and 1.17, respectively, with unit normal test statistics of 1.1 and 1.0, indicating their negligibility. These estimates were obtained with those given in Table 9.4. When estimated with a three-category number of directorships held variable as a measure of market position (i.e., combine the following rows of Table 9.3: 3 with 7, 4 with 8, 5 with 9, and 6 with 10), the parameters have estimated values of 1.24 and 1.34, respectively, with unit normal test statistics of .8 and 2.0, indicating a tendency for senior outside executives to have been listed in the *Social Register*. But when estimated with a two-category constraint–nonconstraint director dichotomy as a measure of market position (i.e., combine the following rows of Table 9.3: 1 with 3 with 5, 2 with 4 with 6, 7 with 9, and 8 with 10), the parameters have estimated values of 1.45 and 1.24, respectively, with unit normal test statistics of 1.8 and 1.4, indicating their negligibility. In short, *Social Register* listings can be generally treated as independent of the market positions and executive roles distinguished in Table 9.3.

[9]There are only 23 rather than the usual 24 degrees of freedom in a ($5 \times 5 \times 2$) table because there are no elite or nonelite nonsenior executives in the sampled manufacturing firms. Rows 6 and 7 are zero in column 1 of Table 9.3, which makes for a zero marginal frequency in the three-way

TABLE 9.4

Interactions between Executive Role and Market Position Holding Social Class Constant[a]

Market position	Executive roles				
	1	2	3	4	5
Nonconstraint directors					
One directorship	4.28	.83	2.10	.30	.45
	(4.1)	(.6)	(2.4)	(2.3)	(3.0)
Two directorships	.64	1.04	1.30	1.08	1.08
	(.8)	(.1)	(.8)	(.2)	(.3)
Three or four directorships	.55	1.49	.68	1.39	1.31
	(.0)	(1.1)	(.7)	(.8)	(.8)
Constraint directors					
Two directorships	1.22	.69	.87	1.80	.77
	(.3)	(.7)	(.2)	(1.3)	(.7)
Three or more directorships	.56	1.13	.62	1.25	2.06
	(1.0)	(.4)	(.9)	(.6)	(2.7)

[a]Executive roles are given in Table 9.2 and interactions between executive role and market position refer to γ^{ME} in the text (see footnote 10). Unit normal test statistics are given in parentheses. Under a two-tail test of a single parameter, a test statistic of two or more would indicate an effect significant at a .05 level of confidence.

Moreover, executive role is contingent on market position in a very simple way. Estimates of the interactions between executive role and market position categories are presented in Table 9.4. These are the $\gamma^{ME}_{i\,k}$ in the model. Unit normal test statistics are given in parentheses. An effect greater than one indicates a combination of market position and executive role categories that occurred more often than would have been expected if the categories were independent of one another.[10] Collectively, these interactions are significant at well beyond the .001 level of confidence. The null hypothesis that executive roles were independent of market position generates a likelihood χ^2 statistic of 94.4 with 32 degrees of freedom. Individually, the effects in Table 9.4 indicate three specific tendencies:

1. Single-seat directors were particularly likely to have been nonsenior executives in one of the sampled manufacturing firms. The effect $\hat{\gamma}^{ME}_{1\,1}$ is signifi-

---

tabulation. A χ^2 of 28.6 with 23 or 24 degrees of freedom is negligible and alternative measures of market position also fail to reject the null hypothesis that listing in the *Social Register* is independent of executive role and market position (see footnote 8).

[10]These effects have been estimated for a saturated model of the frequencies in Table 9.3 (increased by .5 to eliminate the zero cells). See footnotes 7 and 8 to Chapter 4 for details on specification and estimation of effects.

cantly greater than one at well beyond the .001 level of confidence (unit normal test statistic of 4.1).

2. Single-seat directors were particularly unlikely to have been executives elsewhere—especially senior executives. The effect $\hat{\gamma}_{1\,3}^{ME}$ is significantly greater than one, and the effects $\hat{\gamma}_{1\,4}^{ME}$ and $\hat{\gamma}_{1\,5}^{ME}$ are significantly less than one, $\hat{\gamma}_{1\,5}^{ME}$ at the .003 level of confidence.

3. There is a strong tendency for the directors in the most integrative market positions to have been president or chairman of the board in a firm other than the sampled manufacturing firms. The effect $\hat{\gamma}_{5\,5}^{ME}$ is significantly greater than one at a .01 level of confidence (unit normal test statistic of 2.7). More specifically, the estimated value of $\hat{\gamma}_{5\,5}^{ME}$ implies that the observed frequency of these maximally integrative directors was about twice the frequency that would have been expected if market position and executive role were independent.[11]

Note that the interaction is only between senior outside executives holding three or more directorships and spanning severe market constraint. The tendency for senior outside executives to have held three or more directorships without spanning severe market constraint is negligible ($\hat{\gamma}_{3\,5}^{ME} = 1.31$ with a unit normal test statistic of .8). The same tendency is negligible for senior executives within one of the sampled manufacturing firms ($\hat{\gamma}_{3\,2}^{ME} = 1.49$ with a unit normal test statistic of 1.1), and senior executives within the sampled manufacturing firms had no significant tendency to have been constraint directors holding multiple directorships ($\hat{\gamma}_{5\,2}^{ME} = 1.13$ with a unit normal test statistic of .4). The senior outside executives spanning market constraint and holding three or more directorships, in short, stand apart from directors generally as integrative actors in the economy.

This raises the question of how these maximally integrative directors were different from other directors. They were not disproportionately drawn from a social elite. As was true of the sampled directors generally, one in four of these maximally integrative directors was listed in the *Social Register* (11 of the 40, see Table 9.3). They did have disproportionate contact with the 54 large banks and insurance companies in the two-digit sample of firms. Among all 277

---

[11]This interaction is with the market position of spanning severe market constraint and holding three or more directorships, but is slightly stronger with number of directorships. If market position is measured as a three-category variable distinguishing one seat, two seats, and three or more seats (see footnote 8), there is a strong overall tendency for senior outside executives to have held three or more directorships, $\hat{\gamma}^{ME} = 2.09$ with a 3.5 unit normal test statistic. If market position is measured as a two-category dichotomy between constraint directors versus nonconstraint directors (again, see footnote 8), there is a strong overall tendency for senior outside executives to have spanned one or more severe market constraints, $\hat{\gamma}^{ME} = 1.58$ with a 3.1 unit normal test statistic. The bottom line is that senior outside executives tended to span severe market constraint and hold multiple directorships.

sampled directors, there are 40, 14.4%, who fall into the maximally integrative category of cell (5,5) in Table 9.2. Of the 125 directors who held no director-ships in one of the 54 sampled financial firms, however, only 4.8% are the maximally integrative directors. Not only did these maximally integrative direc-tors tend to sit on the boards of financial firms, they were disproportionately drawn from the ranks of finance executives. Of the 25 directors who were executives in one of the 54 sampled financial firms, 32.0% are among the maximally integrative directors. If being one of these maximally integrative directors was independent of having been a finance executive, this percentage would have been the much lower 14.4%.[12] Of course, the fact that the max-imally integrative directors had disproportionately high contact with the sampled financial firms does not imply that they were all representatives from such firms. A majority of the maximally integrative directors were on the boards of the sampled financial firms (34 of 40, or 85%), but a minority actually held execu-tive positions in those firms (8 of 40, or 20%). In contrast to the maximally integrative directors, moreover, directors of the sampled financial firms tended to interlock firms posing negligible market constraint for one another's profits.[13]

[12]The association between contact with financial firms and being a maximally integrative director is statistically strong. In a (2,3) tabulation of being a director in cell (5,5) of Table 9.2 versus not (maximally integrative versus some other kind of director) and three categories of contact with the sampled financial firms (none, nonexecutive director of a finance firm, and finance executive), the null hypothesis of independence can be rejected at beyond the .001 level of confidence (Pearson χ^2 statistic of 19.4 with 2 degrees of freedom).

[13]This statement is based on effects estimated for a three-way tabulation of spanning severe market constraint, holding multiple directorships, and contact with the sampled financial firms. Spanning severe market constraint is a dichotomy (yes, no). Holding multiple directorships is a dichotomy between holding two versus three or more seats (directors of financial firms could not be single-seat directors in this sample). Contact with financial firms is the trichotomy in footnote 12 (none, director only, and executive). The observed frequencies are as follows:

Spanned constraint	Directorships	Contact with financial firms		
		None	Director only	Executive
Yes	3+	11	42	10
Yes	2	17	0	0
No	3+	0	21	6
No	2	17	64	9

Adding a .5 to the observed frequencies and estimating interaction effects (e.g., Goodman, 1972) reveals a strong tendency for directors having no contact to have spanned severe market constraint but held only two directorships. The tendency is significant at beyond the .001 level of confidence. Directors of financial firms and finance executives tended to connect three or more firms in the absence of constraint. This is not surprising since finance executives only appear among the sampled

These results, and those obtained from Tables 9.1–9.4, show that there are a great many more differences among the directors than can be explained by a class perspective on a corporate elite. This is not to say that a class perspective is inadequate because it fails to account for all differences among directors. Recall that market constraint accounts for only a small amount of variation in directorate ties. However, that small amount was systematic across types of ties and market conditions. The class perspective on directors is inadequate because support for it is erratic and occasionally contradictory. To the extent that there was a corporate elite in 1967 as proposed by the class perspective, the sampled directors should have been differentiated in terms of their centrality within the elite. There should have been a systematic tendency for persons at the core of the elite simultaneously to have occupied the most integrative market positions, held executive positions in large firms, and been of sufficient social prominence to appear in the *Social Register*. There should have been a tendency for persons on the periphery of the elite simultaneously to have held the least integrative market positions, held no (or a minor) executive position, and been socially anonymous with respect to the *Social Register*. There is some support for this prediction. Persons were increasingly likely to have been executives to the extent that they held multiple directorships in the large firms sampled and the interlocks they provided spanned severe market constraint. More than tending to have been executives, they tended to have been corporate presidents and chairmen of the board. However, this empirical support for the class perspective is modified somewhat by the tendency for all of the sampled directors to have been executives somewhere. Even the single-seat directors were 66% executives and 33% presidents or chairmen of the board. Most significantly, the class perspective is contradicted in some instances. In contrast to the tendency for executives generally to have occupied the most integrative market positions, executives in the sampled manufacturing firms tended not to have occupied such positions. Senior and nonsenior executives in these large manufacturing firms tended to hold only a single directorship in their home firm. Further, the extent to which a director occupied an integrative market position and the executive role he fulfilled were independent of whether or not he was listed in the *Social Register*.

These results do not reject the idea of a corporate elite in the American economy. There is no clear boundary between members of an upper class and the remainder of society. Any operationalization of who is a member of the "upper class" by virtue of social origin, wealth, or current social affiliations must

---

directors to the extent that they interlock with one of the 42 sampled manufacturing firms, and the finance sector posed negligible market constraint for all manufacturing industries. Every interlock with a financial firm therefore spans negligible market constraint. This only sets the maximally integrative directors in cell (5,5) of Table 9.2 even further apart from finance directors generally since the maximally integrative directors did span severe market constraints.

involve some arbitrary decisions. Evidence for or against the idea of a corporate elite representing upper-class interests must accordingly be open to debate.

What is rejected is the idea that there is a single dimension of differentiation among persons on the directorates of large American corporations. Each of these individuals has a pattern of relations with others that defines his network position in the economy. Differences in the relational patterns defining the positions of different individuals cannot be adequately described by a single axis of centrality. Rather, persons appear to be differentially central in different sectors of the economy, and different patterns appear to be typical of different markets: the patterns of finance executives, for example, are distinct from the patterns of manufacturing executives.

DIRECTOR STRUCTURAL AUTONOMY

As soon as the step is taken to admit segmentation in the system of directors in large firms, the structural autonomy model becomes a guide for research into the relational patterns defining segments as network positions. Under the inference that directorate ties constitute a social market in their own right, an individual director's structural autonomy is determined by social and economic relations, his relational pattern within the social market of directorate ties and the pattern of sales and purchase transactions characterizing his firm's position in the economic market. His involvement in these two types of relations determines his structural autonomy—his freedom to pursue interests without constraint—and that structural autonomy combines with his social prominence and affiliation with a major corporation to give him opportunities to improve his situation. In other words, the director can be viewed as a purposive actor pursuing his own interests, interests that might or might not be the shared interests of other directors within a corporate elite. The network model of structural autonomy would not distinguish directors in terms of the interests they would pursue if they could. Each director is assumed to be interested in improving his own situation, and that situation might be improved in part by enhancing the situations of other directors within some type of corporate elite. More specifically, however, structural autonomy would distinguish directors in terms of their ability to pursue whatever interests they wished. Thinking in particular of the conclusions in Chapter 5, the model can be used to specify parameters in a structural equation model distinguishing the abilities of individual directors to pursue their interests so as to create a social market of directorate ties.

One framework for such a structural equation model is sketched as a path diagram in Figure 9.2 following the diagram specified in Figure 8.2 for individual firms. A director's structural autonomy is defined by his freedom from market constraint and his participation in successful cooptation. This structural

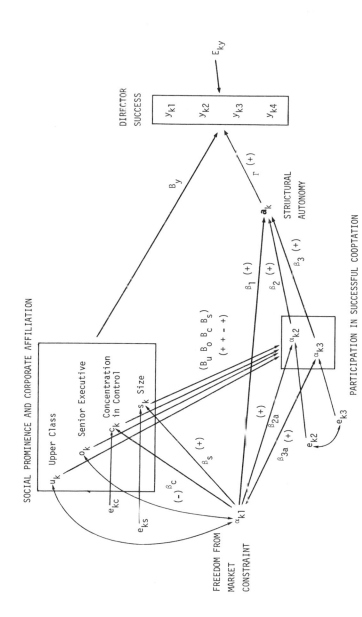

Figure 9.2. A path diagram indicating processes by which individual directors could be responsible for a social market of directorate ties (expected direction of effect given in parentheses).

autonomy combines with his social prominence and corporate affiliation to determine his success in a general sense. Figure 9.2 is provided as a guide for the more detailed discussion to follow. I begin with the determinants of director structural autonomy.

A director would have structural autonomy within the economic market of buying and selling to the extent that the firm with which he is principally affiliated is free from market constraint. This principal affiliation would be the firm in which the director holds his most senior executive position. The director would be free to pursue his own interests without constraint from his firm's competitors, suppliers, or consumers to the extent that his firm's primary establishments were located in structurally autonomous industries. So freed, the individual director could concentrate on the firm's success so as to improve his own position. The closer to one that α_{k1} in Eq. (8.4) is, the less subject to market constraint are the primary establishments of firm k. Where firm k is director k's principal affiliation, therefore, α_{k1} expresses the extent to which his firm offers him a structurally autonomous position within the economic market—at least in comparison to the structural autonomy of directors in other firms.

A director would have structural autonomy within the social market of directorate ties to the extent that he constitutes a personal channel for information, advice, and influence between his principal affiliation and every economic sector potentially a source of market constraint on its profits. In this position, the director provides a strategic interface between the most competitive actors in his corporate environment.[14] There are two manners in which he could fulfill this role.

He could sit on the boards of firms that own establishments in those sectors posing severe market constraint for the industries in which his principal affiliation owns its primary establishments. A measure of the extent to which this is true of a particular director is similar to the measure of cooptive success for an individual firm. Let $b_{qm(k)}$ be zero unless director k interlocks the directorates of firms q and m, whereupon it equals one. In order to exclude the trivial interlock director k provides with his own principal affiliation, firm q, let $b_{qq(k)}$ equal zero.

---

[14]The distribution of persons a firm uses to interface its environment has been studied from the perspective of the firm. "Boundary" personnel are an important feature of Evan's (1966, 1972) discussion of the organization-set connecting a firm with its corporate environment. Hirsch (1972) provides an application of this idea in his description of firms in the communication, broadcasting and amusement sectors. Aldrich and Herker (1977) analytically review implications for organizational performance stemming from the boundary role functions of processing information and representing an organization to its environment. My concern here is only with the perspective of the individual performing the boundary role. This perspective has been used to describe the individual's *intra*organizational power (e.g., Aldrich & Herker, 1977:227, and the review by Pfeffer & Salancik, 1978:230ff). I use that perspective here to describe the *inter*organizational autonomy of an individual holding multiple directorships.

Now the sum $\Sigma_m\, b_{qm(k)}d_{mi}$ equals the number of firms in sector i that director k connects to his principal affiliation q, where d_{mi} is given in Eq. (3.1) as zero unless firm m owns an establishment in sector i, whereupon it equals one. Let w_{ki} equal zero unless director k provides a personal interlock tie with one or more establishments in sector i, whereupon it equals one. This binary cooptive relation provided by director k is defined by this sum:

$$w_{ki} = \begin{cases} 1, & \text{if } \sum_m b_{qm(k)}d_{mi} > 0, \\ 0, & \text{otherwise.} \end{cases}$$

The increased profit margin in industry j to be expected, on average, from a cooptive relation between the industry and some sector i is given in Eqs. (2.12) and (2.13) as negative two times the raw market constraint the sector poses for industry profits, $-2a_{ji}^*$. Under bold ceteris paribus assumptions, the increased profit margin for an industry j establishment that director k could provide through his personal contacts with firms in sector i is then the product $-2a_{ji}^*w_{ki}$ and the sum over all sectors i posing a constraint for profits in the industry is the aggregate increase director k could provide, $\Sigma_i(-2a_{ji}^*w_{ki})$ for all $\mathbf{a}_{ji}$ less than zero. Where δ_{qj} is the proportional weight in Eq. (8.4) indicating the importance to firm q of its primary establishment in industry j, the product $\delta_{qj}\,\Sigma_i(-2a_{ji}^*w_{ki})$ for all $\mathbf{a}_{ji}$ less than zero, measures the increased profit margin director k could provide his principal affiliation's primary establishment in industry j and the following sum across all of his firm's primary establishments is the increased profit margin director k could provide his firm:

$$d(\mathbf{a}_q) = \sum_j \delta_{qj}\left[\sum_i (-2\mathbf{a}_{j\,i}^* w_{ki}) \right] \qquad \text{for all} \quad \mathbf{a}_{ji} < 0. \qquad (9.1)$$

The ratio of this weighted sum of coopted sources of market constraint over the unweighted sum provides a measure of the proportion of market constraint on its primary establishments that firm q might be able to circumvent through the personal connections director k provides to sources of that constraint:

$$\alpha_{k2} = [d(\mathbf{a}_q)] \Big/ \left\{ \sum_j \delta_{qj}\left[\sum_i (-2\mathbf{a}_{j\,i}^*) \right] \right\} \qquad \text{for all} \quad \mathbf{a}_{ji} < 0. \qquad (9.2)$$

Eq. (9.1) states for director k the condition stated in Eq. (8.5) for firm k, and Eq. (9.2) similarly corresponds to the measure of a firm's cooptive success in Eq. (8.6). The index α_{k2} will vary from zero to one as the extent to which director k provides a personal communication channel between his principal affiliation, firm q, and firms operating in every sector potentially constraining profits in the industries where his principal affiliation owns its primary establishments. In other words, α_{k2} is a measure of the extent to which director k is in a position to protect his principal affiliation from the uncertainties of market constraints on profit margins.[15]

In addition to providing personal ties to sources of market constraint from suppliers and consumers, the individual director could provide a personal tie to his principal affiliation's competitors. He could sit on the boards of firms operating establishments in those sectors where his principal affiliation operates its primary establishments. The sum $\Sigma_m \, b_{qm(k)} d_{mj}$ is the number of firms in sector j that director k connects to his principal affiliation firm q. To the extent that the proportional weight δ_{qj} equals one, these firms are all competing with firm q in the production of sector j output. The product $\delta_{qj} \, (\Sigma_m \, b_{qm(k)} d_{mj})$ therefore indicates the significance of competitors to firm q's primary establishment in sector j that can be contacted through personal ties provided by director k. When summed across all sectors j in which firm q operates a primary establishment, the result is an index measuring the extent to which director k provides his firm, q, with personal ties to important competitors:

$$\alpha_{k3} = \left[\sum_j \delta_{qj} \left(\sum_m b_{qm(k)} d_{mi} \right) \right]. \qquad (9.3)$$

The higher this sum is, the more director k provides a personal communication channel for information, advice and influence between his principal affiliation and its competitors.[16] The index is measured as a mean number of competitors

---

[15]This index does not consider the extent to which director k is the *only* personal channel to firms operating in constraint sectors, a condition that would make him especially valuable to his principal affiliation. The sum in Eq. (9.1) could be computed to capture this condition by setting w_{ki} equal to one only if director k is the only person on the board of firm q who sits on the board of some other firm operating in sector i. Two considerations suggest that this operation should not be adopted. First, there can be several different firms operating in sector i, so it would be valuable to firm q to have several directors on the boards of those firms collectively, one director representing each of the major competitors in the sector. Second, although a firm can use its directorate collectively to reach most of the sectors constraining its profits, each director individually is likely to represent only a subset of these sectors. In other words, the expected value of α_{k2} in Eq. (9.2) across all directors k is likely to be much lower than the expected value of α_{k2} in Eq. (8.6) across all firms k. Therefore, it seems premature at this point to limit the sum in Eq. (9.2) to sectors i in which director k provides the only direct interlock tie for firm q even though such a condition would give the director a certain monopoly power over the firm's connection to sector i.

[16]From the perspective of firm q, director k's principal affiliation, it might be useful to have director k represent its major competitors within a single sector i rather than diversifying him across all sectors i in which it owns an establishment. Eq. (9.3) could be modified to capture this quality. The ratio $[\Sigma_m \, b_{qm(k)} d_{mj}]/[\Sigma_m \, d_{mj} - 1]$ is the proportion of sampled establishments in sector j that are owned by firms for which director k is on the board and firm q is a competitor within sector j. This ratio will equal one if director k sits on the board of every sampled firm owning an establishment in sector j and his principal affiliation operates one of its primary establishments in that sector. The index α_{k3} could be defined as the maximum value of this index for director j (maximum across all sectors j), or it could be averaged across the sectors in which his principal affiliation owns primary

reached and will have a high positive value to the extent that it is computed from a large sample of firms owning establishments in a large number of sectors.

These three conditions come together to define a director's structural autonomy as the extent to which the establishments for which he is primarily responsible are free from market constraint and he is integral to their ability to circumvent market constraint. The primary establishments of the firm with which the director is principally affiliated are his immediate concern. To the extent that those establishments are free from market constraint, the director is free to plan for the firm's profits and growth as a determinant of his own well-being. For director k principally affiliated with firm k, this lack of constraint is given by α_{k1} in Eq. (8.4) as the mean profit margin expected in firm k's primary establishments given the market constraints on the industries in which they operate. It would be possible for director k to be successful, in a general sense, within the scope of a single corporation to the extent that α_{k1} is high. The more autonomous his principal affiliation, the more discretion the firm can afford to provide for indi-

---

establishments as is specified in Eq. (9.3) with the proportional weight δ_{qj}. There are at least two reasons for not measuring α_{k3} as a proportionate index.

1. The absolute number of interlock ties to sector j reflects the importance of those ties. As discussed in Chapter 4, intraindustry directorate ties are most useful where there is a moderate level of competition and less useful where it would be either a hopeless task to manage extremely high competition or an unnecessary task to manage extremely low competition. The highest frequency of intraindustry directorate ties and sampled establishments is observed in the moderately competitive industries. On average, therefore, the number of competitor establishments director k can reach will be highest in moderately competitive industries, precisely the industries in which the interlock ties he provides would be most useful to his home firm. A proportionate measure of the extent to which director k reaches all available competitor establishments need not reflect the value of intraindustry interlock ties. Given some upper limit on the number of directorships a single individual can fulfill, the more firms there are operating in a sector (which would be high in moderately competitive industries), the smaller the proportion of them for which person k is a director. It would be easier for a single director to be on the boards of all firms sampled from a sector in which there is very high or very low competition—but there is less value to his principal affiliation in having him reach competitors in such sectors.

2. It is in the director's interest to diversify the sectors he reaches. Having director k specialize in a single sector would make him an excellent source of information on the sector for his principal affiliation, but at the same time it would limit the scope of his information, advice, and influence to that sector and would make him a prime candidate for attention from federal regulatory agencies. In other words, specialization seems to me to be in the interest of the firm, whereas diversification seems to be in the interest of the individual director aspiring to more control within the firm or senior executive positions in other firms. The index in Eq. (9.3) focuses on diversification across firms and sectors in the anticipation that it is diversification that will give director k structural autonomy. The index is high to the extent that director k provides interlock ties to multiple competitors across multiple sectors. This is only an initial guess of course. In an actual data analysis it would be interesting to assess the extent to which director autonomy resulted from the diversification, number, and specialization of interlock ties to competitors that the director provided.

vidual directors to expand its operations to realize each director's interests. Under the principle of conflicting group affiliation used in Chapter 2 to define market constraint, however, a director could derive additional autonomy from being able to exploit the conflicting interests of multiple firms with which he is affiliated so as to increase their mutual profits and derive the benefits typically associated with being responsible for, or integral to, the increase. The opportunities for this source of autonomy would be greatest where the costs for the firms of conducting necessary buying and selling on the open market would be greatest. Those costs would be greatest where market constraint is the most severe. Therefore, a director's structural autonomy would be augmented by his position in the social market of directorate ties to the extent that he connected firms posing severe market constraint for profits in the industries where each operated its primary establishments. The index α_{k2} measures the extent to which director k provides a direct connection to suppliers and consumers constraining the profits of his principal affiliation and α_{k3} measures the extent to which he reaches competitors. To the extent that α_{k1}, α_{k2}, and α_{k3} are high simultaneously, director k would enjoy the structural autonomy of being primarily responsible for establishments free from market constraint and being integral to their ability to circumvent market constraint. He would be in the optimal position to realize his interests without constraint. For the purposes here, let this structural autonomy of director k be given as an additive, linear function of the three components[17]:

$$\mathbf{a}_k = \beta + \beta_1 \alpha_{k1} + \beta_2 \alpha_{k2} + \beta_3 \alpha_{k3}, \qquad (9.4)$$

where β_1 expresses the importance to director structural autonomy of being principally affiliated with a corporation free from market constraint, β_2 expresses the importance of providing interlock ties to supplier and consumer sectors posing a constraint for that corporation's profits, and β_3 expresses the importance of providing interlock ties to the corporation's competitors. The intercept term β is arbitrary since structural autonomy is only meaningful here in a com-

---

[17]I have not specified interaction terms in this equation because they would necessarily complicate the discussion without empirical evidence warranting the complication. In contrast to the structural autonomy model for an individual firm [Eq. (8.7), which contains one interaction term], four interaction terms are possible in Eq. (9.4): a tendency for directors autonomous in the economic market to provide interlock ties to suppliers and consumers ($\alpha_{k1}\alpha_{k2}$); a tendency for them to provide interlock ties to competitors ($\alpha_{k1}\alpha_{k3}$); a tendency for directors generally to provide interlock ties to competitors, suppliers, and consumers ($\alpha_{k2}\alpha_{k3}$); and a third-order interaction ($\alpha_{k1}\alpha_{k2}\alpha_{k3}$). Some or all of these terms could be significant determinants of director autonomy. For example, it is very likely that a director interlocking with suppliers and consumers will simultaneously interlock with competitors given the highly diversified character of large firms, so an interaction effect between α_{k2} and α_{k3} seems probable. Before introducing these possibilities into the discussion, however, it seems prudent to assess their relative importance in empirical research.

parison of the relation autonomy of separate directors, but the three effects β_1, β_2, and β_3 should be positive.

ANALYZING DIRECTOR
STRUCTURAL AUTONOMY

This is an initial model for empirical research. In the same way that the structural autonomy model specified in Eq. (2.4) was an initial model for the analysis of market constraint and the structural autonomy model in Eq. (8.7) would be an initial model for the analysis of individual firms, the structural autonomy model in Eq. (9.4) is an initial model for the analysis of processes by which individual directors are responsible for a social market of directorate ties. As is accomplished in Chapter 8 for individual firms, the model can be used to highlight processes determining and resulting from the structural autonomy of an individual director. Some initial lines of inquiry can be drawn from the analysis of directors sampled from the boards of large manufacturing firms and the discussion of firms in Chapter 8. These lines are sketched in Figure 9.2 as a path diagram.

There is the question of how individual differences between directors account for their differential involvement in successful cooptation. Why do some directors constitute interlock ties across severe market constraints to suppliers and consumers (α_{k2}) and sit on the boards of competitors (α_{k3}) while other directors do neither? Two classes of differences are specified in Figure 9.2 in terms of the following equations predicting the two measures of director k's involvement in successful cooptation:

$$\begin{pmatrix} \alpha_{k2} \\ \alpha_{k3} \end{pmatrix} = \begin{pmatrix} \beta_{2u} \\ \beta_{3u} \end{pmatrix} u_k + \begin{pmatrix} \beta_{2o} \\ \beta_{3o} \end{pmatrix} o_k + \begin{pmatrix} \beta_{2c} \\ \beta_{3c} \end{pmatrix} c_k + \begin{pmatrix} \beta_{2s} \\ \beta_{3s} \end{pmatrix} s_k$$

$$+ \begin{pmatrix} \beta_{2a} \\ \beta_{3a} \end{pmatrix} \alpha_{k1} + \begin{pmatrix} e_{k2} \\ e_{k3} \end{pmatrix},$$

$$\begin{pmatrix} \alpha_{k2} \\ \alpha_{k3} \end{pmatrix} = [B_u]u_k + [B_o]o_k + [B_c]c_k + [B_s]s_k + \begin{pmatrix} \beta_{2a} \\ \beta_{3a} \end{pmatrix} \alpha_{k1} + \begin{pmatrix} e_{k2} \\ e_{k3} \end{pmatrix}, (9.5)$$

where e_{k2} and e_{k3} are residual terms, and variables are measured as deviations from their means. Prestige and position in the economic market are the two considerations specified here to explain the extent to which a director is responsible for the observed patterning of directorate ties by market constraint. Prestige gives the director special opportunities to hold multiple, constraint-spanning directorships. His position in the economic market does that as well as affect his ability to seize those opportunities.

From the class perspective on a corporate elite, differences in the social prestige of individuals should be strongly associated with differences in the number of important directorships they hold. There was no evidence of this among the directors sampled from the boards of large manufacturing firms in 1967 (Table 9.1); however, the class perspective retains support from other research efforts. Given the importance of an integrated economy to the cohesion of a corporate elite, socially elite directors would be expected to be solicited by social elites on other boards so as to end up themselves spanning market constraint and coordinating competitive firms.[18] Let u_k be zero unless director k is listed in the *Social Register*, whereupon it equals one. As one measure of director k's membership in an elite social class, u_k should be associated positively with the two measures of his responsibility for a social market of directorate ties.[19] In other words, the coefficients β_{2u} and β_{3u} contained in B_u in Eq. (9.5) should be positive.

From an organizational perspective, differences in the bureaucratic prestige of individuals should be strongly associated with differences in the number of important directorships they hold. As a simple matter of corporate self-concept, individuals should receive directorship offers to the extent that their senior position as corporate president or chairman of the board would make them an appropriately prestigious outside director.[20] This effect was strongly evident among

---

[18]Extending this inference, directors in family-controlled firms should tend to be *Social Register* listees, and such persons should be especially likely to sit on the boards of other family-controlled firms. Given the common background of the social elite (relative to the overall population) and the control of family firms by a social elite, directors listed in the *Social Register* should have a greater tendency to hold multiple directorships in family-controlled firms than directors not listed there. This suggests that above and beyond the concentration of control measure c_k specified in Eq. (9.5), interesting results could be obtained by expanding the control measure to distinguish family-controlled firms from management-controlled firms from firms controlled by outside financial institutions.

[19]Perhaps the most likely alternative measure of social standing, relative to *Social Register* listings, is membership in exclusive social clubs. In the same sense that comembership in an upper class might endear socially elite directors to one another so as to offer one another directorships when possible, comemberships in exclusive social clubs would give individuals an opportunity to know one another so as to determine who among them would make suitable outside directors. I am not suggesting that club membership per se would result in directorship offers so much as it would provide the setting in which persons who could offer directorships would discover people suitable for such roles. A corporate president put the matter rather succinctly to Mace (1971) in response to the question of how outside directors are selected:

> Here in New York it's a systems club. There is a group of companies that you can see, and you know them as well as I do, where the chief executive of Company A has B and C and D on his board. They are chief executive officers of B, C and D, and he is on their boards. They are all members of the Brook Club, the Links Club, or the Union League Club. Everybody is washing everybody else's hands [p. 99].

[20]This point is nicely illustrated by a statement of corporate policy obtained in Mace's fieldwork on directors. See footnote 7.

directors sampled from the boards of large manufacturing firms in 1967 (Tables 9.2 and 9.4). Let o_k be zero unless director k is the president or chairman of the board in a corporation, whereupon it equals one. With the disproportionate opportunities senior executives receive to sit on the boards of other firms, they should hold a disproportionately high number of directorships and span severe market constraint. In other words, the coefficients β_{2o} and β_{3o} in B_o of Eq. (9.5) should be positive. These coefficients only express the effect of the role of being a senior executive. Director k could be president of a large corporation or president of a small subsidary corporation, and o_k would equal one.

Of course the nature of the firm with which the director is principally affiliated also affects his relative prestige as an outside director. The prestige of being president in a large, autonomous firm like General Motors is greater than that associated with the presidency of a small, constrained firm. Ceteris paribus, directors in large, autonomous firms would be more prestigious than directors generally and so should be given more opportunities to hold multiple directorships. Further, there is the question of corporate policy. The firms most involved in directorate ties in 1967 were large and controlled by diffuse interest groups (Chapter 3). For reasons of prestige and policy, directors in these firms could be expected to have the greatest opportunities to hold multiple directorships spanning market constraint—whether or not the directors occupy the most senior executive positions available.[21] Where c_k is the concentration of control within director k's principal affiliation, in other words, the coefficients β_{2c} and β_{3c} in B_c of Eq. (9.5) should be negative. Where s_k is the size of that corporation, the coefficients β_{2s} and β_{3s} in B_s of Eq. (9.5) should be positive. As discussed in Chapter 8 with respect to Eqs. (8.8) and (8.9), large, diffusely controlled firms would be expected to own primary establishments in structurally autonomous industries. In other words, the size and concentration of control for director k's principal affiliation should increase and decrease, respectively, with the extent to which its primary establishments are free from market constraint, α_{k1}, so that β_s and β_c in Figure 9.2 and Eqs. (8.8) and (8.9) are positive and negative. This means that being affiliated with a structurally autonomous firm has an indirect and a direct positive effect on a director's involvement in successful cooptation.

---

[21]A careful reading of the diagram in Figure 9.2 reveals that there are no covariances specified among the director attributes (u_k and o_k) and the attributes of his principal affiliation (c_k and s_k). This is not to imply that constraints be placed on covariances among them when they are used to predict cooptive success or director success. I am simply unsure of how these four variables will be correlated. There is some evidence of low correlations. Corporate size and concentration in control are uncorrelated in Table 3.1, and senior executive role is independent in Table 9.3 of being listed in the *Social Register;* that is, c_k and s_k may be uncorrelated and u_k and o_k may be uncorrelated. On the other hand, the correlation between s_k and o_k could be quite negative. Given one or two senior executives in every firm, a director is decreasingly likely to be a senior executive to the extent that his firm has a large board. For the purposes of this discussion, I have ignored correlations among the four social prominence and corporate affiliation variables pending further empirical research.

For the same reason that a structurally autonomous firm would be expected to be cooptively successful, a director in such a firm would be expected to participate in that successful cooptation. His firm would provide him with the ability and opportunity to hold multiple directorships spanning market constraint. Moreover, it would be in his own interest to be the person responsible for obtaining information and advice regarding the sectors most threatening industry profits for its principal affiliation. In other words, a director is increasingly likely to interlock with suppliers and consumers [β_{2a} will be positive in Eq. (9.5)] and interlock with competitors [β_{3a} will be positive in Eq. (9.5)] to the extent that his principal affiliation is free from market constraint.[22] At the same time, structurally autonomous firms would be expected to be large, and this increases a director's involvement in successful cooptation; that is, the compound coefficients $\beta_s B_s$ should be positive. They would also be expected to be controlled by diffuse interest groups, which in turn increases a director's involvement in successful cooptation; that is, the products of two negative coefficients, $\beta_c B_c$, should be positive.

In summary, there are five processes distinguished in Figure 9.2 that could account for director participation in a social market of directorate ties: (a) It could result from the opportunities his social prestige provides as captured by β_{2u} and β_{3u}. (b) It could result from the opportunities his bureaucratic prestige as a senior corporate executive provides as captured by β_{2o} and β_{3o}. (c) It could result from the size and distribution of control characterizing the firm with which he is principally affiliated as captured by B_c and B_s. (d) It could result directly from his principal affiliation with a firm operating its primary establishments in structurally autonomous industries as captured by β_{2a} and β_{3a}. (e) It could result indirectly from the extensive involvement of his principal affiliation firm in directorate ties because of the firm's operations in structurally autonomous industries ($\beta_c B_c$ and $\beta_s B_s$). As with the question of successful corporate cooptation, the relative magnitudes of these effects will indicate the relative extent to which each process underlies the documented association between market constraint and directorate ties. The general presumption, however, is that differences in the extent to which directors are involved in successful cooptation can be traced to differences in personal prestige and the extent to which they are affiliat-

---

[22]The association is to be expected because of the distribution of directors across sectors of the economy. As described in Chapter 4, there is a kinked, exponential association between interlock ties between competitors and the lack of market constraint within an industry (e.g., Figures 4.3 and 4.4). Past a criterion level of constraint, interlock ties begin to decrease within an industry. If firms, rather than industries, are taken as a unit of analysis, however, the small number of firms in highly concentrated industries results in an ostensible monotonic association between interlock ties and a lack of market constraint (see footnote 14 to Chapter 4). By extension, a positive monotonic association can be expected across directors as units of analysis sampled from the boards of large firms because few of them will be sampled from oligopolistic industries.

ed with large, structurally autonomous firms controlled by diffuse interest groups.[23]

Turning to consequences, there is the question of how a director's structural autonomy might affect his overall success as a director. It seems likely that directors of large American corporations are relatively well-to-do. Director success could be indexed in terms of sheer volume of assets individual directors possess. However, there are many ways in which an individual could become wealthy in addition to being a successful director. An index of success closer to the role of being a director is the ability to select the firms in which one is a director. The individual with low structural autonomy would be expected to receive few, if any, invitations to be an outside director, but the structurally autonomous director would be expected to receive many. The more structurally autonomous an individual is, according to a_k in Eq. (9.4), the more he would be able to provide valuable information, advice, and influence to any board on which he is an outside director. These are the typical commodities provided by the outside director as discussed in Chapter 3. The structurally autonomous director, in short, would be expected to be disproportionately able to select those directorship offers that would be the most rewarding to him. In turn, the most rewarding directorships would be those that would improve his value as a director in the sense of improving the worth of his information, advice, and influence. This means that directorships in large, profitable firms would be the most valuable. Such positions would be a source of information and advice on the diverse industries in which the firms successfully operate, a prestigious item on one's résumé, and a source of information on corporate growth and executive turnover that would provide opportunities for one's own upward mobility. These rewards of access to information and prestigious association were the items most often mentioned by corporate officers in Mace's (1971) study as reasons for accepting outside directorships. Their comments communicate the flavor of their interests. One person stressed the importance of access to information:

> I do learn something more about business. For a lot of executives who haven't started on the down curve, who are still aspiring, every board meeting is a chance to learn something. One's own business can make you parochial, the industry can make you parochial. There is a lot more to this world of business than our industry and our company [pp. 104–105].

[23]The only caveat here is the possible need to stratify directors into subpopulations within which the parameters in Figure 9.2 would be estimated. Executives in financial institutions interlock so extensively that they could distort processes typical of nonfinancial executives unless they are analyzed separately. Similarly, the results in Tables 9.2 and 9.4 show that there are general differences between the executive directors of the sampled manufacturing firms and the executive directors of other firms, especially with respect to senior executives.

Another person stressed the opportunities presented by holding a position on the directorate of a prestigious firm:

> The important thing is the desirability of getting to know better and be associated with— and in the public eye—well-known people. We like to see our names in a good context. It is good for our morale to be identified with a wise man on the board. And none of us is immune to name dropping. To be able to say, "Yesterday at the XYZ board meeting, Sam Smith (a well-known president of a well-known large New York bank) said he didn't see much lowering of interest rates for some time to come"—that may not be cash income, but friend, that is income [pp. 105–106].

Whatever the value of the exposure gained by directorships, an individual's structural autonomy should affect his success as a director by affecting his ability to obtain the most valued directorships, those in large, profitable corporations.

For the purposes of this discussion, I shall measure director success in terms of the most valued directorships that an individual holds outside of his principal affiliation from the overall value of his outside directorships.[24] The largest, most profitable firm for which person k is an outside director would measure the upper limit on his success. The total size and typical profit margins for the firms in which he is an outside director would measure the scope of his success.

Four measures are available from data already introduced. The binary interlock variable $b_{qm(k)}$ is zero unless director k sits on the boards of firms q and m, whereupon it equals one. For director k principally affiliated with firm q, the product $s_m b_{qm(k)}$ will be zero unless he is an outside director in firm m, whereupon it equals the size of firm m, s_m, measured in dollars of assets or annual sales. Similarly, the product $p_m b_{qm(k)}$ equals zero unless director k is an outside director in firm m, whereupon it equals the profit margin in firm m, p_m. The maximum size and profit margin of firms for which director k is an outside director is then defined by the following two equations across any sampled firm m:

$$y_{k1} = \max (p_m b_{qm(k)}), \qquad (9.6)$$

$$y_{k2} = \max (s_k b_{qm(k)}). \qquad (9.7)$$

---

[24]There are many alternative measures of directorate success here. I have selected four for their face validity and correspondence to the measures of profit and growth used to characterize corporate success in Chapter 8. One interesting alternative here would be a focus on mobility. Given the characteristics of a director's principal affiliation, he could be viewed as successful to the extent that he serves as outside director on firms which increase his opportunities for mobility into larger firms, or more profitable firms, or firms operating in different industries. Success in this sense is measured as the marginal advantage provided by outside directorships. The measures in the text focus on success in the more absolute sense of holding positions on the boards of firms which are large and profitable in comparison to firms in general.

The profit margin typical of the large firms for which k is an outside director could be given as the mean profit margin:

$$y_{k3} = \left[\sum_m p_m b_{qm(k)} \right] \bigg/ \left[\sum_m b_{qm(k)} \right]. \tag{9.8}$$

The total assets or annual sales represented by the firms in which k holds outside directorships is given by the following sum:

$$y_{k4} = \sum_m s_m b_{qm(k)}. \tag{9.9}$$

Across directors with differential prestige affiliated with different types of firms, these four indicators of director success should have a positive association with his structural autonomy.

The profitability of the most profitable firm for which director k is an outside director is a function of his personal prestige (u_k, o_k), the kind of firm with which he is principally affiliated (c_k, s_k), and his structural autonomy ($\mathbf{a}_k$):

$$y_{k1} = [\mathbf{a}_k] + b_{1u}u_k + b_{1o}o_k + b_{1c}c_k + b_{1s}s_k + e_{k1}. \tag{9.10}$$

The other three indicators of director success would be similarly determined. Each indicator, however, could be affected differently by a person's prestige and the nature of the firm with which he is principally affiliated. Add to this the different metrics in which the four indices are measured and it is safe to say that the bs in Eq. (9.10) will vary across different indicators of director success. Further, differences in the scale of the indicators requires an adjustment to the effect of structural autonomy. With these allowances, Eq. (9.10) would appear as follows for the other three indicators of director success:

$$y_{k2} = \gamma_2[\mathbf{a}_k] + b_{2u}u_k + b_{2o}o_k + b_{2c}c_k + b_{2s}s_k + e_{k2}, \tag{9.11}$$

$$y_{k3} = \gamma_3[\mathbf{a}_k] + b_{3u}u_k + b_{3o}o_k + b_{3c}c_k + b_{3s}s_k + e_{k3}, \tag{9.12}$$

$$y_{k4} = \gamma_4[\mathbf{a}_k] + b_{4u}u_k + b_{4o}o_k + b_{4c}c_k + b_{4s}s_k + e_{k4}, \tag{9.13}$$

where the gammas adjust structural autonomy to reflect the varying scales of the four success indicators. The four success indicators would be expected to covary, a director successful in one sense being successful in another sense, so γ_2, γ_3, and γ_4 should be positive. In Figure 9.2, these effects are combined with those in Eq. (9.10) as a matrix of effects:

$$Y_k = \Gamma[\mathbf{a}_k] + B_y X_k + E_k, \tag{9.14}$$

where Y_k is a (4,1) vector of director k's scores on the four success measures, Γ is a (4,1) vector of the gammas ($\Gamma' = 1, \gamma_2, \gamma_3, \gamma_4$), B_y is a (4,4) matrix of the bs in Eqs. (9.10)–(9.13), X_k is a (4,1) vector of director k's scores on the control variables ($X'_k = u_k, o_k, c_k, s_k$), and E_y is a (4,1) vector of residual scores for director k in Eqs. (9.10)–(9.13).

This class of structural equation models appears in preceding chapters. Estimates of the effects in Eq. (9.14) and those defining structural autonomy in Eq. (9.4) can be computed from ordinary least-squares regression coefficients in a canonical correlation analysis. The computations would be similar to those used in Chapter 6 to describe the association between market variables and corporate philanthropy. The same class of models is used in Chapter 8 to describe the association between corporate success and a firm's structural autonomy.[25] Director structural autonomy will be the weighted sum of α_{k1}, α_{k2}, and α_{k3} that is maximally correlated with director success—holding constant differences in director prestige and principal affiliation.

As in the preceding chapters, structural autonomy is being measured in the metric of profit margin. In Chapter 2, an industry's structural autonomy is the profit margin it is expected to have given its pattern of buying and selling transactions. In Chapter 8, a corporation's structural autonomy is the profit margin the firm is expected to have given its freedom from market constraint and its ability to circumvent constraint through directorate ties. In Eqs. (9.4) and (9.14), a director's structural autonomy is the maximum profit margin expected in a firm for which he is an outside director given the extent to which he is primarily responsible for establishments free from market constraint and is integral to their ability to circumvent market constraint through directorate ties.

Also as in Chapter 8, the relative effects of specific processes by which director success results from structural autonomy are apparent when $\mathbf{a}_k$ in Eq. (9.14) is replaced with its definition in Eq. (9.4):

$$Y_k = \Gamma[\beta + \beta_1\alpha_{k1} + \beta_2\alpha_{k2} + \beta_3\alpha_{k3}] + B_yX_k + E_y. \qquad (9.15)$$

In other words, the effects determining a director's structural autonomy are effects determining the maximum profit margin expected in a firm for which he is an outside director. The increased profit margin he can expect from being increasingly responsible for establishments free from market constraint is given by β_1. The increased profit margin he can expect from being increasingly integral to interlock ties to suppliers and consumers for these establishments is given by β_2. The increase he can expect from being increasingly integral to interlock ties with their competitors is given by β_3. These three effects multipled by γ_2 in Eq. (9.11) give the increased size of the largest firm for which he is an outside director that he could expect from the three processes ($\gamma_2\beta_1$, $\gamma_2\beta_2$, and $\gamma_2\beta_3$, respectively). When the three effects are multiplied by γ_3 in Eq. (9.12) or γ_4 in Eq. (9.13) they give the increased average profit margin or total size of the firms

---

[25]Specifically, Eqs. (8.11) and (8.12) correspond to Eqs. (9.10)–(9.13). Computational details are given in footnotes 14 and 15 to Chapter 6 for the model diagrammed in Figure 6.1.

for which director k is an outside director. The key parameters to assessing the consequences of participation in successful cooptation, in short, are β_2 and β_3. To the extent that these two coefficients are significantly positive, director success is contingent, at least in part, on the extent to which directors provide interlock ties spanning market constraint. To the extent that this is true, directors would have an incentive to maintain a social market of directorate ties patterned by constraints on profits in the economic market of purchases and sales.

In summary, the network model of structural autonomy has the potential to guide empirical research on processes by which individual directors could have been responsible for the social market of directorate ties inferred from the analysis in Chapters 2–4. I began with a consideration of directors on the boards of the large manufacturing firms in the two-digit sample. This was sufficient to illustrate the need for a theoretical orientation more refined than the class perspective in which directors are understood to be differentiated in terms of their centrality within a corporate elite drawn from the most integrative market positions, the highest executive positions, and the most prominent social groups. The directors were elites in one sense or another; however, they were differentiated in ways more complex than anticipated by the center–periphery metaphor advanced in class theory. Building on the idea that directors are differentiated in part by their social and corporate prestige, I have used the network concept of structural autonomy to capture the extent to which a director could have exploited his position in the economy so as to pursue his interests without constraint—creating a social market of directorate ties as a byproduct. Equations (9.2) and (9.3) define indices of the extent to which a director is integral to the ability of establishments to circumvent market constraint through interlock ties. These are measures of the director's participation in the successful cooptation generating a social market of directorate ties. Figure 9.2 specifies processes by which this participation could arise, contribute to director structural autonomy, and eventually affect the director's success more generally. An individual's participation in successful cooptation is attributed to his personal prestige and the extent to which he is principally affiliated with a large, structurally autonomous firm controlled by diffuse interest groups. This participation, and the extent to which a director is primarily responsible for establishments free from market constraint, determines the director's structural autonomy as the maximum profit margin expected in firms for which he is an outside director [a_k in Eqs. (9.4) and (9.14)]. That defined ability to pursue interests without constraint in turn affects the director's success more generally in obtaining directorships in large, profitable firms.

APPENDIX

Data on Market Constraint and Directorate Ties

Selected data on two-digit and four-digit market constraints and directorate ties are listed here. Only aggregate market structure data are presented for four-digit industries. The data analyzed as z_{ji}, $\mathbf{a}_{ji}$, and w_{ji} in the text are presented for the two-digit industries. Fractions have been rounded to the third decimal place.

Table A.1 contains the aggregate input–output table, where z_{ij} is the total amount of sales (in millions of dollars) from establishments in sector i to those in sector j. Given with each row are the sequential sector number (1–51), the input–output categories aggregated to correspond to the two-digit SIC categories, and the two-digit SIC industry code. The market transaction data are aggregated from the data in Table 1 of U.S. Department of Commerce (1974). In the published aggregate input–output table, four-digit industries 2251, 2252, 2253, 2254, 2256, and 2259 are classified as apparel rather than textile sectors. I have therefore corrected the price–cost margins and concentration data to take the changes in these two industries into account. The sales from establishments in industries corresponding to multiple input–output categories (e.g., textiles, SIC category 22, corresponds to input–output sectors 16 and 17) are the sum of relevant sales by each component sector as published in the aggregate input–output table by the Commerce Department. Purchases by establishments in these industries have been aggregated similarly.

To the immediate right of each sector name in Table A.1 are the concentration data used in Chapter 2 to compute supplier–consumer constraint indices. These are the values of Y (e.g., Table 2.4) computed as weighted averages of four-digit data:

$$y_j = \sum_k (VS_k C14_k)/VS_j, \tag{A.1}$$

where y_j is the concentration in two-digit industry j, VS_j is the value of shipments for the industry, VS_k is the value of shipments for a four-digit industry k contained within industry j (i.e., $VS_j = \Sigma_k VS_k$), and $C14_k$ is the four-firm concentration ratio, or an approximation to it, for four-digit industry k. Values of Y based on market share approximations rather than the concentration ratios reported in the 1967 *Census of Manufactures* (U.S. Department of Commerce, 1971) are reported in parentheses. Approximations were used to compute Y for the "ordnance" industry (SIC category 19) and all nonmanufacturing sectors.

Table A.2 contains market constraint data for the 327 disaggregate manufacturing sectors in the 1967 input–output study corresponding to unique four-digit SIC categories. These were the industries on which concentration data were reported in the 1967 *Census of Manufactures* and constitute the units of analysis in the text. Industries are listed by SIC code. The manufacturing sectors not corresponding to unique four-digit SIC categories are not listed. Concentration data were needed on these sectors in order to compute constraint indices even though the sectors were not units of analysis in the text. Approximate concentration in these sectors has been computed as a weighted average. The aggregate, or typical, concentration in sector j, y_j, is the weighted mean concentration in each four-digit SIC category k it contains as defined in Eq. (A.1). For nine manufacturing sectors (primary lead, safes & vaults, 7 ordnance) and all nonmanufacturing sectors, concentration data were not available and so have been approximated with eight-firm ratios or number and size data on firms. This underestimates concentration since all firms within a single size category are assumed to be equal in size, but these seem to be the best approximations available. The concentration data used to compute market indices are listed in Table 79 of my unpublished doctoral dissertation in sociology, University of Chicago, 1977. Also given there are the methods used to approximate each ratio based on published data in the *Census of Agriculture, Census of Mineral Industries, Census of Construction Industries, Census of Transportation, Census of Business,* and *Census of Manufactures.* In addition to these approximations from census data, two assumptions were made regarding sectors for which no data were available: (*a*) Retail and final consumption sectors were assumed to be perfectly competitive so that, to three digits, the four-firm concentration ratio in them was zero. (*b*) All government sectors were assumed to be perfectly monopolistic so that the concentration ratio for them was arbitrarily set at .999.

Given $C14$ and $C58$ for manufacturing industries corresponding to unique four-digit SIC categories and given Y for all supplier–consumer sectors in the input–output table, the market constraint indices analyzed in Chapter 2 can be computed. Presented in Table A.2 are the certainty measure of industry oligopoly [Y_1 in Eq. (2.2)], the aggregate measure of supplier–consumer constraint [Y_2 in Eq. (2.3)], the measure of consumer constraint retained in the final model (Y_3 in Table 2.4), and the measure of supplier constraint retained in the final model (Y_7 in Table 2.4). Also presented in Table A.2 are the profit margins computed as price–cost margins corrected for industry capital requirements (p in footnote 3 of Chapter 2) and structural autonomy as the profit margin predicted by market structure for the industry [a in Eqs. (2.5)]. Of the 495 sectors with which these 327 industries could have had market transactions in the disaggregate input–output table, two have been deleted prior to computing constraint indices. Inventory valuation adjustment is deleted because it represents interests neither opposed to nor supporting any industry's interests. Value added is deleted because there is no information readily available on imperfect competition in the labor sector for four-digit industries. Implicit in the constraint indices, therefore, is the assumption that each industry confronts an equally competitive labor force. Of the remaining 493 sectors, 10 are purely consumer sectors composed principally of government final demand. The dollar-flow coefficient z_{ij} from these consumer sectors i is zero for all industries j. In essence then, only 483 sectors could be consumer and/or supplier for any one of the 327 four-digit industries, so I have discussed the detailed input–output table in the text as containing 483 sectors.

The remaining tables present data on the two-digit industries. The market constraint data in Table A.2 for four-digit industries are given in Table A.3 for two-digit industries. Values of Y_1 have been computed as weighted averages of four-digit scores using Eq. (A.1). Table A.4 presents the specific sector to industry market constraint relations [a_{ji} in Eq. (2.6)], where coefficient a_{ji} appears in column j and row i. These coefficients have been multiplied by 1000 to eliminate decimals. Intraindustry coefficients and coefficients analyzed in Chapter 4 as severe market constraints are enclosed in parentheses. Finally, the directorate tie relations discussed in Chapter 3 are presented in the remaining tables. Ownership tie frequencies are given in Table A.5 [$w_{ji(o)}$ in Eq. (3.1)]. Direct interlock ties are reported in Table A.6 [$w_{ji(d)}$ in Eq. (3.3)]. Indirect interlock ties through financial institutions are given in Table A.7 [these are the $w_{ji(i)}$ in Eq. (3.6)].

TABLE A.1

Aggregated Input–Output Table

ID	Categories I–O	Categories SIC		z_{ji} in millions of dollars 1	2	3
1	1		livestock (.000)	5610	1448	96
2	2		other agriculture (.000)	8379	905	105
3	3		forestry and fishery (.000)	0	0	34
4	4		agribusiness services (.000)	603	1335	45
5	5		iron mining (.435)	0	0	0
6	6		nonferrous metal mining (.302)	0	0	0
7	7		coal mining (.025)	4	1	0
8	8		petroleum and gas (.028)	0	0	0
9	9		stone and clay mining (.116)	2	119	0
10	10		chemicals mining (.290)	0	12	0
11	11		new construction (.032)	0	0	0
12	12		maintenance and repair (.033)	233	370	0
13	13	19	ordnance (.083)	0	0	0
14	14	20	food .323	3694	0	24
15	15	21	tobacco .736	0	0	0
16	16-17	22	textiles .380	10	38	59
17	18-19	23	apparel .201	0	43	0
18	20-21	24	lumber .163	3	108	0
19	22-23	25	furniture .185	0	0	0
20	24-25	26	paper .311	17	4	0
21	26	27	printing .189	6	10	0
22	27-30	28	chemicals .417	129	2297	6
23	31	29	petroleum .329	167	905	36
24	32	30	rubber .313	37	165	5
25	33-34	31	leather .251	9	0	0
26	35-36	32	stone, clay & glass .373	8	25	0
27	37-38	33	primary metals .451	1	1	0
28	39-42	34	fabricated metals .283	73	54	48
29	43-52	35	mechanical machines .365	13	13	2
30	53-58	36	electrical machines .462	14	40	2
31	59-61	37	transportation equipment .669	7	14	16
32	62-63	38	instruments .494	0	0	0
33	64	39	miscellaneous .276	2	2	4
34	65		transportation & warehousing (.254)	690	452	40
35	66		communications other than #67 (.060)	75	71	0
36	67		radio and television (.060)	0	0	0
37	68		utilities (.999)	97	205	1
38	69		wholesale and retail (.001)	1333	1527	48
39	70		finance and insurance (.014)	257	314	16
40	71		real estate (.000)	475	2062	13
41	72		personal services (.002)	7	0	0
42	73		business services (.002)	76	1231	0
43	75		automobile services (.001)	124	132	5
44	76		amusements (.004)	0	0	0
45	77		medical & educational services (.000)	183	17	0
46	78		federal government (.999)	3	4	0
47	79		state and local government (.999)	2	0	0
48	80		gross imports (.000)	182	333	505
49	81		expense accounts (.000)	28	40	15
50	82		office supplies (.000)	1	1	1
51	83		scrap (.000)	0	0	0

(continued)

TABLE A.1 *Continued*

ID	z_{ji} in millions of dollars									
	4	5	6	7	8	9	10	11	12	13
1	169	0	0	0	0	0	0	0	0	0
2	507	0	0	0	0	0	0	80	3	0
3	0	0	0	0	0	0	0	0	0	0
4	0	0	0	0	0	0	0	161	19	0
5	0	92	4	0	0	0	1	0	0	0
6	0	33	213	0	0	5	3	0	0	0
7	0	0	1	400	0	6	0	0	0	3
8	0	0	0	1	374	0	0	0	0	0
9	0	4	5	3	0	63	7	670	261	0
10	0	5	3	0	0	2	61	0	0	0
11	0	0	0	0	0	0	0	0	0	0
12	0	30	16	23	476	18	8	26	4	24
13	0	0	0	0	0	0	0	0	0	786
14	44	0	0	0	0	0	0	0	0	0
15	0	0	0	0	0	0	0	0	0	0
16	46	2	0	15	5	2	0	222	3	13
17	5	0	0	3	0	11	0	50	4	13
18	13	4	11	22	0	0	1	4550	396	78
19	0	0	0	0	0	0	0	565	17	0
20	123	0	0	0	0	21	5	247	45	75
21	0	0	0	0	1	0	0	3	0	2
22	21	28	50	50	173	48	27	592	886	252
23	5	4	5	35	33	74	3	1400	624	26
24	0	15	9	27	34	29	9	641	108	88
25	1	0	0	0	0	0	0	0	0	1
26	0	1	3	11	83	119	0	6340	789	17
27	0	46	42	50	120	55	20	3611	325	821
28	14	4	10	56	111	15	3	9378	1797	272
29	3	32	85	129	277	75	19	1456	385	272
30	0	2	1	9	172	6	2	1936	571	507
31	1	6	2	0	0	0	0	4	1	314
32	0	0	0	0	9	0	0	279	24	177
33	0	0	1	0	0	0	0	111	91	5
34	27	103	65	28	146	26	15	2135	478	89
35	0	2	3	5	12	1	4	294	45	103
36	0	0	0	0	0	0	0	0	0	0
37	2	49	41	69	172	74	44	64	9	53
38	28	18	28	68	175	51	15	6503	1723	267
39	2	9	31	32	93	25	9	572	85	29
40	79	133	43	160	2429	89	40	599	101	46
41	0	0	0	0	0	0	0	0	0	15
42	0	62	22	81	242	75	31	4382	529	263
43	1	1	2	6	17	17	1	365	60	16
44	0	0	0	0	0	0	0	0	0	0
45	0	1	1	2	6	0	2	84	13	16
46	0	1	1	2	6	1	2	28	4	13
47	0	0	0	0	0	0	0	29	5	1
48	41	540	318	2	1076	111	90	88	13	60
49	13	3	6	8	37	10	6	532	163	147
50	1	0	1	1	6	1	0	26	4	13
51	0	7	7	18	86	2	0	9	6	0

(*continued*)

TABLE A.1 *Continued*

ID	14	15	16	17	18	19	20	21	22	23	24
					z_{ji} in millions of dollars						
1	19777	0	260	0	0	0	0	0	12	0	0
2	6882	1423	1178	0	123	0	0	0	94	0	0
3	423	0	0	165	1002	0	0	0	16	0	0
4	0	0	0	0	0	0	0	0	0	0	0
5	0	0	0	0	0	0	0	0	47	0	0
6	0	0	0	0	0	0	0	0	71	0	0
7	39	2	16	4	3	3	71	1	105	10	10
8	0	0	0	0	0	0	0	0	49	11556	0
9	8	0	0	0	2	0	57	0	82	63	7
10	4	0	1	0	0	0	26	0	620	0	11
11	0	0	0	0	0	0	0	0	0	0	0
12	257	7	62	29	65	29	146	79	275	363	50
13	0	0	0	0	1	16	0	4	11	0	2
14	14828	1	46	0	0	6	135	0	627	31	6
15	0	1664	0	0	0	0	0	0	0	0	0
16	20	0	6742	7924	18	416	209	87	60	0	780
17	123	2	206	5199	24	57	34	23	36	3	39
18	117	7	5	3	3740	875	1200	6	65	2	42
19	0	0	6	8	41	219	3	4	0	0	10
20	2577	110	130	252	96	114	5574	3386	1143	160	307
21	504	34	11	10	3	3	173	2434	36	3	8
22	758	115	2764	536	239	163	1014	465	11815	725	2832
23	219	2	27	23	107	11	132	40	2019	1831	21
24	638	49	119	111	61	337	333	98	691	58	562
25	1	0	2	93	2	5	3	1	1	1	29
26	1002	0	98	2	105	95	35	0	293	58	103
27	18	0	2	0	48	409	59	50	583	49	60
28	2402	17	9	70	250	497	274	232	917	106	287
29	843	7	139	30	74	62	167	35	438	88	129
30	7	0	13	6	13	23	15	12	35	12	22
31	4	0	2	3	12	17	0	1	22	3	67
32	13	1	7	36	6	35	35	185	70	18	18
33	9	0	19	346	6	25	16	36	37	1	92
34	2592	35	359	178	449	151	802	255	1031	1389	238
35	297	5	41	105	34	39	76	250	176	25	62
36	0	0	0	0	0	0	0	0	0	0	0
37	633	12	211	120	129	51	394	121	886	462	152
38	3286	57	492	776	465	312	686	550	1273	303	440
39	335	16	63	125	82	53	92	134	208	250	56
40	744	50	226	352	114	105	315	965	1163	630	170
41	162	18	9	12	0	5	43	36	96	15	18
42	3100	360	250	416	205	189	492	921	3090	770	436
43	193	1	10	24	58	11	20	55	44	11	13
44	0	0	0	0	0	0	0	0	0	0	0
45	45	1	7	16	5	6	12	44	70	7	9
46	62	13	17	57	7	10	17	278	103	16	12
47	18	0	0	1	2	0	4	2	10	1	1
48	2648	26	467	60	760	33	1369	3	964	1020	388
49	362	41	60	129	38	50	79	280	414	27	120
50	60	2	13	25	7	8	16	55	34	11	11
51	0	1	39	0	0	0	239	0	69	11	16

(*continued*)

TABLE A.1 *Continued*

ID	25	26	27	28	29	30	31	32	33	34
				z_{ji} in millions of dollars						
1	15	0	0	0	0	0	0	0	0	0
2	0	0	0	0	0	0	0	9	10	41
3	0	0	0	0	0	0	0	0	2	3
4	0	0	0	0	0	0	0	0	0	0
5	0	10	1502	1	0	1	0	0	0	0
6	0	12	1109	0	0	7	0	3	0	0
7	2	58	656	7	15	10	20	0	2	7
8	0	0	0	0	0	0	0	0	0	26
9	0	839	70	3	0	0	0	3	4	0
10	0	46	29	7	0	0	0	0	0	1
11	0	0	0	0	0	0	0	0	0	0
12	8	131	361	116	173	142	192	38	23	1307
13	0	0	2	31	59	188	454	22	5	0
14	262	6	9	2	7	0	0	13	17	166
15	0	0	0	0	0	0	0	0	2	0
16	248	70	11	24	19	30	215	95	212	35
17	92	15	33	41	42	35	638	17	36	111
18	47	70	165	138	106	85	364	11	151	2
19	1	17	2	68	29	285	132	18	19	0
20	97	489	60	409	160	497	145	223	419	97
21	3	4	17	153	107	43	8	5	35	50
22	111	398	753	511	155	665	340	347	330	115
23	7	111	164	98	211	99	176	15	28	1999
24	371	214	92	300	559	752	1123	182	363	287
25	1007	3	9	7	9	7	2	5	55	0
26	2	1540	156	206	386	696	550	77	58	52
27	1	179	13939	11070	6266	3482	6141	585	863	327
28	86	142	989	2090	2424	1743	5013	395	275	235
29	23	241	1369	1487	12380	1271	3975	191	59	226
30	4	47	589	296	3472	8942	2183	675	135	130
31	1	15	181	485	928	565	17523	105	47	787
32	14	14	59	130	222	397	535	851	15	50
33	42	48	28	50	51	82	48	42	589	16
34	66	758	1959	559	456	368	935	72	135	5228
35	21	70	139	174	299	508	292	77	46	505
36	0	0	0	0	0	0	0	0	0	0
37	30	494	1249	323	265	311	349	53	49	342
38	233	408	1680	921	1862	1475	1677	370	421	1627
39	34	110	298	205	267	185	210	48	58	781
40	74	280	233	449	1033	768	618	178	151	1369
41	3	11	17	62	40	42	94	13	9	60
42	129	394	1220	750	1166	1385	1289	408	343	862
43	5	37	38	37	61	66	704	12	9	795
44	0	0	0	0	0	0	2	0	0	19
45	6	13	26	26	43	43	44	13	10	46
46	14	14	28	29	54	57	73	15	20	105
47	1	8	9	2	1	5	7	0	0	1446
48	91	272	3467	467	1294	1210	1005	326	627	2259
49	25	93	137	336	604	533	447	141	85	248
50	8	14	27	26	48	46	45	13	13	78
51	0	5	1712	48	60	2	213	0	0	6

(*continued*)

TABLE A.1 *Continued*

ID					z_{ji} in millions of dollars					
	35	36	37	38	39	40	41	42	43	44
1	0	0	0	0	0	1127	0	0	0	52
2	0	0	0	10	0	1200	7	0	0	203
3	0	0	0	0	0	2	0	0	0	0
4	0	0	0	139	0	159	0	0	0	25
5	0	0	0	0	0	4	0	0	0	0
6	0	0	1	1	0	10	0	0	0	0
7	0	0	895	3	1	37	6	1	0	0
8	0	0	2521	0	0	165	0	0	0	0
9	0	0	0	5	0	28	0	0	0	0
10	0	0	0	0	0	6	0	0	0	0
11	0	0	0	0	0	0	0	0	0	0
12	567	6	1137	526	135	7159	188	259	33	104
13	0	0	0	38	0	11	1	0	0	0
14	0	0	2	892	0	138	2	0	0	0
15	0	0	0	9	0	8	0	0	0	0
16	0	0	9	73	0	44	33	9	0	0
17	5	0	8	214	0	54	211	0	17	0
18	0	0	1	199	0	30	11	0	0	0
19	0	0	0	50	0	11	0	0	0	0
20	21	0	37	1577	251	44	142	102	5	9
21	41	1	7	379	445	126	13	9361	0	21
22	2	0	58	565	1	446	550	267	48	40
23	65	1	275	1375	92	720	232	131	178	18
24	24	1	23	714	14	134	197	405	238	3
25	0	0	0	41	0	7	201	14	0	6
26	0	0	1	288	0	55	70	103	203	3
27	10	0	52	77	0	99	10	7	0	0
28	1	0	27	593	0	88	219	596	1114	0
29	0	0	40	522	0	565	70	981	403	0
30	248	42	73	426	8	240	510	164	333	4
31	3	0	3	196	0	177	16	60	1259	1
32	0	3	0	230	2	62	181	291	5	83
33	4	0	0	246	2	35	364	524	4	34
34	41	2	563	1235	115	1096	144	331	113	78
35	143	129	100	1769	973	212	170	1279	89	67
36	0	87	0	0	0	18	0	3053	0	0
37	135	44	6888	2415	392	436	367	201	84	86
38	144	53	202	3382	598	1612	660	1090	1469	200
39	142	17	219	2474	8701	3574	398	365	203	108
40	323	146	155	8608	1961	3654	1441	2149	392	716
41	212	0	53	457	0	519	582	345	14	6
42	631	136	287	8466	3957	3109	604	2541	155	398
43	101	0	48	1764	144	169	337	505	26	31
44	0	812	0	184	3	209	2	173	0	1958
45	19	3	13	230	562	95	68	118	8	22
46	80	4	639	1791	851	411	55	594	7	41
47	6	2	4971	590	128	923	11	9	155	3
48	133	1	145	46	101	0	0	6	0	68
49	131	111	128	2045	807	105	299	1151	69	224
50	70	3	31	340	610	54	34	184	6	14
51	0	0	0	10	1	0	0	0	38	0

(continued)

TABLE A.1 *Continued*

ID	z_{ji} in millions of dollars						
	45	46	47	48	49	50	51
1	17	0	0	0	31	0	0
2	27	389	2	0	115	0	0
3	0	0	0	0	50	0	0
4	0	0	1	0	0	0	0
5	0	0	0	0	0	0	0
6	0	0	0	0	0	0	0
7	10	72	70	0	0	0	0
8	0	0	0	0	0	0	0
9	0	0	0	0	0	0	0
10	0	0	4	0	0	0	0
11	0	0	0	0	0	0	0
12	739	60	1711	0	0	0	0
13	0	0	0	0	16	0	28
14	502	121	0	0	2960	0	0
15	0	0	0	0	187	0	10
16	7	3	1	0	0	0	60
17	55	14	7	0	8	0	12
18	0	0	0	0	4	0	0
19	0	0	0	0	0	0	0
20	118	10	10	0	7	528	55
21	673	29	26	0	14	1485	74
22	1195	23	143	0	79	13	0
23	212	45	96	0	0	0	12
24	150	13	28	0	4	12	10
25	0	2	0	0	39	0	5
26	17	1	7	0	7	1	0
27	0	1	8	0	0	5	362
28	15	5	12	0	6	5	228
29	5	2	30	0	0	13	108
30	22	2	22	0	140	0	96
31	2	12	7	0	0	0	140
32	452	1	5	0	56	176	16
33	181	1	1	0	74	369	19
34	211	1137	115	0	4629	0	57
35	574	20	43	0	0	0	0
36	19	0	0	0	0	0	0
37	1498	132	1136	0	0	0	0
38	951	78	110	0	748	0	1
39	389	87	173	0	0	0	5
40	2704	186	161	0	0	0	0
41	237	3	5	0	1418	0	6
42	1262	199	346	0	0	0	0
43	327	43	30	0	0	0	0
44	31	6	0	0	187	0	0
45	665	1	13	0	71	0	0
46	333	2	13	0	0	0	0
47	50	2	6	0	0	0	0
48	2	342	0	0	356	0	690
49	780	28	48	0	0	0	0
50	160	6	15	0	0	0	0
51	1	0	0	0	0	0	0

Table A.2

Market Structure Indices for Four-Digit Industries (* Marks an Industry Deleted from the Positional Sample)

SIC code	Scores multiplied by 1,000					
	y_{j1}	y_{j2}	y_{j3}	y_{j7}	p_j	$\mathbf{a}_j$
THESE ARE THE FOOD INDUSTRIES (SIC CODE 20)						
2011	192	995	991	355	83	151
2013	130	914	1000	341	139	140
2015	138	1000	1000	432	111	161
2021	140	976	963	660	86	204
2022	328	998	997	877	92	289
2023	197	986	991	828	243	255
2024	239	982	1000	838	236	266
2026	192	999	999	607	179	208
2031	199	995	998	769	230	244
2032	444	986	999	929	334	320
2033	178	987	998	929	275	275
2034	167	995	995	920	262	271
2035	230	987	998	922	248	282
2036	198	998	999	665	173	221
2037	188	996	1000	952	233	282
2041	183	981	964	714	156	222
2042	187	992	1000	929	201	277
2043	819	992	996	907	482	376
2044	83	950	901	392	161	127
2045	428	967	994	822	336	292
2046	302	992	989	750	275	254
2051	198	987	1000	910	268	274
2052	365	989	1000	930	366	307
2071	203	972	1000	911	288	276
2072	614	952	920	890	279	307
2073	782	991	998	945	497	379
2082	142	965	1000	865	335	255
2083	105	863	727	460	135	116
2084	267	994	1000	924	367	289
2085	198	995	1000	930	445	279
2086	122	974	1000	907	327	261
2087	522	973	982	925	522	326
2091	153	974	952	740	91	221
2092	124	968	936	436	92	148
2093	111	972	947	847	146	237
2094	230	966	952	904	212	268
2095	172	997	999	604	306	204
2096	59	961	995	860	175	240
2097	248	979	1000	932	295	288
2098	176	969	998	792	293	245
2099	193	996	999	966	321	286
THESE ARE THE TOBACCO INDUSTRIES (SIC CODE 21)						
2111	619	893	1000	633	483	285
2121	99	896	1000	658	356	203
2131	0	868	998	658	379	186
*2141	154	906	811	482	66	139

(continued)

Table A.2 *Continued*

THESE ARE THE TEXTILES INDUSTRIES (SIC CODE 22)

2241	160	957	975	846	209	249
2251	147	979	999	923	224	269
2252	203	976	999	839	177	260
2253	140	898	871	741	211	205
2254	162	884	839	761	204	205
2259	198	908	874	771	263	218
2256	137	931	917	857	187	238
2284	239	944	966	729	218	234
2291	165	984	986	934	271	272
2292	145	933	891	888	222	241
2293	185	925	872	934	252	251
2294	206	961	927	879	160	253
2295	176	965	958	905	219	261
2296	708	603	526	534	99	89
2297	327	947	900	788	49	242
2298	165	984	988	895	243	264
2299	172	987	982	738	220	229

THESE ARE THE APPAREL INDUSTRIES (SIC CODE 23)

2391	202	935	1000	666	177	222
2392	188	901	999	502	182	184
2393	160	916	917	772	189	222
2394	172	932	938	805	233	235
2395	68	945	943	865	276	235
2396	447	774	621	782	213	161
*2397	121	931	911	842	283	232
2399	163	940	917	894	218	249

THESE ARE THE LUMBER INDUSTRIES (SIC CODE 24)

2411	131	985	971	702	237	213
2421	108	984	996	792	181	233
2426	143	981	990	766	158	232
2429	182	980	980	792	193	242
2431	88	983	996	861	190	245
2432	203	992	997	897	145	272
2433	179	982	977	892	192	263
2491	257	978	990	803	241	259
2499	143	995	998	936	217	271

THESE ARE THE FURNITURE INDUSTRIES (SIC CODE 25)

2511	114	992	995	933	245	265
2512	132	990	999	932	249	268
2514	127	987	999	930	238	267
2515	218	991	1000	917	233	280
2519	173	963	943	826	290	242
2521	162	990	989	952	277	276
2522	208	979	989	928	340	278
2531	179	938	683	966	249	260
2541	59	995	999	953	243	260
2542	201	978	999	908	300	275
2591	183	990	1000	943	255	279

(*continued*)

Table A.2 *Continued*

2599	158	995	1000	968	227	280

THESE ARE THE PAPER INDUSTRIES (SIC CODE 26)

2611	35	951	911	840	189	220
2621	171	983	984	902	187	265
2631	185	930	873	930	271	251
2641	245	984	995	897	294	278
2642	218	965	996	742	240	241
2643	172	977	997	833	207	253
2644	183	987	996	894	258	268
2645	254	970	986	826	229	262
2646	446	985	1000	914	305	317
2647	313	955	999	658	304	239
2649	229	985	999	893	275	276
2661	66	980	976	936	256	255

THESE ARE THE PRINTING INDUSTRIES (SIC CODE 27)

2711	145	975	998	793	336	240
2721	184	987	997	850	413	259
2731	166	957	939	854	516	245
2732	182	964	950	815	262	241
2741	175	990	999	856	379	259
2753	188	960	938	912	290	260
2761	294	957	1000	662	332	237
2771	449	996	999	941	436	323
2782	247	991	998	936	310	288
2789	105	967	944	950	282	258
2791	69	955	971	898	269	246
2793	96	970	977	911	468	254
2794	233	978	968	935	266	279

THESE ARE THE CHEMICALS INDUSTRIES (SIC CODE 28)

2821	190	928	985	690	273	222
2822	185	876	870	718	294	204
2823	759	931	934	842	296	322
2824	752	941	949	843	345	328
2841	564	983	997	897	456	332
2842	236	986	995	938	499	286
2843	214	946	945	868	269	256
2844	208	995	1000	883	601	270
2851	175	976	996	888	292	265
2861	547	984	978	948	293	333
2871	143	968	994	788	224	238
2872	179	806	702	776	171	182
2879	105	940	989	734	355	219
2891	185	979	991	905	289	269
2892	227	724	554	741	227	142
2893	212	952	976	818	251	252
2895	289	896	821	869	408	235
2899	168	969	984	882	360	260

THESE ARE THE PETROLEUM INDUSTRIES (SIC CODE 29)

2951	130	976	993	845	241	248

(*continued*)

Table A.2 *Continued*

2952	48	975	995	365	213	239

THESE ARE THE RUBBER INDUSTRIES (SIC CODE 30)

3011	393	966	989	904	266	303
3021	263	989	999	929	250	289
3031	805	845	733	900	236	236
3069	172	986	992	957	255	279
3079	78	974	998	834	274	238

THESE ARE THE LEATHER INDUSTRIES (SIC CODE 31)

3111	169	944	919	858	165	242
3121	379	986	990	912	298	303
3131	168	982	993	855	205	256
3141	230	984	1000	832	269	263
3142	168	989	999	926	246	273
*3151	205	962	999	627	183	214
3161	233	987	999	924	282	283
3171	95	990	1000	900	231	255
3172	230	991	999	914	271	281
3199	168	989	994	898	215	266

THESE ARE THE STONE, CLAY AND GLASS INDUSTRIES (SIC CODE 32)

3221	294	970	975	893	294	281
3241	155	979	985	929	326	269
3251	130	977	997	936	249	268
3253	49	993	996	908	254	249
3255	119	982	985	930	242	263
3259	152	982	995	939	282	272
3261	179	988	996	943	309	278
3262	393	974	989	914	289	305
3263	84	984	993	937	147	260
3264	64	982	972	910	262	248
3269	224	989	995	951	273	287
3271	40	990	997	907	246	247
3272	105	991	997	934	301	264
3273	59	978	998	829	228	233
3274	140	960	946	934	247	260
3275	655	986	996	900	333	347
3281	160	994	999	897	234	265
3291	317	995	997	961	300	305
3292	144	990	994	944	267	272
3293	227	989	995	942	251	285
3295	208	981	987	856	281	262
3296	495	989	993	942	286	329
3297	134	987	993	948	252	271
3299	230	989	987	947	249	285

THESE ARE THE PRIMARY METALS INDUSTRIES (SIC CODE 33)

3312	162	992	993	967	169	280
3313	503	865	771	902	190	241
3315	197	893	937	695	219	215
3316	175	681	559	609	92	117
3317	210	709	601	635	174	130

(*continued*)

Table A.2 *Continued*

3331	314	963	941	**886**	168	273
3333	0	961	961	873	168	229
3339	193	973	957	648	280	208
3341	177	936	876	775	110	217
3351	69	917	976	774	176	220
3352	381	905	990	614	131	238
3356	156	944	990	826	182	247
3357	183	975	996	910	235	271
3361	210	959	976	864	217	261
3362	158	966	991	892	240	262
3369	223	973	987	894	265	272
3391	227	888	946	664	205	214
3392	666	958	968	897	186	336
3399	129	978	986	931	302	265

THESE ARE THE FABRICATED METALS INDUSTRIES (SIC CODE 34)

3411	561	901	975	652	230	270
3421	550	992	989	902	518	328
3423	178	991	996	955	345	280
3425	124	972	995	880	348	255
3429	183	958	937	951	313	268
3431	162	989	995	945	272	275
3432	187	988	997	939	233	278
3433	182	989	996	951	274	280
3441	125	935	996	747	192	226
3442	96	974	998	913	203	258
3443	256	965	997	862	264	273
3444	96	965	998	862	231	247
3446	230	974	998	884	236	274
3449	179	930	998	720	222	230
3461	325	894	898	784	217	241
3471	49	974	982	908	314	247
3479	162	973	973	898	278	261
3481	105	951	993	788	253	231
3491	162	931	979	760	178	232
3493	156	927	921	852	203	240
3496	0	917	887	871	218	220
3497	90	941	983	818	213	234
3499	131	971	992	895	269	259

THESE ARE THE MECHANICAL MACHINES INDUSTRIES (SIC CODE 35)

3511	813	984	988	956	250	381
3519	170	980	970	968	246	277
3522	248	991	997	954	261	292
3531	239	983	980	961	261	289
3532	195	988	990	957	249	282
3533	163	980	981	946	328	273
3534	307	992	997	958	288	302
3535	223	991	999	953	278	288
3536	167	991	996	962	250	280
3537	226	990	991	965	273	289
3541	172	994	997	947	289	278
3542	172	992	995	962	258	280
3548	182	994	996	969	306	284
3551	178	994	995	964	312	282

(continued)

Table A.2 *Continued*

3552	176	992	990	957	209	279
3553	207	990	995	946	355	283
3554	260	993	996	959	201	295
3555	317	995	995	974	293	307
3559	121	990	988	975	258	274
3561	203	992	991	975	286	287
3562	158	973	986	907	260	264
3564	176	983	987	967	299	281
3565	87	947	922	877	299	237
3566	184	984	982	964	305	280
3567	206	991	998	958	277	286
3569	94	994	994	965	270	268
3572	619	991	987	952	479	349
*3573	479	990	993	952	305	328
*3574	764	983	986	886	317	358
3576	152	991	996	951	328	275
3579	412	985	984	964	383	317
3581	315	992	999	955	337	304
3582	278	977	993	938	254	292
3585	196	979	987	948	281	280
3586	9	990	995	933	289	247
3589	127	991	991	966	287	273
3599	70	988	987	966	292	263

THESE ARE THE ELECTRICAL MACHINES INDUSTRIES (SIC CODE 36)

3611	247	981	974	957	324	287
3512	400	984	997	927	306	311
3613	240	985	995	935	332	286
3621	263	985	984	969	277	294
3622	230	983	979	962	340	287
3523	196	980	993	926	302	276
3524	806	977	968	941	314	367
3629	212	988	995	950	362	285
3631	233	987	999	953	238	290
3632	422	981	977	951	244	314
3633	569	986	999	939	268	343
3634	304	996	999	961	326	303
3635	515	991	997	955	425	337
3636	694	991	988	933	349	357
3639	103	986	997	949	274	267
3641	889	972	990	881	460	379
3642	165	988	986	964	286	278
3651	119	972	999	888	215	256
3652	396	994	998	871	388	299
3661	916	995	994	982	277	408
3652	168	860	746	918	231	221
3674	152	973	965	932	227	265
3679	269	983	970	986	240	296
3691	165	935	986	862	223	256
3692	767	975	973	928	424	361
3693	319	987	991	945	324	300
3694	453	967	955	953	284	312
3699	187	959	937	936	258	266

THESE ARE THE TRANSPORTATION EQUIPMENT INDUSTRIES (SIC CODE 37)

(continued)

Table A.2 *Continued*

3711	890	942	998	804	187	367
3713	182	948	918	941	212	262
3714	437	796	612	953	233	195
3715	190	978	986	937	181	276
3721	339	907	859	822	182	239
3722	308	908	819	984	218	261
3731	168	858	736	954	143	227
3732	170	986	991	950	202	277
3741	964	979	974	962	317	399
3742	212	981	1000	914	113	278
3751	181	997	999	841	233	257
3791	160	993	1000	954	167	278
3799	137	990	999	945	214	272

THESE ARE THE INSTRUMENTS INDUSTRIES (SIC CODE 38)

3811	218	944	897	959	300	266
3821	161	989	984	979	316	280
3822	172	993	993	969	344	282
3831	304	986	986	935	301	294
3841	183	989	995	953	334	281
3842	296	990	987	962	377	299
3843	239	978	996	898	344	278
3851	375	992	997	946	340	311
3861	480	991	991	967	452	331
3871	188	990	988	965	248	282
3872	446	872	775	901	201	239

THESE ARE THE MISCELLANEOUS INDUSTRIES (SIC CODE 39)

3911	211	970	999	838	249	261
3912	208	938	982	810	232	251
3913	176	991	983	667	249	215
3914	336	986	999	926	307	301
3931	112	995	997	944	228	267
3941	198	995	999	933	325	279
3942	160	988	1000	868	239	259
3943	140	981	999	913	252	265
3949	237	996	998	973	292	294
3951	220	994	997	946	367	285
3952	138	985	979	947	240	269
3953	205	991	1000	934	315	281
3955	172	988	994	931	264	274
3961	189	990	1000	939	318	279
3962	168	991	992	805	288	245
3963	192	955	925	938	286	264
3964	276	964	949	924	304	278
3991	230	991	996	937	239	285
3993	59	993	999	957	285	261
3994	199	993	998	957	237	285
3996	827	989	997	921	386	381

TABLE A.3

Market Structure Indices for Two-Digit Industries

ID	SIC code	Industry	y_{j1}	y_{j2}	y_{j3}	y_{j7}	p_j	a_j
					Scores multiplied by 1,000			
14	20	food	202	998	998	813	208	273
15	21	tobacco	434	999	1000	624	353	321
16	22	textiles	226	918	896	817	188	168
17	23	apparel	165	889	944	557	169	191
18	24	lumber	140	988	982	895	193	265
19	25	furniture	146	970	963	904	257	262
20	26	paper	190	980	974	917	230	271
21	27	printing	153	974	999	812	334	257
22	28	chemicals	249	987	984	927	387	290
23	29	petroleum	109	983	980	584	177	204
24	30	rubber	202	954	982	809	269	258
25	31	leather	206	984	990	915	243	286
26	32	stone, clay, & glass	230	984	985	931	289	288
27	33	primary metals	202	962	937	923	193	241
28	34	fabricated metals	220	916	973	681	254	229
29	35	mechanical machines	238	950	950	872	285	236
30	36	electrical machines	313	965	954	920	272	237
31	37	transportation equipment	524	970	976	897	199	293
32	38	instruments	318	979	980	927	368	293
33	39	miscellaneous	197	988	996	921	288	289

TABLE A.4
Market Constraints on Column Industries from Row Sectors

a_{ji} multiplied by 1,000

ID	14	15	16	17	18	19	20	21	22	23
1	(-196)	0	-3	0	0	0	0	0	0	0
2	(-24)	(-387)	(-54)	0	-1	0	0	0	0	0
3	0	0	0	0	(-63)	0	0	0	0	0
4	0	0	0	0	0	0	0	0	0	0
5	0	0	0	0	0	0	0	0	0	0
6	0	0	0	0	0	0	0	0	0	0
7	0	0	0	0	0	0	0	0	0	0
8	0	0	0	0	0	0	0	0	0	(-702)
9	0	0	0	0	0	0	0	0	0	0
10	0	0	0	0	0	0	0	0	-2	0
11	0	0	0	0	(-12)	(-12)	0	0	0	1
12	0	0	0	0	0	0	0	0	-1	-1
13	0	0	0	0	0	0	0	0	0	0
14	(257)	0	0	-4	0	0	(-57)	-1	-5	0
15	0	(469)	0	0	0	0	0	0	0	0
16	0	0	(468)	(-827)	0	(-13)	-1	0	(-60)	0
17	0	0	(-1353)	(301)	0	0	0	0	-1	0
18	0	0	0	0	(184)	(-59)	(-25)	0	0	0
19	0	0	-3	-1	-3	(194)	0	0	0	0
20	-4	-2	-2	-1	(-9)	-1	(244)	(-212)	(-12)	0
21	0	0	0	0	0	0	(-57)	(207)	-1	0
22	(-12)	-3	(-300)	-4	-4	-2	(-32)	-4	(298)	13
23	0	0	0	0	-1	0	-1	0	(-19)	(186)
24	0	-1	(-21)	-1	0	(-9)	-3	0	(-54)	0
25	-1	0	-2	-2	0	0	0	0	0	0
26	-1	0	-1	0	-1	-1	-2	0	-2	0
27	0	0	0	0	0	(-13)	0	0	-7	0
28	-3	0	0	-1	-4	(-21)	-3	-1	-5	0
29	0	0	-1	-1	0	-1	-1	0	-1	0
30	0	0	0	-1	0	(-44)	-3	0	-4	0
31	0	0	-3	(-239)	-2	(-14)	0	0	-2	0
32	0	0	-1	0	0	0	-1	-1	-1	0
33	0	-1	-1	-2	0	0	-1	0	-1	0
34	-4	0	-5	-3	(-13)	-2	(-11)	-1	-4	-1
35	0	0	0	0	0	0	0	-1	0	0
36	0	0	0	0	0	0	0	0	0	0
37	0	0	-2	0	-1	0	-3	0	-3	0
38	-6	-1	-10	-8	(-14)	-8	-8	-6	-6	-1
39	0	0	0	0	0	0	0	0	0	0
40	0	-1	-2	-2	-1	-1	-2	(-17)	-5	-2
41	0	0	0	0	0	0	0	0	0	0
42	-5	(-25)	-2	-2	-3	-3	-4	(-18)	(-36)	-3
43	0	0	0	0	0	0	0	0	0	0
44	0	0	0	0	0	0	0	0	0	0
45	0	0	0	0	0	0	0	0	0	0
46	-1	0	0	0	0	0	0	-1	0	0
47	0	0	0	0	0	0	0	0	0	0
48	-4	0	-9	0	(-36)	0	(-32)	0	-4	-6
49	0	0	0	0	0	0	0	-1	-1	0
50	0	0	0	0	0	0	0	0	0	0
51	0	0	0	0	0	0	-1	0	0	0

(continued)

TABLE A.4 *Continued*

a_{ji} multiplied by 1,000

ID	24	25	26	27	28	29	30	31	32	33
1	0	0	0	0	0	0	0	0	0	0
2	0	0	0	0	0	0	0	0	0	0
3	0	0	0	0	0	0	0	0	0	0
4	0	0	0	0	0	0	0	0	0	C
5	0	0	0	-8	0	0	0	0	0	0
6	0	0	0	-4	0	0	0	0	0	0
7	0	0	0	-2	0	0	0	0	0	0
8	0	0	0	0	0	0	0	0	0	0
9	0	0	(-23)	0	0	0	0	0	0	0
10	0	0	0	0	0	0	0	0	0	0
11	-1	0	(-70)	-2	(-27)	-3	-12	0	-2	0
12	0	0	-2	-1	-1	0	-1	0	0	0
13	0	0	0	0	0	0	-2	-8	-3	0
14	-9	(-18)	(-18)	0	(-18)	-9	0	0	0	0
15	0	0	0	0	0	0	0	0	0	0
16	(-17)	(-16)	0	0	0	0	0	0	-1	-2
17	0	(-37)	0	0	0	0	0	-1	0	(-14)
18	0	-1	0	0	0	0	0	0	0	-1
19	-1	0	0	0	-1	C	0	0	0	0
20	-5	-3	-3	0	-1	0	-1	0	-3	(-8)
21	0	0	0	0	0	0	0	0	-6	0
22	(-237)	-3	-7	-3	-4	-3	-2	0	-8	-5
23	0	0	-1	0	0	0	0	0	0	0
24	(272)	(-42)	-2	0	-1	-1	-3	-3	-2	(-8)
25	-2	(251)	0	0	0	0	C	0	0	0
26	-2	0	(277)	0	0	-1	-2	-1	0	-1
27	0	-1	-2	(292)	(-481)	(-148)	(-71)	(-64)	(-20)	(-35)
28	-4	-2	-1	(-195)	(335)	(-42)	(-17)	(-97)	(-13)	-4
29	-8	-1	-5	(-86)	(-29)	(352)	(-440)	(-326)	(-19)	-1
30	(-18)	-1	(-12)	(-32)	(-14)	(-65)	(459)	(-149)	(-93)	-3
31	(-58)	0	(-11)	(-139)	(-161)	(-422)	(-315)	(612)	(-181)	-1
32	-1	0	0	-1	-1	-1	(-23)	-6	(377)	-1
33	-3	(-17)	0	-1	0	0	-1	-1	0	(237)
34	-3	-1	(-19)	-14	-1	-1	-1	(-154)	-1	-1
35	0	0	0	0	0	0	-2	0	0	0
36	0	0	0	0	0	0	0	0	0	0
37	-1	0	-8	-6	0	0	-1	0	-1	0
38	-5	(-14)	-6	-10	-3	-10	-10	-4	-7	(-8)
39	0	0	0	0	0	0	0	0	0	0
40	-1	-1	-3	0	-1	-3	-3	-1	-2	-1
41	0	-2	0	0	0	0	0	0	0	0
42	-5	-4	-5	-5	-2	-4	-9	-2	-9	-6
43	0	0	0	0	0	0	0	-2	0	0
44	0	0	0	0	0	0	0	0	0	0
45	0	0	0	0	0	0	0	0	0	0
46	0	0	0	0	0	0	0	0	0	0
47	0	0	0	0	0	0	0	0	0	0
48	-4	-2	-2	(-42)	-1	-5	-7	-1	-6	(-18)
49	0	0	0	0	0	-1	-1	0	-1	0
50	0	0	0	0	C	0	0	0	0	0
51	0	0	0	-10	0	0	0	0	0	0

TABLE A.5
Ownership Tie Frequencies

					$w_{ji(o)}$					
ID	14	15	16	17	18	19	20	21	22	23
1	0	0	0	0	0	0	0	0	0	0
2	0	0	0	0	0	0	C	0	0	0
3	1	0	0	0	1	0	1	1	1	0
4	0	0	0	0	0	0	0	0	0	0
5	0	0	0	0	0	1	0	0	1	0
6	0	0	0	0	0	1	0	0	1	0
7	1	0	1	1	0	0	0	0	1	2
8	1	0	1	2	0	1	2	1	4	6
9	0	0	0	0	0	0	0	0	0	0
10	0	0	0	0	0	0	0	0	0	0
11	1	0	1	1	0	2	1	1	2	1
12	1	0	1	1	0	2	1	1	2	1
13	1	0	1	1	0	1	2	0	1	0
14	12	4	2	1	1	1	4	2	9	1
15	4	4	0	0	0	0	1	1	1	0
16	2	0	7	3	1	2	2	0	5	2
17	1	0	3	4	0	1	0	0	2	1
13	1	0	1	0	4	1	4	1	3	0
19	1	0	2	1	1	5	3	1	3	0
20	4	1	2	0	4	3	11	3	8	1
21	2	1	0	0	1	1	3	6	4	0
22	9	1	5	2	3	3	8	4	21	5
23	1	0	2	1	0	0	1	0	5	9
24	4	1	4	3	2	4	7	3	11	4
25	3	0	2	1	0	1	2	0	4	0
26	3	0	3	0	2	1	4	1	6	1
27	4	1	4	1	0	2	2	1	7	3
28	3	1	2	0	0	3	3	3	6	2
29	4	1	3	1	1	3	4	3	7	1
30	3	0	2	1	1	3	4	4	7	1
31	2	0	3	0	0	2	2	3	5	2
32	3	1	1	1	0	3	4	3	5	0
33	3	1	2	1	0	3	4	3	6	0
34	1	0	1	0	1	1	3	0	3	2
35	0	0	0	0	0	0	0	1	0	0
36	0	0	0	0	0	0	0	0	0	0
37	1	0	1	1	0	0	1	0	2	2
38	2	0	2	2	1	0	1	2	4	2
39	0	0	1	1	0	0	1	1	3	3
40	1	0	1	1	0	1	0	0	2	1
41	0	0	0	0	0	1	1	1	0	0
42	3	0	1	1	0	1	0	0	4	1
43	0	0	0	0	0	0	0	0	0	0
44	0	0	0	0	0	0	0	1	0	0
45	0	0	0	0	0	0	0	0	0	0

(*continued*)

TABLE A.5 *Continued*

ID	24	25	26	27	$w_{,i(o)}$ 28	29	30	31	32	33
1	0	0	0	0	0	0	0	0	0	0
2	0	0	0	0	0	0	0	0	0	0
3	0	0	0	0	0	0	0	0	0	0
4	0	0	0	0	0	0	0	0	0	0
5	1	0	0	1	1	1	1	0	1	1
6	1	0	0	1	1	1	1	0	1	1
7	1	0	0	1	0	0	0	0	0	0
8	4	0	1	3	3	4	2	1	2	1
9	0	0	0	0	0	0	0	0	0	0
10	0	0	0	0	0	0	0	0	0	0
11	3	0	0	2	2	2	2	1	2	2
12	3	0	0	2	2	2	2	1	2	2
13	2	1	1	2	2	4	3	2	2	2
14	4	3	3	4	3	4	3	2	3	3
15	1	0	0	1	1	1	0	0	1	1
16	4	2	3	4	2	3	2	3	1	2
17	3	1	0	1	0	1	1	0	1	1
18	2	0	2	0	0	1	1	0	0	0
19	4	1	1	2	3	3	3	2	3	3
20	7	2	4	2	3	4	4	2	4	4
21	3	0	1	1	3	3	4	3	3	3
22	11	4	6	7	6	7	7	5	5	6
23	4	0	1	3	2	1	1	2	0	0
24	17	3	5	6	6	5	7	5	7	6
25	3	4	2	1	1	1	1	1	2	2
26	5	2	9	5	5	5	4	4	3	2
27	6	1	5	13	9	8	6	7	3	4
28	6	1	5	9	13	10	8	8	5	6
29	5	1	5	8	10	17	12	9	6	5
30	7	1	4	6	8	12	16	8	7	6
31	5	1	4	7	8	9	8	11	4	4
32	7	2	3	3	5	6	7	4	9	4
33	6	2	2	4	6	6	6	4	4	8
34	3	1	1	2	1	2	0	1	1	0
35	1	0	1	1	1	1	3	1	2	0
36	0	0	0	0	0	0	0	0	0	0
37	2	0	1	3	1	1	0	0	0	0
38	4	1	3	4	3	3	3	2	2	2
39	4	1	1	2	3	4	5	4	3	1
40	2	0	0	2	1	1	1	0	1	1
41	1	0	0	0	1	1	1	1	1	1
42	2	0	1	3	2	2	2	1	1	2
43	0	0	1	1	1	1	1	1	1	0
44	0	0	0	0	0	0	1	0	0	0
45	0	0	0	0	0	0	0	0	0	0

TABLE A.6
Direct Interlock Tie Frequencies

					$w_{ji(d)}$					
ID	14	15	16	17	18	19	20	21	22	23
1	0	0	0	0	0	0	0	0	0	0
2	0	0	0	0	0	0	0	0	0	0
3	1	0	2	2	1	0	2	2	5	3
4	0	0	0	0	0	0	0	0	0	0
5	0	0	1	0	0	0	0	0	0	0
6	0	0	1	0	0	0	0	0	0	0
7	1	0	1	0	2	0	3	5	6	1
8	6	0	5	1	7	4	13	13	19	0
9	0	0	0	0	0	0	0	0	0	0
10	0	0	0	0	0	0	0	0	0	0
11	2	0	1	0	1	0	1	3	3	0
12	2	0	1	0	1	0	1	3	3	0
13	2	0	1	0	3	1	4	3	7	2
14	2	0	4	3	3	2	5	7	11	5
15	0	0	1	1	0	1	0	0	0	0
16	4	1	2	1	3	1	3	4	6	1
17	3	1	1	0	3	0	3	4	4	0
18	2	0	3	3	2	0	4	3	7	5
19	1	1	1	0	0	0	1	0	1	1
20	5	0	3	3	4	1	7	7	16	9
21	7	0	4	4	3	0	7	4	15	10
22	11	0	6	4	7	1	14	15	29	15
23	4	0	1	0	5	1	8	10	14	0
24	6	0	4	1	6	3	13	6	17	7
25	0	0	1	0	0	0	0	0	0	0
26	5	0	4	4	2	0	5	4	11	7
27	6	0	8	5	4	5	9	6	18	7
28	7	0	7	4	3	2	10	4	21	9
29	12	0	8	4	9	3	16	10	32	13
30	14	0	9	5	6	2	13	8	29	15
31	8	0	3	2	3	3	8	4	21	11
32	6	0	4	1	3	1	6	2	11	5
33	3	0	2	1	2	0	4	3	7	5
34	10	1	10	4	5	4	14	8	24	7
35	4	0	4	2	2	2	4	2	9	5
36	0	0	0	0	0	0	0	0	0	0
37	9	1	7	4	4	8	11	13	21	2
38	11	1	11	10	7	4	18	9	35	12
39	54	8	28	14	25	22	52	34	108	31
40	1	0	1	0	1	0	1	3	2	0
41	1	0	0	1	0	1	2	2	3	0
42	2	1	2	0	2	0	2	4	4	0
43	1	0	1	1	0	0	0	0	2	2
44	1	0	1	1	0	0	0	0	1	1
45	0	0	0	0	0	0	0	0	0	0

(*continued*)

TABLE A.6 *Continued*

ID	24	25	26	27	28	29	30	31	32	33
1	0	0	0	0	0	0	0	0	0	0
2	0	0	0	0	0	0	0	0	0	0
3	3	0	2	2	2	6	5	2	2	2
4	0	0	0	0	0	0	0	0	0	0
5	0	0	0	2	2	3	1	3	0	0
6	0	0	0	2	2	3	1	3	0	0
7	3	0	6	5	5	6	6	4	1	3
8	14	3	11	12	12	17	17	12	8	10
9	0	0	0	0	0	0	0	0	0	0
10	0	0	0	0	0	0	0	0	0	0
11	1	1	2	5	5	6	4	6	1	1
12	1	1	2	5	5	6	4	6	1	1
13	3	0	2	2	3	4	5	2	2	2
14	9	0	7	9	7	14	12	8	6	3
15	0	0	0	0	0	0	0	0	0	0
16	4	1	4	8	7	8	9	3	4	2
17	1	0	4	5	4	4	5	2	1	1
18	6	0	2	4	3	9	6	3	3	2
19	3	0	0	4	2	3	2	3	1	0
20	15	0	7	9	10	18	15	9	7	4
21	6	0	4	5	4	10	8	3	2	3
22	19	0	13	19	19	34	29	21	12	7
23	7	0	7	7	8	13	14	10	5	5
24	12	1	8	14	11	15	12	7	5	3
25	1	0	2	4	3	3	2	1	1	0
26	8	2	4	6	5	9	5	3	4	3
27	15	4	6	12	12	15	14	9	7	8
28	13	3	7	12	11	16	12	9	5	7
29	15	3	10	15	15	23	20	13	8	8
30	14	2	8	15	11	22	17	13	7	5
31	8	1	5	10	10	14	13	5	5	5
32	5	1	4	6	4	7	6	5	2	1
33	3	0	3	7	7	8	5	4	1	2
34	21	3	18	26	19	31	25	16	13	7
35	7	1	4	7	5	6	4	2	2	3
36	0	0	0	0	0	0	0	0	0	0
37	20	6	12	17	18	21	17	16	11	14
38	26	7	17	24	22	29	25	16	10	13
39	69	16	57	79	82	103	90	61	42	37
40	1	0	2	4	4	5	4	5	1	1
41	2	0	2	1	2	4	4	3	4	1
42	1	0	3	4	5	9	7	7	2	1
43	1	0	0	1	0	0	0	0	0	0
44	1	0	0	1	0	0	0	0	0	0
45	0	0	0	0	0	0	0	0	0	0

TABLE A.7
Indirect Financial Interlock Tie Frequencies

	$w_{ji(i)}$									
ID	14	15	16	17	18	19	20	21	22	23
1	0	0	0	0	0	0	0	0	0	0
2	0	0	0	0	0	0	0	0	0	0
3	7	2	5	4	2	2	6	3	12	5
4	0	0	0	0	0	0	0	0	0	0
5	4	1	3	1	1	0	3	3	7	3
6	4	1	3	1	1	0	3	3	7	3
7	8	1	6	5	4	6	12	9	24	7
8	32	4	19	11	20	16	44	28	80	26
9	0	0	0	0	0	0	0	0	0	0
10	0	0	0	0	0	0	0	0	0	0
11	7	1	4	1	3	1	8	8	17	6
12	7	1	4	1	3	1	8	8	17	6
13	15	2	8	4	6	4	13	11	32	11
14	23	3	17	11	15	10	31	22	60	22
15	3	0	4	2	4	2	5	3	9	4
16	17	4	6	4	7	4	14	10	29	11
17	11	2	4	0	6	2	12	8	23	8
18	14	4	7	6	4	4	12	7	22	9
19	8	2	4	2	4	0	7	6	14	8
20	37	6	17	14	13	9	33	25	72	27
21	21	3	10	8	7	6	20	10	41	15
22	63	10	32	25	23	16	63	46	130	46
23	20	4	11	8	9	8	22	15	41	8
24	40	5	20	10	18	9	37	24	79	26
25	8	1	3	2	5	1	9	6	17	6
26	28	6	18	15	14	11	34	22	64	27
27	39	8	29	17	19	17	43	25	83	36
28	53	11	36	24	21	19	52	33	108	45
29	64	10	40	28	27	20	62	40	130	53
30	67	12	37	23	21	20	55	39	123	46
31	39	5	26	19	18	15	39	23	78	33
32	25	2	15	9	10	6	25	18	55	22
33	21	3	9	5	8	4	19	13	42	15
34	58	6	41	24	30	26	66	43	136	52
35	24	5	14	9	6	8	20	13	43	15
36	0	0	0	0	0	0	0	0	0	0
37	34	6	23	16	16	16	42	30	88	28
38	77	13	46	29	33	26	72	45	151	60
39	155	26	95	59	70	55	152	96	300	100
40	6	1	4	1	2	1	7	6	14	5
41	12	0	5	3	4	3	11	10	26	10
42	14	2	10	6	7	3	21	17	39	12
43	4	1	5	3	2	3	6	4	11	6
44	2	1	0	0	0	1	1	1	3	0
45	0	0	0	0	0	0	0	0	0	0

(*continued*)

TABLE A.7 *Continued*

ID	24	25	26	27	28	29	30	31	32	33
					$w_{zi(i)}$					
1	0	0	0	0	C	0	0	0	0	0
2	0	0	0	0	0	0	0	0	0	0
3	10	3	7	8	8	14	11	8	5	4
4	0	0	0	0	0	0	0	0	0	0
5	4	1	5	7	7	8	7	5	2	3
6	4	1	5	7	7	8	7	5	2	3
7	18	5	17	22	27	33	26	20	14	12
8	51	8	44	53	62	88	71	51	36	26
9	0	0	0	0	0	0	0	0	0	0
10	0	0	0	0	0	0	0	0	0	0
11	8	2	11	15	17	21	16	14	7	7
12	8	2	11	15	17	21	16	14	7	7
13	15	4	17	18	22	30	27	15	11	10
14	44	8	30	45	51	70	63	39	26	24
15	5	1	6	8	10	10	11	4	2	3
16	20	3	18	29	33	40	34	23	15	9
17	10	2	15	17	22	28	21	16	9	5
18	18	5	14	19	20	27	20	15	10	8
19	9	1	11	16	17	20	18	12	6	4
20	47	12	39	51	57	76	63	42	31	25
21	24	6	22	24	28	40	34	19	18	13
22	89	20	69	91	104	144	122	77	61	48
23	26	6	27	35	40	53	41	29	22	15
24	40	13	45	51	60	84	67	41	29	22
25	13	0	9	13	15	21	20	12	8	4
26	45	9	30	42	47	67	56	35	29	24
27	52	13	43	61	64	90	76	50	33	29
28	70	18	52	71	70	105	94	59	42	39
29	84	21	67	88	91	126	108	72	51	42
30	77	23	61	83	91	122	103	71	52	44
31	50	14	42	55	59	83	72	45	34	25
32	29	8	29	31	36	51	46	28	18	19
33	22	4	24	28	33	42	38	21	19	12
34	94	23	67	105	109	146	115	92	56	43
35	27	10	19	27	29	38	33	23	17	18
36	0	0	0	0	0	0	0	0	0	0
37	61	13	48	71	78	98	82	59	39	34
38	101	26	80	118	126	169	129	100	60	51
39	200	56	157	228	243	314	262	186	119	104
40	7	2	9	12	13	17	13	10	6	6
41	14	5	13	17	21	25	21	19	11	8
42	22	6	22	29	36	47	38	25	17	18
43	7	2	4	8	8	11	9	7	4	5
44	2	0	1	3	4	2	2	1	2	2
45	0	0	0	0	0	0	0	0	0	0

References

Alba, R. (1982). Taking stock of network analysis: a decade's results. In S. B. Bacharach (ed.), *Research in the Sociology of Organizations*. Greenwich: JAI.

Aldrich, H. E. (1979). *Organizations and Environments*. Englewood Cliffs: Prentice-Hall.

Aldrich, H. E., and Herker, D. (1977). Boundary spanning roles and organizational structure. *Academy of Management Review 2*:217–230.

Aldrich, H. E., and Pfeffer, J. (1976). Environments of organizations. *Annual Review of Sociology 2*:79–105.

Aldrich, H. E., and Whetten, D. A. (1981). Organization-sets, action-sets, and networks: making the most of simplicity. In P. C. Nystrom and W. H. Starbuck (eds.), *Handbook of Organizational Design, 1: Adapting Organizations to Their Environments*. New York: Oxford University Press.

Allen, M. P. (1974). The structure of interorganizational elite cooptation: interlocking corporate directorates. *American Sociological Review 39*:393–406.

Allen, M. P. (1976). Management control in the large corporation: comment on Zeitlin. *American Journal of Sociology 81*:885–894.

Allen, M. P. (1978a). Continuity and change within the core corporate elite. *Sociological Quarterly 19*:510–521.

Allen, M. P. (1978b). Economic interest groups and the corporate elite. *Social Science Quarterly 58*:597–615.

Allison, P. D. (1977). Testing for interaction in multiple regression. *American Journal of Sociology 83*:144–153.

Armentano, D. T. (1982). *Antitrust and Monopoly: Anatomy of a Policy Failure*. New York: Wiley-Interscience.

Arrow, K. (1974). *The Limits of Organization*. New York: W. W. Norton.

Bacon, J. (1979). *Corporate Directorship Practices: The Audit Committee*, Report #766. New York: National Industrial Conference Board.

Bacon, J. (1980). *Corporate Directorship Practices: Compensation 1979*, Report #778. New York: National Industrial Conference Board.

Bacon, J., and Brown, J. K. (1975). *Corporate Directorship Practices: Role, Selection and Legal Status of the Board*, Report #646. New York: National Industrial Conference Board.

Bacon, J., and Brown, J. K. (1977). *The Board of Directors: Perspectives and Practices in Nine Countries*, Report #728. New York: National Industrial Conference Board.

Barnard, C. (1938). *The Functions of the Executive*. Cambridge: Harvard University Press.

Baty, G. B., Evan, W. M., and Rothermel, T. W. (1971). Personnel flows as interorganizational relations. *Administrative Science Quarterly 16:*430–443.

Bearden, J., Atwood, W., Freitag, P., Hendricks, C., Mintz, B., and Schwartz, M. (1975). The nature and extent of bank centrality in corporate networks. Paper presented at the annual meetings of the American Sociological Association.

Bennett, J. T., and Johnson, M. H. (1980). Corporate contributions: some additional considerations. *Public Choice 35:*137–143.

Beresford, D. R., Busch, R. W., and Neary, R. D. (1978). *SEC Form 10-K: A Guide to Financial Reporting*. New York: Mathew Bender.

Berkowitz, S. D., Carrington, P. J., Kotowitz, Y., and Waverman, L. (1979). The determination of enterprise groupings through combined ownership and directorate ties. *Social Networks 1:*391–413.

Berle, A. A., and Means, G. C. (1932). *The Modern Corporation and Private Property*, 1968 ed. New York: Harcourt Brace.

Bick, W., and Müller, P. J. (1978). Stable patterns within a network of urban bureaucracies: domains or positions? Paper presented at the annual meetings of the American Sociological Association.

Blau, P. M. (1955). *The Dynamics of Bureaucracy*. Chicago: University of Chicago Press.

Blin, J. M., and Cohen, C. (1977). Technological similarity and aggregation in input–output systems: a cluster-analytic approach. *Review of Economics and Statistics 59:*82–91.

Brittain, J. W., and Freeman, J. H. (1980). Organizational proliferation and density dependent selection. In J. R. Kimberly, R. H. Miles and Associates, *The Organizational Life Cycle*. San Francisco: Jossey-Bass.

Brooks, D. G. (1973). Buyer concentration: a forgotten element in market structure models. *Industrial Organization Review 1:*151–163.

Burch, P. H., Jr. (1972). *The Managerial Revolution Reassessed*. Lexington, MA: D. C. Heath.

Burt, R. S. (1977). Power in a social topology. *Social Science Research 6:*1–83.

Burt, R. S. (1979a). Disaggregating the effect on profits in manufacturing industries of having imperfectly competitive consumers and suppliers. *Social Science Research 8:*120–143.

Burt, R. S. (1979b). A structural theory of interlocking corporate directorates. *Social Networks 1:*415–435.

Burt, R. S. (1979c). Relational equilibrium in a social topology. *Journal of Mathematical Sociology 6:*211–252.

Burt, R. S. (1980a). Autonomy in a social topology. *American Journal of Sociology 85:*892–925.

Burt, R. S. (1980b). Models of network structure. *Annual Review of Sociology 6:*79–141.

Burt, R. S. (1980c). On the functional form of corporate cooptation: empirical findings linking the intensity of market constraint with the frequency of directorate ties. *Social Science Research 9:*146–177.

Burt, R. S. (1980d). Cooptive corporate actor networks: a reconsideration of interlocking directorates involving American manufacturing. *Administrative Science Quarterly 25:*557–582.

Burt, R. S. (1982a). *Toward a Structural Theory of Action: Network Models of Social Structure, Perception, and Action*. New York: Academic Press.

Burt, R. S. (1982b). A note on cooptation and definitions of constraint. In P. V. Marsden and N. Lin (eds.), *Social Structure and Network Analysis*. Beverly Hills: Sage Publications.

Burt, R. S. (1983a). Range. In R. S. Burt and M. J. Minor (eds.), *Applied Network Analysis*. Beverly Hills: Sage Publications.

Burt, R. S. (1983b). Corporate philanthropy as a cooptive relation. *Social Forces 61:* In Press.

Burt, R. S., Christman, K. P., and Kilburn, H. C. (1980). Testing a structural theory of corporate cooptation: interorganizational directorate ties as a strategy for avoiding market constraints on profits. *American Sociological Review 45:*821–841.

Burt, R. S., and Minor, M. J., eds. (1983). *Applied Network Analysis: A Methodological Introduction*. Beverly Hills: Sage Publications.

Carter, A. P. (1967). Changes in the structure of the American economy, 1947 to 1958 and 1962. *Review of Economics and Statistics 49:*209–224.

Carter, A. P. (1970). *Structural Change in the American Economy*. Cambridge: Harvard University Press.

Caves, R. E. (1982). *American Industry: Structure, Conduct, Performance*. Englewood Cliffs: Prentice-Hall.

Caves, R. E., and Porter, M. E. (1980). The dynamics of changing seller concentration. *Journal of Industrial Economics 29:*1–15.

Chandler, A. D., Jr. (1962). *Strategy and Structure*. Cambridge: MIT Press.

Clevenger, T. S., and Campbell, G. R. (1977). Vertical organization: a neglected element in market structure–profit models. *Industrial Organization Review 6:*60–66.

Coase, R. H. (1937). The nature of the firm. In G. J. Stigler and K. E. Boulding (eds., 1952), *Readings in Price Theory*. Chicago: Richard D. Irwin.

Collins, N. R., and Preston, L. E. (1968). *Concentration and Price-Cost Margins in Manufacturing Industries*. Berkeley: University of California Press.

Collins, N. R., and Preston, L. E. (1969). Price–cost margins and industry structure. *Review of Economics and Statistics 51:*271–286.

Commission on Private Philanthropy and Public Needs (1977). *Research Papers*, 5 Volumes, Department of the Treasury. Washington, DC: Government Printing Office.

Corporate Directors Conference (1975). *The Corporate Director: New Roles—New Responsibilities*. Cambridge: Arthur D. Little.

Delacroix, J., and Carroll, G. (1982). Organizational mortality in the newspaper industries of Argentina and Ireland: an ecological approach. *Administrative Science Quarterly 27:*169–198.

Domhoff, D. W. (1967). *Who Rules America?* Englewood Cliffs: Prentice-Hall.

Dooley, P. C. (1969). The interlocking directorate. *American Economic Review 59:*314–323.

Emmet, B., and Jeuck, J. E. (1950). *Catalogues and Counters: A History of Sears, Roebuck and Company*. Chicago: University of Chicago Press.

Evan, W. M. (1966). The organization-set: toward a theory of interorganizational relations. In J. D. Thompson (ed.), *Approaches to Organizational Design*. Pittsburgh: University of Pittsburgh Press.

Evan, W. M. (1972). An organization-set model of interorganizational relations. In M. F. Tuite, M. Radner, and R. K. Chishold (eds.), *Interorganizational Decision-Making*. Chicago: Aldine.

Evans-Pritchard, E. E. (1940). *The Nuer*. New York Oxford University Press.

Feldstein, M. S., and Clotfelter, C. (1976). Tax incentives and charitable contributions in the United States: a microeconomic analysis. *Journal of Public Economics 5:*1–26.

Feldstein, M. S., and Taylor, A. (1976). The income tax and charitable contributions. *Econometrica 44:*1201–1222.

Fennema, M., and Schijf, H. (1979). Analysing interlocking directorates: theory and methods. *Social Networks 1:*297–332.

Fienberg, S. E., and Wasserman, S. S. (1981). Categorical data analysis of single sociometric relations. In S. Leinhardt (ed.), *Sociological Methodology 1981*. San Francisco: Jossey-Bass.

Fischer, C. S. (1982). *To Dwell among Friends: Personal Networks in Town and City*. Chicago: University of Chicago Press.

Fischler, H. (1980). Monopolies, market interdependencies and the logic of collective action: some critical comments on Mancur Olson's group theory. *Public Choice 35:*191–195.

Galaskiewicz, J. (1979). *Exchange Networks and Community Relations*. Beverly Hills: Sage Publications.

Galaskiewicz, J. (1982). Networks of resource allocation: corporate contributions to nonprofit organizations. In P. V. Marsden and N. Lin (eds.), *Social Structure and Network Analysis*. Beverly Hills: Sage Publications.

Galaskiewicz, J., and Marsden, P. V. (1978). Interorganizational resource networks: formal patterns of overlap. *Social Science Research 7:*89–107.

Galaskiewicz, J., and Wasserman, S. S. (1981). A dynamic study of change in a regional corporate network. *American Sociological Review 46:*475–484.

Galbraith, J. K. (1952). *American Capitalism: The Concept of Countervailing Power*. New York: Houghton Mifflin.

Galbraith, J. K. (1973). *Economics and the Public Purpose*. New York: Houghton Mifflin.

Goodman, L. A. (1970). The multivariate analysis of qualitative data: interactions among multiple classifications. *Journal of the American Statistical Association 65:*226–256.

Goodman, L. A. (1972). A general model for the analysis of surveys. *American Journal of Sociology 77:*1035–1086.

Goodman, P. S., and Pennings, J. M. (1977). *New Perspectives on Organizational Effectiveness*. San Francisco: Jossey-Bass.

Grossack, I. M.(1972). The concept and measurement of permanent industrial concentration. *Journal of Political Economy 80:*745–760.

Guth, L. A., Schwartz, R. A., and Whitcomb, D. K. (1976). The use of buyer concentration ratios in tests of oligopoly models. *Review of Economics and Statistics 58:*488–492.

Guth, L. A., Schwartz, R. A., and Whitcomb, D. K. (1977). Buyer concentration ratios. *Journal of Industrial Economics 25:*241–258.

Hannan, M. T., and Freeman, J. (1977). The population ecology of organizations. *American Journal of Sociology 82:*929–964.

Hanushek, E., and Jackson, J. (1977). *Statistical Methods for Social Scientists*. New York: Academic Press.

Harris, J. F., and Klepper, A. (1976). *Corporate Philanthropic Public Service Activities,* Report #688. New York: National Industrial Conference Board.

Harriss, C. L. (1977). Corporate giving: rationale, issues and opportunities. In Commission on Private Philanthropy and Public Needs, *Research Papers,* Volume III, Department of the Treasury. Washington, DC: Government Printing Office.

Hauser, R. M. (1972). Disaggregating a social-psychological model of educational attainment. *Social Science Research 1:*159–188.

Hauser, R. M., and Goldberger, A. S. (1971). The treatment of unobservable variables in path analysis. In H. L. Costner (ed.), *Sociological Methodology 1971*. San Francisco: Jossey-Bass.

Hirsch, P. M. (1972). Processing fads and fashions: an organization-set analysis of culture industry systems. *American Journal of Sociology 77:*639–659.

Hirsch, P. M. (1975). Organizational effectiveness and the institutional environment. *Administrative Science Quarterly 20:*327–344.

Holland, P. W., and Leinhardt, S. (1981). An exponential family of probability distributions for directed graphs. *Journal of the American Statistical Association 76:*33–50.

Internal Revenue Service (1971). *Statistics of Income: Corporation Income Tax Returns*. Washington, DC: Government Printing Office.

Johnson, O. (1966). Corporate philanthropy: an analysis of corporate contributions. *Journal of Business 39:*489–504.

Kaysen, C., and Turner, D. F. (1959). *Antitrust Policy*. Cambridge: Harvard University Press.

Keim, G. D., Meiners, R. E., and Frey, L. W. (1980). On the evaluation of corporate contributions. *Public Choice 35*:129–136.

Khalilzadeh-Shirazi, J. (1974). Market structure and price–cost margins in the United Kingdom manufacturing industries. *Review of Economics and Statistics 56*:67–76.

Kilburn, H. C. (1981). A note on the existence of a corporate elite. Unpublished paper, Department of Sociology, State University of New York, Albany.

Kile, O. M. (1948). *The Farm Bureau through Three Decades*. Baltimore: Waverly Press.

Klepper, A. (1977). *Annual Survey of Corporate Contributions, 1975*, Report #720. New York: National Industrial Conference Board.

Knoke, D., and Kuklinski, J. H. (1982). *Network Analysis*. Beverly Hills: Sage Publications.

Koenig, T., Gogel, R., and Sonquist, J. (1979). Models of the significance of interlocking corporate directorates. *American Journal of Economics and Sociology 38*:173–186.

Koontz, H. (1967). *The Board of Directors and Effective Management*. New York: McGraw-Hill.

Kotz, D. (1978). *Bank Control of Large Corporations in the United States*. Berkeley: University of California Press.

Kwoka, J. E., Jr. (1979). The effect of market share distribution on industry performance. *Review of Economics and Statistics 61*:101–109.

Larner, R. J. (1970). *Management Control and the Large Corporation*. Cambridge: Dunellen.

Laumann, E. O. (1973). *Bonds of Pluralism: The Form and Substance of Urban Social Networks*. New York: Wiley-Interscience.

Laumann, E. O., Galaskiewicz, J., and Marsden, P. V. (1978). Community structure as interorganizational linkages. *Annual Review of Sociology 4*:455–484.

Leontief, W. (1951). Input–output economics. In W. Leontief (ed.), *Input–Output Economics*, 1966 ed. New York: Oxford University Press.

Leontief, W. (1968). Input–output analysis. In *The Encyclopedia of the Social Sciences*. New York: Free Press and Macmillan.

Levine, J. H. (1972). The sphere of influence. *American Sociological Review 37*:14–27.

Levy, F. K., and Shatto, G. M. (1978). The evaluation of corporate contributions. *Public Choice 33*:19–27.

Light, I. H. (1972). *Ethnic Enterprise in America*. Berkeley: University of California Press.

Lindblom, C. E. (1977). *Markets and Hierarchies*. New York: Basic Books.

Litwak, E., and Rothman, J. (1970). Towards the theory and practice of coordination between formal organizations. In W. Rosengren and M. Lefton (eds.), *Organizations and Clients*. New York: Charles Merrill.

Louden, J. K. (1982). *The Director*. New York: Amacom.

Lustgarten, S. H. (1975). The impact of buyer concentration in manufacturing industries. *Review of Economics and Statistics 57*:125–132.

Lustgarten, S. H. (1976). The use of buyer concentration ratios in tests of oligopoly models: reply. *Review of Economics and Statistics 58*:492–494.

Mace, M. L. (1948). *The Board of Directors in Small Corporations*. Boston: Division of Research, Graduate School of Business Administration, Harvard University.

Mace, M. L. (1971). *Directors: Myth and Reality*. Boston: Division of Research, Graduate School of Business Administration, Harvard University.

Malinowski, B. (1922). *Argonauts of the Western Pacific*. London: George Routledge & Sons.

Mariolis, P. (1975). Interlocking directorates and control of corporations: the theory of bank control. *Social Science Quarterly 56*:425–439.

Means, G. C., Chairman (1939). *The Structure of the American Economy: Basic Characteristics*, National Resources Committee. Washington, DC: Government Printing Office.

Merton, R. K. (1957). Continuities in the theory of reference groups and social structure. In R. K. Merton, *Social Theory and Social Structure*, 1968 ed. New York: Free Press.

Metcalf, L., Chairman (1978). *Voting Rights in Major Corporations,* U.S. Senate Committee on Governmental Affairs, Subcommittee on Reports, Accounting and Management. Washington, DC: Government Printing Office.

Mills, C. W. (1956). *The Power Elite.* New York: Oxford University Press.

Mintz, B., and Schwartz, M. (1981a). The structure of intercorporate unity in American business. *Social Problems 29:*87–103.

Mintz, B., and Schwartz, M. (1981b). Interlocking directorates and interest groups. *American Sociological Review 46:*851–869.

Mitchell, J. C. (1969). The concept and use of social networks. In J. C. Mitchell (ed.), *Social Networks in Urban Situations.* Manchester: University of Manchester Press.

Mizruchi, M. S. (1982). *The American Corporate Network, 1904–1974.* Beverly Hills: Sage Publications.

Moch, M. K., and Seashore, S. E. (1981). How norms affect behaviors in and of corporations. In P. C. Nystrom and W. H. Starbuck (eds.), *Handbook of Organizational Design, 1: Adapting Organizations to Their Environments.* New York: Oxford University Press.

Mokken, R. J., and Stokman, F. N. (1979). Corporate–governmental networks in the Netherlands. *Social Networks 1:*333–358.

Mueller, R. K. (1978). *New Directions for Directors.* Lexington: D. C. Heath.

Mueller, W. F., and Hamm, L. G. (1974). Trends in industrial market concentration, 1947 to 1970. *Review of Economics and Statistics. 54:*511–520.

National Industrial Conference Board (1956). *The Why and How of Corporate Giving.* New York: National Industrial Conference Board.

Neale, A. D. (1970). *The Antitrust Laws of the United States of America: A Study of Competition Enforced by Law.* Cambridge: Cambridge University Press.

Nelson, R. L. (1970). *Economic Factors in the Growth of Corporate Giving,* Occasional Paper #111. New York: National Bureau of Economic Research.

Newcomer, M. (1955). *The Big Business Executive.* New York: Columbia University Press.

Nystrom, P. C., and Starbuck, W. H., eds. (1981). *Handbook of Organizational Design, 1: Adapting Organizations to Their Environments.* New York: Oxford University Press.

Ornstein, M. D. (1980). Assessing the meaning of corporate interlocks: Canadian evidence. *Social Science Research 4:*287–306.

Ornstein, M. D. (1982). Interlocking directorates in Canada: evidence from replacement patterns. *Social Networks 4:*3–25.

Ouchi, W. T. (1980). Markets, bureaucracies, and clans. *Administrative Science Quarterly 25:*129–142.

Palmer, D. (1983). Broken ties: interlocking directorates and intercorporate coordination. *Administrative Science Quarterly 28:*40–55.

Patman, W., Chairman (1968). *Commercial Banks and Their Trust Activities: Emerging Influences on the American Economy,* U.S. House of Representatives Committee on Banking and Currency, Subcommittee on Domestic Finance. Washington, DC: Government Printing Office.

Pennings, J. M. (1980). *Interlocking Directorates: Origins and Consequences of Connections among Organizations' Boards of Directors.* San Francisco: Jossey-Bass.

Pfeffer, J. (1972a). Size and composition of corporate boards of directors. *Administrative Science Quarterly 17:*218–228.

Pfeffer, J. (1972b). Merger as a response to organizational interdependence. *Administrative Science Quarterly 17:*382–394.

Pfeffer, J., and Leblebici, H. (1973). Executive recruitment and the development of interfirm organizations. *Administrative Science Quarterly 18:*449–461.

Pfeffer, J., and Nowak, P. (1976). Joint ventures and interorganizational interdependence. *Administrative Science Quarterly 21:*398–418.

Pfeffer, J., and Salancik, G. (1978). *The External Control of Organizations: A Resource Dependence Perspective*. New York: Harper & Row.

Phillips, A. (1960). A theory of interfirm organization. *Quarterly Journal of Economics 74:*602–613.

Poensgen, O. H. (1980). Between market and hierarchy. *Zeitschrift für die gesamte Staatswissenschaft 136:*209–225.

Porter, M. E. (1974). Consumer behavior, retailer power and market performance in consumer goods industries. *Review of Economics and Statistics 56:*419–436.

Porter, M. E. (1979). The structure within industries and companies' performance. *Review of Economics and Statistics 61:*214–227.

Porter, M. E. (1980). *Competitive Strategy: Techniques for Analyzing Industries and Competitors*. New York: Free Press.

Ratcliff, R. E. (1980). Banks and corporate lending: an analysis of the impact of the internal structure of the capitalist class on the lending behavior of banks. *American Sociological Review 45:*553–570.

Rhoades, S. A. (1973). The effect of diversification on industry profit performance in 241 manufacturing industries: 1963. *Review of Economics and Statistics 55:*14–155.

Rhoades, S. A. (1974). A further evaluation of the effect of diversification on industry profit performance. *Review of Economics and Statistics 56:*557–559.

Riker, W. H., and Ordeshook, P. C. (1973). *An Introduction to Positive Political Theory*. Englewood Cliffs: Prentice-Hall.

Sahlins, M. (1972). *Stone Age Economics*. Chicago: Aldine.

Schwartz, R. A. (1966). Corporate philanthropic contributions. *Journal of Finance 23:*479–497.

Seider, M. S. (1974). American big business ideology: a content analysis of executive speeches. *American Sociological Review 39:*802–815.

Selznick, P. (1949). *TVA and the Grass Roots: A Study in the Sociology of Formal Organization*. New York: Harper & Row.

Sevaldson, P. (1970). The stability of input–output coefficients. In A. P. Carter and A. Brody (eds.), *Applications of Input–Output Analysis*. Amsterdam: North-Holland Publishing.

Shapley, L. S., and Shubik, M. (1954). A method for evaluating the distribution of power in a committee system. *American Political Science Review 48:*787–792.

Shepherd, W. G. (1970). *Market Power and Economic Welfare*. New York: Random House.

Shepherd, W. G. (1975). *The Treatment of Market Power: Antitrust, Regulation, and Public Enterprise*. New York: Columbia University Press.

Simmel, G. (1908). On the significance of numbers for social life. In K. Wolf (trans., 1950), *The Sociology of Georg Simmel*. New York: Free Press.

Sonquist, J. A., and Koenig, T. (1975). Interlocking directorates in the top U.S. corporations: a graph theory approach. *Insurgent Sociologist 5:*196–229.

Soref, M. (1976). Social class and a division of labor within the corporate elite: a note on class, interlocking, and executive committee membership of directors in U.S. industrial firms. *Sociological Quarterly 17:*360–368.

Stigler, G. J. (1951). The division of labor is limited by the extent of the market. *Journal of Political Economy 59:*185–193.

Stinchcombe, A. L. (1965). Social structure and organizations. In J. G. March (ed.), *Handbook of Organizations*. Chicago: Rand-McNally.

Taussig, F. W., and Joslyn, C. S. (1932). *American Business Leaders: A Study in Social Origins and Social Stratification*. New York: Macmillan.

Thompson, J. D. (1967). *Organizations in Action*. New York: McGraw-Hill.

Tucker, I. R., and Wilder, R. P. (1977). Trends in vertical integration in the U.S. manufacturing sector. *Journal of Industrial Economics 26:*81–94.

Turk, H. (1977). *Organizations in Modern Life: Cities and Other Large Networks.* San Francisco: Jossey-Bass.

Turner, E. W., counsel (1978). *Interlocking Directorates Among the Major U.S. Corporations,* U.S. Senate Committee on Governmental Affairs, Subcommittee on Reports, Accounting and Management. Washington, DC: Government Printing Office.

U.S. Department of Commerce (1971). *1967 Census of Manufactures, Concentration Ratios in Manufacturing.* Washington, DC: Government Printing Office.

U.S. Department of Commerce (1973). *Annual Survey of Manufactures, 1970–1971.* Washington, DC: Government Printing Office.

U.S. Department of Commerce (1974). Input–output structure of the U.S. economy: 1967. *Survey of Current Business 54:*24–55.

Useem, M. (1978). The inner group of the American capitalist class. *Social Problems 25:*225–240.

Useem, M. (1979). The social organization of the American business elite and participation of corporation directors in the governance of American institutions. *American Sociological Review 44:*553–572.

Useem, M. (1980). Corporations and the corporate elite. *Annual Review of Sociology 6:*41–77.

Useem, M. (1982). Classwide rationality in the politics of managers and directors of large corporations in the United States and Great Britain. *Administrative Science Quarterly 27:*199–226.

U.S. Federal Trade Commission (1951). *Report on Interlocking Directorates.* Washington, DC: Government Printing Office.

Vaccara, B. N. (1970). Changes over time in input–output coefficients for the United States. In A. P. Carter and A. Brody (eds.), *Applications of Input–Output Analysis.* Amsterdam: North-Holland Publishing.

Vance, S. C. (1964). *Boards of Directors: Structure and Performance.* Eugene: University of Oregon Press.

Vasquez, T. (1977). Corporate giving measures. In Commission on Private Philanthropy and Public Needs, *Research Papers,* Volume III, Department of the Treasury. Washington, DC: Government Printing Office.

Warner, W. L., and Unwalla, D. B. (1967). The system of interlocking directorates. In W. L. Warner, D. B. Unwalla, and J. H. Trimm (eds.), *The Emergent American Society: Large Scale Organizations.* New Haven: Yale University Press.

Watson, J. H. III (1972). *Biennial Survey of Company Contributions,* Report #542. New York: National Industrial Conference Board.

Weber, M. (1925). *Social and Economic Organization.* A. M. Henderson and T. Parsons (trans., 1947). New York: Free Press.

Wellman, B. (1978). The community question: the intimate networks of East Yorkers. *American Journal of Sociology 84:*1201–1231.

White, H. C., Boorman, S. A., and Breiger, R. L. (1976). Social structure from multiple networks, I, blockmodels of roles and positions. *American Journal of Sociology 81:*730–780.

Williamson, O. E. (1975). *Markets and Hierarchies: Analysis and Antitrust Implications.* New York: Free Press.

Williamson, O. E. (1981). The economics of organization: the transaction cost approach. *American Journal of Sociology 87:*548–557.

Zald, M. N. (1969). The power and function of boards of directors: a theoretical synthesis. *American Journal of Sociology 75:*97–111.

Zeitlin, M. (1974). Corporate ownership and control: the large corporation and the capitalist class. *American Journal of Sociology 79:*1073–1119.

Zeitlin, M. (1976). On class theory of the large corporation: response to Allen. *American Journal of Sociology 81:*894–903.

Ziegler, R. (1982). *Market Structure and Cooptation.* München: Institut für Soziologie, Ludwig-Maximilians-Universität.

Index

QUANTITATIVE STUDIES IN SOCIAL RELATIONS